*THE IMAGINATION OF DISASTER*

# THE
# IMAGINATION
# OF DISASTER

Evil in the Fiction of Henry James

*BY* J. A. WARD

UNIVERSITY OF NEBRASKA PRESS

LINCOLN          1961

The publication of this book was assisted by a grant
from the Ford Foundation.

Publishers on the Plains

UNP

*for*
ANN

# *Preface*

The purpose of this book is to investigate what seems to me a major yet relatively neglected aspect of James's fiction. It has often been remarked that evil in James usually takes the form of what Hawthorne in "Ethan Brand" calls the "Unpardonable Sin," the malign intervention of one person in the life of another; but there has been no systematic consideration of the forms and implications of this evil or of its relevance to James's general fictional purposes. Likewise, several critics have observed—but usually in other connections—that in the development from the early to the late fiction, the words "villain" and "hero" become increasingly less applicable to James's characters. One of my intentions is to reveal the changes and patterns in James's characterizations of the evildoer, and thus to shed light on a subject that has been illuminated only in part.

My emphasis is literary rather than theological or moral. The subject "evil" is a means to an end; it serves as a new focus for an explication of James's fiction. Therefore I do not concern myself with evil as such; and the definition of evil which I presuppose throughout is intentionally broad, so as to protect me from any arbitrary limitation of subject matter. Paul Siwek, a Jesuit, in *The Philosophy of Evil* provides the most inclusive and succinct definition of evil that I have seen:

> [Evil is] all that opposes the intrinsic finality of a being. Therefore it is all that hinders the being's full development, all that thwarts its tendencies, all that resists the drive from the depths of that being toward full expansion, toward that completion which it would attain to in its ideal type, the archetype of its own nature (p. 50).

This definition is more satisfactory, because more philosophical, than those which define evil as that which destroys or which causes suffering. Furthermore, it crosses over a number of philosophical and theological boundaries, because, at least out of context, it leaves open the question of what "full expansion" is, and does not specify "all that opposes . . . finality."

However, with the implicit identification of good with growth, the definition seems especially useful for the consideration of a writer

vii

fundamentally in the tradition of nineteenth-century romanticism. For James, as for Wordsworth, Shelley, Emerson, and Thoreau, good is constant, unending development, and evil is stasis, or restriction of development. Growth in James's fiction is not nearly so natural as in a writer like Whitman: development for James requires a delicate balance between self and society, not a rejection of human institutions in the name of freedom or self-expression. In the main, evil in James is the complex of forces, internal and external, which prevents the individual from moving toward completion, always moral and spiritual, and sometimes intellectual, emotional, and aesthetic, toward which his nature strives.

This book is in no way intended to be a complete account of James's productions, although most of the major novels are discussed and some of the minor ones are treated rather extensively. The plays have been excluded because, though they are useful for a study of James's fictional technique, they at best only parallel and at worst soften the moral issues of the fiction. As Leon Edel makes clear in his introduction and notes to *The Complete Plays of Henry James*, the plays have an obviousness and conventionality seldom present in James's fiction.

After an introductory chapter dealing with general characteristics of James's treatment of evil, the subsequent chapters attempt to apply these generalizations successively to the four major divisions of James's writing: the early international fiction (1870–1889); the English, or "middle period," fiction (1890–1901); the later international fiction, that of the "major phase" (1902–1904); and the scattered fiction of James's last years (1905–1916). In spite of its obvious limitations, this scheme has seemed the most workable for the purposes of this study. For example, *The Bostonians*, set entirely in America, is treated under the general heading of the international theme, because this novel offers a revelation of James's critical attitude toward America which does much to clarify the moral opposition of America and Europe. The order is only generally chronological; within each of the four main divisions the order followed is that which seems most appropriate to the topic.

# Acknowledgments

In the course of writing and rewriting this book, I have received much valuable assistance and advice. I especially wish to acknowledge the wisdom, generosity, and patience of Professor Richard Harter Fogle of Tulane University, who first encouraged me to deal with the subject, guided my work to completion in its first form as a doctoral dissertation, and carefully read the revised version I prepared for publication. Professors Richard P. Adams, John D. Husband, and George W. Meyer of Tulane, Professor Richard T. Wagner of the University of Southwestern Louisiana, and Professor B. R. McElderry, Jr. of the University of Southern California have also read the manuscript in entirety; to each of these I am very grateful. The notes suggest the extent of my indebtedness to all the critics and scholars whose work has helped my understanding of James.

I also wish to thank the editors and directors of the following journals and presses for permission to reprint portions of this study which first appeared in article form: *Twentieth Century Literature* for "Henry James and the Nature of Evil," slightly enlarged as Chapter One; *Mississippi Quarterly* for "Henry James's America: Versions of Oppression," slightly altered as part one of Chapter Two; *Texas Studies in Literature and Language* for "The Ineffectual Heroes of James's Middle Period," slightly enlarged as part one of Chapter Three; *Arizona Quarterly* for "Social Criticism in James's London Fiction," slightly altered as part two of Chapter Three; The Regents of the University of California and the University of California Press, publishers of *Nineteenth-Century Fiction*, for "The Ambassadors: Strether's Vision of Evil," © 1959 by The Regents, slightly enlarged as part one of Chapter Three; the Wayne State University Press, publishers of *Criticism*, for "Social Disintegration in *The Wings of the Dove*," copyright 1960 by Wayne State University Press, slightly enlarged as part two of Chapter Four; and the *Western Humanities Review* for "Evil in *The Golden Bowl*," slightly altered as part three of Chapter Four.

I am indebted to the following publishers for permission to quote from materials on which they hold copyright: to the American Book Company, for a quotation from the introduction to *Henry James: Representative Selections*, by Lyon N. Richardson; to E. P. Dutton & Co., Inc., publishers of *The Pilgrimage of Henry James*, by Van Wyck Brooks; to George W. Stewart, publisher of *The Great Tradition* by F. R. Leavis; to Grove Press, Inc., for permission to quote from *The Sacred Fount* by Henry James and the Introduction to *The Golden Bowl* by R. P. Blackmur; to Harper & Brothers, publishers of *The Wind Blew from the East* by Ferner Nuhn; to Holt, Rinehart and Winston, Inc., publishers of *The Question of Henry James: A Collection of Critical Essays*, edited by F. W. Dupee; to the Houghton Mifflin Company, publishers of *The Question of Our Speech and The Lesson of Balzac* by Henry James and *Henry James: Man and Author* by Pelham Edgar; to the *Journal of Aesthetics and Art Criticism*, for permission to quote from "The Relativism of Henry James" by Joseph J. Firebaugh; to the *Kenyon Review*, for permission to quote from "The Sacred Fount" by R. P. Blackmur and "Myth and Dialectic in the Later Novels" by Austin Warren; to the J. B. Lippincott Company, publishers of *Henry James: The Untried Years* by Leon Edel; to The Macmillan Company, publishers of *The Crooked Corridor: A Study of Henry James* by Elizabeth Stevenson and *The American Novel: 1789–1939* by Carl Van Doren; to *The New Republic*, for permission to quote from "The Choice So Freely Made," by Leon Edel; to the Oxford University Press, publishers of *Henry James: The Major Phase* by F. O. Matthiessen and *The Notebooks of Henry James;* to Paul R. Reynolds & Son, representative of the Henry James estate, for permission to quote from the volumes of *The Novels and Tales of Henry James* which it controls and for Canadian distribution rights; to Charles Scribner's Sons, publishers of *The Novels and Tales of Henry James, A Small Boy and Others, Notes of a Son and Brother, The Art of the Novel: Critical Prefaces by Henry James*, edited by Richard P. Blackmur, and *The Letters of Henry James*, edited by Percy Lubbock; to *The Sewanee Review*, for permission to quote from "*The Golden Bowl* Revisited" by Francis Fergusson; to the University of Chicago Press, publishers of *The American Adam* by R. W. B. Lewis, © 1955 by the University of Chicago; to the *University of Kansas City Review*, for permission to quote from "*The Turn of the Screw* as Poem" by Robert B. Heilman; to The Modern Language Association of America, publishers of *PMLA*, for permission to quote from "Henry James's World of Images" by R. W. Short; to the Ronald Press Company, publishers of *The Philosophy of Evil* by Paul Siwek, copyright 1951 by The Ronald Press Company; to The Viking Press, Inc., publishers of *Craft and Character in Modern Fiction* by Morton Dauwen Zabel; and to William Sloane Associates, Inc., publishers of *Henry James* by F. W. Dupee, copyright 1951 by William Sloane Associates, Inc.

Finally, I wish to express my thanks to the Ford Foundation, whose grant made possible the publication of this book.

# Contents

*THE IMAGINATION OF DISASTER*

### CHAPTER ONE

# The Consciousness of Evil

HENRY JAMES is a realist in fiction, one who conceives of his art as an end, not as a means, and whose effort is to dramatize life, to depict life, and to give form to life, not to present a religious or philosophic system. Evil is present in his fiction as it is embodied in concrete characters and situations and as the characters reflect upon these. James's concern with evil is a concern with an aspect of reality, and therefore it is dealt with imaginatively rather than theologically or moralistically.

It is a testimony to James's consistent artistic development that there is in his works a distinct movement toward detachment in his treatment of evil. Just as the villains of his early stories are simply conceived, so his own condemnation of them is unequivocal. In "Madame de Mauves" (1874), for example, James employs an almost primitive imagery of black and white to convey moral values. Likewise his admiration for the heroine, Euphemia Cleve, whose unflinching righteousness offends the modern reader, and his disapproval of the duplicity and adultery of Richard de Mauves, establish an absolute moral dualism (possibly qualified by the ambiguous ending of the story) that is characteristic of many of James's early pieces. In his more mature stories of the early period, however, James maintains a disinterested position through an ironic approach to his heroes and heroines: Christopher Newman and Isabel Archer meet evil through weakness of character as well as through unfortunate circumstances. James achieves full detachment in his middle period when he replaces the stage villainy of the Bellegardes and Osmond with the ambiguous characterizations of Mrs. Gereth, Rose Armiger, and Mrs. Brookenham.

*The Other House* (1896) reveals the shift in James's view of

3

evil; it is the novel in which James continues to convey the horror of evil, and yet divests the evildoer of the simple blackness that often takes the place of realistic characterization in the early works. *The Other House* is especially notable and unusual in that it is about a crime of violence—specifically, the murder of a child. Yet the villainess, Rose Armiger, is a subtle creation, looking forward to the ambiguous "bad heroines" of later works, especially Kate Croy. Her evil is tempered and thus made credible by certain admirable traits. Rose's tremendous passion and vitality, her grace and style are inseparable from her cruelty. James treats Rose's evil as a psychologist rather than a moralist, and in doing so makes her heinous crime believable.

The objective dramatic form of *The Other House* serves James in his realism, but the toleration and qualified admiration for the evildoer carry over to the last novels, which are subjective rather than objective in approach. The later versions of the European villain—Mme. de Vionnet, Kate Croy, and Prince Amerigo—bear little resemblance to the earlier versions—Richard de Mauves, Urbain de Bellegarde, and Gilbert Osmond. Moral conflict, however, becomes no less significant in the later works, but James's ambiguity, complexity, and detachment prohibit critical literalism and moralism.

In 1876, James wrote of Baudelaire that

> He knew evil not by experience, not as something within himself, but by contemplation and curiosity, as something outside of himself, by which his own intellectual agility was not in the least discomposed, rather indeed . . . flattered and stimulated. . . . evil for him begins outside and not inside, and consists primarily of a great deal of lurid landscape and unclean furniture. . . . Evil is represented as an affair of blood and carrion and physical sickness—there must be stinking corpses and starving prostitutes and empty laudanum bottles in order that the poet shall be effectively inspired. . . . he was, in his treatment of evil, exactly what Hawthorne was not—Hawthorne, who felt the thing at its source, deep in the human consciousness.[1]

It is important to establish that for James evil resides primarily inside the human consciousness, for except in the background of his early fiction and in the foreground of *The Other House* there is little of stock horror and villainy in James's work. Stuart P. Sherman, accustomed to conventional nineteenth-century fictional techniques, accuses James of replacing genuine evil by bad manners: "[James's] controlling principle is a sense of style, under which vice, to adapt Burke's words, loses half its evil by losing all its grossness." [2] But in his critique of Baudelaire James makes explicit what is implicit in his fiction, his belief that the literary artist should deal with the evil which exists "deep in human consciousness." Though James gives evil external form, it originates in the will or the intellect and reveals its force by causing suffering that is not physical but emotional and mental. Moreover, evil partakes of the forms of civilization. It is detectable in the motives which bring it about and in the suffering which it causes, but in itself it may seem hardly significant or even nonexistent. One cannot accuse Dr. Sloper, Mme. Merle, or Christina Light of criminal action or even of conduct intrinsically reprehensible: our judgment of these and other "villains" must be based on their motivations and on the anguish they cause others.

Evil in James's fiction is not so much a problem as it is an inexorable, ever-present reality that cripples and destroys; it is present at the base of every human situation, and it is at least latent in every man. Critics frequently describe James as having a "sense of evil" (rather than an "idea of evil" or a "concept of evil"); and the term is accurate, for it suggests that to James evil is obscure and indefinite. In his works the reaction to evil often strikes us as vague and unrelated to specific action or character, or we may feel, as does Yvor Winters toward some of the novels, that the sense of evil far outweighs what the presented facts merit. [3] This sense of evil in James, this "imagination . . . clouded by the Pit," as Graham Greene terms it, [4] is based on or is equivalent to an imaginative recognition of a sin that, if it is not "original," is certainly fundamental to the human situation. James once wrote, ". . . I have the imagination of disaster and see life indeed as ferocious and sinister." [5] To R. P. Blackmur his fiction conveys "the menace of life itself." [6] A stoic who rejected the easy solutions of the optimist, James unquestionably shared the feeling of Mr. Vetch of *The Princess Casamassima:*

> The idea of great changes . . . took its place among the dreams of his youth; for what was any possible change in the relations of men and women but a new combination of the same elements? If the elements could be made different the thing would be worth thinking of; but it was not only impossible to introduce any new ones—no means had yet been discovered for getting rid of the old. The figures on the chess-board were still the passions and jealousies and superstitions and stupidities of man, and their position with regard to each other at any given moment could be of interest only to the grim invisible fates who played the game—who sat, through the ages, low-backed over the table (VI, 104).[7]

Significantly, James found one of Emerson's limitations to be his "ripe unconsciousness of evil"; [8] similarly he thought Hawthorne "most creative" when he showed "that we are really not by any means so good as a well-regulated society requires us to appear." [9] In one of his most profound letters he advised Grace Norton to "content yourself with the terrible algebra of your own [life]." [10] He considered his father's theological system invalidated by an "optimism fed so little by any sense of things as they were or are." [11] Probably James's most explicit comment on evil occurs in his essay on Turgenev: "Life *is*, in fact, a battle. On this point optimists and pessimists agree. Evil is insolent and strong; beauty enchanting but rare; goodness very apt to be weak; folly very apt to be defiant; wickedness to carry the day; imbeciles to be in great places, people of sense in small, and mankind generally, un-happy." [12]

James's acceptance, imaginative rather than literal, of "some terrible aboriginal catastrophe," to use Newman's phrase,[13] that made evil, if not a natural element of human life, certainly a permanent reality, takes the form in his novels of what theologians term "sin" rather than of what they term "evil," or of "moral evil" rather than "natural evil." Natural evil, which is beyond the realm of human control, the caprices and cataclysms of nature, the unavoidable facts of disease and death, is, according to Reinhold Niebuhr, "an irrelevance and a threat of meaninglessness in the realm of human history." [14] In James the emphasis on natural evil is equally slight. It is of course an accepted reality, and instances of it set many of his stories in motion: the illness and death of Ralph Touchett and Milly Theale and such circumstantial misfortunes as the poverty of Kate Croy and Merton Densher are central to James's plots. But such matters are never treated for their own value; they merely serve as bases for stories which have moral evil at their center. James has so little concern for natural evil that he very often makes death the result of moral rather than of natural evil—as in *The Wings of the Dove,* "The Author of Beltraffio," and "The Death of the Lion," in which the deaths through natural causes of Milly Theale, Mark Ambient, and Neil Paraday symbolize the spiritual suffering caused by unwarranted human intervention. Other deaths, like those of May Bartram in "The Beast in the Jungle" and Mrs. Pynsent in *The Princess Casamassima,* are of little emotional or thematic value in themselves; they are necessary simply to accentuate moral situations. May Bartram's death causes John Marcher to realize that his life has been a spiritual death; the death of Mrs. Pynsent makes it possible for Hyacinth Robinson to visit the continent and thereby gain new awareness. [15]

In James's fiction man is not in a condition of absolute depravity, but he possesses a latent capacity for evil that is dreadful even when unrealized. Perhaps central to James's treatment of evil is this pervasive awareness of "the sin that dwelleth within me," the strange and horrible existence of latent sin. James rarely treats this sense of potential personal evil in his fiction directly, but it lies at the center of many of his ghost stories, in which the ghosts are "manifestations of a darker power inherent in the order of things"; [16] or, as R. P. Blackmur states, ". . . James's ghosts represent the attempt to give objective rational form—knowledgeable form—to all the vast subjective experience of our 'other,' our hidden, our secret selves which we commonly deny, gloss over, or try to explain away." [17]

The central passage in James's work suggesting his consciousness of hidden personal evil is contained in his autobiographical volume *A Small Boy and Others*, in which he describes

> the most appalling yet most admirable nightmare of my life. The climax of this extraordinary experience . . . was the sudden pursuit, through an open door, along a huge saloon, of a just dimly-descried figure that retreated in terror before my rush and dash (a glare of inspired reaction from irresistible but shameful dread,) out of the room I had a moment before been desperately, and all the more abjectly, defending by the push of my shoulder against hard pressure on lock and bar from the other side. The lucidity, not to say the sublimity, of the crisis had consisted of the great thought that I, in my appalled state, was probably still more appalling than the awful agent, creature or presence, whatever he was, whom I had guessed, in the suddenest wild start from sleep, the sleep within my sleep, to be making for my place of rest.[18]

The pattern of the terrified person finding himself even more terrifying than the hideous monster who confronts him is a buried motif in much of James's fiction, especially the late works. For example, in *The Ambassadors* Strether's confrontation of Chad is a case in which the appalled person is ultimately revealed as "still more appalling than the awful agent." In *The Ambassadors* Strether carries with him the evil of the New England conscience; in *The Awkward Age* the character paralleling James in his nightmare is Vanderbank, whose sin is pride: in each case, and in many others, the character who in the beginning seems the victim emerges as the source of evil.

James regularly makes evil latent and unconscious of itself. It is often a power beyond will, beyond knowledge, beyond identity. It is this obscure and irrational quality in his sense of evil that links James to modern novelists like Kafka, whose Joseph K. is on trial for an unnamed, unknown crime of which he yet is guilty. It also links him to the diarists of the Puritan theocracy, who relentlessly reflected on their own sins, and to Hawthorne, many of whose characters were obsessed by their own guilt.

A resemblance that James noted between Hawthorne and the Puritans also holds true for his own fiction: "To him as to them, the consciousness of *sin* was the most importunate fact of life." [19] Evil in James is rarely isolated from the personal consciousness of it: either the subjective response of the disinterested observer (as in "The Two Faces," in which the cruel treatment of a girl by a jealous woman is not seen directly, but through the consciousness of a spectator, whose revulsion from the woman's behavior establishes the moral tone of the story), the consciousness of the guilty person (as in "Mora Montravers," in which the scornful uncle who abuses the innocent Mora is the reflector of the action), or the consciousness of the victim (as in *The American*, in which Christopher Newman suffers the effect of the villainy of the Bellegarde family).

Though James seems to be in the Puritan tradition in his subjective treatment of evil, there are some important modifications, alterations, and changes in emphasis in his works. James tends to concentrate on the good man's reaction to evil, rather than on the guilty man's obsession with his own sin. Thus the vision of evil in James more often resembles that of, say, Hilda in Hawthorne's *The Marble Faun*, the innocent made aware of evil, than it resembles the concern of Miriam with her own guilt. When James allows the reader to see into the mind of a villain, his emphasis differs from Hawthorne's. He is little interested in the sinner's sense of morality or in his feelings of guilt after the sin. Like most of the villains, the Bellegardes in *The American* and Gilbert Osmond in *The Portrait of a Lady* are never dealt with subjectively. We are permitted to see into the mind of Kate Croy, the instigator of the plot against Milly Theale in *The Wings of the Dove*, but we find no concern with sin or guilt. We perceive the subjective moral condition of Merton Densher, her accomplice, only when he regains the will to assert his temporarily suppressed sense of decency. In *The Golden Bowl* neither Charlotte Stant (whose mind we are not allowed to enter) nor Prince Amerigo seems conscious of his guilt. Nor is there any apparent struggle between will and conscience in these characters; the perpetrators of the evil cease their disruptive affair not because, like Arthur Dimmesdale of *The Scarlet Letter*, they are too burdened by conscience to continue, but simply because they are defeated by Maggie Verver.

The evil character in James is almost never reflective. The characters who fully understand a situation are reduced to inactivity because of their knowledge. This knowledge is mainly a moral awareness that enables the perceiver to grasp the full implications of a situation and thus to recognize the moral limitations of any sort of private action. In this respect James is an Aristotelian: to him the will is subservient to the intellect; behavior and thought must be in accordance. Nearly all the James characters who have achieved total moral awareness are markedly passive; their sole action is to accept their conditions. They renounce escape, revenge, marriage, or any other course of action which would relieve pain or improve their situations. The less perceptive characters, on the other hand, are limited to a selfish view of life, and as a result their wills control them. As James says of "the awful Mona Brigstock" of *The Spoils of Poynton*, she "is *all* will, without the smallest leak of force into taste or tenderness or vision, into any sense of shades or relations or proportions." [20] In James's fiction it is nearly axiomatic that the good are reflective and passive, and the evil irreflective and active.

Though his villains are usually active, evil to James is a negative reality. In this respect James, more in the tradition of Emerson than that of Hawthorne and Melville, deviates from the modified Manicheanism prevalent in much of American literature. In James's fiction evil is not an active principle in the universe; there are no Chillingworths or Ethan Brands, no Babos or Claggarts; there is no "evil according to nature" and no devotion to evil for its own sake. The James character who injures others does so through pursuit of good. James does not characterize pure egotism, as does Hawthorne; rather he delineates characters whose perception is limited—to art, as with Osmond; to social decorum, as with Mme. Merle; to material goods, as with Mona Brigstock; or to physical passion, as with Ida Farange. Evil comes about through the imperception of those who either do not recognize or ignore the effects of their activity on others. Thus Osmond's devotion to aesthetics, in itself a good, brings misery to his wife.

Furthermore, evil in James does not exist beyond human relationships. Occasionally melodramatic techniques lead James to invest a particular family or civilization with a pervasive miasma, suggestive of ineradicable evil; but in these cases theme and setting conflict. The house of Pyncheon and the house of Usher symbolize hereditary evil inevitably destroying each member of the family. Unlike Hawthorne or Poe, however, James does not treat evil beyond the level of psychology. Even in *The American*, James's most melodramatic novel, hereditary evil operates merely as an inclination, not a compulsion, which can be rejected by each family member.

James follows the melodramatic, though not strictly Manichean, convention of dramatizing conflicts between good and evil. The Jamesian innocent, an embodiment of the principles of Emersonian transcendentalism, cannot be identified with a total goodness, but he represents an ultimate moral achievement.[21] "Life [for James] was good and it was evil," writes Leon Edel; "people were innocent, sometimes *bon enfant* and good natured, or, on the other hand, predatory and destructive." [22] If the good characters reflect a high view of human nature, we are never allowed to forget that they form only part of the total picture and that experience necessitates the encounter with evil, the supreme test of the good nature.

Evil in James's world is ubiquitous only in the sense that it is latent in every man. Nevertheless, it is unavoidable; it derives from the fundamental human condition of limited perception. Thus evil has its source in a part of existence more permanent and essential than the vice of individuals.[23] It is not merely accidental that Isabel Archer encounters Mme. Merle and that Milly Theale becomes acquainted with Kate Croy. James's adventurers are doomed from the beginning, because of the nature of the world in which they live, to meet and be defeated by the force of evil.

Therefore, if the heroes and heroines are good, they rarely achieve happiness or success. Often the complexity of life itself is the villain, but evil is most often revealed in the stupidity, the self-righteousness, or the rapacity of an individual or of a society. Evil is unavoidable and universal, but it is centered in the human soul and manifests itself in the harmful domination of one person over another. Many James critics [24] have observed that the principal sin in James is "[the violation of] the sanctity of the human heart." [25] This element of personal violation, which has been described as "emotional cannibalism" [26] and by James himself as "omnivorous egotism," [27] is James's version of Hawthorne's "Unpardonable Sin" and the major evil in his works. James's inclination to associate egotism with imperception is not shared by Hawthorne, but the effects of egotism are the same in both authors—an emotional and spiritual crippling of the victim.

Though the resemblance between the treatments of sin by Hawthorne and James is striking, James did much to alter both the appearance and the activity of Hawthorne's villains. Especially in James's later works, in which the evildoer loses his conventionally melodramatic features, his villains are lifelike, whereas Hawthorne's rarely have an air of actuality; they are embodiments of a principle of evil. Even in such early works of James as *Roderick Hudson* and *The American*, the reprehensible characters, Mrs. Light and Urbain de Bellegarde, are motivated by common human desires—pride, greed, and revenge. Such Hawthorne villains as Roger Chillingworth and Judge Pyncheon are Satan figures; they personify evil. As James is usually more successful in giving solidity to his villains and their villainy, he also attempts to translate the "Unpardonable Sin" into natural human action,[28] so that the villainy is not remote and vague, but familiar and specific. In James the "Unpardonable Sin" is both embodied in and indistinguishable from concrete human action, such as adultery or theft or duplicity.[29]

James describes many kinds of personal violation, which are the same in essence and effect but different in type. The victimizer may be a false set of social values, as in many of the international stories: Daisy Miller is destroyed by the artificial mores of a decadent society. In most cases the sin takes the form of a person or group of persons improperly using another individual: Maisie Farange is little more than a pawn in the hands of her corrupt elders as they use her to their own advantages.

James inevitably compounds the sin of personal violation by associating it with betrayal. Gilbert Osmond, Paul Muniment, Rose Armiger, Kate Croy, and nearly all the malefactors in James are Judas-like in exploiting and destroying those whose confidence they have gained. Improper intervention in the life of another is virtually the only sin that interested James. Specific human actions, considered in isolation from other matters, are never in themselves evil (in this respect James is a moral relativist); the only criterion is the injury of another person. But in James's world of complex social relationships, human action does not take place in a vacuum, and the choice of one person inevitably results in either good or evil for others. Thus, deception (like that of Kate Croy and Merton Densher in *The Wings of the Dove*), theft (like that of Haughty Vint in *The Ivory Tower*), and adultery (like that of Beale Farange in *What Maisie Knew*) take their human tolls.

It is unnecessary to catalogue all the forms that personal violation assumes in James's fiction; in later chapters consideration is given to James's treatment of the common sins of pride, greed, and lust, and to the less common sin of ignorance. It is appropriate, however, to point out that evil in James is frequently a social rather than an individual force. His recognition of evil in institutionalized society, usually that of Europe, where in spite of its cultural and aesthetic graces, there is the "blackness of an old-world social order," [30] is usually reflected in fiction that reveals that appearances are deceptive: that manners are not morals and righteousness is not virtue. Whether James indicts the hypocrisy of French aristocracy, as he does in "Gabrielle de Bergerac" and *The American*, the degeneracy of such sophisticated milieux as those in *The Awkward Age* and "In the Cage," or the greed of such materialistic societies as those in *The Ivory Tower*, he reveals the disparity between the attractive exterior—the wealth, the manners, the social graces, and the evidences of culture—and the evil center. He repeatedly exposes what Maggie Verver calls "the thing hideously *behind*, behind so much trusted, so much pretended, nobleness, cleverness, tenderness" (XXIV, 237).

The sense of evil beneath the gilded surfaces of society is paralleled by the detection of evil in moral righteousness. Often this notion is portrayed comically, especially in such Puritanical Americans as Mr. Babcock, the itinerant New England minister

in *The American,* and Waymarsh in *The Ambassadors,* but more
often than not James points out the power for evil of the self-
righteous. James treats this theme too by contrasting appearance
and reality. In any number of stories he shows the ostensibly
"good," those whose behavior is approved by society, to be in
fact capable of the worst kind of evil. Thus the narrow-minded
wife of Mark Ambient in "The Author of Beltraffio" sacrifices
both husband and child in adherence to her warped notion of
morality. Mrs. Newsome in *The Ambassadors* and Olive Chancellor of *The Bostonians* are additional illustrations of the tyranny
of self-righteousness.

In all of James's fiction, if the villains are motivated by common
and frequently vulgar desires, the human damage is irreparable.
The victim suffers for more than loss of material possessions. He
suffers loss of love, as does Newman, or loss of life, as does Isabel
Archer spiritually and Milly Theale physically. Fleda Vetch's loss
of the spoils of Poynton and of Owen Gereth causes not only
solitude and poverty but intense spiritual suffering. The effect of
evil is usually to cut off the victim from free experience and
permanently ruin his chances for happiness.

Though James alters the traditional Puritan consideration of
evil by focusing on the sinned-against rather than the sinner, he
perhaps even more than Hawthorne reflects a Puritan view of
life in the dominant pattern of his novels, his view of life as a kind
of pilgrimage. We may well be reminded of Bunyan or the New
England historians in following a James hero through his experience, in which he is called upon to exercise supreme moral discrimination on a road beset with evil. Like Milton, James rejected
the notion of a "cloistered virtue" and sent his innocents into the
world to prove themselves: not simply to resist temptation but to
encounter experience, to face evil, to suffer, to endure, to exercise
and retain the moral view of life, and by doing so ultimately to
achieve salvation. Obviously the doctrinal ideas of the Puritan
allegorists and historians are not present in James, but his view of
life as the trial of the individual is essentially the same.

The notion of life as a trial is implicitly related to one of James's
primary themes: the necessity of experience. The exhortation of

Strether to Bilham in *The Ambassadors*—"Live all you can; it's a mistake not to. It doesn't so much matter what you do in particular, so long as you have your life" (XXI, 217)—is neither a plea for hedonism nor for aestheticism, and certainly not a plea for personality development through a variety of secular experiences. Isabel Archer of *The Portrait of a Lady* explains the Jamesian principle of experience:

> "I'm not bent on a life of misery. . . . I've always been intensely determined to be happy, and I've often believed I should be. . . . But it comes over me every now and then that I can never be happy in any extraordinary way; not by turning away, by separating myself . . . from life, . . . from the usual chances and dangers, from what most people know and suffer" (III, 187).

To miss experience, as does John Marcher of "The Beast in the Jungle," "the man of his time, *the* man, to whom nothing on earth was to have happened" (XVIII, 125), is to stultify one's self, to make moral development impossible, to starve the consciousness, to become sterile and spiritually dead.

James's principle of experience represents a belief in the expansion of consciousness, for the subjective life of the individual, his reflections and recognitions, his emotional responses to experience, comprise the essential life of James's fiction. The maturing of the moral consciousness through experience enables James's heroes and heroines to triumph over evil spiritually though they are otherwise defeated by it. Proper moral growth can occur only with an encounter with evil. Though the exposure of the innocent to evil involves loss and suffering, the result—the expanded consciousness—represents an ultimate victory.

The suggestion that James's fiction has the recurrent theme of the "fortunate fall" leads almost inevitably to a reference to R. W. B. Lewis's *The American Adam*, which fully examines the uses of "the Adamic mythology" in American literature, and in a few pages relates James to the tradition. Professor Lewis writes, "The form which life assumed in James's fiction reflected the peculiarly American rhythm of the Adamic experience: the birth of the innocent, the foray into the unknown world, the collision with that world, 'the fortunate fall,' the wisdom and the maturity which suffering produced."[31] Self-development, however, regardless of how spiritual and moral that development may be, in no way negates the ugliness of the evil which helped bring it about. James's fiction represents, if not the synthesis, certainly the coexistence of a Puritan concern with evil and a transcendentalist concern with experience.

Evil in James's fiction acquires its intensity not by the mere documentation of facts, but by the means employed to make the facts significant. Throughout his career James employed a variety of fictional methods to intensify situations and to give them universal implications. He grew increasingly adept at utilizing imagery and symbolism and at suggesting mythical parallels to his plots in order to give his material the widest relevance.[32] He frequently relied on such primitive plot substructures as the fairy story, the fable, and the melodrama[33] in order to reveal that beneath the impeccable manners and sophisticated dialogue of his characters there lurked the most basic of conflicts, that between good and evil; and his many methods enabled him to dramatize that conflict in its elemental force.

James's principal means of intensifying evil, however, was to reveal its emotional effect on the character who is its victim. "Henry James mentalized phenomena," writes A. C. Orage.[34] When James converts the concrete fact of evil into a kind of impalpable essence, the effect is not to diminish its reality but to intensify it by making it mysterious—even vaguely supernatural. Even when the nature of a crime is specified, like the duplicity of the Bellegardes or the parasitism of Gilbert Osmond, the sense of the evil far transcends the recorded facts, for as the evil impresses itself on the consciousness of the victim, the reader is compelled to realize its full force through the emotional reaction of the sinned-against. Sometimes, as in "The Turn of the Screw," the precise nature of the offense is not told us. James explains in the preface to the tale that to describe "the offered example, the imputed vice, the cited act" is to make evil limited and credible; "Only make the reader's general vision of evil intense enough . . . and his own experience, his own imagination, his own sympathy . . . and horror . . . will supply him quite sufficiently with all the particulars. Make him *think* the evil, make him think it for himself, and you are released from weak specifications." [35] James accomplishes these ends in this tale by making full use of the consciousness of the governess, whose terror colors her response to the experience and passes it on in turn to the reader.

Subjective response to evil is not simply a means of gaining intensity; it is related to James's notion that phenomena are only important when the private consciousness contains them. In a sense evil does not exist outside the mind of the spectator, who may be either a victim or witness. Probably the most intense sense of evil in James's fiction occurs at those times, which are frequent, when we witness the individual sensibility reacting to evil. In such scenes as that in which Isabel Archer sits before the fireplace and reflects upon Osmond's deception of her, we see what L. C. Knights terms James's "preoccupation with the plight of the trapped creature," the person who can only passively suffer. It is this "sense of suffocation" [36] that isolates the spectator from the movement of life that testifies most fully to James's imaginative grasp of the power of evil.

### CHAPTER TWO

# Evil and the International Theme

IT IS NOT difficult to explain Henry James's preoccupation with the international theme. As a historian of his times, James found considerably more meaning and interest than his contemporaries in the spectacles of international marriages and American tourists in Europe. Furthermore, James habitually saw human experience in terms of contraries. Through his repeated use of the international theme he gave cultural and national embodiment to the oppositions of innocence and experience, self and society, and good and evil which provide the dramatic tensions in all his works. The international theme offered James an inherent contrast between the most significant and extensive realities of his time.

"On the interest of *contrasted* things any painter of life and manners inevitably much depends, and contrast, fortunately for him, is easy to seek and to recognize," James writes; "the only difficulty is in presenting it again with effect, in extracting from it its sense and its lesson." [1] The "sense" and the "lesson" of the international theme are the moral issues involved in a conflict of representative national figures; for, while social comedy rules a story like "The Point of View," moral drama rules the more typical "A London Life." In most of his international fiction James penetrates the comic surface to the ethical conflict beneath. Thus such stories as "Daisy Miller," "The Reverberator," and "An International Episode," which expose American provincialism and offended European propriety, derive their "sense" and their "lesson" from James's profound concern with the nature of good and evil.

In the international fiction James identifies both good and evil

with specific nations and cultures; more precisely, there are versions of good and evil peculiarly American, and versions peculiarly European. Though the Europeans are no matches for the
Americans in ethical conduct, both have their generic malignities.
Thus it is far from adequate to hold that James's America is good
and his Europe evil, though it is generally true that the evil of
Europe is more prominent than that of America. Actually James
gains variety and subtlety in his international fiction through his
concern with the many forms of evil he finds in American life,
while there is a certain sameness and melodramatic obviousness in
his treatment of the evil of Europe.

The basic pattern of James's international fiction is well known
and requires only a brief description here. The American has an
instinctive moral sense; yet he is offered no means for experience,
no possibility of development. When he journeys to Europe, the
American is exposed to a rich complexity of art, history, and
manners, but also to an evil inseparable from the age and beauty
which he has sought. The American responds either by renouncing Europe on account of its evil, or by renouncing the moral
sense on account of Europe. The pursuit of happiness and experience leads to the crucial moral choice—the decision between
the world and the self. No synthesis between American innocence
and European experience is possible.

## AMERICA: VERSIONS OF OPPRESSION

As complexity is the most obvious characteristic of James's
Europe, simplicity is the most striking feature of his America. It
is a simplicity which excludes not only all the social and cultural
advantages catalogued in the well known passage in James's
*Hawthorne*, but also the evil inherent in traditional society. In
"An International Episode" (1879), two English visitors to Newport gain impressions of

> images of early breezy shining hours on lawns and piazzas
> that overlooked the sea; of innumerable pretty girls saying
> innumerable quaint and familiar things; of infinite lounging
> and talking and laughing and flirting and lunching and din-
> ing; of a confidence that broke down, of a freedom that

pulled up, nowhere; of an idyllic ease that was somehow too
ordered for a primitive social consciousness and too innocent
for a developed; of occasions on which they so knew every
one and every thing that they almost ached with reciprocity;
of drives and rides in the late afternoon, over gleaming
beaches, on long sea-roads, beneath a sky lighted up by
marvellous sunsets; of tea-tables, on the return, informal,
irregular, agreeable; of evenings at open windows or on the
perpetual verandahs, in the summer starlight, above the warm
Atlantic and amid irrelevant outbursts of clever minstrelsy.
. . . it was all the book of life, of American life, at least; with
the chapter of "complications" bodily omitted (XIV, 320).

The simple beauty of the idyllic pastoral scene is consistent with,
if not symbolic of, the innocence of its inhabitants. At its best
James's America is a kind of Eden, in which refinement, intelligence, and morality are natural endowments, uninhibited by any
external social or religious code. This to James is the perfectly
organic society, for there can be no distinction between man as
social creature and man as individual. Society derives its character from the individuals comprising it; no system of manners and
morals shapes the members or limits them.

In *A Small Boy and Others* (1913), in which James recollects
the charm of the America of his youth, he speaks of his cousin
Helen as a representative of this uncomplicated society: "I note
with appreciation that she was strenuously, actively good, and
have the liveliest impression both that no one was ever better, and
that her goodness somehow testifies for the whole tone of a society, a remarkable cluster of private decencies." Some pages
later James writes, "The social scheme, as we knew it, was, in its
careless charity, worthy of the golden age . . . ." The merit of
this ideal American society is that its principles of conduct are
private rather than public, spontaneous rather than cultivated,
simple rather than complex; in the narrow sense of the word it is
no society at all, rather a kind of anarchy: "How as mere detached unaccompanied infants we enjoyed such impunity of
range and confidence of welcome is beyond comprehension save
by the light of the old [American] manners and conditions, the

old local bonhomie, the comparatively primal innocence, the absence of complications . . . ." [2]

The America of "An International Episode" and *Notes of a Son and Brother*, as well as other of James's works, is the idealized myth, the America of the romancer, concerned with spiritual rather than surface truth; and, as R. W. B. Lewis has made clear, the mythology is Adamic.[3] The central reality beneath the romantic surface is the innocence of the American, an innocence nurtured and guarded by the very lack of "a complex social machinery" [4] that James found necessary for the artist. But if freedom and innocence are negative virtues, they are inestimable ones and abound in "a little world of easy and happy interchange, of unrestricted and yet all so instinctively sane and secure association and conversation, with all its liberties and delicacies, all its mirth and earnestness protected and directed so much more from within than from without . . . ." [5]

The conflict, or dialectic, of the international theme involves the collision of the internal code with the external. In "An International Episode," for example, the American, Bessie Alden, is snubbed by the mother of the British nobleman who has proposed to her. Bessie's inherent sense of honor leads her to reject the proposal: British pride in name and station clashes with American pride in self.

Aside from the simple and innocent America of the Adamic myth, there is also the America of oppression and evil in James's work. In the main, James finds evil, like good, to be a product of freedom: it is an effect of self-coercion rather than external pressure. It is the moral sense gone wrong and innocence perverted; it comes from a consideration of American negations as fulfillments and inflexible codes. In extreme, the evil of America is an intense provincialism that breeds aggressive narrow-mindedness; in moderation it is a complacent ignorance of the value of foreign experience.

The New England conscience, even though James frequently exposes it comically, is a source of evil in his fiction. Through Benjamin Babcock of *The American* (1877) James parodies the excessive moral timidity of the overdeveloped conscience, but even in the case of Babcock there is evidence of an evil, for though his shortsightedness is foolish to Christopher Newman, it is oppressive to Babcock, who is attracted to art by his aesthetic sensibilities and pulled away from it by his inclination to suspect all pleasure and beauty.

In *The Europeans* (1878), the Puritan temperament is for the most part either absurd or quaint. A characteristic touch is the conversation between Mr. Wentworth, with his inherited distrust of art and leisure, and the European Felix Young, who requests that he be allowed to paint the old man's portrait:

> "I think sitting for one's portrait is only one of the various forms of idleness," said Mr. Wentworth. "Their name is legion."
>
> "My dear sir," cried Felix, "you can't be said to idle when you are making a man work so!"
>
> "One might be painted while one is asleep," suggested Mr. Brand, as a contribution to the discussion.[6]

The Wentworth household is ruled by a fixed idea. Here is a case in which innocence does not imply freedom; the family's hostility to free experience makes moral maturity impossible. There is only physical freedom among the Wentworths, no intellectual freedom. A number of death images suggest the real condition of the family: Felix tells his sister, "My uncle, Mr. Wentworth . . . looks as if he were undergoing martyrdom, not by fire, but by freezing"; later Felix "perceived that there was something almost cadaverous in his uncle's high-featured white face"; to the Baroness, Felix's sister, "Gertrude seemed . . . most funereal . . . ."[7]

The Wentworths' rigid morality, which just falls short of being intolerance, expresses their fear of experience. Since life is tainted by evil, the Wentworths choose not to live at all; they shelter themselves from their European guests, who in turn invite them to share in the happiness and fullness of their lives. Felix Young is the normative character, opposed on the one hand by his sister, an adventuress who is not above deception, and on the other by the Wentworths, who equate happiness with evil. Felix admires the freshness but regrets the gloominess of the Americans. He tells Gertrude,

"You seem to me very well placed, for enjoying. You have money and liberty and what is called in Europe a 'position.' But you take a painful view of life, as you may say."

"One ought to think it bright and charming and delightful, eh?" asked Gertrude.

"I should say so—if one can. It is true it all depends on that," Felix added.

"You know there is a great deal of misery in the world," said his model.

"I have seen a little of it," the young man rejoined. "But it was all over there—beyond the sea. I don't see any here. This is a paradise.". . .

"To 'enjoy,' " [Gertrude said,] "to take life—not painfully, must one do something wrong?"

Felix gave his long light laugh again. "Seriously, I think not. And for this reason, among others: you strike me as very capable of enjoying, if the chances were given you, and yet at the same time as incapable of wrong-doing." [8]

Gertrude then, according to Felix, should view life as an opportunity rather than a discipline.

Among the Americans in *The Europeans*, only Gertrude breaks away from the stiff moral environment to seek a fuller experience; she marries Felix and goes with him to Europe, where conceivably her innate virtue and intelligence will be allowed to mature. Mr. Wentworth is beyond salvation; he is, as Felix observes, spiritually dead. Charlotte, Gertrude's sister, and Mr. Brand, the clergyman who unsuccessfully courted Gertrude, are alike unchanged by the Europeans and remain incapable of moral growth. Robert Acton, a neighbor of the Wentworths but apparently far more liberal and sophisticated than they, is equally subdued by his conscience. He falls in love with the Baroness Münster and thinks of marrying her. The Baroness, whose motive in visiting her relatives is to gain a fortune, would welcome the marriage, for Acton is very wealthy. Acton rejects the Baroness when he discovers that she is capable of lying; but the Baroness's lies are harmless, usually motivated by good manners.[9] As Rebecca West points out, "poor Eugenia fails altogether in an environment where a lie from her lips is not treated as *un petit péché d'une petite femme*, but remains simply a lie." [10] Acton is really worse than the Wentworths in that he is compelled by conscience to chastise others as well as shelter himself.

In Acton's repudiation of the Baroness, the inflexible virtue of the New Englander has become perverted and destructive; negative virtue has become active evil. For the most part the New England conscience is evil only to the extent that it prohibits experience. But it cannot be assumed that such an abstract basis of morality as the Wentworths' remains simply quaint when transferred to foreign soil or when influenced by alien codes. Thus Gertrude shows that she has no adequate substitute for the discipline she has abandoned. The New England morality is the only morality she knows; she has no personal resources to fall back upon. James clearly shows that the marriage of Gertrude and Felix is far from an ideal union of American innocence and European experience, for Gertrude from the start uses her newly found freedom to injure the representatives of her old code. She crudely insults Mr. Brand and Charlotte, and is brash and inconsiderate to everyone. It is not simply that Gertrude knows nothing of delicacy or tact, but that she is unable to reconcile her old standards of moral decency with the exuberant experience that Felix makes attainable.

*The Europeans* ends when Gertrude marries, and we are not told what she experiences in Europe. But in "A London Life" (1888), there is an American woman very much like Gertrude whose response to her European experience reveals the grave limitations in American innocence. Laura Wing, a young sheltered American with a New England conscience, visits her sister in London, where she finds herself in the midst of a thoroughly scandalous situation: her sister and her brother-in-law are both openly engaged in adultery. Laura is shocked and on the point of collapse. But her conduct surpasses indignation: to keep herself above any suspicion of impropriety she hysterically exhorts her relatives to reform and crudely tries to persuade a young American to marry her. James's opinion of his heroine is necessarily ambiguous, however, for as the center of consciousness in the story the righteous Laura is not inclined to question her own conduct. There is only one occasion when Laura considers that her interference might be reprehensible:

> Was she all wrong after all—was she cruel by being too rigid? . . . ought she only to propose to herself to "allow" more and more, and to allow ever, and to smooth things down by gentleness, by sympathy, by not looking at them too hard? It was not the first time the just measure seemed to slip from her hands as she became conscious of possible, or rather of very actual, differences of standard and usage (X, 372).

Laura, however, chooses intervention over endurance. Though her reckless attempts at reform are explicable in terms of her emotionally starved and morally rigorous past, Laura has something in common with the sophisticated evildoers of *The American* and *The Portrait of a Lady*: that is, she will not be content until she imposes her own narrow standards on others. It is nearly an inflexible rule in James's fiction that regardless of one's intentions he must respect the freedom of others. Through her meddling, Laura brings shame and hostility only to herself, yet she demonstrates the potential power for evil in the innocent who takes it upon himself to generalize from his own creed and to judge and reform others.

The New England ethos is more specifically under attack in *The Bostonians* (1886). Olive Chancellor's devotion to the abstract cause of woman's rights leads her to frustrate the impressionable Verena Tarrant's impulses to love. Oppression is clearly the dominant mood of *The Bostonians*. As opposed to the fresh and open scene of *The Europeans*, the settings in *The Bostonians* are for the most part musty and enclosed. In Olive's parlor the hero, Basil Ransom, thinks he has "never seen an interior that was so much an interior as this queer corridor-shaped drawing room of his new-found kinswoman . . . ." Most of the story takes place in such rooms, or in narrow, low-ceilinged lecture halls, where the audience has "an anxious, haggard look, though there were sundry exceptions—half a dozen placid, florid faces." Boston itself is cold, decayed, and drab:

The western windows of Olive's drawing room, looking over the water, took in the red sunsets of winter; the long, low bridge that crawled, on its staggering posts, across the Charles; the casual patches of ice and snow; the desolate suburban horizons, peeled and made bald by the rigour of the season; the general hard, cold void of the prospect; the extrusion, at Charlestown, at Cambridge, of a few chimneys and steeples, straight, sordid tubes of factories and engine-shops, or spare, heavenward finger of the New England meeting house. There was something inexorable in the poverty of the scene, shameful in the meanness of its details, which gave a collective impression of boards and tin and frozen earth, sheds and rotting piles, railwaylines striding flat across a thoroughfare of puddles, and tracks of the humbler, the universal horse-car, traversing obliquely this path of danger; loose fences, vacant lots, mounds of refuse, yards bestrewn with iron pipes, telegraph poles, and bare wooden backs of places.[11]

Ransom attempts to liberate Verena from Olive and from Boston. Symbolically his meetings with her occur in parks or on the Harvard campus, where Verena can not only breathe fresh air, but also enjoy a freedom from the movement which supports her liberty. The central situation of Olive's repression of Verena, not to mention her far more perverse self-repression, fuses with the New England urban setting to reveal the moral decay of Boston in a way that looks forward to poetic treatments of the same theme by T. S. Eliot and Robert Lowell.

In his remark that "the society of Boston was and is quite uncivilized but refined beyond the point of civilization," T. S. Eliot [12] refers to the New England tendency to dissociate morality from experience, the same habit of mind which James exposes in *The Europeans*. In *The Bostonians* he exposes a later generation of New Englanders, involved in post-Civil War urbanization and commercialism, rabidly progressive rather than primly conservative. The Calvinistic zeal has found political and secular expression. But, to return to Eliot's observation, the moral and social barbarism of the Boston James depicts is but the outgrowth of the refinement of a slightly earlier stage of New England culture. In neither era has the New England conscience adapted itself to the demands of personal liberty and social experience.

The world represented by Verena Tarrant's parents is the world of money. In their gross commercialism, Selah Tarrant, a fake mesmerist who exploits his daughter's public-speaking ability, and his wife, a tawdry social climber who hopes to crash society through Olive's adoption (actually purchase) of her daughter, reveal the ultimate corruption of New England Puritanism. The Tarrants seem remote from both the serene dignity of the Wentworths and the misguided idealism of Olive. If Mr. Wentworth and Olive represent a society which has abstracted ethics from experience and morals from manners, the Tarrants represent a society supported by neither ethics nor manners. They repel morally and aesthetically. They are the end product of a people who have never been able to reconcile the demands of the world with those of religion.

When morals go wrong in New England, and to some degree in America as a whole, James implies, the result is an intolerable vulgarity as well as a destructive evil. For the most part James's European malefactors pay great heed to manners, to a civilized style; indeed they repeatedly sacrifice conscience to form. But New England has a long tradition of hostility to beauty, and thus when it changes from a leisurely to an acquisitive society it can only be vulgar. In good and evil alike, the New Englander has no concern for appearances; they always correspond with reality.

The Tarrants, therefore, are an implicit criticism of the New England mind. But more specifically they cast a shadow on the liberalism of Miss Birdseye, Olive, and their fellow enthusiasts. The Tarrants are knaves and the others fools, but both feminism and mesmerism oppress the innocent, Verena, and both are condemned by the wise witness, Ransom.

The Tarrants are perhaps the most appalling examples of vulgarity in James's fiction, mainly because their lack of any aesthetic sense is all but identical with their lack of any moral sense. This, however, is using the term "vulgarity" in a simpler way than James himself uses it. "Vulgarity," in his fiction, is a term of both moral and aesthetic disapprobation. James frequently describes moral or immoral conduct in aesthetic terminology: "ugly" is almost synonymous with "evil," and "beautiful" with "good." This practice, however, should not be interpreted to mean that James considers vulgarity per se evil, and refinement per se good. It is incorrect to assume with H. R. Hays that "James really felt that bad manners was worse than murder," [13] or with Ernest A. Baker that in James's fiction "Vulgarity is the flesh and the devil." [14] James is in the tradition not of Oscar Wilde ("It is absurd to divide people into good and bad. People are either charming or tedious" [15] but in the tradition of Emerson ("Beauty is the mark God sets upon virtue" [16]).

In James's fiction vulgarity is mainly an American trait. At times it accompanies provincialism, as with the unsophisticated and self-satisfied Marcellus Cockeral of "The Point of View" (1882), who complacently rejects all of Europe: "They talk about things that we've settled ages ago, and the solemnity with which they propound to you their little embarrassments makes a heavy draft on one's good nature" (XIV, 599). At other times vulgarity indicates moral barbarism. Just as the bad manners of Verena Tarrant's parents reflect their greed, fraudulence, and indecency, so George Flack, an American correspondent for the scandal sheet *The Reverberator*, in the story of the same name (1888), has a brashness and indelicacy which mirror his moral corruption. As a journalist—one of many in James, all of whom (except Merton Densher) commit the arch crime of invading privacy—he delights in betraying confidences and exposing secrets. It is difficult to point out where Flack's vulgarity—his passion for money, scandal, and publicity—ends and where his immorality—his violation of privacy—begins; he is vulgar because he is immoral and immoral because he is vulgar.

Frequently vulgarity is accompanied by acquisitiveness: not the desire for experience, for the sense of the past, or for happiness which incites so many of James's American heroines on their European pilgrimages, but simply a greed for things. The wife and daughter of Mr. Ruck, the American business man in "The Pension Beaurepas" (1879), are devastating caricatures of a century of American woman tourists in Europe, armed with cameras and checkbooks, and blind to all but size and quantity. James's treatment, however, goes beyond caricature, for he reveals in the Ruck women a vicious selfishness and an unquenchable avarice that horrify rather than amuse. Mrs. Ruck and her daughter wish simply to buy Europe—to get as many of its clothes and jewels as possible. James dramatizes the sordid as well as the preposterous nature of this undertaking by showing the effect of the lavish spending on the pitiable husband. As one of the characters in the story says,

> To get something in a 'store' that they can put on their backs—that's their one idea; they haven't another in their heads. Of course they spend no end of money, and they do it with an implacable persistence, with a mixture of audacity and of cunning. They do it in his teeth and they do it behind his back; the mother protects the daughter, while the daughter eggs on the mother. Between them they're bleeding him to death (XIV, 460).

Vulgarity and immorality both stem from the same source, a fundamental blindness to all but the grossest of values. The Ruck women's tastelessness is but the converse of their disrespect for Mr. Ruck. Virtue always stands in some relation to awareness in James. In some cases aesthetic awareness may exist without moral awareness (for example, in Gilbert Osmond and Mrs. Gereth); in other cases a commonplace moral awareness may exist without aesthetic awareness (for example, in Henrietta Stackpole and Owen Gereth); but James's superior creatures combine the two (for example, Isabel Archer and Fleda Vetch). If the highest morality requires the unified sensibility, the basest immorality often results from some kind of imbalance between the aesthetic and the moral understanding, or from a deficiency in both.

The inoffensive vulgarians in James, those with a kind of moral sense, are agents of a mild evil. They oppress themselves. For good is necessarily imperfect in James unless it masters experience; and the vulgar by definition are incapable of experience. They see life superficially and they cannot participate in the refining and maturing process which the complex civilization offers. "Daisy Miller" (1878) is a story in which an apparently inoffensive, even charming, vulgarity is a moral limitation. Most commentators have stressed the victory of American innocence over narrow European standards. But Daisy does not profit from her experience; she is a pure child of nature, whose response to trivial and grave challenges alike is impulsive. Without conscious reflection Daisy disregards the dicta of the American colony in Rome that she should not appear in public with a gentleman unescorted, that she should not violate curfews, that she should not treat her courier as an equal. Daisy "does what she likes" because there is no other motivation in her simple nature. Innocent and good as she is, she has no moral, not to mention aesthetic, consciousness. She has neither receptivity nor potency. Her European travels, her relation to Winterbourne and to the offended Americans, and her indifference to convention are ultimately meaningless to her. She is a person on whom everything is lost.

The business man in James has the same basic deficiency. Though James confessed that his inadequate knowledge of "the huge organized mystery of the consummately, the supremely applied money-passion" precluded his treating "nineteen-twentieths" [17] of American city life, another reason is probably James's belief that for the business man the "money-passion" is the only passion, that his business denies him the physical and intellectual freedom necessary for the enriching experience of Europe. Daisy Miller's father remains in Schenectady making money; Mr. Dosson of "The Reverberator," when not sitting idly in his hotel room, likes Europe because he can spend part of his fortune there: "he was never content on any occasion unless a great deal of money was spent . . ." (XIII, 50). Business is not a base activity to James until such late works as "The Jolly Corner" and *The Ivory Tower*, but in his early fiction it consistently stifles the spirit and the sensibilities. Ferner Nuhn, among other critics, has commented on James's "curious attitude toward money, which made the possession of worldly means—and a comfortable amount of it!—virtually a prerequisite for the good life, but the acquisition of it an almost necessarily damning activity." [18] The possession of money is a condition of freedom, and the earning of it a condition of slavery.

Thus money-making, like the New England conscience and provincial vulgarity, causes or reflects the deadened consciousness. An apt illustration is Mr. Ruck of "The Pension Beaurepas," described by a fellow tourist as "a broken-down man of business. He's broken-down in health and I think he must be broken-down in fortune. He has spent his whole life in buying and selling and watching prices, so that he knows how to do nothing else" (XIV, 460). There is some comedy in Mr. Ruck's pathetic incompatibility with the leisurely and cultured life in Europe: "Well, we certainly saw the cathedral. I don't know as we're any the better for it, and I don't know as I should know it again. But we saw it anyway, stone by stone—and heard about it century by century" (XIV, 440). But there is minor tragedy in the old man's approaching bankruptcy as his wife and daughter spend the last of his dollars on clothes and jewelry which they will never use. Mr. Ruck is figuratively and literally killed by money, by the possession of it and by the lack of it.

In James's early work the wealthy business man is usually seen as an innocent soul spiritually blighted by his work. The unsuccessful business man, however, is most often a conniver and a scoundrel. George Fenton of *Watch and Ward* (1878) and Morris Townsend of *Washington Square* (1880), both failures in business, try to marry for money. When James returned to the American scene in his later years his critical insight into the nature of business deepened, so that he went beyond the rather limited—and unmistakably middle-class—attitude of regarding business success as a certain key to morality and business failure as a clear indication of immorality.

Fenton and Townsend are exceptions, however, to the general rule that evil in American life comes from prohibition and restraint, rather than aggression and intervention. Thus commercialism is usually a negative rather than a positive evil: it is hostile to experience and moral development. All of James's Americans who commit themselves to a specific code or cause—whether it be New England Puritanism, feminism, commercialism, or nationalism—are incompletely human. And in this respect James shares the belief of his philosopher-theologian father, who, as his novelist son was to write, insisted that "What we were to do . . .

was just to be something, something unconnected with specific doing, something free and uncommitted, something finer in short than *being that*, whatever it was, might consist of." [19] Those who choose to be something specific are unable to be themselves; by adhering to an external system they unfit themselves to live the inner life.

James's fictional portraits of America and Americans give abundant support to the observation of M. D. Zabel that "The American mind, rooted in hereditary conscience, had never escaped its hauntings by darker powers, its stirring of ancestral guilt, what Howells was presently to call 'the slavery implicated in our liberty.' " [20] Some of James's stories imply the existence of an evil inherent in American life beyond individual control and considerably less tangible than the various evils of commerce, vulgarity, and Puritanism, although it is perhaps the ultimate source of them. In remembering his American youth, James reflects on "the relics of those we have seen beaten," on "the chronicle of early deaths, arrested careers, broken promises, orphaned children," and on those who "in spite of brilliant promise and romantic charm, ended badly, as badly as possible." [21] Pertinently, Van Wyck Brooks writes, "To the end of his life . . . America, to James, signified destruction and failure. It was the dark country, where the earth was a quicksand, where amiable uncles ended in disaster, where men were turned into machines, where genius was subject to all sorts of inscrutable catastrophes." [22] James interpreted the failures and disasters of his friends and relatives as somehow symbolic of an intrinsic treachery in America.[23]

Thus the evil of America in "A Passionate Pilgrim," "Europe," "Four Meetings," and *Washington Square* cannot be explained as the effect of self-suppression; the protagonists of these stories are suppressed by various external, rather than internal, agencies. In his discussion of *The Portrait of a Lady*, Pelham Edgar complains (rather unreasonably) that

> There is not much to be gained by portraying a woman with a mind, if that mind is ultimately to be cramped in its opportunity for growth, nor in emphasizing the value of

experience, if experience is to lead in the end to a spiritual prison in which the natural impulses of the heart must suffer an inevitable decay.[24]

According to his own standards, Edgar should find even more intolerable those James stories in which persons of sensibility and intelligence must accept spiritual imprisonment from the start. Such characters are never allowed to reach the point where they can choose to renounce or accept happiness; they are thwarted, not by free will, but by something like fate.

One example is Clement Searle, the decayed, brittle, and sensitive hero of "A Passionate Pilgrim" (1871) who is deprived of his hereditary right to an English manor by a proud cousin who schemes to keep the estate in his own hands. Because he is poor, Searle is unable to leave America. His bad health symbolizes the effect of American life on his spirit. When Searle finally comes to England, believing he can recover his estate, the incivility of the British relative is all that is needed to kill both body and spirit. Searle, then, who requires a richness of culture and manners to sustain his fine consciousness, is to a large degree destroyed by the aesthetic poverty of America.

"Four Meetings" (1877) and "Europe" (1899) are slight and ironic stories of frustration; each deals with a young woman of imagination and intelligence who is prevented—in "Four Meetings" by inadequate finances and in "Europe" by family obligations—from going to Europe, an experience which, James implies, is necessary for the spiritual and intellectual growth of each. The irony in these stories is that the generosity of these two women keeps them from fulfilling their ambitions. Jane Rimmle, who has an intense "sense of life" (XVI, 354), wastes away in New England caring for her mother, who is constantly ill but never dies; Caroline Spencer, a New England schoolteacher, uses her life savings to take a trip to Europe, but she gets only as far as Le Havre, where she gives her money to her worthless cousin so that he may pay his debts.

Catherine Sloper of *Washington Square* (1880) is James's most fully realized portrait of the person frustrated by external forces. Catherine is coerced by her father, who if not a tyrant is a cold-blooded analyst who trades upon the respect Catherine has for him, by Miss Penniman, her witless and meddlesome aunt, and by Morris Townsend, the adventurer who wants to marry the unattractive Catherine for her money. Catherine is betrayed by her innocence and unawareness and by the essentially well intentioned interference of her father and aunt as much as she is by the deceit of Townsend. Unlike most of James's heroines, Catherine is not allowed the freedom to make a mistake. Though her father's judgment is correct, we feel that he creates for Catherine a harsher and sadder life than she would have had with Townsend. If she is sheltered from disillusion, she is also sheltered from the moral experience of making a decision and living with it.

Like Caroline Spencer and Jane Rimmle, Catherine misses "living" partly because she is good; she is incapable of disobeying her father. While in *The Portrait of a Lady* the native moral sense prevents an unqualified acceptance of "the ampler experience" [25] of Europe, in *Washington Square* it prevents the slightest movement toward experience. Unlike the Wentworths, Catherine is restrained, not by a New England conscience, but by a clear-headed concept of loyalty. Were Catherine to disobey her father, she would certainly lose our sympathy. Nor should we think that a deficiency in intellect is the major impediment to Catherine's development; rather it is a deficiency in freedom.

In the end Catherine accepts her fate, her life-in-death. Her experience has been one solely of suffering and frustration:

> From her own point of view the great facts of her career were that Morris Townsend had trifled with her affection, and that her father had broken its spring. Nothing could ever alter these facts; they were always there, like her name, her age, her plain face. Nothing could ever undo the wrong or cure the pain that Morris had inflicted on her, and nothing could ever make her feel toward her father as she felt in her younger years. There was something dead in her life, and her duty was to try and fill the void.[26]

Catherine can rise above self-pity, but not above suffering, the permanent scar of evil. But her suffering is almost entirely gratuitous, the effect of environment rather than free choice. Catherine acquires a kind of moral strength and stoic wisdom through her sad history, but her life is primarily one of wasted sensibilities.

In the main, however, the American protagonist has the freedom to realize his ideals. But just as the evil which can oppress the American is most often a negation, so too the free American possesses a good which is negative: [27] he is blissfully ignorant of evil; he is uninfluenced by weighty codes of manners and ethics. The ideal American is capable of "living," of responding to the splendor of Europe, and of enriching his moral-aesthetic consciousness through the experience it offers.

Among the Americans who have the freedom and the intelligence to seek the prizes of Europe there are different character types and modes of behavior. There are those who either respond too much to Europe or not enough, and those who maintain the delicate balance between conscience and experience. Implicit in the international theme is the tension between what Elizabeth Stevenson calls

> the conscious individual and the raw material of life. That person has two duties in living: the first, to expose himself to as much of the great unconscious force of life as he is able to endure; the second, to hold firm to that irreducible core which is himself, to be what he is with all his might.[28]

Most of the Americans who are cramped by a literal and dogmatic morality stay in America; but if they go to Europe, their major concern is to protect themselves from any personal involvement. They remain uncommitted and untested. Rowland Mallet, for example, can gain experience only vicariously, through his protégé Roderick Hudson. He enjoys the art and culture of Europe, but shies away from any human relationship, so that in the end his fear of life has prevented him from marrying.

At the opposite pole is Winterbourne of "Daisy Miller." Like Mallet he is restrained from marriage by a perversion of scruples, but his suspicion and aversion are caused not by an exaggeration but by a withering of the American moral sense. He is an American who, in repudiating Daisy Miller, commits the arch European crime of judging on appearances. If Mallet, and also Robert Acton

of *The Europeans,* remain unmarried for having been too long in
New England, Winterbourne's fault is that he has lived too long
in Europe.

But the American can be too indiscriminate. Thus it is that the
Europeanized American is more often the agent of evil than the
European in James. There are the Americans who, far from remaining passive and suspicious, are unrestrained in their greed for
the riches of Europe. In *Roderick Hudson* (1875) both Mrs.
Light and her daughter Christina so totally adopt European
values that they deny American values. Mrs. Light coerces her
daughter into a profitable marriage to an Italian nobleman; Christina is so reckless and conscienceless in her craving for sensations
that she ruins Roderick Hudson and—in *The Princess Casamassima*—Hyacinth Robinson.

The American abroad exposes himself to the alternate possibilities of being betrayed by Europe and of losing his native integrity. He can become either victim or agent of evil. The European
is more restrained in his treachery, for the American retains his
freedom when he loses the rectitude usually coordinate with it.
The European must at least respect his own conventions, and his
aesthetic sense prohibits overt grossness. The Bellegardes' code of
honor may seem narrow and amoral; but the Osmonds and Lights
have no traditional codes.

Furthermore, James seems more interested in America than in
Europe in his international works. He reveals the many forms the
American character can assume when exposed to the complexity
of Europe. On the other hand, his Europeans are by contrast both
less interesting and less important; they form a kind of uniform
background to the multifaceted American temperament.

## THE AMBIGUITY OF EUROPE

The foremost European sin is exclusiveness. The reprehensible
Europeans derive their standards externally, and betray and exploit in order to uphold them. Both the merits and the faults of
Europe are social rather than private. Europe represents culture,
civilization, art, and manners. One cannot make a simple distinction—as do James's more parochial Americans—between the
form and the content of Europe, and conclude that the form is

superficial because it masks the evil beneath. In James's Europe the exterior beauty always permits and frequently depends upon treachery. Yet the surface has a reality of its own. European culture can be defined only as an ambiguity: it elevates normal human intercourse and social existence to a relation with beauty and style, and yet private moral conduct inevitably undergoes a degradation in order for the relation to be maintained. Ultimately James finds perversion in the sacrifice of morals to manners, but he never questions the importance of manners. His international fiction explores the dilemma but never resolves it; the dialectical opposition of American innocence and European experience is unresolvable. In Ferner Nuhn's terms, "Europe is form without spirit, America is spirit without form"; [29] and those who deny the importance of form are as wrong as those who deny the importance of spirit. James's international fiction implies the failure of western civilization, for its most searching implication is the discord between individual and society. The self-determined individual must deny the wellsprings of his being to partake of the civilized society; those who refuse to make the compromise—the Isabel Archers and Christopher Newmans—have no alternative other than social and spiritual isolation.

The American's experience with Europe is one of disillusion, for each must make his own discovery of the disparity between appearance and reality. Laura Wing's recognition is typical:

> The contrast was before her again, the sense of the same curious duplicity (in the literal meaning of the word) that she took in at Plash—the way the genius of such an old house was all peace and decorum and yet the spirit that prevailed there, outside the schoolroom, contentious and impure. She had often before been struck with this—with that perfection of machinery that can still at perfect times make English life go on of itself with a stately rhythm long after corruption is within it (X, 292).

The innocents themselves err in holding an impossible ideal— their faults as well as their merits are idealistic. Clement Searle assumes that the majestic exterior of an English country house represents an ultimate kind of happiness; Euphemia Cleve is deluded by her romantic temperament into taking the faultless appearance and manners of the aristocrat Richard de Mauves at face value. Even before he meets European evil, the American is, in a sense, victimized by his own innocence.

The sense of evil is both more extreme and more apparent in Europe than in America. Employing—no doubt excessively—the melodramatic techniques of Dickens and Hawthorne, James suggests evil through scene rather than action. The once glittering aristocracy is now, quite literally, dark and crumbling. The spaciousness of the American's background contrasts with the narrowness of the European scene, just as American emotional spontaneity contrasts with European formality.

In "Madame de Mauves" (1874), for example, James develops meaning through scene; he depicts rather than dramatizes an evil considerably more extreme than the transgressions of Richard de Mauves—his marrying for money and his infidelity. James gains a certain depth and scope by suggesting that the heroine, symbolically named Euphemia, is coming into contact not with an isolated European but with the essence of European culture, so that the evil she experiences is one endemic to a civilization. Much of the story occurs in twilight, the time of day that is both night and day, or evil and good—suggesting the complexity of a society which offers external advantages if one is willing to accept the basic evil. The betrayed heroine consistently "linger[s] through the thickening twilight" (XIII, 220), inextricably trapped in the dense moral atmosphere. Originally Euphemia had been attracted to de Mauves because of the age of his family and home; it is, however, the evil of the past, decayed and corrupt, which injures her. The old formal garden is a kind of prison for her:

> She lived in an old-fashioned pavilion, between a high-walled court and an excessively artificial garden, between whose enclosure you saw a long line of tree-tops. . . . Presently she would come out and wander through the narrow alleys and beside the thin spouting fountain, and at last introduce [Longmore] to a private gate in a high wall, the opening to a gate which led to a forest (XIII, 244).

The forest means the same to Euphemia as Washington Square means to Catherine Sloper and the Harvard campus to Verena Tarrant: specifically it means freedom. But the forest is permanently closed to Euphemia, who must live out her life in the death scene, the walled-in formal garden with the ancient pavilion. She refuses to compromise her integrity to the code of the French family. In her white dress, she is the center of a picture: "her intrinsic clearness shone out . . . through the darker cast over it" (XIII, 251). The imagery throughout the story is conventional and its effectiveness is dubious, but James's effort to suggest that evil is inseparable from the European past is unmistakable.

It is noteworthy that whereas James frequently uses imagery of coldness, darkness, and imprisonment to symbolize the mysterious and pervasive evil of Europe, he is less concerned with scenic effects in those stories in which the Americans avoid injury by the Europeans. In "An International Episode," for instance, the situation is similar to that in *The American,* but the treatment is entirely different. The snobbish Duchess of Bayswater tries to prevent the marriage of her son to the American Bessie Alden. But since the Duchess is sketched in light rather than dark colors, her mistreatment of Bessie seems closer to bad taste than to evil; there is nothing to suggest a malignity more extreme than the overt—therefore limited—unpleasantness of the Duchess. The American can avoid suffering only from the less menacing forms of European culture. When he gets the better of the Europeans—notably in "An International Episode," "The Siege of London," "The Reverberator," and "Miss Gunton of Poughkeepsie"—he touches the surface of Europe, not the depths beneath.

## THE AMERICAN

In *The American* (1877) James fully utilizes the inherent comic situation of the swaggering Californian in Europe: his ignorance of art and manners, his excessive good nature and optimism contrast sharply with his new environment. Christopher Newman is not only conventional and characteristic in his touring methods—in making Paris his headquarters and visiting the Louvre and the opera; he is also typically American in his attitude

toward Europe—in being candid and unashamed of his nationality, in desiring to "get something out of Europe," and in being
confident that he can conquer the world even though he knows
nothing about it. There is comedy and tragedy in James's drama
of the American abroad, but the common denominator or principle of unity is Newman's moral naïveté, his childlike ignorance
of the ways of the world. His gauche reactions to paintings and
cathedrals and the protocol of Parisian society are for the most
part highly comic; but his insensibility to European evil brings
about the moral struggle.

In the beginning Newman harbors the illusion that the world
is good, and evil nonexistent; he also assumes that he is a completely free agent, whose sole responsibility is to be as happy as
he possibly can. "The world [is] a great bazaar where one might
stroll about and purchase handsome things" (II, 87), Newman
believes. When he meets evil and suffers from it, Newman acquires a moral education; he is made to see the folly of his innocent illusions. One of the points of the novel is that, as in *Oedipus
Rex*, an ignorance of evil is a moral failure. It is the same message
Melville dramatizes in "Benito Cereno," in which the morally
immature Captain Delano is unable to recognize and understand
the evil inherent in the situation in which he is involved.

Newman wishes to take the best of Europe without dealing
with the worst of it. In Europe he wants "the biggest kind of en-
tertainment a man can get" (II, 33), and also

> "a great woman. I stick to that. That's one thing I *can*
> treat myself to, and if it's to be had I mean to have it. What
> else have I toiled and struggled for all these years? I've suc-
> ceeded, and now what am I to do with my success? To make
> it perfect, as I see it, there must be a lovely being perched on
> the pile like some shining statue crowning some high monu-
> ment. She must be as good as she's beautiful and as clever as
> she's good. I can give my wife many things, so I'm not afraid
> to ask certain others. . . . I want, in a word, the best article
> in the market" (II, 49).

The business metaphor is not accidental; it points to Newman's
basic fault, his tendency to deal with Europe and Europeans, if

not with life, as commodities for which he has the money to pay. Newman's good nature and boyish concern with fair play do not disguise his vanity. His self-satisfaction is finally identical with his innocence, for he cannot see that life ultimately demands more self-denial than that which the honest business man brings to bear in his purchases and sales.

In the beginning Newman never relaxes his view of his European experience as a holiday. He interrupts his stay in Paris to tour Europe, an excursion which dramatizes Newman's moral inadequacy for his approaching personal involvement with European values. Newman, tastelessly and greedily, tries to take as much of Europe with him as he can; yet he is perfectly content with himself: he has no desire to emerge a European. Indeed, he superimposes the American values of efficiency and materialism upon everything he sees.

Newman meets the Reverend Benjamin Babcock, an arch representative of the New England conscience, and travels with him for several months. James uses the absurd Babcock to illuminate a serious deficiency in Newman. Newman "liked everything, he accepted everything, he found amusement in everything; he was not discriminating, his values were as vague and loose as if he had carried them in his trousers pocket" (II, 91). Babcock, on the other hand, "detested Europe and felt an irritated need to protest against Newman's easy homage to so compromised a charmer. . . . He mistrusted the 'European' temperament. . . . 'European' life seemed to him unscrupulous and impure" (II, 92). Babcock has in excess the very qualities which Newman lacks: responsibility and restraint. The two Americans are alike, however, in their innocence, for neither is prepared to face the decadence of Europe.

Newman's inability to recognize evil is a steady motif in the novel. "Isn't [Claire], as a married woman, her own mistress?" (II, 109) he asks Mrs. Tristram when he learns of the authority the Bellegardes assume over her. When he hears more about Claire's forced marriage, he remarks, "It's like something in a regular old play" (II, 111), and asks, "Is it possible . . . that they can do this sort of thing over here?" (II, 111). Not until the end does he learn to take the evil of the Bellegardes seriously as a part of the world in which he lives. Up to that point he oversimplifies and underestimates his antagonists: "What should I be afraid of? You can't hurt me unless you kill me by some violent means" (II, 303), Newman tells Valentin, with characteristic naïveté. Even when he is wronged by the Bellegardes, he does not comprehend the meaning of their crime against him:

> And to be turned off because one was a commercial person! As if he had ever talked or dreamed of the commercial since his connexion with the Bellegardes began. . . . Granted one's being commercial was fair ground for one's being cleverly "sold," how little they knew about the class so designated and its enterprising way of not standing upon trifles (II, 421).

Newman makes the mistake of considering the Bellegardes' evil as somehow to be explained rationally—either as a mistake or a "trick."

When Newman learns from Mrs. Bread of the murder which the Bellegardes have committed, he realizes the gravity of the evil he is dealing with. The murder explicitly relates bad manners to bad morals. James permits the reader to discover with Newman that the surface capriciousness of the Bellegardes is in fact linked with an evil that is invincible and incomprehensible (to the very end Newman cannot fully understand the motivation and meaning of the Bellegardes; he can only accept them as a fact).

James does not define the evil of the Bellegardes—much of their malignity depends on their mystery—but he describes it in several ways. There is but limited effectiveness in the horror of the family curse and the Gothic murder; nor is much gained by the imagery of darkness, coldness, and complexity which suggests the miasma that surrounds the Bellegardes in both time and space. James conveys the evil of the Bellegardes most effectively through dramatic action. He establishes the connection between the depravity and the aristocratic tradition of the family more through Valentin and Claire, the morally superior Bellegardes, than through the obvious villains, Mme. de Bellegarde and Urbain. When Valentin dies defending his honor—killed by a Ger-

man brewer in a duel caused by a dispute over a worthless co-
quette—the ugliness of family pride is forcefully conveyed. This
subordination of sense to an archaic notion of honor is "unnatural
and monstrous" (II, 388) to Newman, and clearly James is in
agreement.

When Claire quietly acquiesces to the will of her mother and
brother, she demonstrates her acceptance of their guilt:

> "I ought to have convinced you [she tells Newman] that I
> was doomed to disappoint you. But I *was*, in a way, too
> proud. . . . I'm too proud to be honest. . . . I'm afraid of
> being uncomfortable. . . . It's not marrying you; it's doing
> all that would go with it. It's the rupture, the defiance, the
> insisting upon being happy in my own way. What right have
> I to be happy when . . . others have so suffered?" (II,
> 411–412).

Newman, of course, cannot understand that Claire is by birth implicated in the evil of her family and must atone by renouncing
Newman and the freedom he proposes.

The traditional code of the European has the maturity and wisdom of age just as it has the evil which James usually associates
with age, for it holds as a first premise that a belief in happiness is
fallacious. To the Bellegardes personal contentment is neither a
desirable nor an attainable goal. Claire's mother and brother reject
the easy comfort of Newman's millions because they cannot
reconcile the source of the money with family honor. Newman
cannot comprehend Claire's renunciation, for he, till the conclusion of his experience, believes happiness to be the primary goal
in life. When Newman burns the note that would give him revenge, he reveals his maturity—he recognizes the superior value
of endurance; he denies himself the right to happiness through
self-assertion; and he realizes that evil is irremediable. Newman
has invaded Europe to reap its treasures, but he leaves it with a
higher sense of ethical values, a code of life closer to stoicism
than his original hedonism, and a knowledge of evil. In Newman's
case this knowledge produces a fineness of response that counter-
balances the anguish of humilation and loss.

### THE PORTRAIT OF A LADY

Like the other American heroines in James, Isabel Archer of *The Portrait of a Lady* (1881), an enormous self-seeker who believes that reality corresponds to her ideals, whose innocence is her strength as well as her weakness, is doomed to failure. James repeatedly dramatizes the inadequacy of romance as a guide to life.[30] He consistently shows the impossibility of complete success for his Newmans, Euphemia Cleves, and Isabel Archers, and permits them to achieve only equivocal moral triumphs through endurance of suffering. Isabel Archer's history assumes this pattern, but in *The Portrait of a Lady* James also treats a number of more commonplace marriages. There is the marriage of the expatriates Mr. and Mrs. Touchett, two different American types whose marriage is all but a total failure. Mr. Touchett preserves the quiet and honest dignity of his American nature in his English estate, while his wife is quick to seek European values and friends. There is the adulterous tie between the other expatriates, Osmond and Mme. Merle. There is the marriage of the American Henrietta and the English Bantling, both comic figures, whose union is an ironic counterpart to Isabel's, for it gives all indications of being the only successful marriage in the book. The marriage of Edward Rosier and Pansy Osmond is thwarted by Osmond. Ralph Touchett, clearly in love with Isabel, is confined to the role of a spectator by his illness. Finally, there is the Countess Gemini, Osmond's sister, who has left America in her youth and married a third-rate Italian nobleman. Her marriage is more or less in the background of the novel, but it casts a grim shadow over the proceedings in the foreground, for the Count Gemini is an impoverished gambler and the Countess has become an adulteress.

The marriage of Henrietta and Bantling is the only successful one, and this seems to be mainly a comic contrast to the failure of the others. The marriages not prevented by circumstances or intervention end in futility or disaster. James's meaning is that though theoretically the union of America—which represents morality, innocence, and spirit—with Europe—which represents manners, experience, and form—is an ideal arrangement, in actuality it can mean only misery. James recurrently explored the possibilities of a workable union of America and Europe. Perhaps Felix Young of *The Europeans* embodies this ideal synthesis, but Young is the only character of his type in James's fiction. He is somewhat like Valentin Bellegarde of *The American*, yet Valentin is too intimately associated with the traditional values of his country to realize the freedom he desires. F. R. Leavis maintains that Ralph Touchett

> is the centre, the key-figure, of James's 'system'—the poise of harmony. . . . He is neither American nor English—or he is both: that is, he combines the advantages, while being free from the limitations. He can place everyone, and represents the ideal civilization that James found in no country.[31]

What Leavis overlooks is that Touchett is a ruined man. His incurable illness, which associates him with those Americans who are denied experience by physical, economic, or other handicaps, symbolizes impotence. Touchett can live only vicariously; he is, in effect, outside the action of the novel. More important, as Elizabeth Stevenson points out, "his living and dying as he does is a kind of reference to reality for Isabel."[32] Like Mercutio in *Romeo and Juliet* or Angela and the Beadsman in "The Eve of Saint Agnes," he is a kind of *memento mori*.

The failure of every marriage except Henrietta's also points to James's abiding conviction that isolation is the ultimate lot of every man. Social existence precludes love, friendship, and sympathy. The James character requires completion, and, just as *The Portrait of a Lady* illustrates the limitations of Isabel and Osmond by contrasting them, it stresses the futility of any attempt at a reconciliation of opposite qualities. At best—as in the case of Isabel and Warburton—there is no alteration in either person; at worst—as in the case of Isabel and Osmond—one person's deficiency injures the other. The morally superior person is thus driven further back into himself, forced to rely on his innate strength, forever estranged from a significant social relationship.

There is clearly a revelation of an intrinsic evil in the novel's emphasis on man's inevitable conditions of isolation and failure. But in *The Portrait* James is also concerned with the process of man's decline from innocence to depravity. Nearly all James's novels treat to some extent the theme of the Fall of Man—the single theme which dominated so much of nineteenth-century American literature—but no one work so explicitly as *The Portrait of a Lady.*

In James's version of the Fall myth America is Eden. As Felix Young says of the society of the Wentworths in *The Europeans,* "It's primitive; it's patriarchal; it's the *ton* of the golden age." [33] The idyllic American paradise suits the moral innocence of the Americans. The innocents leave their paradise of their own will. If they are expelled from Eden, the force is their own selfhood, a pride which urges them to master experience. In spite of the language of Emersonian transcendentalism with which James's Americans consider their goals, they are clearly motivated by an unhealthy egotism. Isabel, for example,

> had an unquenchable desire to think well of herself. She had a theory that it was only under this provision life was worth living; that one should be one of the best, should be conscious of a fine organization (she couldn't help knowing her organization was fine), should move in a realm of light, of natural wisdom, of happy impulse, of inspiration gracefully chronic. . . . She spent half her time in thinking of beauty and bravery and magnanimity; she had a fixed determination to regard the world as a place of brightness, of free expansion, or irresistible action . . . (III, 68).

Such pride, based on a belief in the goodness and possibility of unlimited emotional and intellectual expansion, is also an active aggressiveness that can easily become evil. What distinguishes the Americans and the Europeans in *The Portrait of a Lady* is that the Americans are ambitious to possess something or someone. In this sense, the aims of Isabel and Osmond are similar, for both wish to satisfy their own cravings. But Isabel's pride is untainted by malice; rather it stems from her "meagre knowledge, her inflated ideals, her confidence at once innocent and dogmatic" (III, 69). When Isabel leaves the Edenlike America, she seeks a total knowledge and freedom; disillusion comes with the awareness that the two are mutually exclusive. As Leon Edel points out, "twice in the book James uses Miltonic words to describe the extent of Isabel's freedom—as if she were Eve standing at the portals of Paradise, which are closing behind her."[34] Though Isabel is more innocent than Eve at the beginning of her adventure, her innocence is ambiguous; it combines a false notion of personal independence with an obliviousness to evil. In this sense her original sin is simply innocence, but an innocence coordinate with pride.

It is significant that *The Portrait of a Lady* concludes with Goodwood offering Isabel a way out of her misery:

> "It's too monstrous of you to think of sinking back into that misery, of going to open your mouth to that poisoned air. . . . Why shouldn't we be happy—when it's here before us, when it's so easy? . . . We can do absolutely as we please. . . . Were we born to rot in our misery? . . . The world's all before us—and the world's very big. I know something about that" (IV, 434–435).

The point is that Goodwood knows nothing about the world, for his pleas recall the former beliefs of Isabel, who at this point has so matured through her contact with evil that she can reply, "The world's very small" (IV, 435). Goodwood proposes an enormous temptation, as only now does Isabel realize the worth of the happiness that Goodwood offers: "She had wanted help, and here was help; it had come in a rushing torrent" (IV, 435). Isabel's renunciation of escape from Osmond and of happiness with Goodwood is a triumph of her (and James's) idealism; it avows the supreme dignity of the human being. James does nothing to minimize the suffering with which Isabel must spend the rest of her life, but he suggests that the acquired wisdom, the expansion of consciousness, represents a development far higher not only than her life in America but higher than her life with Warburton or Goodwood would have been. When Isabel partakes of the Tree of Knowledge in the world of experience she is made forcefully aware of the presence of evil, but in a sense her earlier ambitions are fulfilled. She was perhaps correct in pursuing her ideals, in accepting nothing but the fullest experiences that life can offer.

From the beginning Isabel vaguely realizes that her restlessness for knowledge will not be satisfied until she faces evil. When she tells Ralph, ". . . I don't wish to touch the cup of experience. It's a poisoned drink! I only want to see for myself" (III, 213) (echoing Rowland Mallet), she speaks of impossibilities, and Ralph spots the flaw in her wish: "You want to see, but not to feel" (III, 213). But for the most part Isabel's quest is far from superficial; she tells Warburton after rejecting his proposal, "I can't escape unhappiness. . . . In marrying you I shall be trying to" (III, 186). Here Isabel knows unhappiness only abstractly, but she realizes that she must experience it to fulfill her mission. On several occasions she asks Ralph to show her the ghost of Gardencourt. Ralph's reply to her first request is significant:

> Ralph shook his head sadly. "I might show it to you, but you'd never see it. The privilege isn't given to every one; it's not enviable. It has never been seen by a young, happy, innocent person like you. You must have suffered first, have suffered greatly, have gained some miserable knowledge. In that way your eyes are opened to it. I saw it long ago," said Ralph.
>
> "I told you just now I'm very fond of knowledge," Isabel answered.
>
> "Yes, of happy knowledge—of pleasant knowledge. But you haven't suffered, and you're not made to suffer. I hope you'll never see the ghost" (III, 64).

This is light banter, but it serves to point up a serious shortcoming in Isabel: she wants a total knowledge, including a knowledge of evil, but cannot recognize that an association with evil will require her to compromise her enormous goals.

Knowledge, especially a knowledge of evil, proves to be a recompense for sorrow. The Fall of Man is basically (i.e., morally) fortunate because through experience Isabel loses the characteristics of her innocence which caused her to be ignorant and proud, to believe that she could exercise an unlimited freedom in the world. Through experience she is enabled to realize the finer qualities of her innocence—a sense of decency, a generosity of spirit, a capacity to give—and she has learned the great lesson that one should neither renounce his ideals nor make life conform to them, that the ultimate achievement in life is the preservation of the integrity of the human character. For, after all, Isabel is the winner in the end; by accepting Goodwood's offer she would in effect be rejecting her freedom, her belief in the value of her own decision.

In spite of the European setting, *The Portrait of a Lady* is mainly about America. James takes a gallery of American types, removes them from the limited American environment, in which they have no opportunity to change, and places them in Europe, where they are free to indulge in the fine art of living and susceptible to experience that tests their moral stability. Caspar Goodwood and Henrietta Stackpole are closed from experience by their protective Americanism; both distrust Europe and refuse to recognize its advantages over America. Ralph Touchett and Mr. Touchett are more sensitive; yet they neither assimilate European values nor reject them, for they are destined to inactivity, Ralph by his illness and his father by his business and his age. Edward Rosier, the thwarted lover of Pansy, is of little importance in himself as his function is mainly technical. Generally, however, his response to Europe is limited to an appreciation of its art. The other expatriates, except Isabel, repudiate America entirely and fully accept European standards of conduct. Mrs. Touchett, Gilbert Osmond, Mme. Merle, and the Countess Gemini are outstanding examples of the thoroughly Europeanized American.

Mrs. Touchett is neither good nor evil. Yet she represents negatively the defects of Europe and its injurious effects on the American. She is in many ways like the American women who persecute Daisy Miller; she resembles Osmond and Mme. Merle in her total devotion to forms and convention. But with Mrs. Touchett—and unlike Mme. Merle and Osmond—the polished surface does not disguise an inner evil. Rather it covers a kind of emptiness, an emotional vacuum. At the deaths of her husband and her son, she is repellingly unfeeling. After Ralph's death she "appeared to be absorbed in considering, without enthusiasm but with perfect lucidity, the new conveniences of her own situation"

(IV, 422). Mrs. Touchett's cool rationality leads Isabel to wonder if her aunt "were not even missing those enrichments of consciousness and privately trying—reaching out for some aftertaste of life, dregs of the banquet; the testimony of pain or the cold recreation of remorse" (IV, 406–407). James's Americans are most often heart characters: they readily respond to intuitions and feelings. But in *The Portrait of a Lady* Mrs. Touchett and the other long-time expatriates are almost completely head characters. It is as if their excessive devotion to manners has dried up all feeling.

Also Mrs. Touchett is a rover. She is rootless and unattached, aloof from her son and husband and devoted to travelling. She is a seeker of culture and manners who is content to remain on the surface of life. Though her ideal is more realistic than Isabel's —she seeks the attainable—it is also more superficial and less valuable, for Isabel, to misuse Henrietta Stackpole's phrase, is interested in "the inner life," a knowledge of more than forms.

The combined characteristics of formalism, rootlessness, and rationalism are most evident in Mme. Merle and Osmond. These two, however, are incontestably evil. Their capacity for evil is partly explained by their nationality. The American is capable of a greater malignity than the European because of his freedom. Furthermore, as F. W. Dupee observes, the Americans are all self-seekers,[35] aggressive in their plunder of Europe. The Europeans—characters like Richard de Mauves and Urbain de Bellegarde—are conservatives who resort to evil to preserve their old values and possessions. More often than not, their sins are sins of exclusion; they betray not in an effort to gain, but in a refusal to give.

The significant difference between Isabel and Osmond is that when Isabel realizes that her demands on life are exorbitant she withdraws; Isabel learns through experience that unrestrained acquisitiveness—emotional, intellectual, or material—is inconsistent with her high moral code, as she learns that her duty is to give rather than to receive. Osmond, on the other hand, employs his refined awareness of the complexities of life to further his self-seeking ends. To put it somewhat differently, Isabel's knowledge of the world is complemented by self-knowledge, so that her ultimate awareness is one of moral as well as social truth, whereas Osmond's is solely of social truth.

Osmond and Isabel also differ in their ways of knowing. Isabel responds to experience emotionally and spontaneously, eventually replacing all her dangerous abstract beliefs about freedom, experience, and happiness by a kind of pragmatic insight, an experiential grasp of what is real and of what is right. "I've only one ambition," Isabel says, "to be free to follow out a good feeling" (IV, 73). In complete contrast, Osmond lives in a world governed by impersonal ideas. Osmond's manner derives from his conception of what it should be; it accords with a social rather than a personal ideal. His conduct is from beginning to end totally calculated, from his initial project to ensnare Isabel to his posture when he forbids Isabel to visit the dying Ralph. Negatively Osmond's coldly intelligent manner—similar to that of the Hawthorne villain, especially Chillingworth and Rappacini—is revealed in the absence of love and sympathy in his dealings with those who are most intimate with him: with Isabel, whom he marries for money; with his daughter, whose love for Edward Rosier he suppresses; with his one-time mistress, Mme. Merle, whom he uses as a piece of machinery to better his position. Positively, Osmond's narrow but keen intellect is revealed in his shrewd operations to gain Isabel's favor. There is a special horror in his calculated abuse of Isabel's feelings; Osmond knows emotions only abstractly, but he knows them well. Stephen Spender has noted that in *The American* evil is "Elizabethan in its mechanism"; [36] and in *The Portrait of a Lady* Osmond suggests Iago. His conquest of Isabel is intrigue in its purest form. Like Iago Osmond sets a series of traps and carefully plans his approach. After Osmond and Mme. Merle prearrange the marriage behind Isabel's back, each works separately to carry out the plan. The strategy is brilliant: Mme. Merle advises Isabel that the Countess Gemini is a habitual liar, thus nullifying the Countess' own strength, for the latter knows of the previous liaison between Mme. Merle and Osmond, and Mme. Merle fears that she may tell Isabel; Osmond arranges for Isabel to visit Pansy in Florence, well knowing that his daughter's innocent charm will captivate Isabel and influence her towards him. Isabel is completely fooled.

Rarely in James—Maggie Verver is possibly the only exception—
is there a complete balance between the head and the heart. The
good are duped by the worldly-wise, who in turn lack the
instinctive charity of the good. When one combines these virtues
—as does Ralph Touchett—he is compelled to remain outside the
story as a kind of chorus.

Gilbert Osmond's formalism is a paradoxical kind of egotism.
More than anyone else in the book he stands for the impersonal
values of tradition, convention, and society. Isabel Archer, for
all her self-esteem, is no match for Osmond as an egotist. In his
devotion to convention he has a hostility to freedom; his byword
is exclusion. He marries Isabel not just to get her money, but to
bend her spirit, to possess her heart and mind. "The real offence,
as she ultimately perceived, was her having a mind of her own at
all. Her mind was to be his—attached to his own like a small
garden-plot to a deer-park" (IV, 200). Not only is Osmond
repelled by Isabel's independence, but he wishes to subjugate her
as he has subjugated himself to convention. Osmond wishes to
possess art, tradition, and manners: for him they are not attributes
of a meaningful and well regulated society but matters to be
appropriated exclusively as his own. His interest in art is especially perverse, for, unlike Edward Rosier, also a collector, who
sells his valuable possessions out of love for Pansy, Osmond col-
lects treasures for the sake of owning them and making it impossible for others to own them. As Joseph J. Firebaugh observes,
"Isabel comes to realize that he values beauty, not as a mode of
knowledge of human life, but as a symbol of traditional power
and inherited wealth." [37] He has made an unnatural distinction
between aesthetic values and human values: "He's the incarnation
of taste," Ralph Touchett observes. "He judges and measures,
approves and condemns, altogether by that" (IV, 71). Just as
Osmond's conduct and speech are perfect representations of
traditional manners, his physical presence is hardly distinguishable from the works of art that surround him. When he accuses
Isabel of treachery as she asks his permission to visit Ralph at his
deathbed, Osmond is characteristically engaged in copying an
antique coin.

But for all of Osmond's veneer, he is ultimately revealed as common. The gravity of his evil is obvious from its contagious effects on Isabel and Pansy, and even on Mme. Merle and Edward Rosier. Its grossness is also apparent, however, in his brutal control of Isabel. When he drops the veil of cultivation and speaks from his nature, the superficiality of his refinement becomes clear. Towards the end of the book, when Isabel learns the full truth, she finds that beneath Osmond's sophistication is the sordidness of an adulterous connection with Mme. Merle and that Osmond's supposed superiority to normal human desires is a fiction: "She found herself confronted . . . with the conviction that the man in the world whom she had supposed to be the least sordid had married her, like a vulgar adventurer, for her money" (IV, 330). Contrasted with the elegance of Osmond and Mme. Merle, the Countess Gemini's exposure of them gains added force, for beneath the glamorous surface we find only the coarsest of animal impulses. Osmond insults Isabel in their final meeting with particular crudity; also he ridicules Caspar Goodwood in an act of gratuitous malice. At the end there is little doubt that Osmond's celebrated superiority is meretricious.

The Countess Gemini and Mme. Merle are also mainly characters of surface. "The Countess seemed [to Isabel] to have no soul; she was like a bright rare shell, with a polished surface and a remarkably pink lip, in which something would rattle when you shook it" (IV, 225–226). The Countess represents an extreme decadence, the result of a lifetime of sterile existence in a corrupt society. She is neither good nor evil; she resides in the background of the story, aware of the sins of the past but incapable of redeeming the present. She does not tell Isabel the truth about Osmond and Mme. Merle until it can only make Isabel's pain even greater.

Mme. Merle resembles the Countess in her hollowness. As with Mrs. Touchett, "Emotion . . . had become with [Mme. Merle] rather historic; she made no secret of the fact that the fount of passion, thanks to having been rather violently tapped at one period, didn't flow quite so freely as of yore" (III, 268). Later she makes it clear that the source of her coldness is Osmond: "You've not only dried up my tears; you've dried up my soul" (IV, 334), she tells him. Aside from Osmond's responsibility for her corruption, other factors tend to modify her evil. For she is at least partly motivated in her deception of Isabel by a regard for her daughter, Pansy: she knows not only that Isabel's money will enable Pansy to marry well, but also that Isabel's influence will counterweight Osmond's. Mme. Merle has nothing to gain from her part in the intrigue. Most important, she is finally, like Lady Macbeth, overcome with guilt. In her final scene with Osmond, she alone accepts guilt and renounces any further implication in their mutual crime. "I don't know how we're to end. I wish I did! How do bad people end?—especially as to their *common* crimes. You have made me as bad as yourself" (IV, 335). Mme. Merle ends by going to America to accept a kind of penance, an atonement for the evil of the past. Nonetheless, Mme. Merle is a creature of free will; no extenuating circumstances can lessen her guilt. Her perception of her own baseness indicates not that she is saved, but that she is damned—and that she knows it.

As Osmond lives for art, Mme. Merle lives for society. "She's the great round world itself!" (III, 362). She lives "exclusively for the world" (IV, 144). A creature of brilliant surface, she has achieved a state of social completeness. Ralph Touchett says that Mme. Merle "pushes the search for perfection too far—that her merits are in themselves overstrained. She's too good, too kind, too clever, too learned, too accomplished, too everything. She's too complete, in a word" (III, 361). Isabel's analysis of her friend is also acute:

> If for Isabel she had a fault it was that she was not natural;
> . . . her nature had been too much overlaid by custom and
> her angles too much rubbed away. She had become too
> flexible, too useful, was too ripe and too final. She was in a
> word too perfectly the social animal that man and woman
> are supposed to have been intended to be; and she had rid
> herself of every remnant of that tonic wildness which we
> may assume to have belonged even to the most amiable per-
> sons in the ages before countryhouse life was the fashion.
> Isabel found it difficult to think of her in any detachment or
> privacy, she existed only in her relations, direct or indirect,
> with her fellow mortals (III, 273–274).

Mme. Merle has the same distrust of personal resources that Osmond has; she is a slave to propriety. In a crucial passage Mme. Merle remarks to Isabel that no one is important in himself but in "the whole envelope of circumstances. There's no such thing as an isolated man or woman; we're each of us made up of some cluster of appurtenances" (III, 287). In Mme. Merle's belief that man is entirely a social animal, she is sharply contrasted to Isabel, who modifies but never rejects her belief in the supreme value of personal resources: "Nothing that belongs to me is any measure of me; everything's on the contrary a limit, a barrier, and a perfectly arbitrary one" (III, 288). Like Emerson and Thoreau before him, James holds that evil consists in adopting the world's values before one's own. For Mme. Merle's devotion to the ways of the world necessarily involves her repudiation of the moral sense, which transcends convention and external systems. The James character must find his salvation by retaining and exercising his natural moral faculty in an environment which emphasizes the unnatural social values. Obviously Mme. Merle and Gilbert Osmond have sacrificed their richest American trait in order to participate in the ambiguous glory of Europe.

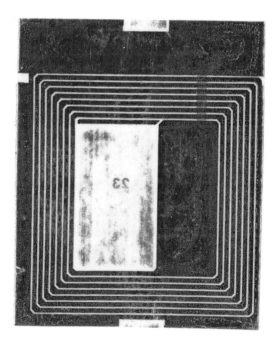

### CHAPTER THREE

# Evil in London

## THE INEFFECTUAL HERO

*THE PRINCESS CASAMASSIMA* (1886) is a bridge between the international fiction of the eighties and the London novels of the nineties. James has switched the scene from the European continent to London, the hero's nationality from American to British, and his economic condition from wealth to poverty. But the basic elements of his character and adventure are the same: the intelligent and imaginative person is introduced to a world of culture and wealth which takes him into its confidence and then betrays him. James's major alteration in *The Princess Casamassima* and most of his novels of the next fifteen years is to diminish the stature of the hero. He is not only poor, but he is also powerless. Unlike the Americans who invade Europe with dynamic vigor and confidence, the heroes of the London novels are armed only with their sensibilities.

Christopher Newman and Isabel Archer are allowed an initial triumph before encountering disaster, but the London hero makes no progress; he is thwarted from the beginning. Isabel gains a qualified victory over her antagonists. Her innate charm, dignity, and intelligence contrast favorably with the acquired finesse of the expatriate Americans. Her moral superiority to Mrs. Touchett, Mme. Merle, and Gilbert Osmond is unequivocal. She loses happiness, but she acquires spiritual nobility. After Isabel, James's heroes and heroines become progressively less attractive, so that with "The Turn of the Screw" and *The Sacred Fount* they become as perverse and grotesque as their adversaries.

In James's fiction of the 1890's, goodness reaches its nadir.

If good is ineffective and subject to treachery in *The Portrait of a Lady*, it is nevertheless accorded dignity. But in *The Princess Casamassima*, where there is only Hyacinth Robinson (unless we count the inept Mrs. Pynsent and Mr. Vetch) to uphold the moral sense in a corrupt world, there are no characters equivalent to Ralph Touchett, Henrietta Stackpole, Pansy Osmond, and Caspar Goodwood, individuals who, though they do not offset the evil of Osmond and Mme. Merle, present a formidable array of private virtue. Also isolated in a world of various shades of egotism, Fleda Vetch of *The Spoils of Poynton* (1897) has only the "pointlessly active and pleasantly dull" (X, 9) Owen Gereth as an ally. Mrs. Gereth and Mona Brigstock possess all the force.

It is especially significant that in *The Spoils of Poynton* virtue itself is not entirely admirable, as it is in *The Portrait of a Lady*. Fleda's virtue is so incongruous with the society in which she exercises it that the effect is to make her seem overscrupulous, perhaps even ridiculous. Mrs. Gereth tells Fleda, "[I] fail to comprehend the inanity of a passion that bewilders a young blockhead [Owen] with bugaboo barriers, with hideous and monstrous sacrifices. I can only repeat that you're beyond me. Your perversity's a thing to howl over" (X, 225). Mrs. Gereth, whose uncompromising practicality is as immoral in its way as Mona Brigstock's greed, certainly does not speak for James, nor does James give any indication that he doubts the validity of the private conscience. But nowhere in *The Portrait of a Lady* does Isabel Archer appear so foolish as Fleda Vetch. It may simply be that Isabel's problems are far weightier than Fleda's, as are her ambitions and adventures, so that delicate moral discrimination is necessary for her situation. In *The Spoils of Poynton* Mrs. Gereth's ridicule of Fleda is in many ways paralleled by the dramatic action of the novel. In a European society based on tradition and manners, Isabel adheres to the accepted code by refusing to repudiate Osmond. The world of *The Spoils of Poynton* is the modern world, where tradition gives way to expediency and customs support passions. Thus Fleda's insistence on the old rules strikes Mrs. Gereth as out of date and Mona Brigstock as absurd.

The American hero of the early international fiction is young,

successful, sensitive, and intelligent. Because of his ignorance of
the ways of the world, he is deceived and betrayed. But in his
state of innocence he is magnanimous, and in his state of experience he gains an inner strength through full awareness. The hero
of James's middle period is unsuccessful from the beginning of
his life. He is also unattractive. Even when exercising the moral
sense he is likely to be self-consciously priggish. Thus Fleda
Vetch, with a kind of pride singularly absent in Newman and
Isabel Archer, decides to renounce marriage to Owen and possession of the spoils:

> Nothing was really straight but to justify her little pensioned
> presence by her use; and now, won over as she was to
> heroism, she could see her use only as some high and delicate
> deed. She couldn't in short do anything at all unless she could
> do it with a degree of pride, and there would be nothing to
> be proud of in having arranged for poor Owen to get off
> easily (X, 106).

At this point Fleda's act of pride, especially from Mrs. Gereth's
point of view, is extremely perverse, for Fleda betrays the kindness shown to her by directly counteracting her benefactress's
plans.

In the novels from *The Spoils of Poynton* to *The Awkward
Age*, moral refinement appears at times as a kind of immorality in
itself. That is, renunciation of happiness is no longer a purely
personal matter, as it is for Newman and Isabel. Since the London
heroes are less free from restricting circumstances than their
predecessors, their acts of self-denial affect others as well as themselves. To renounce Owen, Fleda must necessarily betray Mrs.
Gereth; to renounce Sir Claude, Maisie must distress Mrs. Wix.

In his middle period James is refocusing his picture of the
individual and the world, so that the opposition between the two
loses its clarity. In other words, James has revised his conception
of moral reality: in appearance good and evil are not clearly
distinct; good is so weak and incongruous with its environment
that it may seem grotesque; the honorable man is objectively
perverse and queer. Moreover, moral conduct often necessitates
the violation of inadequate, if not false, moral systems recognized

by society. To try to reconcile the demands of conscience with those of society—to be moral in an immoral world—may cause one to become corrupted himself. Thus there exists an utter inversion of moral conduct: good may appear evil and evil may appear good. Because modern social existence is based on false principles, it is often necessary to be false regardless of motive and intention.

Thus, in *The Spoils of Poynton*, Fleda Vetch must appear freakish, even perhaps mad, in her extreme scrupulosity. To do less than she does—to accept Mrs. Gereth's bribe, to allow Owen to break his pledge to Mona—would be to accept Mrs. Gereth's utilitarian values as her own. But for Fleda to do the opposite— to adhere to a superior code which she knows to be right—she must, first, betray the confidence Mrs. Gereth has placed in her, and, second, tell a direct lie. Mrs. Gereth, of course, places Fleda in the awkward position of having to appear ungrateful and of having to lie, because it is she who commits the initial crime of adopting Fleda for her deceitful purposes: she frankly "uses" Fleda to lure Owen away from Mona. Having gratefully accepted Mrs. Gereth's seemingly innocent proposal that she live with her, Fleda, in order to remain free from complicity in her benefactress's plot, must necessarily refuse to cooperate. Correspondingly, Fleda must lie to Mrs. Gereth—must falsify what she knows to be true, that Mona Brigstock will not marry Owen unless Mrs. Gereth returns the treasures to Poynton—in order to prevent her from refusing to return the spoils and disrupting the marriage. When she learns of Mona's decision from Owen, Fleda is fully conscious of the curious position she is in:

> If she should now repeat his words this wouldn't at all play the game of her definite vow; it would only play the game of her little gagged and blinded desire. She could calculate well enough the result of telling Mrs. Gereth, how she had had it from Owen's troubled lips that Mona was only waiting for the restitution and would do nothing without it. The thing was to obtain the restitution without imparting that knowledge. The only way also not to impart it was not to tell any truth at all about it; and the only way to meet this last condi-

tion was to reply to her companion as she presently did. "He told me nothing whatever. He didn't touch on the subject" (X, 119–120).

A fundamental trait of Fleda is her alienation from human society—a common limitation with James's middle period heroines. Fleda is clothed only with an idea, Mrs. Gereth thinks, and the novel shows her to be one of James's typical seeking heroines, with a large appetite for experience. Her imagination, her responsiveness to art and society, along with her deep moral sense, align her with Isabel Archer, Milly Theale, and a dozen other "heiresses of all the ages." She shares, however, the particular limitations of the English protagonist of the middle period in that she is sealed off in a tightly restricted society—by poverty, by friendlessness, and mainly by the impersonality and dense materialism of London itself.

There is a spectrum of intelligences in *The Spoils of Poynton*. At the lowest point is the absolute willfulness of Mona Brigstock. Mona sees only that the furniture and art objects of Poynton— to her more than anyone they are "spoils"—are valuable: they must be, since Mrs. Gereth regards them highly and they have been praised in the society columns. Mrs. Gereth herself has a fine aesthetic awareness, which places her above Mona; but the action finally reveals her to be more like Mona than like Fleda: she sees only what she wants. She has taste—she knows why the spoils are valuable; and she is clever—she has gotten them at the best prices; also she is ingenious in devising ways to prevent Mona from getting them. But in the final analysis, she has perversely subordinated intelligence to will. Owen Gereth is a kind of *tabula rasa:* neither will nor thought directs him; and thus he is manifestly weak, the easy tool of the three women in his life. Repeatedly seen in images of the natural man, he acts through casual instincts only. Finally, Fleda herself has maximum—though certainly incomplete—awareness. Her appreciation for the art objects and splendid trappings of Poynton is not a compartmentalized activity of the mind; rather it is the same grasp of reality that presents her with moral scruples.

It is not farfetched to say that *The Spoils of Poynton* dramatizes the position of *logos*—or contemplation—in a world of *ethos* —or action. The characters who act do so blindly; thus the one person who thinks is prohibited from action. Through a series of almost maddening moral dilemmas, the novel leads Fleda to the point of moral anarchy, where the very terms of her principles have been obscured, converted, and rendered all but meaningless.

Fleda's isolation from social intercourse of any sort is only gradually revealed, but it is her condition from the start of the book. One wonders how she was ever invited to Waterbath, where Mrs. Gereth first meets her, since she seems to be on close terms with no one other than her pitiful father and newly married sister. In any event, Mrs. Gereth, in the familiar role of Jamesian fairy godmother, impresses Fleda with what seems a kindred sensitivity to beauty, and shortly afterwards attempts to manipulate Fleda into attracting Owen away from Mona. The book rapidly shows Fleda accepting two—mutually contradictory—loyalties: to Mrs. Gereth, who has taken her to Poynton and befriended her; and to Owen, who in his simplicity asks Fleda to "bring Mommy around" to accepting Mona. Separate from these loyalties, which become increasingly more demanding and involving, is Fleda's own notion, strong from the beginning, that Owen cannot in honor ignore his pledge to Mona. Fleda, of course, is thoroughly involved in Mrs. Gereth's life, both in her intrigue to keep the spoils from falling to Mona, and in her charm, grace, and taste. She has unwittingly committed herself to Mrs. Gereth and more knowingly committed herself to Owen, whose position she alone sees to be a moral one.

Once involved in Mrs. Gereth's schemes, Fleda, quite literally, cannot escape; and she frequently tries. The pattern of the novel is that of Fleda's withdrawing and being brought back by one or the other of the Gereths, each urging her to align herself against the other. She is also, of course, partly restrained from complete withdrawal by her growing love for Owen, her sensibility to Poynton, and her fondness for Mrs. Gereth. Thus, after she realizes that Mrs. Gereth is using her as bait to lure Owen from Mona, Fleda feels that "she couldn't possibly remain after being offered to Owen" (X, 33). And yet she does—for a fortnight; and then she proceeds with Mrs. Gereth to Ricks. Back in her

father's house, she is again drawn to the Gereth affair by meeting
Owen in the street. However, it is only after Mrs. Gereth plun-
ders Poynton to stock Ricks that Fleda attempts to escape: she
shelters herself in her father's house. At this point James clearly
conveys Fleda's dilemma:

> She had neither a home nor an outlook—nothing in all the
> wide world but a feeling of suspense. . . . only a horrible
> sense of privation. She had quite moved from under Mrs.
> Gereth's wide wing; and now that she was really among the
> penwipers and ash-trays she was swept, at the thought of all
> the beauty she had forsworn, by short wild gusts of despair
> (X, 145).

At her father's, where she has determined to communicate with
neither Owen nor his mother, Fleda is visited, first by Owen, who
proposes marriage to her and urges that she allow him to break
off from Mona, and then by Mrs. Brigstock, who finds her in a
compromising meeting with Owen. When she again tries to escape—this time to her sister's house outside of London—she is
again pursued by Owen and also receives a telegram from Mrs.
Gereth urging Fleda to visit her. Significantly, the novel concludes with Fleda once more travelling, this time to Poynton,
where she sees only the black smoke of its destruction and the
end of everything.

Unlike those novels in which the journey motif provides a
structural symbol of a journey to knowledge, to liberation, or to
maturity, in *The Spoils of Poynton,* the withdrawal and return
pattern, accentuated by Fleda's homelessness and mixed feeling
toward the Gereths, comes to symbolize her unavoidable involvement in a world not of her own making.

When she leaves for her sister's, Fleda feels that

> She required for this step no reason but the sense of neces-
> sity. It was a strong personal need; she wished to interpose
> something, and there was nothing she could interpose but
> distance, but time. If Mrs. Brigstock had to deal with Owen
> she would allow Mrs. Brigstock the chance. To be there, to
> be in the midst of it, was the reverse of what she craved: she

had already been more in the midst of it than had ever entered into her plan. At any rate she had renounced her plan; she had no plan now but the plan of separation. This was to abandon Owen, to give up the fine office of helping him back to his own . . . (X, 179).

The renunciation is, of course, thwarted by Owen, just as it was he who previously had sought her out. Thus it is that Fleda's travels come to symbolize her undesired moral involvement in others' lives, her perilous passivity that must in the long run be converted to action. Fleda has the imagination of the free spirit, but is simply unable to remain free. To allow Owen to break his pledge to Mona is tantamount to ignoring the dictates of conscience by which she knows the dishonor of such an act. Nor can she leave Owen free to do what he wishes, for she is part of his plans. She must interfere with him, tell him he must honor his pledge, in order to avoid complicity. It should not be forgotten that the engagement is of Owen's and not of Fleda's making; it is not she who consigns him to a life of misery with Mona Brigstock. Fleda simply cannot be a part of the violation herself. It is Owen who repeatedly seeks her out, just as it is Mrs. Gereth who makes demands upon her. Fleda should be accused neither of interference in the lives of the Gereths, nor of narrow self-righteousness. She has really no alternative between a complete abandonment of scruples and a perverse, even incomprehensible, renunciation.

In less subtle stories than *The Spoils of Poynton*, James exposes the limitations of his middle-period protagonists through irony. Most of his London tales are told from the point of view of the protagonists, who consistently evaluate their own conduct as heroic and rarely suspect their own flaws. James's ironic treatment of his leading character is most apparent in "In the Cage" (1898), the story of a girl who works in a telegraph office, where she takes messages from the upper-class men and women of London's West End. Shut off from any rich experience of her own by poverty and a sterile personal life, she takes vicarious pleasure in handling the communications of her social superiors. There is a certain pathos in the girl's "spending, in framed and wired confinement, the life of a guinea-pig or magpie" (XI, 367), but her adolescent devotion to those who give her messages to send is not only juvenile but self-destructive. James makes this obvious in several ways: first, the girl cannot help but know from the implications of the communications she transmits that the people she admires are, as she herself says, "selfish brutes" (XI, 400), ostentatious in their lavish spending, unconcerned with the plight of the less fortunate, and primarily interested in their own illicit love affairs; secondly, because of her foolish loyalty to people who are hardly aware of her existence, the girl ignores her responsibility to Mr. Mudge, the substantial if unromantic grocer to whom she is engaged.

It is significant that James never reveals the girl's name. And, as with the anonymous narrators of "The Turn of the Screw" and *The Sacred Fount*, the point is that she really has no identity, for she exists not in herself, but only in others. Again a comparison with *The Portrait of a Lady* should clarify the alteration of the Jamesian protagonist. Isabel idealizes Europe, which she knows to offer a rich experience and believes to be no more immoral than her own America; the girl telegraphist idealizes West End society, which she knows to be permanently closed to her, which she knows to be immoral, and which offers no valuable experience. Likewise, Isabel's adventure in Europe is personal, whereas the telegraphist's adventure in the cage is vicarious. Isabel is fully committed to Gilbert Osmond; the telegraphist is engaged to Mr. Mudge and infatuated with Captain Everard.

The innocence of such American women as Euphemia Cleve and Isabel Archer manifests itself in their easy enchantment with Europe. Their stories record their progress from illusion to disillusion. The plots of "In the Cage" and "The Turn of the Screw" develop the same basic progression, but, with America replaced by London slums or country villages and the European aristocracy by a vulgar upper class, much of the objective beauty and meaning of the world is gone. Not even in the beginning is the reader's sympathy fully with the heroine as it is with Isabel, whose innocence and illusions are readily excused. In James's middle period, he frequently stresses the immaturity more than the incorruptibility of his innocent protagonists.

These are most often children or adolescents: Morgan Moreen of "The Pupil," Maisie Farange of *What Maisie Knew,* the telegraphist of "In the Cage," the governess and children of "The Turn of the Screw," and Nanda Brookenham of *The Awkward Age.* The child in these works has a definite ambivalence. James emphasizes both the innocence and the ignorance of his immaturity: when the child is passive he is helpless and pure; when he is active he is stupid and inept. On the one hand, James achieves a pathos foreign to his earlier international tales by exposing children to corruption. In a world defiled by adults, the child has little opportunity for spiritual expansion. He can only withdraw from the world into himself: to retreat from the cage with Mr. Mudge, to retreat from Sir Claude with Mrs. Wix, to retreat from Mrs. Brook with Mr. Longdon. To remain in the world too long is either to be destroyed by it, like Morgan Moreen, or to become an adult and therefore corrupt oneself, like Little Aggie of *The Awkward Age.*

When the burden of goodness is placed on the child the impossibility of its triumph is emphasized. When the children act in society their efforts are either misdirected or ineffectual. Maisie thinks she is doing everyone a service when she brings together Sir Claude and Mrs. Beale, but she is only a valuable, though innocent, means of aiding an evil she cannot possibly understand. The telegraphist, more naïve than her years would indicate, wishes to assist her beloved customer, Captain Everard, and, when she is able to recall the wording of an old telegram, enables him to avert a scandal. But such practical aid is no more commendable than that given by Maisie. Nanda Brookenham tries to protect Little Aggie from corruption, and persuades Mitchy to marry her. When the marriage fails—Aggie readily submits to adultery—Mitchy's distress is certainly Nanda's fault. In each of these cases, goodness, combined with ignorance, leads directly to evil.

A notable characteristic of much of James's work is the frequency with which characters offer to "save" others. In his middle period, James employs the theme of salvation ironically. He shows apparent good to conceal real evil. First, there are those whose supposedly charitable missions conceal the most malicious plans. In "The Middle Years" (1893), Miss Vernham demands that the novelist Dencombe leave Bournemouth, where he is convalescing from a serious illness, in order that his disciple, Doctor Hugh, may be free to return to his patient, the Countess. The Countess has taken a great liking to the doctor and given assurance of leaving him a fortune. Miss Vernham is in love with the doctor and feels that nothing should prevent him from getting the money. But the effect of the girl's interference is calamitous, for by compelling Dencombe to leave she causes his death. In reference to the girl's action, James speaks of "the brutality of her good conscience" (XVI, 100). Her effort to "save" Doctor Hugh, which is mainly motivated by selfishness, causes disaster. The telegraphist and Nanda Brookenham both act from laudable motives—to save others. Although the interference by the telegraphist causes no personal injury, it abets an immorality. Nanda's meddling is more culpable, for it establishes Aggie in society and gives her the liberty to corrupt herself; more important, it destroys Mitchy's life.

Fleda Vetch succeeds in saving Owen Gereth from dishonor and Mrs. Gereth from theft, but the practical result of her conscientiousness is that both are faced with a lifetime of unhappiness. But Fleda Vetch is closer in intelligence and maturity to Isabel Archer than she is to Nanda Brookenham, because Fleda's motive is to remain free herself from external influences and not to shelter others. Her interference, more negative than positive, in the affairs of the Gereths is an unavoidable result of her adherence to personal integrity. But, given the nature of society, any interference in the lives of others, regardless of motive, produces disorder and suffering. The reasons are that society itself is based on evil principles and that the innocent is unable to foresee the consequences of his action. His imperception, however, is not due entirely to the disparity between appearance and reality (for example, the disparity between Little Aggie's outward behavior and her latent nature), but also to his own serious deficiencies.

James's most ironic and most elaborate treatments of the "salvation" theme are "The Pupil," "The Turn of the Screw," and *The*

*Sacred Fount.* In each, evil is either unimpeded or increased by the person whose role it is to try to save others from destruction. Each of the three stories concerns an uninvolved character who finds himself in the midst of a situation in which a person or group of persons is being corrupted by another person or group of persons.

Pemberton, of "The Pupil" (1891), is the tutor of a bright and sensitive child, Morgan Moreen, whose parents are perpetually on the brink of poverty. The Moreens are social climbers who travel about Europe in an unsuccessful attempt to form attachments with rich, titled families in order to satisfy their social pretensions and arrange advantageous marriages for their older children. The main effect of their wandering is that the neglected Morgan lacks the love from his parents necessary to sustain him. The Moreens are not active agents of evil, and their malignity is negative rather than positive. But the child dies when the parents completely divorce themselves from him and ask the tutor to adopt him. The tutor himself is badly misused by the Moreens; they pay him no salary and exploit his affection for Morgan, whom they leave entirely to his care. The tutor sacrifices his own life to save the child from the influence of his parents. He provides for him materially as well as he can from his meager savings and attempts to compensate for the love denied the child by his parents. Thus the story amounts to a kind of morality tale, in which good and evil struggle for the possession of a human soul.

Pemberton, the tutor, not only sacrifices his own promising future to save Morgan, but also is an emotionally mature person whose dealings with Morgan delay the child's eventual demise. Also, unlike Mrs. Wix, the governess in *What Maisie Knew* (1897), Pemberton has no selfish reasons for remaining with Morgan; he is motivated by love only. The power of evil is stronger than the power of good in "The Pupil," but good, as represented by Pemberton, is unequivocal and valuable.

The governess in "The Turn of the Screw" (1898), however, has obvious emotional and intellectual shortcomings. Her position parallels Pemberton's. She finds herself in the midst of an unspeakable evil, for she discovers that the children she is to instruct are visited by the ghosts of two dead servants who try

to gain possession of them. In "The Turn of the Screw" and
*The Sacred Fount*, the outsider, whose mission it is to save the
threatened innocents, faces an evil far more menacing than in
"The Pupil." But the outsider himself is far less adequate. The
governess differs from Pemberton in being emotionally like the
telegraphist of "In the Cage." Unlike Pemberton, who accepts
his position strictly as an economic matter, the governess is attracted to her job because of a foolish romantic attachment to her
employer. And as the girl in the cage wishes to "do something"
for Captain Everard in order to justify her existence in his world,
so the governess soothes herself after her first encounter with
Quint's ghost:

> . . . I was giving pleasure—if he ever thought of it!—to the
> person to whose pressure I had yielded. What I was doing was
> what he had earnestly hoped and directly asked of me, and
> that I *could*, after all, do it proved even a greater joy than I
> had expected (XII, 174).

Like the telegraphist, the governess is an easy victim of illusion.
Idealizing Bly, she is enchanted by the beauty of the picturesque
old country house and the surrounding landscape: ". . . I had
the view of a castle of romance inhabited by a rosy sprite, such a
place as would somehow, for diversion of the young idea, take
all colour out of story-books and fairy tales. Wasn't it just a story-
book over which I had fallen a-doze and a-dream?" (XII, 163).
James develops a terrifying irony by revealing the true nature of
Bly and contrasting the ugly real ghosts with the imagined garden
of bliss. But the controlling irony is psychologically justified, for
in the prologue to the story James characterizes the governess as
immature and highly imaginative. "She was young, untried, nervous" (XII, 155), the daughter of a country minister, overly
sensitive to both beauty and ugliness, and inclined to be naïve and
excessively emotional in her reactions to new experience.

Like Pemberton, the governess, once exposed to the malignity
of Quint and Miss Jessel, conceives of her duty as essentially
moral: "The children in especial I should thus fence about and
absolutely save" (XII, 195); "I was there to protect and defend
the little creatures in the world the most bereaved and the most

loveable, the appeal of whose helplessness had suddenly become only too explicit . . ." (XII, 199). In "The Turn of the Screw" the issues are the same as in "The Pupil," but in the former James isolates the metaphysical aspect of evil: "It was like fighting with a demon for a human soul . . ." (XII, 303). James dramatizes the struggle of good and evil in abstraction; he deals with the morality play theme in its largest dimension.

Robert B. Heilman's essay *"The Turn of the Screw* as Poem" suggests that James has stressed the disparity between the governess's moral purpose and her achieved results. Through careful analysis of imagery and diction, Heilman demonstrates that the story parallels the Fall of Man legend. The recurrent light imagery suggests "the dawn of existence"; the children suggest "the childhood of the race." Bly is described as an Eden; the movement of the seasons from June to November reflects the moral movement from innocence to fall. Quint has "the characteristics of a snake"; Miss Jessel resembles the Miltonic fallen angel. After submitting to evil, the children reveal a precocious awareness, indicative of their having eaten of the Tree of Knowledge. What seems most significant is that

> From the start the words used by the governess suggest that James is attaching to her the quality of a savior, not only in a general sense, but with certain Christian associations. She uses words like "atonement"; she speaks of herself as an "expiatory victim," of her "pure suffering," and at various times—twice in the final scene—of her "torment." [1]

Though somewhat overingenious, Heilman's interpretation of "The Turn of the Screw" is persuasive. Yet it ignores the irony that James achieves by his references to the governess as a Christlike savior. The governess, for all her devotion and agony, not only does not save the children; she also helps to damn them.

The governess shows her deficiencies in both understanding and action. For the most part, the children completely deceive her. She realizes too late that their "angelic" appearances conceal corrupted souls. Their various tricks and deceptions invariably succeed; little Miles is especially charming so that Flora can meet Miss Jessel. But it is in her behavior that the governess's weakness

becomes most obvious. She is rarely other than impetuous and
hysterical. Her judgment is usually mistaken and her direction of
the children incompetent. Her overprotectiveness gives Miles the
weapon he needs to escape her and gain free access to Quint,
for he rightly insists that he is not being treated as a normal boy
of his age. When the governess accuses Flora of meeting Miss
Jessel by the lake, the child feigns innocence and fear of her
protectress, and thereby gains the right to be taken away from
her.

In the dramatic concluding scene, the governess attempts to
save little Miles by eliciting a confession from him. She recognizes the difficulty of her plan:

> I could only get on at all by taking "nature" into my con-
> fidence and my account, by treating my monstrous ordeal
> as a push in a direction unusual, of course, and unpleasant,
> but demanding after all, for a fair front, only another turn of
> the screw of ordinary human virtue (XII, 295).

The governess has the will but not the means to save Miles. In a
situation requiring supreme delicacy, she confronts the child, who
wavers precariously between salvation and damnation. While
Quint and the governess both strive for his soul, the child himself
is in a state of utmost spiritual distress, so that only a kind of
divine intervention can bring him to the side of good.

In the final scene with Miles, the governess's weakest human
quality is emphasized—her self-concern. Not only is there no
grace, but the human agent of good is fallible. In her pride the
governess thinks not of Miles so much as of herself. After Miles
confesses to stealing the letter which she has written to his uncle,
the governess's first thought is not of the spiritual significance,
not of the magnanimity of Miles's confession, but of "my personal
triumph" (XII, 305). As the child blurts out his repentance, the
governess continues to think primarily of herself, of the fact that
her previous inductions were correct. "He almost smiled at me in
the desolation of his surrender, which was indeed practically, by
this time, so complete that I ought to have left it there. But I was
infatuated—I was blind with victory . . ." (XII, 306). In her
exhilaration, the governess, as she realizes, proceeds imprudently.

She questions and accuses Miles with brutality.[2] James makes it clear that through her indelicacy, she forces Miles to look elsewhere for support—to Quint, who is standing behind the boy on the other side of the window. When she questions the child about the crimes which caused him to be expelled from school, her enthusiasm makes her reckless:

> But the next after that I must have sounded stern enough. "What *were* these things?"
> My sternness was all for his judge, his executioner; yet it made him avert himself again, and that movement made *me*, with a single bound and an irrepressible cry, spring straight upon him. For there again, against the glass, as if to blight his confession and stay his answer, was the hideous author of our woe—the white face of damnation. I felt a sick swim at the drop of my victory and all the return of my battle, so that the wildness of my veritable leap only served as a great betrayal (XII, 308).

Gripped by hysteria, the governess simultaneously shelters the child and questions him, with even more anxiety and terror. When Miles asks her whom she is staring at, whether "It's *he*," the governess

> was so determined to have all my proof that I flashed into ice to challenge him. "Whom do you mean by 'he'?"
> "Peter Quint—you devil!" His face gave again, round the room, its convulsed supplication. "*Where?*"
> They are in my ears still, his supreme surrender of the name and his tribute to my devotion. "What does he matter now, my own?—what will he *ever* matter? *I* have you," I launched at the beast, "but he has lost you for ever!" Then for the demonstration of my work, "There, *there!*" I said to Miles (XII, 309).

The governess's anxiety to have her suspicions and actions justified, her solipsism, has a terrifying effect on Miles. Her excessive self-concern emerges in her determination "to have all my proof," her hasty and irreflective "Whom do you mean by 'he'?" and her stress on "his tribute to my devotion." The climax of the scene occurs when the governess, egotistically and disastrously, points out Quint to Miles with her "There, *there!*"—for the demonstration of her work. Thus she literally turns the child over to Quint. In view of the governess's misdirected goodness and rashness, Miles's "you devil" has double significance. The phrase not only indicates, as Heilman observes, that the child has lost all moral perception, so that in his state of damnation good is evil and evil good,[3] but also that the governess is doing the work of the devil, for she is certainly aiding rather than hindering Quint, and that she is, if not a malignant force like the demons, a grotesque person who would seem Satanic to any child. Edmund Wilson overstates the case when he writes that "the governess has literally frightened him to death,"[4] but she has so terrified him that he gives himself over to Quint.

It is unnecessary to rely on Wilson's Freudian interpretation of the governess's behavior, for not only are her final witless efforts in accordance with James's characterization of her and with the logic of the story, but also she resembles those other outsiders or agents of good who frequent the fiction of James's middle period. Usually characterized as emotionally and intellectually inadequate, they stand for human imperfection. They are objective portraits of James's conception of the ineptitude and weakness of good in a world dominated by evil. In addition, they represent a harsher evaluation of the romantic view of life, based on illusion rather than good sense—a view shared by James's earlier American protagonists, who do not, however, significantly cause ill to others. Since there is no divine providence, no grace, no supernatural good, the agent of salvation is bound to fail—so much so that he may contribute to the victory of evil.[5]

There are several links between "The Turn of the Screw" and *The Sacred Fount* (1901). While in "The Pupil" and "The Turn of the Screw" the outsider occupies an inferior social position—as tutor and governess—and the victims of evil are in both cases children, in *The Sacred Fount* the outsider is a gentleman spending a weekend at a country house and the victims are adults. But the observer's relation to evil is essentially the same as in the previous two stories. The narrator is himself uninvolved in the malignant tangle—which in *The Sacred Fount* is sexual—but is the only person fully aware of the meaning of the superficially tranquil activities at Newmarch.

Unlike the governess, however, the observer of *The Sacred Fount* is inactive, concerned not with restoring good but only with understanding evil. But even more than the governess, he is unpleasant, if not obnoxious. He is an egotist whose concern with the affairs of others is purely intellectual. As soon as he boards the train for Newmarch, the narrator begins to scrutinize his fellow guests. He recognizes that Grace Brissenden, whom he has known to be far older in appearance than in years, has undergone a remarkable transformation, so that she now appears unnaturally young. Correspondingly, he detects a marked alteration in Gilbert Long, who has always in the past been dull and boorish, but who now amazes the narrator with his wit and intelligence. Upon arriving at Newmarch, the narrator finds an unfortunate change in Guy Brissenden, Grace's husband, who, previously youthful in appearance, now seems an old man. The observer tries to find a logic in these three transformations and induces that Grace Brissenden is draining her husband, sapping his youth and vitality. Therefore, he reasons that for the pattern to be complete there must be a source for Long's new-found wit and, after a lengthy search, concludes that the source is May Server. In this fantasy, James objectifies his notion of the depleting power of sex.[6] But the other theme of the tale is that of the narrator, whose scientific interest in the corruption of Newmarch is, as he recognizes, "wanting in taste." [7]

As the narrator of "The Turn of the Screw" craves to prove that the horrible deeds and visions she has seen actually existed, so the narrator of *The Sacred Fount* always searches for evidence that his surmises correspond with reality. In the process of his investigation, he reflects, "I had created nothing but a clue or two to the larger comprehension I still needed, yet I positively found myself overtaken by a mild artistic glow." Carried away by his mental accomplishments, much like the governess in her final scene with Miles, the narrator is involved only with his own ingenuity: his reference to "my private triumph" echoes the governess's "my personal triumph." His egotism emerges as the narrator, dispassionately studying the morbid relationships among the other guests and realizing that his own speculations have a basis in fact, thinks, "It was the coming true that was the proof of the enchantment, which, moreover, was naturally never so great as when such coming was, to such a degree and by the most romantic stroke of all, the fruit of one's own wizardry." [8]

Though his pride of knowing is almost a pathological obsession, only through knowing can the narrator exist at Newmarch (which, like many of James's country-house settings, may be taken as a microcosm of all society). To become involved is to become either sinned-against or sinner. Knowledge, however, is a kind of action, for, just as the governess can save Miles only by eliciting a confession from him, the "I" of *The Sacred Fount* can save the predatory Mrs. Briss only by forcing her to admit her guilt. (It must be kept in mind that whereas the governess's motive is to save the children, the houseguest's is to satisfy his curiosity.) There is a striking similarity between the last scenes of the two novels. The climax of each is reached when the observer confronts the sinner with his guilt. As is always the case with James, evil is inconsistent with knowledge—the good characters are incapable of perpetrating evil because they fully understand; therefore, if Miles and Grace Brissenden would acknowledge their guilt they would be saved.

In an excellent essay on *The Sacred Fount*, R. P. Blackmur finds in the narrator a personification of the consciences of the other characters; he is, in effect, the alter ego of the social group at Newmarch. Blackmur writes that in the narrator's climactic scene with Grace Brissenden he "has given [Grace] the butter and honey of his imagination to eat, so that . . . she might know to refuse the evil, and choose the good." On the symbolic level, then, the narrator is "the projected image of conscience," [9] though on the literal level he is an overly curious snooper.

Like the governess, the all-observant guest is impersonal. He is nameless and characterless (it is not entirely clear whether he is a man or a woman). In "In the Cage" James stresses the self-destructiveness of the vicarious impersonal life. But in "The Turn of the Screw" and *The Sacred Fount* there are no counterparts of the girl's Mr. Mudge, the person with whom she may live a life of her own. The governess and the snooping guest are denied the personal life. They are faced with the dilemma either of becoming fully human by taking part in a society they know to be corrupt or of remaining aloof from life as incomplete human beings. F. O. Matthiessen suggests that the real function of such people resembles that of Tiresias,[10] doomed to know and to suffer for the sins of all, but unable to restore good. Like Eliot's Prufrock, Tiresias-like himself, James's observer may be fastidious, even ridiculous; and like the Tiresias of *The Waste Land* he may find intelligence a liability. Although extreme in his ineffectualness, the narrator of *The Sacred Fount* is nevertheless a characteristic hero of James's middle-period fiction.

### THE GREAT GREY BABYLON

James's London differs obviously from the America and Europe of his earlier international fiction. Unlike Newport or Schenectady, London is tightly organized and tends to submerge the individual; unlike Paris or Rome, it has no immediate connection with the past and is devoted to modernity rather than tradition. James describes it as a society in which the old world forms are dead; there is no more concern for dignity, for honor, for politeness, for loyalty. The Bellegardes of *The American* are partly redeemed by their adherence to an ancient system. With the decline of the *noblesse*, however, expediency replaces tradition, and sheer material greed, rather than pride of name, becomes the dominant principle of a society.

In his notebooks James writes of

> the great modern collapse of all the forms and 'superstitions' and respects, good and bad, and restraints and mysteries—a vivid and mere showy general hit at the decadences and vulgarities and confusions and masculinizations and feminizations—the materializations and abdications and intrusions, and Americanizations, the lost sense, the brutalized manner —the publicity, the newspapers, the general revolution, the failure of fastidiousness.[11]

Certainly much of James's feeling stems from his own fastidiousness, his religious devotion to forms and admiration for the past.

Yet much of his social criticism in the London novels has a valid basis. For at the heart of his indictment of "the great grey Babylon" [12] of London is his revulsion from its egotism, its materialism, and its pragmatism. Manners transcend the self; they implicitly subordinate it to the larger social whole. Likewise the old manners of Europe deprecate material acquisition for its own sake and combat mere efficiency. Modern society promotes the passions of greed and lust, whereas the old world supports a nobler concept of human nature.

In his preface to "The Altar of the Dead," James refers to London as "the densest and most materialized aggregation of men upon earth, the society most wedded by all its conditions to the immediate and the finite." [13] Its passion for adultery, for money, for status are unmodified by delicacy or tact. Removed from a system of manners, such conduct represents the norm of society rather than its aberrations. Therefore, when James points out the tastelessness and the modernity of his characters he establishes their grossness of conduct as well. The vulgarization of standards in the society of *The Awkward Age* indicates moral deterioration:

> "beauty, in London . . . staring glaring obvious knock-down beauty, as plain as a poster on a wall, an advertisement of soap or whiskey, something that speaks to the crowd and crosses the footlights, fetches such a price in the market that the absence of it, for a woman with a girl to marry, inspires endless terrors and constitutes for the wretched pair (to speak of mother and daughter alone) a sort of social bankruptcy. London doesn't love the latent or the lurking, has neither time nor taste nor sense for anything less discernible than the red flag in front of the steam-roller. It wants cash over the counter and letters ten feet high" (IX, 25).

Most of James's Londoners are members of the leisure class, either of the aristocracy or of the wealthy commercial set. James was oppressed by the decline of the British nobility, the neglect of the old sense of high standards and obligations. Such country-house gatherings as those in *The Sacred Fount* and *The Awkward Age* have nothing of the easy cultured life and graceful manner of the society of Gardencourt in *The Portrait of a Lady*. They even lack the fierce loyalty to family and name that marks the English gentry in "A Passionate Pilgrim" and "An International Episode." Sir Claude has none of the dignity and stature of Lord Warburton. James expresses his feeling toward the British upper class in a letter:

> The condition of that body seems to me to be in many ways very much the same rotten and *collapsible* one as that of the French aristocracy before the revolution—minus cleverness and conversation; or perhaps it's more like the heavy, congested and depraved Roman world upon which the barbarians came down. In England the Huns and Vandals will have to come *up*—from the black depths of the (in the people) enormous misery, though I don't think the Attila is quite yet found—in the person of Mr. Hyndman. At all events, much of English life is grossly materialistic and wants blood-letting.[14]

Most often James exposes London society from the point of view of the individual Londoner surrounded on all sides by either sordidness or meaninglessness. His children are all more or less "in the cage," estranged in the midst of "a society in which for the most part people [are] occupied only with chatter . . ." (XI, 6). His decayed old men like George Stransom and Mr. Longdon embody an older period of history in which values dictated behavior and meaning stood behind appearances. To James modern civilization is a threat to the self. Not only is the sanctity of the individual person jeopardized by the decline of refinement and subtlety and the rise of the crass vehicles of public communication, but the mechanical nature of society—cold, harsh, and efficient—threatens to defeat the precious human elements. Thus, for James, the replacing of the formal letter by the informal note symbolizes London at the end of the nineteenth century:

> Good manners are a succession of details, and I don't mean to say that she [London] doesn't attend to them when she has time. She has it, however, but seldom—*que voulez-vous?*

Perhaps the matter of note-writing is as good an example as another of what certain of the elder traditions inevitably have become in her hands. She lives by notes—they are her very heart-beats; but those that bear her signature are as disjointed as the ravings of delirium, and have nothing but a postage stamp in common with the epistolary art.[15]

Condensation and efficiency, for James, are incompatible with the human and the meaningful. They necessitate the elimination of the intelligent and the sensitive approaches to life; they deprive human intercourse of the finer intellectual basis that gives it value.

In a notebook entry James records the *donnée* of a possible story:

> Yesterday at the Borthwicks', at Hampstead, something that Lady Tweedmouth said about the insane frenzy of futile occupation imposed by the London season, added itself to the hideous realization in my own mind—recently so deepened—to suggest that a 'subject' may very well reside in some picture of this overwhelming, self-defeating chaos or cataclysm toward which the whole thing is drifting. The picture residing, exemplified, in the experience of some tremendously exposed and intensely conscious individual—the deluge of people, the insane movement for movement, the ruin of thought, of life, the negation of work, of literature, the swelling, roaring crowds, the 'where are you going?,' the age of Mrs. Jack, the figure of Mrs. Jack, the American, the nightmare—the individual consciousness—the mad, ghastly climax or denouement. It's a splendid subject—if worked round a personal action—situation.[16]

This passage, written in 1895, might well serve as the "germ" for all of James's London fiction. It is a striking observation, close to much of recent literature in its sense of the present, in its perception of the sickness of modern society. The world of pointless movement in Eliot's "The Hollow Men" parallels the London world James describes. This passage also shows that James's point of view is outward from the sensitive person. The world is evil insofar as it causes suffering. In itself thoroughly dehumanized, it can corrupt only the superior person, whose values are on a higher plane—the human rather than the commercial or the animal. James's sensitive London characters all live "under the awful doom of general dishumanization." [17]

What James finds to be inhuman about London is its neglect of the simple yet important matters of living: such essential human relationships as those between husband and wife, parent and child, and living and dead are perverted or destroyed. The basis of "The Pupil," *What Maisie Knew*, and *The Awkward Age* is the subordination of family responsibility to greed or lust. As Sir Claude says in *What Maisie Knew*, "there *are* no family women —hanged if there are! None of them want any children—hanged if they do!" (XI, 61). *The Spoils of Poynton* concerns an antagonism between mother and son. *The Awkward Age* deals with the corruption of marriage. *The Sacred Fount*, *What Maisie Knew*, and "The Turn of the Screw" also treat varying perversions of love. As normal human intercourse is reduced to the telegraphed communication in "In the Cage," so parental and marital relationships are settled in the law courts in *The Spoils of Poynton* and *What Maisie Knew*.

In James's middle period the blackness of the past is replaced by the grossness of the present. Thus the divorce court, rather than the ancestral manor, is the symbol of a corrupt society. The social acceptability of divorce represents for James the decline of marriage. Though both Gilbert Osmond and Urbain de Bellegarde pervert marriage out of egotism, they nevertheless recognize its inviolability and sanctity. From *What Maisie Knew*, as well as "A London Life," it is apparent that James finds little difference between adultery and divorce: both are equally grave violations of the marriage vow. Sexual relations dominate James's London fiction in a peculiarly lurid way. The symmetrical compounding of matches in *What Maisie Knew*, the welter of cryptic telegrams between the lovers in "In the Cage," perversion and the suggestion of homosexuality in "The Turn of the Screw," [18] and the intrinsic horror of sex in *The Sacred Fount*—all point to James's habit of identifying sex per se with the ugly and the unnatural.

Usually, however, James links physical passion with divorce

and adultery, which, in his essential conservatism, he considers
serious wrongs. Sexual relations are more often indirectly than
directly evil, since they disrupt marriage and lead to the dereliction of responsibility. The gravity of the sexual offense is more
apparent in its disastrous effect on the outsider to the relationship
—usually the innocent child—than, as in *The Sacred Fount*, on
the participant.

In those London stories in which divorce and adultery do not
provide the sordid background—most prominently in *The Spoils
of Poynton*—the sin is greed for material possessions. In his
preface to *The Spoils* James writes:

> One thing was . . . in the sordid situation, on the first blush,
> and one thing only . . . the sharp light it might project on
> that most modern of our current passions, the fierce appetite
> for the upholsterer's and joiner's and brazier's work, the
> chairs and tables, the cabinets and presses, the material odds
> and ends, of the more labouring ages.[19]

In themselves, of course, the "things" are neither good nor evil.
Yet the possession of them and the means by which one gains
possession of them may be evil. Only Fleda Vetch holds moral
principles over acquisition: both Mona Brigstock and Mrs. Gereth
injure others to gain the spoils.

Whether one is devoted to sexual lust or material greed, his
egotism has the effect of crippling the life of another, usually
an innocent child deserted by his parents. The theme of the
dereliction of parental duty is inseparable from the theme of lust
and greed in *What Maisie Knew*, "The Pupil," and *The Awkward Age*. The children in these stories need love to survive, but
their elders subordinate responsibility to passion. The other notable children of James's London fiction are also neglected: Miles
and Flora of "The Turn of the Screw" are orphaned children,
wards of an uncle who never sees them, placed in the care of an
obtuse maid and a hysterical governess.

In the London stories there are no single villains; society itself
is the villain. In the world of *The Portrait of a Lady*, Mme. Merle
and Henrietta Stackpole as well as Gilbert Osmond and Lord

Warburton can exist and prosper as independent persons. The social situation is fluid and spacious enough to contain a multitude of different types. Paradoxically, in James's London, in which the manners which have upheld the older society are dead, a higher consistency is demanded on the part of the characters. The social structure of *The Awkward Age* is far more rigid than that of any continental group. Adherence to the ways of modern life restricts individual freedom more than adherence to the ways of the aristocracy.

Therefore the dominant figures of London society are merely typical. Such characters as Sir Claude and Mrs. Brookenham represent the whole tone of a society. They have no independent selves; removed from their environments they are nothing. Society is an artificial form of existence, for it makes no provision for the personal element. As Scott Homer of "Mrs. Medwin" says, in reference to those who live in and for society, "They're dead" (XVIII, 491); they can exist only as social creatures and not at all as persons.

For this reason the symmetrical pattern of divorces and re-matches in *What Maisie Knew* indicates more than James's concern for structural balance. Rather the ludicrous regularity with which Maisie's parents pair off establishes the sameness of their lives. In *The Awkward Age* the stylized conversation cramps the individual. Vanderbank and Mitchy stand slightly aloof from the immorality of Mrs. Brook's group, but Petherton, Lady Fanny, the Duchess, Tishy Grendon, and Mrs. Brook herself differ only in the accidental matters of appearance, intelligence, and economic status.

In such a society the individual who is not absorbed by the group is either excluded or preyed upon. Sir Claude must finally decide whether to adhere to his weak moral sense and to his liking for Maisie or to his illicit attachment to Mrs. Beale. His decision is between self and society: to reject Mrs. Beale for Maisie would be equivalent to isolating himself from an environment which recognizes adultery as normal. Drawn into her mother's group, Nanda must retreat with Mr. Longdon to preserve her independence of thought and judgment. In short, as

James puts it (with considerable understatement), London society is one in which "individual appreciations of propriety have
not been formally allowed for." [20]

London society of the 1890's lacks the obvious sinister quality
of the Europe which ensnared Newman and Isabel. There are no
ancestral curses, no gloomy chateaux, no mysteries, no Gothic
overtones. No superificial veneer disguises the precise nature of
the vain and avaricious Londoners. Appearance and reality correspond in such characters as Mrs. Brook and Beale Farange.
Here, for example, is James's description of Maisie's mother:

> The sole flaw in Ida's beauty was a length and reach of arm
> conducive perhaps to her having so often beaten her ex-
> husband at billiards, a game in which she showed a superior-
> ity largely accountable, as she maintained, for the resentment
> finding expression in his physical violence. Billiards was her
> great accomplishment and the distinction her name always
> first produced the mention of. Notwithstanding some very
> long lines everything about her that might have been large
> and that in many women profited by the licence was, with a
> single exception, admired and cited for its smallness. The
> exception was her eyes, which might have been of mere
> regulation size, but which overstepped the modesty of na-
> ture; her mouth, on the other hand, was barely perceptible,
> and odds were freely taken as to the measurement of her
> waist. She was a person who, when she was out—and she was
> always out—produced everywhere a sense of having been
> seen often, the sense indeed of a kind of abuse of visibility,
> so that it would have been, in the usual places, rather vulgar
> to wonder at her (XI, 7–8).

This description approaches caricature. Certainly Ida lacks both
the superficial attraction of an Osmond and the portentousness of
an Urbain de Bellegarde. Ida is blatantly ludicrous in both appearance and behavior.

The prevading tone of *What Maisie Knew*, like that of *The
Spoils of Poynton* and *The Awkward Age*, is that of light comedy
of manners. But James does not lessen the gravity of the transgres-

sions of his comic characters. *The Awkward Age* has all the glitter and brilliance of dialogue of a Wilde comedy, plus the light approach toward marriage. Were it not for the presence of the innocent (Nanda), the tone of the society would set the tone of the novel. But the innocent requires that the entire proceedings be judged on moral grounds. Actually, to James, the presence of a superior person and the effect of the frivolous group on the person give the society meaning. In his preface to *Maisie* James remarks that without Maisie the other characters would have no interest:

> They become, as she deals with them, the stuff of poetry and tragedy and art; she has simply to wonder, as I say, about them, and they begin to have meanings, aspects, solidities, connexions—connexions with the "universal!"—that they could scarce have hoped for. Ida Farange alone, so to speak, or Beale alone, that is either of them otherwise connected—what intensity, what "objectivity" (the most developed degree of *being* anyhow thinkable for them) would they have? How would they repay at all the favour of our attention? [21]

Through the agency of Maisie, James shows the objectively comic to be subjectively tragic and the superficially pleasant to be essentially evil. Quentin Anderson points out that one of James's fictional methods is to convert the reader, to change his attitude toward the subject matter. [22] Maisie's presence transforms social comedy into personal tragedy, as the light approach to marriage by the adults is demonstrated to be inadequate.

But if the Londoners are comic they are also—and obviously—unimportant. They lack the stature of the early villains, just as their deeds are sins of the weak rather than sins of the strong. Like Isabel Archer and Euphemia Cleve, the telegraphist and Maisie are betrayed by illusion, each finding a glamorous superiority in a man who is little more than a pompous and stupid fop. To find value in the appearance of Captain Everard and Sir Claude—men whom Isabel Archer would easily see through—requires an extreme naïveté, a quality which James stresses in his child victims. The easily duped victims are far more vulnerable than their

American predecessors precisely because of their naïveté. They are readily taken advantage of without the assistance of elaborate intrigue or calculation by the adults. It is unnecessary for Maisie's parents to deceive her as Osmond deceives Isabel. Because appearance and reality correspond, the innocent must be given the simplicity and credulity of a child.

Since society bears no sinister appearance, James employs scene to suggest its deviation from a norm. In his British fiction nature plays a major role in establishing moral tone. The pastoral settings of country-house activity ironically contrast with the sordidness of the characters. The observer frequently becomes entranced by the surrounding beauty of a social gathering, so that his apprehension of what the scene conceals comes as a shock. In his early American stories James uses the placid and harmonious countryside to symbolize the quiet, graceful lives of such families as the Wentworths. He uses scene for the opposite purpose in *The Awkward Age*. A rented country house seems to suggest a relaxed and eminently humane social entity:

> The lower windows of the great white house, which stood high and square, opened to a wide flagged terrace, the parapet of which, an old balustrade of stone, was broken in the middle of its course by a flight of stone steps that descended to a wonderful garden. The terrace had the afternoon shade and fairly hung over the prospect that dropped away and circled it—the prospect, beyond the series of gardens, of scattered splendid trees and green glades, an horizon mainly of woods. . . . The scene had an expectant stillness that [Nanda] was too charmed to desire to break; she watched it, listened to it, followed with her eyes the white butterflies among the flowers below her, then gave a start as the cry of a peacock came to her from an unseen alley (IX, 203).

What begins to take on the appearance of a Garden of Eden soon becomes a kind of Garden of Gethsemane;[23] Nanda meets the nervous, patronizing Vanderbank and realizes that he will neglect her and leave her to struggle for her own existence in her mother's circle.

In *The Sacred Fount* the description of nature surrounding

Newmarch emphasizes an unnatural calmness and stillness. Here, as Elisabeth Luther Cary has observed, "the tortured real is corrected by the calm ideal, and abstract synthetised beauty hangs like a brooding angel over the tangled human spectacle." [24] Yet nature not only provides a sharp contrast with the frenzied human activity, but also it suggests, through its own frozenness, the grimness of the world it surrounds:

> There was a general shade in all the lower reaches—a fine clear dusk in garden and grove, a thin suffusion of twilight out of which the greater things, the high tree-tops and pinnacles, the long crests of motionless wood and chimnied roof, rose into golden air. The last calls of birds sounded extraordinarily loud; they were like the timed, serious splashes, in wide, still water, of divers not expecting to rise again. [25]

The startling concluding metaphor, and those like it which now begin to appear frequently in James's work, suggest, as F. W. Dupee writes, "the realm of the physical and the elemental, of latent horror, of 'the thing hideously behind'." [26] Clearly James is using scene for purposes radically different from those in his earlier work. Instead of relying on conventional Gothic or pastoral settings, he creates a world in which objects of nature correspond to states of mind.

More than ever before, James in his London fiction uses the personal vision of things to convey significance. Thus meaning cannot always be clearly stated in rational terms, because it is inseparable from the emotion of the witness. The horror of the governess, the frenzied intellectualism of the weekend guest, the morbid anguish of Stransom: such feelings convey the inner corruption of James's Londoners.

Physical passion exists only in the background of James's fiction, but its moral significance is explored fully in the foreground. There is not so much as a kiss or a suggestive glance in *The Sacred Fount*, James's one novel whose major theme is physical love, but there is no escaping the full horror of sexual relations. From a glance at Mrs. Server, the victim of Gilbert Long's predatory love, the narrator grasps the quality of that love:

I saw as I had never seen before what consuming passion can
make of the marked mortal on whom, with fixed beak and
claws, it has settled as on a prey. She reminded me of a
sponge wrung dry and with fine pores agape. Voided and
scraped of everything, her shell was merely crushable.[27]

With surrealistic effect, mental images replace concrete delinea-
tion. The avoidance of graphic description of physical passion is
more than compensated for by the concreteness of the images
which convey its ravaging effects.

There are four major character types in James's middle-period
fiction: the victimized innocent, the weak man, the fool, and the
clever woman. Each in his own way has a large capacity for evil.
The innocents are too rarely intelligent and thus injure through
ignorance. The men are most often dependent, indecisive creatures, who prefer to ignore crises rather than face them. Owen
Gereth has a kind of boyish tenderness; Sir Claude and Vanderbank have an obvious but unalloyed charm; some others, like
Edward Brookenham, are so negative as to seem completely
innocuous. Yet, in their retreat from all positive action, these men
implicitly commit themselves to the decisions of the women who
govern their lives; by default they contribute to the moral ugliness of society. The fools, on the other hand—invariably women
—are violently aggressive. James writes that "the fixed con-
stituents of almost any reproducible action are the fools who
minister, at a particular crisis, to the intensity of the free spirit
engaged with them." [28] Among the fools is the philistine, the
woman who, through stupidity or crassness, kills the artist. A
major example is Mona Brigstock, a massive force, concerned
only with the grossest of material possessions. In a world largely
controlled by fools, there are also the more dangerous, because
more intelligent, women, who manipulate weak and foolish alike,
and exploit the sensitive. None of James's stories contains a full-
scale portrait of a fool, but many have as central characters those
women of great exterior attraction who combine will and social
(but not moral) intelligence to achieve worldly success.

Just as the evil of the fools is somewhat disguised by their absurdity, the evil of the clever women is so fused with their personal charm and social grace as to be concealed. Furthermore, these women command admiration for their remoteness from the shallowness and tastelessness of the worlds they inhabit. Even the murderess in *The Other House*, Rose Armiger, can hardly be termed a complete villainess.[29] But, though her evil is not unmixed, it is obvious. Mrs. Gereth and Mrs. Brookenham, however, though just as willful as Rose, and ultimately as predatory, are far more ambiguous characterizations.

Both are intelligent and delightful, mistresses of society, and expert manipulators of people. Mrs. Gereth's refined love of *objets d'art* reflects taste and sensibility, in themselves admirable traits. In manner she is genuine and gracious, capable of respect and friendship for Fleda Vetch. She gains sympathy because of the repulsiveness of her antagonists: the insensitive Mona Brigstock, who strives to possess the objects Mrs. Gereth has spent a lifetime collecting, and the brutal, unflinching injustice of the British law, which provides that the "things" rightfully belong to Mona. But when Mrs. Gereth takes the offensive she violates the Jamesian ethical code: she attempts to have Fleda gain Owen's love and win him over from Mona, thereby disregarding her son's pledge and exploiting Fleda. Thus, in spite of Mrs. Gereth's praiseworthy ambitions and sympathetic situation, she is, as James states in his notebooks, blinded to moral reality by her aggressiveness: "*She sets the girl on him*—cynically, almost, or indecently (making her feel AGAIN how little account—in the way of fine respect—she makes of her. Touch *that*, Mrs. G.'s unconscious brutality and immorality, briefly and finely). She presses Fleda— yes—upon him . . . ."[30]

In *The Spoils of Poynton* the unethical is natural and the ethical unnatural. Mona instinctively snatches at the spoils; Owen is willing to break his pledge; Mrs. Gereth is unaware of the moral limitations of her intrigue; even Fleda is tempted to follow Mrs. Gereth's lead and seek happiness before honor. When Fleda renounces happiness, she seems perverse; she goes counter to human nature. The inclination to evil is part of human nature; guilt is universal.

The ultimate spiritual implication of *The Spoils of Poynton* and most of James's London fiction becomes the theme of "The Turn of the Screw." The main irony of "The Turn of the Screw" is the disparity between the reality and the appearance of the children. Described as angelic, even divine, in their beauty, the children are not innocent, as they seem, but corrupted. The story does not show, as Robert B. Heilman suggests, good becoming evil and youth becoming age, but evil existing under the appearance of good. Charles G. Hoffmann writes that "in *The Turn of the Screw* innocence and evil coexist as evil-in-good." But the good is mere illusion. The children themselves consciously appear most innocent at the very moments when they are in communication with the demons. As Oliver Evans comments, "the 'rose flush of innocence' is never so intense as when [Miles] is most actively engaged in positive evil." In other words, "the lambs are not lambs at all, but tigers; the children are not really children, but, as Mrs. Grose perceives in the end, as old as evil itself." [31]

The ultimate theme of "The Turn of the Screw" is Original Sin. The governess speaks of the children as "blameless and foredoomed" (XII, 217). They are blameless because foredoomed; that is, the children are evil—or inclined to evil—because of a kind of natural depravity. With all of James's characters evil is either active or latent. For all except those of "the finer grain" it dictates the natural course of activity. The others must make extreme effort to remain free from complicity. Personal evil can be avoided only by a retreat from the world—the ultimate course for Maisie and Nanda. If one—like Fleda Vetch—is to act for good it follows that he must seem perverse, for such conduct is not only abnormal, but literally unnatural. In the society of a fallen world innocence cannot survive.

"The Turn of the Screw" concerns a pair of children plagued from infancy by evil, which they willingly accept when they first understand its meaning. In his other stories about children, James also treats "the death of . . . childhood." [32] Like Miles and Flora, Maisie and Nanda are exposed to contaminating influences. Their stories deal with the period in their lives when they acquire knowledge. What Maisie finally knows is that her elders are corrupt and that to remain uncorrupted herself she must reject them. But Maisie always possesses the capacity to damn herself, as does Nanda, for whom her mother's circle, with its adulteries, intrigues, and treacheries, presents a constant temptation. The latent power for evil emerges in Little Aggie when she ceases to be a child. Even with the free spirits there is often a pride which modifies the purity of the moral sense. Fleda Vetch, the governess, and the telegraphist cannot divorce self-interest from right conduct.

In James's world of "blameless and foredoomed" people, it is not surprising to find a number who are basically honorable—who do not injure others—yet so limited as to be in part evil. In his middle period James catalogues a number of characters guilty of pride, not the gross egotism of an Osmond or even the unconscious egotism of a Mrs. Gereth, but the less offensive vanity that has the effect of blighting the self.

In a notebook entry James makes a distinction between "the pride that can harden and stiffen its heart . . . and the pride that suffers." [33] The former is the pride of John Marcher of "The Beast in the Jungle" (1903), whose excessive self-concern prohibits him from loving May Bartram; the latter is the pride of Fleda Vetch, whose loyalty to principles prevents her happiness. But Fleda does not allow her heart to harden; she would become callous and insensitive only by rejecting her higher values and pursuing mere pleasure. Many characters like Marcher enter the stories of James's middle period. George Stransom's exclusion of his betrayer, Acton Hague, causes his devotion to the dead to be imperfect. Not until he forgives Hague is Stransom's altar of the dead complete, for he still shares in the self-destroying egotism of the world he rejects. Vanderbank, of *The Awkward Age*, however, becomes increasingly hardened by a pride that leads him to find too many faults in the woman he loves. The brief "Broken Wings" (1900) is a light treatment of the theme of pride. Two lovers do not see each other for ten years because each is ashamed of his failure in his chosen career and believes the other to be successful. Meeting by accident, they realize that both have experienced the same misfortune. "What had come out . . . was that each, ten years before, had miserably misunderstood and then had turned for relief from pain to a perversity of pride" (XVI, 158). When they realize the destructiveness of their attitudes, they reunite and plan to marry, "with a final abandonment of pride that was like changing at the end of a dreadful day from tight shoes to loose ones" (XVI, 161). This is not the large and dynamic pride of Isabel Archer, through which she believes that all the world exists for her, but a narrowing rather than an expansive pride, a weakness of spirit that excludes and limits.

Just as Stransom and the couple in "Broken Wings" are essentially moral in spite of their limitations, there are other characters whose selfishness does not outweigh their goodness. Mrs. Wix, Maisie's governess, gains by contrast with Maisie's elders, but it is clear that, to emphasize Maisie's isolation, James qualifies Mrs. Wix's goodness by pointing out that her devotion to Maisie is far from selfless. Her passion for Sir Claude is ridiculous only to others; to herself the relationship with Maisie is a means of meeting and possibly winning him. Also, Mrs. Wix is desperately poor, too incompetent to be assured of regular work. To her, caring for Maisie means, among other things, steady employment. When she considers that Maisie may become the sole property of Mrs. Beale and Sir Claude, her concern is not for the welfare of the child, but for herself: "They'll take you, they'll take you, and what in the world will then become of me?" (XI, 118).

Mrs. Wix shares in the universal sin of selfhood. And with the rest of James's Londoners she inhabits a fallen world, where evil is normal and good perverse, where total good is a fiction, where the sensitive moral person cannot exist.

## THE AWKWARD AGE

*The Awkward Age* (1899) is a study of a social situation: an awkward period during which a young single girl is exposed to the advanced conversation of her elders. According to the rules of the society, she must marry as soon as possible, before she loses her innocence of mind and thus becomes unattractive to prospective suitors. James constructs around this central theme a number of secondary issues along with a full set of characters, in order to amplify the basic *donnée*. From the situation of the girl's awkward age, the nature of a society is revealed through its relation to the situation, which in turn is given meaning because of its connection with the larger whole. The problem of the daughter, Nanda, is also her mother's; and the field of operations is Mrs. Brookenham's circle. James achieves complexity and depth through full characterization of the circle, which is a microcosm of the London world, with its indecencies, indelicacies, betrayals, intrigues, pettiness, and ugliness. Marriage, the major concern of Nanda and her mother, is, as in *The Portrait of a Lady*, also the dominant interest of the other characters: to Mrs. Brook and the Duchess, marriage is a matter of political intrigue; to the shadowy figures in the background of the novel—Cashmore, Petherton, Lady Fanny, and Mrs. Donner—it is a matter of frivolity; to Vanderbank, it is a matter of self-effacement; to Mr. Longdon, who represents the mores of a previous age, it is a matter of sacred trust and devotion.

As in *The Sacred Fount* and *What Maisie Knew*, we are never allowed to overlook the immorality of the society, because of the constant suggestion of irregular sexual behavior. Three adulteries unmistakably establish the tone of the society: Cashmore has an affair with Mrs. Donner; his wife, Lady Fanny, is about to leave for Italy with a Captain Dent-Douglas; and Lady Fanny's brother, Lord Petherton, is the Duchess's lover. This tangled web of marital and extramarital relationships exists within an even tighter circle than in *What Maisie Knew;* and, as in the earlier novel, though with less symmetry, there is also the pairing off and rematching. Petherton neglects the Duchess and takes up with her niece, Little Aggie; Lady Fanny decides not to leave with Dent-Douglas because of her attraction for Mrs. Brookenham's son, Harold; and Cashmore makes an unsuccessful bid for Nanda's favor.

While sexual promiscuity pervades the background of Mrs. Brook's circle, the foreground is dominated by the equally immoral, though less sordid, activity of the major characters. Too poor to operate with ease in her society, Mrs. Brook is forced to plot to gain a fortune. Thus, like Mrs. Gereth of *The Spoils of Poynton*, she exploits others in order to insure her own material comfort. Though Nanda loves Vanderbank, her mother promotes her marriage to Mitchy, for not only is Van poor and Mitchy wealthy but Mrs. Brook wants Van, a key figure in her circle, for herself. The novel chronicles Mrs. Brook's numerous maneuvers to acquire a large income and keep Van, all the while neglecting the interests and desires of Nanda. But the monetary theme enters the novel in other ways as well. Harold Brookenham, one of James's children who do not preserve innocence, has the function of revealing his mother's true nature, for he has her ambitions and unscrupulousness, unredeemed by her wit and grace. Harold continually and systematically takes money from his mother's friends and parasitically invites himself—at his mother's urging— to other people's houses. Petherton bleeds Mitchy of his wealth; Vanderbank is sorely tempted to marry Nanda for money.

To James's mind unrestrained commercialism indicates the depravity of a culture. In *The Awkward Age* the decline of manners is in inverse ratio to the increased association of human institutions with money. Thus Mr. Longdon, who represents the moral norm of the novel,[34] is shocked when he learns that Mitchy has rented a country house:

> "Now this sudden invasion of somebody's—heaven knows whose—house, and our dropping down on it like a swarm of locusts: I dare say it isn't civil to criticise it when one's going too, so almost culpably, with the stream; but what are people made of that they consent, just for money, to the violation of their homes?"
>
> Nanda wondered. . . . "But haven't people in England always let their places?"
>
> "If we're a nation of shopkeepers, you mean, it can't date, on the scale on which we show it, only from last week? No doubt, no doubt, and the more one thinks of it the more one seems to see that society—for we're *in* society, aren't we, and that's our horizon?—can never have been anything but increasingly vulgar. The point is that in the twilight of time— and I belong, you see, to the twilight—it had been made out much less how vulgar it *could* be" (IX, 219–220).

Manners are an indication of morals in *The Awkward Age*. The tastelessness of the furnishings in Tishy Grendon's parlor prepares us for the immoral behavior which occurs there. Most of the overt activity of Mrs. Brook's circle is bad-mannered. In his preface James notes that the custom of allowing the innocent daughter to participate in adult conversation is a vulgarity— "as far as possible removed even, no doubt, in its appealing 'modernity,' from that of supposedly privileged scenes of conversation twenty years ago." [35] The conversation recognizes no limits imposed by good taste; rather it delights in analyzing the illicit behavior of others, in promoting scandals, in destroying character. In his fastidiousness James—through Mr. Longdon— calls attention to the modern practice of lying about one's daughter's age to better her chances for marriage; and the crisis of the novel has as its basis the revelation that Nanda has read a French novel.

Yet *The Awkward Age* does more than condemn modern vulgarity, for behind the bad manners there is generally gross conduct. The society of *The Awkward Age* sacrifices the meaningful to the artificial, and in order to be urbane it destroys the humane. Not only is marriage made a business and a game and the child a victim of the parent's opportunism rather than a recipient of his love, but friendship, loyalty, and sincerity are replaced by betrayal and hypocrisy, or else they become so superficial as to amount to their opposites. Mrs. Brook's group is bound by a joint interest in good talk, which is good precisely because of its ironies and innuendoes, its callousness to privacy, its wit at the expense of others' foibles. At one point the Duchess remarks, "What are parties given in London for but that enemies may meet?" (IX, 103). Mr. Longdon's observation would be considered by the insider as irrelevant, but it strikes at the heart of both the merits and weaknesses of the circle: after Vanderbank casually remarks, "What's London life after all? It's tit for tat," Mr. Longdon replies, "Ah but what becomes of friendship?" (IX, 20). Vanderbank, who recognizes the inadequacy of Mrs. Brook's circle, but—like Prufrock—is too weak and dependent to withdraw from it, later crystalizes Mr. Longdon's objection: "What you mean at any rate . . . is that we're cold and sarcastic and cynical, without the soft human spot" (IX, 34). As her group overlooks the province of the heart in human intercourse, so Mrs. Brook is coldly rational in promoting Nanda's marriage.

Closely allied to the absence of friendship is the absence of

loyalty. Mr. Longdon's priestlike loyalty to the dead Lady Julia
serves as an instructive contrast to the betrayals that characterize
Mrs. Brook's coterie. Vanderbank betrays Mr. Longdon's trust
and Nanda's chances for happiness by refusing to marry her out
of pride and squeamishness. Mr. Longdon is loyal to the memory
of Lady Julia: he shelters her granddaughter from her environment, while Vanderbank vainly decides that Nanda is beyond
possible salvation. In order to embarrass Van and keep him from
marrying Nanda, Mrs. Brook betrays his confidence; she informs
Mitchy of Mr. Longdon's proposal to give Nanda a fortune if
Van will marry her. Mitchy is betrayed by Little Aggie, who is
unfaithful to him immediately after their marriage. Most important, Mrs. Brook betrays Nanda: she humiliates her before Mr.
Longdon and the entire circle. On the other hand, the finer
characters—those removed from or on the periphery of the circle
—act from nobility and loyalty. In her own curious way Nanda
is loyal to Mitchy when she takes responsiblity for his hapless
marriage, which he originally agrees to out of loyalty to Nanda.
Finally, Nanda, with Mitchy's aid, reveals a loyalty to the very
people who betray her: she urges Van and Mitchy not to desert
her mother; she urges Mr. Longdon to forgive Van. Mitchy and
Mr. Longdon together agree to provide Van with money so that
he will not have lost by not marrying Nanda.

Sincerity and honesty in human dealings are replaced by
deception and indirection. The series of intrigues and counter-
intrigues depends on clandestine maneuvering and false appearances. Sincerity becomes perverted when Mrs. Brook hypocriti-
cally justifies her exposure as an act of sincerity: "If the principal
beauty of our effort to live together is . . . in our sincerity, I
simply obeyed the impulse to do the sincere thing. If we're not
sincere we're nothing" (IX, 302). The episode resembles the
scene in *The Golden Bowl* in which the Prince and Charlotte,
while speaking of their sacred duty to be faithful to their *sposi*,
embrace and begin their illicit relationship. Mitchy, Van, and
Mrs. Brook all know that the latter's manner is totally insincere,
for it is her method of keeping Van from marrying Nanda; the
conversation disguises the real nature of the incident. Thus the
three carry the scene to its conclusion, and their emphasis on the

importance of simplicity and sincerity is in complete contrast with their actual feelings and motives. Mitchy is obviously embarrassed by Mrs. Brook's audacity; Van feels exposed and defeated; and Mrs. Brook herself is uneasy after her blow. The episode stresses the false camaraderie of the group and the perversion of honesty. Mrs. Brook's final attempt to restore tranquility strikes a particularly false note:

> "The thing is, don't you think?"—she appealed to Mitchy— "for us not to be so awfully clever as to make it believed that we can never be simple. We mustn't see *too* tremendous things—even in each other." She quite lost patience with the danger she glanced at. "We *can* be simple!" (IX, 303).

After this proclamation, feeling that the smoke has been cleared and her frankness justified, Mrs. Brook proceeds to annihilate Van and further her plans for Nanda by callously referring to her own attachment to Van and to Van's feelings about Nanda.

Mrs. Brook's set is "past saving" (p. 20) because of its talk, however, rather than its behavior. Although she ironically defeats her own purposes, Mrs. Brook is motivated by her desire to hold her school of wits together. Thus the problem of the "awkward age" is hers more than Nanda's, for, with Nanda downstairs, she is faced with the (to her) disastrous necessity of reducing the high level of talk in order to keep Nanda sheltered. She chooses to compromise Nanda rather than compromise her conversational standards. To preserve her own circle Mrs. Brook must keep Van and she must have money: thus she sacrifices Nanda. ". . . I often feel as if I were a circus-woman, in pink tights and no particular skirts, riding half a dozen horses at once" (IX, 188), Mrs. Brook says, and without her circus she cannot exist. Mrs. Brook, in a sense, reduces life to a kind of art. She values life as a source of intellectual enjoyment, and, if need be, will injure others in order to preserve her circle.

Mrs. Brook's dealings with Cashmore and his wife, Lady Fanny, well illustrate her total devotion to wit. Early in the novel Cashmore complains to her that Lady Fanny has been accepting gifts from unknown donors. Mrs. Brook, who, as she explains, has "a kind of vision of things, of the wretched miseries in which you all knot yourselves up . . ." (IX, 164–165), shrewdly analyzes Cashmore's marital difficulties. She contends that Lady Fanny is a magnificent pagan who acts entirely on instinct; she is thus not to be judged on standard moral grounds. Cashmore, however, as Mrs. Brook observes, must rationalize his own profligacy: he feels justified in his affair with Carrie Donner only as long as he believes his wife to be equally unfaithful. But Mrs. Brook will not give him the support he wants, for she does not condemn Fanny. Thus she keeps the situation in balance; things remain unresolved and indefinite.

Mrs. Brook's intention has not been to soothe Cashmore, to prevent scandal, or to promote a moral code, but to ensure the continuation of what she and her circle find intellectually exciting. Her moral neutrality, rather her total freedom from what she would probably consider "vulgar" personal concerns, allows her to encourage her son Harold to pursue Lady Fanny, and Cashmore to pursue Nanda, so that the tension might continue and Lady Fanny might be prevented from leaving.

In contrast, the Duchess, who is a seeress and a moderator on a lesser scale, has motives which are personal and opportunistic; and Mr. Longdon, more remote but equally formidable as a kind of stage manager, is prompted by his chivalric love for Nanda and respect for Vanderbank. In this network of intrigues, both Mrs. Brook and Mr. Longdon demonstrate the inadequacy of the Duchess's motives and methods of interference. Mrs. Brook's and Mr. Longdon's intentions, however, are mutually critical, for if the former lack love, the latter lack art, but ultimately Mr. Longdon's moral bias is shown to take precedence over Mrs. Brook's intellectual bias.

The talk is objectionable not simply because it is too free, but because it is abstracted from life. In the typical James novel, as Jacques Barzun has pointed out, dialogue is both dramatic and emotional; it is a substitute for physical action and is full of passion and feeling.[36] With the sophisticated intellectual chatter of *The Awkward Age*, however, talk exists almost in a vacuum. In his final scene with Nanda, Vanderbank, second only to Mrs. Brook as a master of wit and conversation, is speechless in a genuinely human situation. His constant shaking of his foot and inane banter reveal his incapacity to be other than superficial. As we have seen, in the episode in which Mrs. Brook tells Mitchy of Mr. Longdon's proposal to Van, the talk is divorced from the actual feelings and thoughts of the characters. Mrs. Brook once remarks, "And yet to think that after all it has been mere *talk!*" Vanderbank replies, "Mere, mere, mere. But perhaps it's exactly the 'mere' that has made us range so wide." And Mrs. Brook answers, "You mean that we haven't had the excuse of passion." Van's "There you are" (IX, 313) underlines her remark, which sums up the weakness of the circle. Here, then, is form without content, gesture without motion—the mark of a hollow, decadent society.

Within this circle James creates characters alike in their modernity and their reliance on the head rather than the heart, but different in the ways in which they show their degeneration. Mrs. Brook, the major figure, although her immorality is partly redeemed by her energy, her wit, her superiority, and her skill, is nevertheless damned by her perversion of values—her sacrifice of Nanda to her self-interest. Her intellectual supremacy disguises the grossness of her misdeeds, for even her scandalous humiliation of Nanda at Tishy Grendon's, which is a brutal act of personal violation, comes as the result of a carefully planned and well executed intrigue.

One is tempted to admire if not condone Mrs. Brook because of her intellectual as well as moral superiority to her foil, the Duchess. Mrs. Brook and the Duchess play the same game, but they use different rules. Mrs. Brook plots to marry Nanda to Mitchy, and the Duchess tries to snare him for her niece, Little Aggie. But the Duchess is deceptive and hypocritical, whereas Mrs. Brook, for all her scheming, is above the vulgarity of the Duchess's methods. The Duchess educates Aggie in the continental system; that is, she totally shelters her from her elders. The Duchess feigns a complete devotion to Aggie, while Mrs. Brook frankly admits that she has no interest in self-sacrifice. The Duchess has an affair with Petherton; Mrs. Brook, though in love with Vanderbank, does not have an affair with him.[37] The Duchess's hypocrisy emerges in other ways also, for she schemes to have Mitchy marry Aggie in order to acquire his fortune, though she says that Mitchy, the son of a shoemaker, is beneath her social level. She is hypocritical because she wishes to make Mrs. Brook —who wants Mitchy for Nanda—feel unopposed. The Duchess's methods are vulgarly blunt. Mrs. Brook tries to win Mitchy only by suggesting tactfully to Nanda that she consider him, but the Duchess, who never bothers to consider Aggie's desires—if she has any—suggests that Mr. Longdon make it worth Van's while to marry Nanda, virtually forces Mitchy to meet and talk with Aggie, and compels her lover, Petherton, to praise Aggie's merits ("he must like *her*. Make him feel that he does" [IX, 115]). Though the Duchess tells Mr. Longdon, "I can only work Mitchy through Petherton, but Mrs. Brook can work him straight" (p. 254), she overestimates her adversary's vulgarity. Mrs. Brook can work Mitchy straight, but she refuses to do so. Because of her devotion to subtlety and wit, Mrs. Brook abhors bluntness, which she associates with tastelessness; her method of keeping Van for herself is indirect and relatively delicate, and her attempt to gain Mitchy for Nanda recognizes limits of propriety. Even when she is blunt—as when she makes herself hideous before Mr. Longdon —her obvious behavior conceals a subtle method, since her intention is to appear so odious that Mr. Longdon will take Nanda. Even Mrs. Brook's exposure of Nanda is less culpable than the Duchess's cloistering of Aggie, because it is not only straightforward but also more beneficial to Nanda, who is allowed to know in order to choose. The Duchess treats Aggie as a puppet, while Mrs. Brook respects Nanda's mind and judgment.

Mrs. Brook also gains through contrast with Vanderbank, who is a trimmer, capable of moral discrimination (Mitchy says, "He's very much the best of us" [IX, 125]), but incapable of converting his principles into action, and finally unable completely to break with Mrs. Brook's circle or completely to join it. Vanderbank's personal drama is one of indecision. After months of inconclusive consideration of Mr. Longdon's offer to marry Nanda, Van finally withdraws, not because of his own decision but because of Mrs. Brook's interference. Like the Duchess, Vanderbank represents a pseudo-traditionalism. For, as the Duchess pretends to follow an older code, Van is ultimately too old-fashioned to condone Nanda's behavior. Mr. Longdon gives the lie to both because, in his genuine traditionalism, he knows the difference between the literal and the real, the overt and the actual. Thus Van rejects Nanda because he suspects that she has been too exposed, though Mr. Longdon recognizes that Nanda's corruption is superficial. He accepts Nanda as she is because he has the understanding to see through the appearances that prove a barrier to Van. But Van's primary shortcoming is his pride—Mrs. Brook terms him "awfully conceited and awfully patronising" (IX, 248) —which Mrs. Brook exploits in order to stop him from marrying her daughter. She tells Mitchy in Van's presence that Van "won't want to have the pecuniary question mixed up with the matter: to look in short as if he had had to be paid. He's like you, you know—he's proud . . ." (IX, 300). Mrs. Brook thwarts Van; she cleverly raises an issue that had heretofore been of secondary importance to him. Now he feels that to marry Nanda will damage his reputation. Van's foil, Mitchy, has no such self-damaging pride: out of devotion to Nanda he willingly makes himself appear a fool by marrying Aggie. Vanderbank is related to John Marcher of "The Beast in the Jungle" in that he is incapable of selfless love. Though Van is attracted to Nanda, he too readily admits impediments, so that his own selfishness, masked as high propriety, is the factor without which Mrs. Brook's interference with Nanda would have been unsuccessful.

Mrs. Brook acquires stature when contrasted with the Duchess and Van, but her basic immorality is most apparent when she is contrasted with Nanda. Nanda resembles the other innocents of James's London fiction. She is sealed up in a restricting environment; she is victimized by her parents; she has certain unattractive traits; and her positive action for good (her persuasion of Mitchy to marry Aggie) creates evil. James belittles Nanda in the beginning by showing that she suffers by contrast with both her mother and her grandmother. She is not so worldly-wise as her mother; she is not so good as her grandmother. Furthermore, she is grim: "She's as bleak as a chimney-top when the fire's out" (IX, 452); she is also solemn: the jovial Mitchy never knows quite what to make of her.

She is strangely old—older than her mother, even older than Mr. Longdon—in her tragic awareness of things. She differs most

from her fellow heroines in that there is nothing romantic about
her; she is no victim of enchantment and has no illusions about
her world and her life. "What I am I must remain," she tells
Vanderbank; "I haven't what's called a principle of growth . . . .
I'm about as good as I can be—and about as bad. If Mr. Longdon
can't make me different nobody can" (IX, 214). She has inherited
her mother's uncanny perception, so that she knows from the beginning that she is fated to unhappiness: ". . . I shall be one of
the people who don't. I shall be at the end . . . one of those who
haven't" (IX, 232).

Like Maisie, Nanda has the talent for understanding what goes
on about her. Yet, unlike Maisie, she is prim and quaint rather
than pliable and fresh. She knows only disaster. She can reconcile neither joy nor good humor with her insight. However, her
perception shelters her from the intense personal grief that Isabel
Archer must live with and from the sudden shock of evil that
destroys Morgan Moreen. Nanda, after her mistreatment by her
mother and Van, is peculiarly calm; she even steals the scene as
she directs Van and Mitchy to comfort her mother. She is composed because she is inured to suffering and through experience
can bear the shock of reality which destroys her mother.

In spite of her acquaintance with her mother's group and Tishy
Grendon, Nanda is essentially innocent. Mr. Longdon realizes
that Nanda's differences from her grandmother are superficial and
environmental. Nanda tells him, "If [Lady Julia and I are] both
partly the result of other people, *her* other people were so different. . . . Granny wasn't the kind of girl she *could*n't be—and
so neither am I" (IX, 230–231). Forced against her will into her
mother's universe, thrown into association with Tishy Grendon so
that her mother might be free to live her own life (like the innocents of "The Turn of the Screw," Nanda is "blameless and foredoomed"), Nanda has in her awkward period developed a consciousness of reality that enables her to distinguish good and evil.
An irony of the novel is that although Van rejects Nanda for
knowing too much, it is only because of her knowledge that she
is able to achieve genuine, tested goodness. Her counterpart, Little Aggie, has the appearance of innocence; Nanda has the ap-

pearance of worldliness. Until her marriage, Aggie is an unknown
quality:

> Decidedly [Aggie] was . . . an angel, and there was a
> wonder in her possession on this footing of one of the most
> expressive little faces that even her expressive race had ever
> shown. . . . Formed to express everything, it scarce ex-
> pressed as yet even a consciousness. All the elements of play
> were in it, but they had nothing to play with (IX, 240).

Nanda's surface immorality corresponds to that of Maisie, whose
initial approval of her elders shocks Mrs. Wix but disguises an
innocence. Though Nanda may appear both grim and corrupted,[38] her very awareness and involvement support the moral
sense, while Aggie, inexperienced, is immediately corrupted upon
her introduction to the adult world. Thus Nanda's withdrawal
contrasts with Aggie's entrance. It is a withdrawal prompted not
only by devotion to Mr. Longdon and her mother—she feels
obliged to do her part so that her mother may receive money
from Mr. Longdon—but by her insistence on remaining free
(Cashmore is ready to step in now that Van is out of the picture).
Nanda's retreat is no renunciation, for she has nothing to renounce; yet in her final scenes with Van, Mitchy, and Mr. Longdon, she dramatizes the Jamesian doctrine that the self matures
through knowledge of good and evil. Since she can have no personal happiness, she now devotes herself to patching the lives of
others. When Nanda achieves full understanding of her situation,
she loses self-consciousness. She has inherited the goodness of her
grandmother; here she shows that she can put to proper use what
she has learned from her mother. But when Nanda "squares" Van,
Mitchy, Mr. Longdon, and even Mrs. Brook, her queenly control
of others has a purity that comes from its total divorce from self-
concern. Nanda's serenity, however, does not disguise the malignity of the world which she abandons. Her selflessness is an ironic
contrast to the destructive egotism of her mother.

### CHAPTER FOUR

# Evil and the Major Phase

WHEN, in the first years of the twentieth century, James again took up the international theme, he used the same broad situation that had served him in the eighteen-seventies and eighties—the conflict of America and Europe against a European background. However, he so radically altered his treatment that his late international fiction must be considered not so much an extension of the earlier work as a distinct category. After the tightly restricted settings and unheroic protagonists of James's London novels, the international settings and international heroes of *The Ambassadors*, *The Wings of the Dove*, and *The Golden Bowl* significantly extend the scope of James's fiction. In the London fiction James was limited by subject matter and theme. The cramped Londoners with minor ambitions and, by comparison, petty problems, stand for man at his least heroic. The international theme offered James the setting for large-scale conflicts and characters of heroic dimensions.

Yet the novels of James's major phase are not so pointedly international as those of his earlier period. Not only do they contain little satire of American Puritanism and Philistinism, but also they stress moral rather than cultural differences.[1] It is significant, for example, that James planned *The Wings of the Dove* as a purely English novel.[2] Yet to provide his heroine with a moral strength that he found lacking in the English woman, he made Milly Theale an American. While Fleda Vetch and Nanda Brookenham are like the American heroines in their innocence and moral sense, they differ strikingly in being weak and unattractive. James looked to America to supply his heroines of stature, to complement morality with strength of character.

102

The American replaces the Londoner as hero because, at least potentially, he has the wisdom and the strength to survive in Europe. What is required for success is a maturing of the moral sense, an added perception, and a new power. It seems that James's own moral attitudes have changed with those of his heroes and heroines. The distance between Euphemia Cleve of the early "Madame de Mauves" and Maggie Verver of *The Golden Bowl* is as extreme as that between the Puritanical conception of morality which informs the first and the pragmatic conception which informs the second. Euphemia Cleve is virtue shocked and indignant at her husband's infidelity; she is adamant and unforgiving. Isabel Archer is disillusioned and hurt by Osmond, and like Euphemia she finds no alternative to sealing herself off from the world. Fleda Vetch marks a major deviation from this pattern: she cannot run away when she learns the truth about Mrs. Gereth, and tries to restore good. Maggie, like Euphemia and Isabel, finds herself betrayed and victimized. Unlike them, however, she does not withdraw. Like Fleda she combats the evil; but, unlike Fleda, she achieves high success.

For the American to counteract evil—and by doing so to retain a relationship with his immediate society—he must rise above the legalism of Puritanism and the squeamishness of innocence. The matured moral sense aligns itself with aspects of American life that James had either ignored or found wanting in America of the mid-nineteenth century. The new American is pliable. Isabel Archer lacks the rigidity of Euphemia Cleve and Gertrude Wentworth, but only to a point. She easily accepts cultural differences and welcomes new experience, to which she readily responds. But to the evil of Osmond and Mme. Merle Isabel reacts by rejecting the freedom which has brought her suffering. To the early James such renunciation represents high morality; to the late James it signifies a moral deficiency.

The later protagonists either possess or acquire an imagination which can penetrate surface facts and which can gain a transcendent understanding of things. Such an imagination rises above personal indignation and insistence on justice. James makes far greater demands upon native American idealism than he made in *The American* and *The Portrait of a Lady*. Positive virtue, such as that demonstrated by Maggie Verver, requires selflessness, a capacity for suffering, and a sense of social duty. The early hero-ines find their principal duty to be to themselves—to adhere unswervingly to their own ethical standards. The later heroines find their principal duty to be to others—to sacrifice themselves to the well-being of society.

The first requirement for the maintenance of a stable social relationship is the recognition of evil as an ineluctable condition of life. Furthermore, intelligence must be supported by resolute-ness and resourcefulness. Up to *The Golden Bowl*, James's Americans are critically handicapped by their ignorance of the conditions of life. Even in *The Golden Bowl*, the innocent, Mag-gie Verver, is unaware of evil at the beginning of her European adventure, but once she gains her vision of evil, she uses her new insight to restore good, or at least to keep her marriage from col-lapsing. To lesser degrees and with less success, Lambert Strether and Milly Theale also acquire more than knowledge from their encounters with evil. Their knowledge enables, rather compels, them to *act*, and with considerable effectiveness. This is a new role for the Jamesian protagonist, whose characteristic tragic position has in the past been passivity.

Milly Theale uses the transcendent imagination to subdue evil. Though she dies a victim of treachery, her spiritual love for those who destroy her has the practical effect of converting an agent of evil to good. Maggie uses the transcendent imagination and the empirical intelligence to achieve both an ideal and a real triumph over those who have wronged her. James tends to asso-ciate both spiritual and intellectual power with wealth. (His inept Londoners are poor.) His Americans now have behind them not only the Puritan and Transcendental traditions, but also late nine-teenth-century American financial strength. James vaguely iden-tifies the American commercial empire with a native power that can produce not only the fortunes of the Newsomes, the Theales, and the Ververs, but also the deeds of spiritual and intellectual strength that enable Milly Theale and Maggie Verver to impede the evil of Europe.

Although James alters his picture of the American to include a greater generosity and a greater power, he seems to realize, far more than before, the American capacity for evil. With *The Ambassadors* he especially reveals the ugliness of American intolerance as well as the guilt that must accompany American wealth. With *The Wings of the Dove* he is concerned with the flaws of Milly Theale's innocence: her pride, her excessive reliance on money, and her hesitance to face life in its fullness. With *The Golden Bowl* he explores fully the underside of both American wealth and American innocence; the novel shows the essential destructiveness of imperception and immaturity. What was before often comic or pathetic becomes serious and tragic. In addition, James's later Americans prove not only extremely limited in themselves, but also menaces to the values and achievements of Europe.

Most of the malefactors in James's earlier international novels are impelled toward evil because their ambitions are social rather than private. For the sake of upholding a tradition, of adhering to a convention, or of maintaining a social position, they injure others. The evildoers of the late international novels are self-reliant; and, unlike the earlier Mme. Merle and Mrs. Brookenham, they neither adopt impersonal goals nor strive to satisfy external codes. James's late Europeans embody both national and personal qualities; they do not thoughtlessly conform to European mores. Maud Lowder of *The Wings of the Dove* belongs to the world of *The Awkward Age*; she is the British middle-class woman aspiring towards gentility. She stands alone in James's final international trilogy[3] as a European whose concern is primarily social. Mme. de Vionnet, Kate Croy, and Prince Amerigo surpass her in stature and dignity because they go beyond the demands of the world to seek a fulfillment that is personal.

Just as James's heroes and heroines become less legalistic and doctrinaire in their reactions to the evil of Europe, James himself shows hesitance to define and judge that evil. Evil in the novels of James's major phase is far more mysterious and ubiquitous than in his earlier works. The major reason is that it is less specifically linked to the sins of particular persons. Human differences, human weaknesses, and the complexity of life cause suffering and calamity, but the origin and the location of the evil are unspecified. In *The Golden Bowl*, in which each of the major figures contributes to the creation of the evil situation, the apparent source—the combined offenses of four people—seems disproportionate to the effects. Only in *The Wings of the Dove* is the crime terrible in itself. In *The Ambassadors* and *The Golden Bowl* there is neither an obvious crime nor an obvious villain, but the results of seemingly minor transgressions indicate that an extreme evil has been admitted to the scene. There is no superficial manifestation of villainy in the later novels. Furthermore, the offenders are as much as possible forgiven. Mme. de Vionnet, Kate Croy, and Charlotte Stant are placed in extremely difficult and compromising situations. To avoid the sins that they eventually commit would require a supreme virtue and a saintlike abnegation of happiness. Through his emphasis on the details of Kate Croy's background, James makes the reader sympathize with her, even though her plot against Milly Theale is inhumanly cruel. Likewise, since the American heroes do not apply their own moral codes dogmatically to the behavior of the Europeans, the effect is that James does not so much judge or condemn as simply reveal. Evil does not develop because of the sins of the malignant, but because of those of the weak. Yet the force of evil is not diminished; rather it is strengthened; for it is universal.

The agents of evil in the late novels remain aesthetically and intellectually fine specimens. The early villains have only a superficial and acquired attractiveness, which vanishes once they are found out. Yet Mme. de Vionnet actually gains charm and beauty when her sins are discovered; Kate Croy has a physical beauty and an intellectual strength which are not diminished by her monstrous crime; and Prince Amerigo epitomizes the grace of his ancestry. These characters have merits neither because of nor in spite of what they do. Unlike Sarah Pocock, Maud Lowder, and Fanny Assingham, the major evildoers are ladies and gentlemen whose dignity, charm, and good will are neither accidental nor superficial, but inherent in their natures. They are neither gross nor base; their being is separable from their behavior. James not only treats human character as far more complex than in his earlier works, but he also sees evil as far less explicable and identifiable. It is not removed or removable from human beings or human relationships, but no comfortable conclusions can be drawn about the evildoer. He is an agent of evil, but he is also much else.

In James's aesthetic sense of morality, all undesirable behavior is ugly, but with the later novels it is possible for one to be highly civilized and at the same time commit a great crime. In such case the sin is ugly, but the sinner remains beautiful. Mme. de Vionnet is genuinely beautiful—in an aesthetic and even a moral way—though she is the agent of an extreme evil. In respects other than her deception of Strether and intimacy with Chad, she has a high sense of responsibility and honor in human dealings. She is, as Strether recognizes, well worth saving.

Though it is not the only or even the main source of evil in James's late novels, deception is the most obvious cause of suffering. But this suffering does not consist simply of disillusion and resultant despair. The consciousness of the heroes and heroines is overwhelmed by mystery and confusion. The deceit of others combines with the mystery latent in Europe to create a severe anguish. With final knowledge there is disillusion and a more intense pain, but the dark journeys of James's protagonists do not end at this point, as do those of their predecessors. For Strether, Milly, and Maggie must continue to make their ways without retreat or the comfort of complete despair. Much of the obscurity in James's later works derives from the difficulty the characters have in going through the ordinary motions of life. One has the sense in reading *The Ambassadors, The Wings of the Dove,* and *The Golden Bowl*—especially the latter—that for a character to refer explicitly to the pressing situation that everyone is aware of but no one dares mention would be to shatter the lives of all. For the involved individuals to continue to live as social creatures, the evil that surrounds them must be kept from engulfing them. The indirection, nuances, and illusory surface calm of the later novels reflect the life of the novels. It is the struggle to preserve appearances that makes living a trial.

Behind James's emphasis on the importance of keeping up appearances—even though they directly contradict the reality of a situation—lies his recognition of the necessity of form—of manners. Though in the ideal society appearance and reality should correspond, one should preserve the appearance of the good and the beautiful even though it is an illusion. In 1908 James advised Edith Wharton to

> *go through the movements of life.* That keeps up our con-
> nection with life—I mean of the immediate and apparent life;
> behind which, all the while, the deeper and darker and unap-
> parent, in which things *really* happen to us, learns, under that
> hygiene, to stay in its place. Let it get out of its place and it
> swamps the scene; besides which its place, God knows, is
> enough for it![4]

Latent and suppressed evil is more terrible than overt evil. But, paradoxically, evil must be concealed if there is to be any basis for living.

The appearance of life is not the full or even the adequate life; it makes deception, hypocrisy, insincerity, and artificiality in-evitable. In his grasping for a workable relationship between in-dividual and society, James rejects the simple solution of renun-ciation—the abandonment of social relationships out of ethical scruple—and shows the necessity of a stoic endurance of things as they are. Also, appearances have a reality of their own. For James, style and manners, as well as surface humanity and recog-nition of basic amenities, are prerequisites for civilization. They are not enough to relieve isolation, but they provide grounds for social intercourse.

The late novels are really about the disintegration of western civilization. They reflect what James's letters and notebooks fre-quently state—his vision of "this overwhelming, self-defeating chaos or cataclysm toward which the whole thing is drifting." [5] One way of defining James's ideal of civilization is to say that not only should society offer the individual a contact with the aes-thetic and social values of history—art and manners—but also that these values must be consistent with actual human behavior. In the late novels Americans and Europeans alike undermine and at the same time struggle to maintain the values of the past. Forms, surfaces, and manners have become all but incompatible with the human standards they should ideally reflect.

In *The Ambassadors, The Wings of the Dove,* and *The*

*Golden Bowl*, James varies slightly his dominant theme of appearance and reality to dramatize his vision of the American-European world straining to preserve itself from internal destruction. Appearance, the historical heritage of art and manners, is no longer reality: at best it is a thin disguise lending meretricious splendor to a behavior alien to it; at worst it is a thing to be kept in museums, a refuge from reality. The reality of greed, with its mechanics of intrigue and duplicity, seeks the appearance of art and manners. There is a consistent dichotomy between the form and the content of civilization, between past and present, between society and individual. When the form collapses, society becomes anarchy and merely the sum-total of individual grasping egos. The value of the form is ambiguous, for it adds the horror of deceit to the evil of economic and human plunder; but also it is a restraint: it provides a uniformity of standards and a social cohesiveness without which there would be no community at all. Society and civilization collapse together when Strether sees the duplicity of Mme. de Vionnet and Chad, and when Lord Mark reveals Densher's plot to Milly. In *The Golden Bowl* Maggie Verver has her vision of reality, but instead of withering she struggles successfully to maintain appearances. But in *The Ambassadors* and *The Wings of the Dove*, the perceptions of Strether and Milly of the hollowness of form bring about the death of civilization.

Such are the Jamesian moments of exclusion, in which the individual finds himself isolated, unsupported by values outside of himself, unable to define himself through his social and historical position. The nature of the relationship between the innocent seeker and the cultured world of experience has significantly changed since a novel like *The Portrait of a Lady*. Isabel Archer's problem is to reconcile the values of a traditional society with her personal ideals. At opposite poles are Henrietta Stackpole, whose limitations are measured by her absolute hostility to Europe, and Mme. Merle, who is morally deficient because she lives "exclusively for the world" (IV, 144). Mme. Merle tells Isabel, "There's no such thing as an isolated man or woman; we're each of us made up of some cluster of appurtenances" (III, 287). The novel reveals the need for synthesis between the personal and the social code.

The norm is clearly Ralph Touchett, who appreciates the need for "appurtenances" to the self—that is why he persuades his father to make Isabel rich—and yet is ultimately self-reliant in his moral judgments. In the world of a novel like *The Wings of the Dove*, however, no such compromise is possible. Thus the moral person is forced back on himself, denied any kind of meaningful social relationship. James's last novels treat the dual movements of society's dissolution and the individual's recognition of his essential isolation. They dramatize the reality of evil overcoming the appearance of beauty.

## THE AMBASSADORS

In *The Ambassadors* James fully achieves what he had approached in many of his earlier works: the identification of action with vision. Although the protagonist, Lambert Strether, is one of James's spectator heroes, he is not held back from life by the debility of a Ralph Touchett or the intellectual pride of a Vanderbank. In the person of Strether vision is action; it represents a full participation in experience. It is dynamic, dramatic, and personal.

Strether's relation with Europe is dynamic and dramatic because it is personal. Strether is in Europe as the emissary of Mrs. Newsome, who has sent him from Woollett, Massachusetts, in order to retrieve her son, Chad, whom she and the rest of Woollett suspect to have become involved with a disreputable French woman. When he arrives in Europe, Strether carries with him a strong sense of obligation to fulfill his mission; and he also holds the Woollett attitude toward Paris. He believes it to be a modern Babylon, in which Chad has been seduced into the conventional and vulgar vices. Moreover, Strether is motivated by more than a sense of duty. His future happiness depends upon his success in bringing Chad home. Strether, a widower in his mid-fifties, has obtained neither wealth nor success. He is a friend to the Newsome family and for years has edited the literary magazine which the wealthy and influential Mrs. Newsome has subsidized. Strether has reason to believe that Mrs. Newsome will marry him if he is successful as her ambassador to Europe. Therefore, even though Strether is almost entirely a spectator, he is personally involved in the situation he observes.

James traces the development of Strether's understanding of a particular Parisian social group. Before Strether sees Chad, he discovers the beauty of Paris: its cultural, aesthetic, and architectural richness, which indicates a way of life more satisfying than that of Woollett. Even before he meets Chad, his prejudices begin to be modified, and after he meets Chad they all but vanish. James dramatizes Strether's awakening in visual terms. Strether "sees" truth: in the architecture of Chad's home and in Chad's appearance in a theater box. Each successive impression forces Strether to shift his moral position, to consider the relation of the new impression to his duty to Mrs. Newsome; by seeing one thing differently he is made to see other things differently.

Midway in the novel Strether, in the process of comparing the life of his new Parisian friends to his own starved past and equally bleak future, reveals to Little Bilham, Chad's companion, the startling influence of Paris on him. In his advice to Bilham to "live," Strether shows his realization of his own situation ("It's too late" [XXI, 217]). Now unable to live actively and immediately, he can live passively and remotely. He is not, however, experiencing life merely vicariously. Through seeing and through understanding, he does "have his life." In Strether's mind, scenes create impressions and impressions give rise to insights.

Strether must deal with two kinds of evil: the evil of Europe and the evil of America. His growth involves a rejection of the evils of America which he has brought with him to Europe and an acceptance of the evils of Europe which he gradually discovers. To achieve self-fulfillment, he must cast off the American evils of prejudice, intolerance, narrowness, and smugness. James exposes Puritanism in *The Ambassadors* not only through Jim and Sarah Pocock and the felt presence of Mrs. Newsome, but also through Strether himself, who gradually abandons the worst aspects of his Puritan heritage. In the beginning his fault is simply his ignorance and his prejudices; he accepts without serious consideration the Woollett view of Paris and of Chad. Even when he realizes the fallacy of such notions, he still retains subtler but equally dangerous traits of New England Puritanism.

In *The Ambassadors* James equates the New England fear of experience with evil. He delves into the psychological basis of the

New England conscience and its related evils by showing them
to be manifestations of a fear of the unknown. For such a New
Englander as Waymarsh the foreign is to be feared and hated because it is unknown. Thus, comically but significantly, Waymarsh
becomes shocked and fearful when, early in the novel, Strether
begins to make casual advances into European life. The purchase
of a pair of gloves in a British shop portends horrors to Waymarsh:

> Mere discriminations about a pair of gloves could . . . rep-
> resent . . . possibilities of something that Strether could
> make a mark against only as the peril of apparent wantonness.
> He had quite the consciousness of his new friend [Maria
> Gostrey], for their companion, that he might have had of
> a Jesuit in petticoats, a representative of the recruiting inter-
> ests of the Catholic Church. The Catholic Church, for Way-
> marsh—that was to say the enemy, the monster of bulging
> eyes and far-reaching quivering groping tentacles—was
> exactly society, exactly the discrimination of types and tones,
> exactly the wicked old Rows of Chester, rank with feuda-
> lism; exactly in short Europe (XXI, 41).

Strether is the only New Englander who can accept his fear of
the unknown as a fear, instead of converting it into a rigid antagonism, justified on flimsy moral grounds. In the beginning he can
admit to Maria Gostrey his dread of his forthcoming adventure:
"I'm always considering something else; something else, I mean,
than the thing of the moment. The obsession of the other thing is
the terror" (XXI, 19). Strether's honest attempt to discover truth
without a priori judgments involves a painful conquest of his fear
of life. With the other ambassadors, there is no such honesty.

What appears quaintly provincial in *The Europeans* becomes
aggressive and dangerous in *The Ambassadors*. The Wentworth
family is rendered by its Calvinistic heritage incapable of moral
maturity because it is unable to absorb new experience. In *The
Ambassadors* James views New England Puritanism, coupled
with the force of New England industrial power, as capable of a
greater evil. What is ignorance in the Wentworths becomes intolerance in the Pococks. New England loses the dignity of its mid-

nineteenth-century patriarchal society and replaces it by the inhumanity of its late-century commercialism.

Strether is saved from being a complete New Englander by his imagination and by his lack of economic and social success. Unable to participate fully in New England wealth and culture, Strether partly escapes its deadening effects, so that his wisdom is allowed, if not to grow, to remain latent until Europe can nurture it. Mrs. Newsome, the Pococks, and Waymarsh, however, like many of James's morally deficient Americans and Europeans, allow their personal attitudes to be replaced by pervasive regional or cultural attitudes. Accordingly, Mrs. Newsome's dominant trait is her inflexibility.

James's exposure of Puritanism as a malignant force is equivalent to linking ignorance with sin. Maria Gostrey tells Strether that Sarah Pocock's vilification ("Do you consider her even an apology for a decent woman?" [XXII, 202]) of Mme. de Vionnet cannot be justified by ignorance. "She imagined meanly," she tells Strether. "He had it, however, better. 'It couldn't but be ignorantly.' 'Well, intensity with ignorance—what do you want worse?'" (XXII, 225). In themselves ignorance and fear are merely negative deficiencies, but in practice they lead directly to the kind of dynamic intolerance which the later James sees as the source of a far greater evil than Europe.

In the early chapters of *The Ambassadors*, James stresses the baseness of American capitalism. The Newsome fortune far exceeds that of the earlier Christopher Newman, whose methods of acquisition, while perhaps undignified, were never unethical. In speaking with Maria Gostrey about the Newsome fortune, Strether says, "The source of [Chad's] grandfather's wealth—and thereby of his own share in it—was not particularly noble" (XXI, 62). A bit later, Strether refers to the manner in which Mrs. Newsome uses her wealth: ". . . her money is spent, her life conceived and carried on with a large beneficence." Maria's reply is immediate and devastating (she dares constantly to mention realities which Strether shies from considering): "That's a kind of expiation of wrongs" (XXI, 63).

Just as Mrs. Newsome and Sarah Pocock embody the brute strength of American wealth, so Jim Pocock and Waymarsh manifest its crippling effect. Waymarsh and Jim Pocock, unlike the earlier Mr. Ruck, the business man in "The Pension Beaurepas," are not simply pathetic. Though they are comic in their vulgarity and their inability to enjoy Europe, they are not simply victims of a fierce economic system, but are so emotionally and morally deranged by their backgrounds that they have become agents of evil. Waymarsh, whose provincialism is at first comic, emerges in the course of the novel as sinister. His distorted sense of values and perverted notion of duty cause him to betray his friendship to Strether by surreptitiously reporting his activities to Mrs. Newsome and by callously siding with the Pococks. Jim Pocock, whose lack of dignity and moral stature is partly a result of his own business activities and partly of his domination by the women of the Newsome household, lacks the ethical rigidity of his wife and mother-in-law, but he is equally repulsive because of his coarseness. Jim Pocock is the American business man blighted and dehumanized, made bestial through his activity in industry. He is an enemy of the fine and the noble. His raucous delight in a Paris which he imagines a center of licentiousness and debauchery is but the counterpart of his wife's prejudiced denunciation of Paris. As Van Wyck Brooks notes, "Jim Pocock's face is the same face of horror that Spencer Brydon ["The Jolly Corner"] encountered when the ghost of his American self dropped its hands." [6] Brydon, like Abel Gaw of *The Ivory Tower*, has been turned into a monster by his life of commerce.[7]

Enabled to profit from a new experience because of his incomplete connection with Woollett, Strether gradually acquires a new set of values. Initially Strether learns of the positive values of Europe and of the evils of Woollett; later he learns of the evils of Europe. His first major step is his liberation from the narrow-mindedness of New England: an evil and dangerous tendency to condemn the foreign. Strether gradually replaces condemnation by suspicion, and finally judgment by sympathy. Before he even meets Chad, he has learned through acquaintance with his friends and his surroundings that his preconceived notions were false and oversimplified. He can honestly reconsider his position: "He must approach Chad, must wait for him, deal with him, master him, but he mustn't dispossess himself of the faculty of seeing things as they were" (XXI, 118). Strether proceeds cautiously, and he begins to realize the necessity for making distinctions undreamed of in Woollett. By observing the remarkable and beneficial alteration in Chad, who has gained a culture and a refinement far superior to that of the New Englander, Strether recognizes that he is dealing not with the broad caricature of Paris and of "life" that Woollett accepts as fact, but with a complex, subtle phenomenon that has much of value and nothing of vulgarity. Strether realizes that "to live" is certainly not to be evil in the Woollett sense of the word: "experience was what Chad did play on him, if he didn't play any grossness of defiance. Of course experience was in a manner defiance; but it wasn't, at any rate—rather indeed quite the contrary!—grossness; which was so much gained" (XXI, 155).

Strether's readjustment represents a rejection of personal pride —a pride that justifies fear and ignorance. His moral aid to Chad and Mme. de Vionnet requires self-surrender. When he decides to renounce the happiness and security promised by Mrs. Newsome to "save" Chad and Mme. de Vionnet, he tells Maria Gostrey, "I seem to have a life only for other people" (XXI, 269). In spite of his personal renunciation, however, Strether retains up to the very end of his experience some dangerous New England traits. Like the governess of "The Turn of the Screw," he is capable of asking unpleasant and compromising questions in order to justify his own behavior. He questions Bilham as to the precise nature of the relation between Chad and Mme. de Vionnet, demanding to know whether it is a "virtuous attachment" (XXI, 181). Later he questions Miss Barrace about Mme. de Vionnet: "Will you answer me a plain question? Will she ever divorce?" (XXI, 265). It becomes clear from Strether's more mature behavior at the conclusion of his experience, when he acquires the taste to respect the dignity of others and the imagination to perceive the fallacy of judging from the obvious, that such legalistic probings are tainted with pride.

Strether becomes attracted to Europe for aesthetic reasons. He rejects his New England morality not because he encounters a

superior morality in Europe, but because he recognizes the shortsightedness of the conventional Woollett evaluation of Europe.
He sides with Europe rather than with America because he is
greatly impressed by European beauty. Strether errs in making
an unconscious equation between art and morality: first, he applies New England principles to European life, and later, after he
has repudiated Mrs. Newsome, he tends to see aesthetic grace as a
kind of morality in itself. Not till the end of his adventure does
Strether realize the proper relationship between art and morality,
when he finds that evil is an attribute of beauty.

Because Strether is a spectator rather than a participant and because his vision is his major faculty, his viewpoint is mainly aesthetic. As his perception increases and more things come into its
ken, he discovers the true content of beauty. Strether first "sees"
Chad, in terms of art, as an "irreducible young pagan" (XXI,
156–157). But Strether is betrayed by his vision, for while he is
vastly pleased by the bearing of Chad, he is blinded by the surface to the moral essence of Chad. Strether realizes much later
that Chad is a pagan—i. e., faithless, capricious, materialistic—
in reality as well as in appearance. Thus Strether too casually dismisses his original fears about Chad. Although Strether thinks of
Chad's new manner as smooth, he overlooks the implications of
superficiality in the term.

Strether's renunciation of Woollett occurs at the crucial scene
in Gloriani's garden, in which Strether is introduced to the splendor of Parisian culture and is so impressed that he urges Bilham to
experience life to its fullest. Here is life as art—in the scene itself,
in Gloriani, and especially in Mme. de Vionnet. At the beginning
of the party, Strether is painfully conscious of his "odious ascetic
suspicion of any form of beauty" (XXI, 193–194), but in the
course of the afternoon he all but completely dispels this Calvinistic hostility.

The scene in Gloriani's garden occurs in a carefully delineated
setting, which is filtered through Strether's consciousness in a
series of impressions which suggest that there is more to Parisian
culture than simply beauty. Thus, as Strether gains a panoramic
impression of the area about the garden, he thinks of it in religious terms:

Strether had presently the sense of a great convent, a convent of missions, famous for he scarce knew what, a nursery of young priests, of scattered shade, of straight alleys and chapel-bells, that spread its mass in one quarter; he had the sense of names in the air, of ghosts at the windows, of signs and tokens, a whole range of expression, all about him, too thick for prompt discrimination (XXI, 196).

Strether has the sense of being initiated into the old and the beautiful. But the curious image of "a nursery of young priests" [8] suggests that Strether considers his approaching experience with Europe as both a retreat from the mediocrity and anxiety of the world and an introduction to an ideal condition of innocence. It is a mark of Strether's inexperience that he believes the aesthetic life to be a sanctuary from all forms of evil.

Immediately after this "assault of images" (XXI, 196), Strether is introduced to Gloriani himself, the complete European aesthete, and in the scene James continues to suggest the inseparability of beauty from evil. After observing Gloriani, Strether realizes that beneath the fine surface culture of the artist there is something of the fierce and the terrible. When he sees Gloriani in conversation with a duchess, he receives a distinct impression:

Were they, this pair, of the "great world"?—and was he himself, for the moment and thus related to them by his observation, *in* it? Then there was something in the great world covertly tigerish, which came to him across the lawn and in the charming air as a waft from the jungle. Yet it made him admire most of the two, made him envy, the glossy male tiger, magnificently marked (XXI, 219).

Strether associates the sensuousness of the artist with the sensuousness of the man. The image of the tiger stands for sexual passion. Gloriani symbolizes the whole of European culture, and, as physical beauty is inseparable from sexual energy in him, the same is true of Europe as a whole, and particularly of Mme. de Vionnet, the embodiment of its beauty.

Strether's sudden and only half-conscious perception of Gloriani is but a short-lived awareness. He reverts to idealizing the aesthetic life of Europe without accepting its suggested components.

Such life, Strether eventually realizes, is associated not with a retreat from reality, but with elements of reality that he finds unpleasant. When Strether urges Bilham to "have your life," he is only partly aware of the implication of his statement.

Strether still harbors dim suspicions of Mme. de Vionnet's guilt and Chad's deception. He is not yet morally prepared for total knowledge. It is ironic that when Strether finally does accept unreservedly the cause of Chad and Mme. de Vionnet, he does so in true Woollett fashion: he believes he has evidence of their innocence. When he sees Mme. de Vionnet in Notre Dame Cathedral he naïvely reasons:

> [Mme. de Vionnet's] attitude fitted admirably into the stand he had privately taken about her connexion with Chad on the last occasion of his seeing them together. It helped him to stick fast at the point he had then reached; it was there he had resolved that he *would* stick, and at no moment since had it seemed as easy to do so. Unassailably innocent was a relation that could make one of the parties to it so carry herself. If it wasn't innocent why did she haunt the churches? —into which, given the woman he could believe he made out, she would never have come to flaunt an insolence of guilt (XXII, 10).

Strether here projects New England attitudes toward religion and morality. Nevertheless his tacit pledge of loyalty is a sincere one, and it enables him to withstand the shocks that follow, when he discovers that the relationship between Chad and Mme. de Vionnet is sexual.

Preliminary to his discovery of the nature of the relationship, Strether learns from Mme. de Vionnet that she is planning a marriage for Jeanne, her daughter. Up to this point, Strether, convinced of Chad's innocence, has believed that Jeanne and Chad will eventually marry. The sudden knowledge shocks him. He feels the oppression of the "cold chambers of the past" (XXII, 127), of a way of life which allows the prearranged marriage and condones a union not entirely innocent between a married woman and a younger man. He has the sense of "being further and further 'in' " (XXII, 127–128), of being "concerned in something

deep and dim. He had allowed for depths, but these were greater
. . . . It was—through something ancient and cold in it—what
he would have called the real thing" (XXII, 129).

Most significant in Strether's development is that after receiving the information about Jeanne from Mme. de Vionnet, he replies, "How *much* I have to judge!" (XXII, 131). The comment
indicates that though Strether has gone far, he has still farther to
go. He must renounce judging entirely. Though it will entail
extreme suffering and involve painful self-effacement, he must
accept reality as it is, for he will soon be called upon to exercise
a sympathy and an understanding utterly incompatible with the
pride which allows one to judge his fellow man.

Strether's experience is one of developing awareness: of
beauty, of history, of culture. For his experience to be complete
his perception must be all-inclusive. Therefore he must come to a
knowledge of evil. Since all his knowledge has been acquired
through seeing, it is appropriate and significant that his perception
of evil be literally visual. Journeying through the countryside
near Paris, Strether stops at an inn, and, while sitting in the garden, he notices Chad and Mme. de Vionnet together in a boat.
When they come to shore and join Strether in dinner, it becomes
apparent that they have planned to spend the night in the inn. In
handling the scene in which Strether discovers the intimacy between Chad and Mme. de Vionnet, James reveals that the incident, along with its implications, points to the essential nature of
European culture. The incident is a part which stands for the
whole. As Strether begins his short journey, he is intent upon
discovering a pastoral scene "that would remind him of a certain
small Lambinet that had charmed him, long years before, at a
Boston dealer's and that he had quite absurdly never forgotten"
(XXII, 245). He happens upon a landscape that fills the requirements. Thus Strether, at the time of the excursion seeking art in
life, is most conscious of the aesthetic side of Europe. The limits
of his vision provide the framework of a painting. Viewing the
river, he finds a harmony usually found only in art. When his
revery is disturbed by the sight of the couple in the boat, his perception of Europe becomes complete. Beauty and truth become
one. Neither Strether nor the reader is allowed to dissociate the

ugly from the beautiful, for both are essential to Europe. The harmony of Strether's projected canvas is not destroyed but completed and deepened.

Strether, Maria Gostrey tells us, possesses "treasures of imagination" (XXII, 225), a power of mind capable of transcending prejudices and surfaces to a knowledge of reality. In the pastoral scene he exercises the faculty which enables him to see that Europe is neither simply good nor simply evil, but something which contains both, a luxuriant complexity in which life approaches art but remains life. He reconciles what had been the conflicting opposites of moral reality and aesthetic reality, and creates a unity that transcends both.[9] Strether's adventure is virtually ended, for it has been a drama of the expanding consciousness; and when it encounters the ugly and the evil, it assimilates them with the beautiful and the good. The result is not a less valuable awareness, but a more valuable one, for it is complete.

*The Ambassadors* does not end when Strether discovers that the relationship between Chad and Mme. de Vionnet is not "a virtuous attachment." Strether has further dealings with the participants, and his final attitude toward Mme. de Vionnet especially suggests the redemptive effect of his full and complex vision—of which evil is an essential component—upon his moral character. Strether's involvement in the affairs of Chad and Mme. de Vionnet has been personal, not only because he has sacrificed the advantages of Woollett in order to defend Chad, but also because his sympathy and affection, especially for Mme. de Vionnet, have acted as a bond, connecting his life with hers. In his effort to "save" her, he has become attached in an essential way to the life she represents. When he discovers her intimacy with Chad, he does not sever himself from her, but accepts the evil of which she is an agent as endemic to the world in which she lives. Initial shock and disillusion are replaced by a kind of sober recognition of universal human frailty. While walking the streets of Paris and posting a letter, Strether thinks of his close identification with the city and with what it now represents to him:

> After he had put in his paper he had ranged himself, he was really amused to think, on the side of the fierce, the sinister,

the acute. He was carrying on a correspondence, across the great city, quite in the key of the *Postes et Télégraphes* in general; and it was fairly as if the acceptance of that fact had come from something in his state that sorted with the occupation of his neighbors. He was mixed up with the typical tale of Paris, and so were they, poor things—how could they all together help being? They were no worse then he, in short, and he no worse then they—if, queerly enough, no better. . . .

. . . if he lived on thus with the sinister from hour to hour it proved an easier thing than one might have supposed in advance. He reverted in thought to his old tradition, the one he had been brought up on and which even so many years of life had but little worn away; the notion that the state of the wrongdoer, or at least this person's happiness, presented some special difficulty. What struck him now rather was the ease of it—for nothing in truth appeared easier (XXII, 271–272).

In his final scene with Mme. de Vionnet, Strether not only refuses to judge her, but also displays an overriding sympathy that amounts to a kind of love. While earlier he had helped Mme. de Vionnet in order to repay her for what she had done for Chad ("a criterion savoring of Woollett," as F. W. Dupee remarks),[10] now he helps her because she needs Chad. And Strether's desperate efforts to prevent Chad from deserting her attest his devotion to her.

The nature of the evil of Europe is less explicit in *The Ambassadors* than in any other James novel. Far clearer is the evil of Woollett. It is ironic that even though Mrs. Newsome and Sarah Pocock are right in believing their suspicions of adultery to be well founded, they are no less immoral for their condemnation of Strether and Mme. de Vionnet. They are wrong not only in their prejudices and in their blindness to beauty, but also in their unequivocal and easy identification of adultery with evil and in their condemnation of the adulterer. Before his initiation into Europe, Strether possesses the typical New England attitudes toward physical passion. In the process of his awakening—once he is convinced that Chad's affair is pure—he tends to ignore the existence of passion. But in the meantime he has become so impressed with the superior humanity of Mme. de Vionnet that even the shock which reveals her to be engaged in adultery cannot erase the previous image.

In effect James treats the adultery without ethical consideration, for he, like Strether, refuses to judge. He does, however, link the adultery with ugliness, but an ugliness that resides solely in the illicit passion and not in the participants. To both James and Strether, adultery is as coarse as it is to Woollett; yet the adulterers themselves are not coarse. Thus, what Strether had observed earlier in Gloriani—a combination of aesthetic beauty and sexual energy—he finds also in Mme. de Vionnet. Eventually Strether realizes the inseparability of the sensuous and the sensual in Paris.

Mme. de Vionnet is further exculpated because James treats her love for Chad as almost beyond her control, so that she is more a victim of sin than a sinner. In his final scene with her, Strether finds that she regrets and despises the weakness which causes her to love Chad:

> "What I hate is myself—when I think that one has to take so much, to be happy, out of the lives of others, and that one isn't happy even then. . . . The wretched self is always there, always making one somehow a fresh anxiety. What it comes to is that it's not, that it's never, a happiness, any happiness at all, to *take*" (XXII, 282–283).

Mme. de Vionnet is pathetic not only in her painful self-knowledge and unhappiness, but also in her dependence on Chad. The sympathy that James displays for her in her sorrow and abjection is a sympathy for man's weakness and human suffering. Maria Gostrey has the last word on the situation: "I'm sorry for us all" (XXII, 303).

Just as the evil and ugliness of adultery are transcended by the personal beauty of Mme. de Vionnet, in the same way her deception of Strether is transcended by the manner in which she deceives him. Strether understands that "their eminent 'lie,' Chad's and hers, was simply after all such an inevitable tribute to good taste as he couldn't have wished them not to render . . . . That is he could trust her to make deception right. As she presented things the ugliness—goodness knows why—went out of them . . ." (XXII, 277). It is not simply that Mme. de Vionnet's grace excuses her behavior or that she is led to deceive Strether because of an uncontrollable passion, but that the deception itself, though it amounts to a betrayal of Strether and causes him suffering, is an inevitable effect of the original evil—the adultery. Certainly Mme. de Vionnet and Chad gain Strether's favor under false pretenses; yet Strether's original prejudice was at least equally wrong. Maria Gostrey, in effect, deceives Strether by not telling him the truth about Chad and Mme. de Vionnet, which she has known from the beginning. But, as Strether ultimately realizes, immediate knowledge of the literal facts would have meant to him "a revulsion in favour of the principles of Woollett" (XXII, 296). Maria saves Strether from spiritual decay by deceiving him. Bilham lies to him when Strether blatantly asks him whether Chad's friendship is innocent. Strether justifies Bilham's deception through appreciation of the superior morality of loyalty and prudence ("Little Bilham had lied like [a gentleman]" [XXII, 299]). Strether defends the admitted evil of Mme. de Vionnet's deception by seeing it as an act of "good taste." The forms of civilization are worth preserving at all costs. Once a situation is grounded in evil, other evils must follow. In *The Ambassadors*, Strether himself, by abetting an adultery—at first ignorantly and then knowingly—commits himself to making the best of a corrupt situation. Strether chooses the complexity of beauty and ugliness in Europe for the sake of beauty. Therefore Mme. de Vionnet's deception has the ultimate effect of saving, albeit temporarily, a valuable though imperfect mode of life and of allowing Strether to have his life. Beyond this, James and his mature characters recognize the value of appearances and of keeping the evil hidden beneath the surfaces. Strether's accidental discovery prevents a successful containment of evil, and after his discovery, when the evil comes to the surface, a civilization dies. Shame, sorrow, and revulsion do not replace but become fused with grace and beauty.

Strether's experience amounts to a discovery of the fullness of life, for Europe itself, which embodies the deeds of man at his

finest and of man at his worst, provides not merely a special kind
of experience and an enriching one, but an experience without
which one is incomplete. James uses Mme. de Vionnet as a personal symbol of Europe—its past, its art, its complexity, its mystery, its evil. She is identified pictorially with Europe. When he
first visits Mme. de Vionnet, Strether finds

> himself making out, as a background of the occupant, some
> glory, some prosperity of the First Empire, some Napoleonic
> glamour, some dim lustre of the great legend; elements cling-
> ing still to all the consular chairs and mythological brasses
> and sphinxes' heads and faded surfaces of satin striped with
> alternate silk (XXI, 244).

As here she is associated with the First Empire, at other times
she is linked to the Renaissance, an association especially suggestive of the aesthetic wealth of the past: "Her head, extremely fair
and exquisitely festal, was like a happy fancy, a notion of the
antique, on an old precious medal, some silver coin of the Renaissance . . ." (XXI, 270). The allusion to the Renaissance leads directly to a more remote antiquity: "He could have compared her
to a goddess still partly engaged in a morning cloud, or to a sea-
nymph waist-high in the summer surge" (XXI, 270).

James associates the grace and beauty, along with the mystery,
of Mme. de Vionnet with the Renaissance and the tradition of
classical art. In both periods of history there are connotations of
sensuality which James subtly invokes in order to achieve an
additional connection between Mme. de Vionnet and her heritage.
But the evil that vaguely lurks about Mme. de Vionnet and her
situation is more often related, scenically and metaphorically, to
the period of the First French Empire, which suggests to James
violence and horror. On one occasion, when Strether takes his
leave from Mme. de Vionnet's rooms, he gains a startling impression: "He stopped, he looked back; the whole thing made a vista,
which he found high melancholy and sweet—full, once more, of
dim historic shades, of the faint far-away cannon-roar of the
great Empire" (XXII, 125). The sense of Paris, of the evil of its
past, permeates the novel, and toward the end of his experience
Strether is especially aware of the closeness of the evil of the past.

The streets and buildings of Paris remain beautiful and picturesque, but they suggest the darkness as well as the light of the past, particularly of the period of the revolution:

> Strether had all along been subject to sudden gusts of fancy in connexion with such matters as these—odd starts of the historic sense, suppositions and divinations with no warrant but their intensity. Thus and so, on the eve of the great recorded dates, the days and nights of revolution, the sounds had come in, the omens, the beginnings broken out. They were the smell of revolution, the smell of the public temper —or perhaps simply the smell of blood (XXII, 274).

In spite of his ultimate revelation, there is still much that remains mysterious to Strether. He has his facts and he has his impressions, but his logic and ethics are powerless to reconcile them in any intelligible way. He can do nothing but accept his vision as truth. Through his own experience he has met but not penetrated the mystery of the past, and he can feel but awe and contribute but sympathy. Soon after his arrival, while conversing with some of Chad's friends, Strether feels that "Nothing . . . could well less resemble a scene of violence than even the liveliest of these occasions" (XXI, 173). He is yet to learn that the violence of the past still exerts an influence in the most superficially innocuous and casual scenes and occasions. With his imaginative ability to see beyond the literal, Strether can associate Mme. de Vionnet and his entire experience not simply with the beauty of the past, but also with its evil. In his last interview with Mme. de Vionnet, Strether sees her

> dressed as for thunderous times, and it fell in with the kind of imagination we have just attributed to him that she should be in simplest coolest white, of a character so old-fashioned, if he were not mistaken, that Madame Roland must on the scaffold have worn something like it . . . . The associations of the place . . . were at first as delicate as if they had been ghostly . . . . He knew in advance he should look back on the perception actually sharpest with him as on the view of something old, old, old, the oldest thing he had ever personally touched . . . (XXII, 275–276).

At the very end, Strether "felt what he had felt before with her, that there was always more behind what she showed, and more and more again behind that" (XXII, 283).

The evil of Europe then is ultimately indefinable, but its effects are concrete and definite, especially in the acute suffering of all the persons who are affected by it. The conclusion of the novel stresses suffering. Strether's final deed is an effort to prevent Chad from deserting Mme. de Vionnet. Chad, in spite of the surface culture which he has acquired through intimacy with Mme. de Vionnet, lacks the dignity and nobility of her character. He deserts her because she is old and exposed and because his own interests lie in the gross materialism of Woollett and in another woman. Mme. de Vionnet's tragedy is that she is too fine for Chad, who, unlike Strether, is incapable of appreciating her, and yet too dependent on him, for she cannot endure the loss of him. She is weak and mortal humanity, redeemed by beauty and grace.

### THE WINGS OF THE DOVE

*The Wings of the Dove* (1902) [11] treats a later stage in the collapse of western civilization than *The Ambassadors*.[12] *The Ambassadors* deals with the last gasping breath of the old order; by the time of *The Wings* the old order is dead, visible only in its decay. Strether is the last Jamesian pilgrim to gain a relationship with what James has termed the *"visitable* past," [13] as Mme. de Vionnet is the last European whose beauty is not solely a pretense, a false allure.

The scene of *The Wings of the Dove* is the western world: the New York home of Milly Theale [14] and the London and Venice settings embrace the moral as well as the geographical limits of western culture. The England which has its center in Lancaster Gate (ironically the entrance to the English past leads but to hideous modernity) is given over completely to materialism. Its art has degenerated to the colossal vulgarity of Maud Lowder, the "Britannia of the Market Place" (XIX, 30) in whom "There was a whole side of Britannia, the side of her florid philistinism, her plumes and her train, her fantastic furniture and heaving bosom, the false gods of her taste and false notes of her talk . . ." (XIX, 31). The England of Maud Lowder has found the aristocratic legacy of manners at odds with the material drive, and has thus drained it of content. Force it finds more effective. Imperial and gross, Maud is a lioness; she is imagined as outfitted with "a helmet, a shield, a trident and a ledger" (XIX, 31). The emblematic Maud is blind to all but mass and quantity. She is "the most remarkable woman in England" (XIX, 180) because she sets the tone for an empire, because she is "unscrupulous and immoral" (XIX, 31) in an absolute way. The lesser figures about her, Lord Mark and Lionel Croy, are less typical only in that they are less effective. Maud Lowder's London is essentially the same as the London of *What Maisie Knew* and *The Awkward Age*, with the major difference that in *The Wings* James has made it unmistakably clear that the part stands for the whole.

Money is the controlling force in *The Wings of the Dove;* in the London world the economic drive is the normal motivation. Milly recognizes early that her English friends "appeared all . . . to think tremendously of money" (XIX, 195). Economic values subvert human values throughout, not just in Kate's identification of Milly with her wealth, the easy assumption that leads to the central action of the novel, but in the systematic reduction of all quality to quantity. For example, Kate's father and sister reject Kate's offer of family loyalty in favor of her potential cash value as Aunt Maud's ward. Aunt Maud visualizes Kate as a financial hold: ". . . I've been keeping [Kate's presence] for the comfort of my declining years. I've watched it long; I've been saving it up and letting it, as you say of investments, appreciate, and you may judge whether, now it has begun to pay so, I'm likely to consent to treat for it with any but a high bidder" (XIX, 82). Milly to Maud also has negotiable value, as a bribe to Densher: "The pieces fell together for him as he felt her thus buying him off, and buying him . . . with Miss Theale's money" (XX, 67). The relationship between Kate and Densher gradually becomes corrupted through association with the acquisitive drive; the natural has been made unnatural, so much so that Kate's visit to Densher's rooms is thought of by both as a payment for services rendered. Densher fondly thinks of "The force of the engagement, the quantity of the article to be supplied, the special solidity of the contract, the way, above all, as a service for which the price

named by him had been magnificently paid . . ." (XX, 237).
Kate, before she formulates her plan, predicts that "Milly would
pay a hundred per cent—and even to the end, doubtless, through
the nose . . . (XIX, 180)." Milly, though she is morally detached from her wealth and innocent in spite of her millions, dies
a victim of economic competition.[15]

It is particularly significant that Milly's great deed consists of a
bestowal of her money. It is an act of love, an expression of for-
giveness, and a transcendence of self. Nevertheless, since money
is the destructive force in the novel, the nature of the act is
tainted, although its motive is not. Milly's benevolence cannot
purify her money. It is appropriate that the practical result of her
gift is to sever Kate and Densher, for it was a want of money
that kept them from marrying in the beginning. Milly is not corrupted by her money; yet the possession of it causes her destruction. Money destroys those who are associated with it—those
who have it, those who desire it, those who contend for it.

Thus, one's moral stature is determined by the degree to which
he is free from money. Maud Lowder is surely damned from
the beginning; and Kate demonstrates her own damnation at the
end, when she rejects spirit for matter, when she burns the unread
letter of grace but rips open the envelope containing the check. In
giving her the money, Densher gives "poor Kate her freedom"
(XX, 396): the ambiguity of her being poor spiritually when rich
materially and enslaved morally when free economically points
the hard lesson of James's novel. Milly grows dependent on
money only when social pressures compel her to buy the sanctuary of Palazzo Leporelli and the protection of Eugenio. She uses
her wealth as "a counter-move to fate" (XX, 142). Yet she gains
her lasting salvation only when she renounces money utterly.

Money and manners conflict throughout. In a society in which
the only reality is money, traditional forms of intercourse—which
should ideally reflect honor, sincerity, and intelligence—are necessarily false and hollow; and yet they constitute the last barrier
against barbarism. The ambiguity of manners in *The Wings of
the Dove* is well conveyed when Milly confronts Densher, just
returned from his American tour, and Kate in the National Gallery. Having been suspicious all along of Kate's closeness to Den-

sher and continually embarrassed by Kate's concealment of the intimacy, Milly is placed in the false position of having to pretend surprise at the discovery of their attachment. Kate and Densher are discomfited also; yet they too must carry on the pretense. The weight of the unspoken—the real—oppresses Milly. She sadly recognizes that the incident obviates any closeness in her future dealings with Kate and Densher. Yet, without the elaborate pretense that all is just as it should be—with the jointly maintained lie that Densher's visit to the United States is an appropriate conversation piece—the entire situation would collapse: all would be exposed and isolation would be total. If manners, what Densher calls "The mere aesthetic instinct of mankind" (XX, 299), are strained and deceptive, they yet remain necessary for social existence.

For Maud and Kate manners are the machinery for economic gain; for Densher and Milly they prohibit sincerity and intensity in personal relationships. Milly and Densher are among the first of James's protagonists to seek beauty and truth not in human institutions, now sterile and meaningless, but in human nature itself. James's approach is the same in *The Wings of the Dove;* he can define neither good nor evil in terms of national or social contexts. Milly's capacity for good is not so much a native American trait as it is a purely spiritual, literally a supernatural, power. Evil springs not from a rotten aristocracy, as in *The American*, or from the abandonment of national innocence, as in *The Portrait of a Lady*, but quite simply from human nature. Taken singly, the "villains" of *The Wings* have nothing of the absolute malignity that James finds in persons like Gilbert Osmond, who is ego-driven to an absolute degree and ruthless in his tyranny. Nothing of the same can be said of the malefactors in *The Wings*, whose actions or inactions are caused by common human failings: Aunt Maud is driven by social ambition, Kate by the need to rise above her unfortunate circumstances, Densher by weakness of will, and Lord Mark by stupidity and spite.

Evil in *The Wings* is the evil of the normal, and yet it produces such a monstrous catastrophe that the imbalance between suggested cause and obvious effect is extreme. James implies that though evil exists only in human relationships, it does not origi-

nate entirely in man's will; it is in the very scheme of things.[16] The
intrigue against Milly is planned by Kate, but the plot derives
ultimately from circumstances beyond the control of any of the
characters. Stephen Spender has said of James's last novels that
they contain no villains, that the situation is the villain.[17] This is
largely true, even though James, neither a determinist nor a
fatalist, holds his agents of evil morally responsible for their
crimes.

The ancestral curse is James's metaphor for the evil in the
world beyond the power of the human will. Both Milly and Kate,
we are told, are destined to suffer for the sins of their ancestors,
Milly by dying early and Kate by committing a great sin. Milly's
family has been plagued by a long history of early deaths and
widespread disaster. Kate also partakes mysteriously in the failure and disaster that have visited all her relatives and ancestors.
Early in the story, Kate thinks of her family: "Why should a set
of people have been put in motion, on such a scale and with such
an air of being equipped for a profitable journey, only to break
down without an accident, to stretch themselves in the wayside
dust without a reason?" (XIX, 4). Here James suggests the
capriciousness of fate, the inevitability of failure and unhappiness.
In *The Wings of the Dove* James associates the destinies of his
characters with a specific world-view more explicitly than in any
other novel. He suggests, if not the intervention of malign gods,
at least the prevalence of a law of life which cripples the deserving from the start.

While Milly is foredoomed to be a victim of evil, Kate is foredoomed to be an agent of evil. She shares mysteriously in the
unnamed crime of her father. She tells Densher that her father's
crime is "a part of me" (XIX, 68). The suggestions of ancestral
guilt and hereditary predestination are slight in *The Wings of the
Dove*, but they are significant; they support James's stress on the
general malignity of fallen human nature, rather than the evil of
particular villains.

Milly Theale's death is the effect of both illness and betrayal;
eventually physical and emotional pain become indistinguishable.
The point is that through Milly, James shows the relationship
between Kate's crime and the common frailty of man. The

inevitable and the calculated merge to kill Milly. Milly draws universal meaning from her illness: she identifies her doomed state with that of mankind. In his preface James speaks of "the communities of doom" [18] which surround Milly; to Milly everyone is in a "community of collapse with her" (XIX, 290). When she leaves Sir Luke's office knowing that she is fated to an early death, she projects her despair into the world about her. Milly wanders through the grimiest section of London and identifies herself with the children she sees playing:

> Here were benches and smutty sheep; here were idle lads at games of ball, with their cries mild in the thick air; here were wanderers anxious and tired like herself; here doubtless were hundreds of others just in the same box. Their box, their great common anxiety, what was it, in this grim breathing-space, but the practical question of life? (XIX, 250).

Milly's sense of the menacing relates the attitudes and actions of Kate, Densher, and Aunt Maud—each of whom represents a different kind of human weakness—to the general human fate.

When the civilized community falls apart James and his intelligent characters must transcend the temporal and the local to try to understand experience in terms of unchanging human nature and the permanent conditions of life. Kate, Milly, and Densher reach the point where they can no longer exist as morally free creatures in terms of manners or money, and therefore must acknowledge or renounce their humanity. Since society is dehumanized, to be human is to be socially isolated. Only through morality—and not through manners or money—can humanity be achieved.

Milly Theale's assumption that her siege of London will mean full nourishment of the sensibilities is an ironic illusion. She soon recognizes that her celebrated "success" is cheap and false. The great world, or the great English world, has simply crumpled beneath the weight of materialism. Unlike Strether and Maggie Verver, she recognizes rapidly that the old forms of civilization are empty. Soon after leaving her Alpine peak and plunging into the "abyss" [19] of the London world, she finds "society," in the sense of traditional and splendid styles of conduct, to be superficial and pretentious. Lord Mark's surface is soon penetrated: "Why did he hover before her as a potentially insolent noble? . . . she had, on the spot, with her first plunge into the obscure depths of a society constituted from far back, encountered the interesting phenomenon of complicated, of possibly sinister motive" (XIX, 152–154). Milly's "banquet of initiation" in London society is primarily an introduction to the false, substanceless manners that thinly disguise the greed beneath. Even in the early London chapters we look forward to Densher's wry reflection on the world he finds himself in: "He had supposed himself civilised; but if this was civilisation——! One could smoke one's pipe outside when twaddle was within" (XX, 44). Or we may look forward to the central image of a later James novel, the cracked crystal bowl gilded in gold.

Cut off in the beginning from any real relation with "all the ages" (XIX, 109), Milly seeks meaning in art. She finds "largeness of style" (XIX, 208) not at Lancaster Gate but at Matcham, and not through society but art. Milly leaves the Alps for London because "it had rolled over her that what she wanted of Europe was 'people'. . ." (XIX, 134). In the overstuffed vulgarity of Lancaster Gate, however, the reality of egotism is unrelieved and virtually undisguised by the appearance of art. But at Matcham people and scene merge into a single vision—a picture. "The great historic house had, for Milly, beyond terrace and garden, as the centre of an almost extravagantly grand Watteau-composition, a tone as of old gold kept 'down' by the quality of the air, summer full-flushed but attuned to the general perfect taste" (XIX, 208). Here life comes up to art—in a single splendid illusion for Milly: "Everything was great, of course, in great pictures, and it was doubtless precisely a part of the brilliant life—since the brilliant life, as one had faintly figured it, just *was* humanly led—that all impressions within its area partook of its brilliancy . . ." (XIX, 209). The "mild common carnival of good nature—a mass of London people together" (XIX, 218) gains immensely through the atmosphere of beauty, so that Milly unconsciously dismisses her earlier impressions of ugliness. If society were art, she thinks, then "to accept it without question might be as good a way as another of feeling life" (XIX, 219). The empty chatter of Lord

Mark and the banalities of people named Lord and Lady Aldershaw are transformed by the transcendent beauty of the Bronzino. "Once more things melted together—the beauty and the history and the facility and the splendid midsummer glow: it was a sort of magnificent maximum, the pink dawn of an apotheosis coming so curiously soon" (XIX, 220). The apotheosis is personal and prophetic, rather than social and actual; it suggests that only through death and suffering can Milly approach the magnificence of art, that, according to a basic metaphor of the novel, Milly can go up only by going down, that she can be reborn into the immortal beauty of the portrayed woman only by being, like her, "dead, dead, dead" (XIX, 221).

But until her apotheosis art and life remain the separate poles of Milly's experience. There are several efforts at reconciliation, with results always tenuous and implications always ironic. In the National Gallery, Milly finds refuge from an English society that Kate had but shortly before described to her as "a strange and dreadful monster, calculated to devour the unwary, to abase the proud, to scandalize the good . . ." (XIX, 277). The relief afforded by "the quiet chambers, nobly overwhelming, rich but slightly veiled" (XIX, 287–288), clashes startlingly with the revelation of the real. The scene parallels the recognition scene in *The Ambassadors*, when Strether's imaginative Lambinet—Europe as art—fuses with his vision of evil—Europe as life. A tourist's oblique observation that what she sees is "In the English style" (XIX, 291) at first is taken by Milly to be a reference to a painting, but she soon sees that the subject of the comment is Merton Densher. Life intrudes upon art, and unlike the situation in *The Ambassadors*, in which a synthesis occurs, here there is only clash. The relief of the gallery gives way to the pain of social existence.

Beginning with Book Sixth the strain of maintaining appearances drives Milly to art—to her rented Venetian palace, which is inadequate because its beauty, its inherent traditional values, its silent profundity reflect nothing of the Europe of the early twentieth century. James dramatizes throughout the second volume the meaning of Venice in the modern world: it, like London, has made the sacrifice of art to matter (James may be invoking the

commercial as well as the aesthetic past of the Italian city), so that
Palazzo Leporelli has the same relation to the controlling ethos of
Venice as does Matcham to that of London. "Palazzo Leporelli
held its history still in its great lap, even like a painted idol, a solemn puppet hung about with decorations" (XX, 135). The
imagery suggests artificiality and sterility, for the essential Venice is better represented by the shady commercialism of Eugenio
and Pasquale. Although granted a luster by Susan Stringham's
journalistic imagination and by Milly's presence, the old palace
along the Grand Canal is but a relic of a decayed past.[20]

The Venetian past is purposefully present not in its beauty,
but in its evil—the two components of Europe that formed an
inseparable unity to the earlier James. Densher, the man of intellect, sees the Venetians of the present as "members of a race in
whom vacancy was but a nest of darknesses—not a vain surface,
but a place of withdrawal in which something obscure, something always ominous, indistinguishably lived" (XX, 256). When
Lord Mark awakens Milly to the monstrous plot against her, the
Venetian scene reflects the personal catastrophe and gives it extensive dimensions. The great black storm means tumult and
cataclysm. "It was a Venice all of evil that had broken out . . . a
Venice of cold lashing rain from a low black sky, of wicked wind
raging through narrow passes, of general arrest and interruption
. . ." (XX, 259). The Piazza San Marco, symbolic of European
civilization as a whole, is darkened to blackness and overwhelmed
by violence: "the whole place, in its huge elegance, the grace of
its conception and the beauty of its detail, was more than ever like
a great drawing-room, the drawing-room of Europe, profaned
and bewildered by some reverse of fortune" (XX, 261). The
effort of all to contain evil by appearances fails. Milly Theale's
death is the death of a civilization: the grey of a London dominated by materialism and the black of a Venice traditionally malign combine to kill her.

Milly believes that she can resist pain only by remaining in the
fortress tower of her palace, surrounded by the sterile formali-
ties of art. "Ah not to go down—never, never to go down" (XX,
147), she sighs to the uncomprehending Lord Mark. The idea of
"remaining aloft in the divine dustless air" (XX, 147) is a false

approach to the ideal, for purification and apotheosis require for James, as for Conrad, immersion in the destructive element. Thus when Milly does "come down" (XX, 203), literally to "the great saloon" (XX, 203) beneath her rooms in Palazzo Leporelli, figuratively to the abyss of human life, she discards for the first time "her almost monastic, her hitherto inveterate black" (XX, 214), the color of death, for white, the color of life. The incident is a picture: Milly diffusing "in wide warm waves the spell of a general, a kind of beatific mildness" (XX, 213); Densher and Kate speaking, for the first time, of the unspeakable—"Since she's to die I'm to marry her?" (XX, 225). Just as the historic grandeur of Matcham has transformed the ugly into the beautiful, so the splendor of the descent of the dove brings to the scene of betrayal the enveloping atmosphere of art. For once Susan Stringham's extravagant imagination has validity: "It's a Veronese picture, as near as can be . . ." (XX, 206), she tells Densher. But unlike her tower, Milly's surroundings below have human composition. "You're in the picture" (XX, 207), Kate tells Densher, and so is everyone. Life and art fuse when Milly goes down: ". . . Milly, let loose among them in a wonderful white dress, brought them somehow into relation with something that made them more finely genial; so that if the Veronese picture of which he had talked with Mrs. Stringham was not quite constituted, the comparative prose of the previous hours, the traces of insensibility qualified by 'beating down,' were at last almost nobly disowned" (XX, 213). Surrounded by her conspirators, the white-robed Milly begins to live just as she begins to die. "Since I've lived all these years as if I were dead, I shall die, no doubt, as if I were alive . . ." (XIX, 199), she had said earlier. It is then not the art  of the gallery or of the palace that will enable Milly "to live," but the moral response to immoral humanity, which becomes in itself spiritual beauty.

Through Milly's developing awareness of the irrelevance of the art of the past to modern life, James dramatizes the disintegration of civilization. Throughout the novel he reveals the ever widening breach between individual needs and the social framework. One inevitably finds himself in a position where he must define himself through either his social position or his isolated self. De-

prived of access to meaning through art or manners, Maud
Lowder derives her motivations and morality from British culture
in general. We find her in the beginning as we find her in the end
—a loyal apostle to money. But Kate, Densher, and Milly are, in
the beginning, undefined by status or creed. The novel records
their efforts and decisions toward achieving identity. For each the
existing situation is inadequate.

Kate's personal qualities are great: she esteems family loyalty
over private gain, the need for love over the need for profit, and
moral freedom over moral commitment. But her father, her sister,
and her aunt comprise for her a world in which selfhood and
vulgarity set the tone, in which the material urge is unrefined by
sentiment or sensibility. Thus, in her visit to her father's squalid
rooms, we find Kate for the most part glancing into the mirror,
holding fast to that which is herself.

In Kate's case the standard Jamesian ambiguity towards
money has an added twist. The ordinary dilemma is there: to
acquire money is ugly, but the possession of it is the *sine qua non*
for the good life. In most of James's novels, however, the social
scene itself remains aloof from the economic process: fortune-
hunter and business man alike are anomalies, inconsistent with
the placid solemnity of age and beauty. But the London world
can be understood only in terms of money. To pursue magnificence Kate has no choice but to accept the code of Aunt Maud.
Her effort to reconcile the human value of love and the barbaric
value of money must fail. In her struggle to avoid Aunt Maud
and yet gain a fortune, she becomes an Aunt Maud herself. Therefore, when she seeks her own image in Densher's mirror in the
novel's final scene, she signalizes her separation from her lover,
whose own renunciation of money forces Kate to retreat to the
damning security of wealth.

Kate's initial conflict is between acceptance of family poverty
for the sake of loyalty and acceptance of Aunt Maud's wealth for
the sake of magnificence. When Kate, rebuffed by her father and
sister, moves to Lancaster Gate, she hesitates to surrender her
will to Maud. In "her actual high retreat" (XIX, 56–57) above
Maud's "counting-house" (XIX, 30), she is precariously detached
and uncommitted. The parallel to Milly in her tower is clear

enough. Here Kate's relation to Maud forecasts Milly's eventual relation to Kate. But when Kate descends she reconciles the standards of Maud with her love for Densher, and thus becomes converted to society; whereas Milly holds firm to her personal values, her moral integrity.

What we find in Kate is a great will that accepts and then uses society on its own terms. Her object is money and her method is manners. Once she initiates her plot, from the moment she decides not to tell Milly about her engagement to Densher, she remains inflexible. To Densher, Kate is "deep" (XIX, 175), "a whole library of the unknown, the uncut" (XX, 62), but ironically there is nothing beneath the surface but the will: the moral intelligence has surrendered itself to money.

To the very end Densher marvels at Kate's "high sobriety and her beautiful self-command. . . . she had her perfect manner, which *was* her decorum" (XX, 316). Because of her mastery over manners, her skillful control of appearances, her intrigue almost succeeds. But the lady of appearances pays the great price of being definable only through appearances; she is magnificent only in contrast with the cheap and the showy. In Venice Kate's brilliance pales before Milly's: "As a striking young presence she was practically superseded . . ." (XX, 216). Later, when Densher meets Kate at Marion's wretched house, he observes that "Kate wouldn't have been in the least the creature she was if what was just round them hadn't mismatched her . . ." (XX, 365). The conclusion of course reveals Kate's magnificence for what it is—a thing of death—in contrast with the life-giving spiritual magnificence of Milly.

If Kate commits herself to Aunt Maud, Densher commits himself to Kate. But his association always admits the possibility of his detachment. For one thing, Densher becomes involved not through strength of will, but through weakness of will; for another, his motivation is not greed, but love. His loyalty to Kate, like Kate's loyalty to Maud, is an imperfect moral standard, but it is supported by affection rather than a prudent concern for appearances.

Densher too at the beginning is uncommitted. His James-like continental education has given him, if not a moral firmness, at least a detachment from the English trait of regarding money excessively. In his quest for identity, Densher—through Milly's grace—choses the hitherto unrealized self over the materialism of his age. Through indecision he becomes implicated in Kate's scheme. His good nature and gentlemanliness carry him through to deceive Milly. But when he finds the demands of appearance too oppressive, he finds the necessity of self-assertion compelling. In his brooding walks about Venice, Densher faces fully "the interesting question of whether he had really no will left" (XX, 177). His problem is really very much the same as Milly's, for, unlike Maud and Kate, both require the sustenance of immediate and honest personal relationships, which are by definition unattainable in a society held together by appearances. Since the association with Kate has been beclouded by duplicity, he seeks out—half-consciously—the companionship of Milly. Densher's passion and Milly's love are both frustrated by Kate's scheme of appearances.

Densher is a forerunner of a dominant character type of modern literature: he leads to Eliot's Prufrock, Conrad's Heyst, and Greene's Scobie. He is the nonheroic yet perceptive man, driven to self-understanding by his weakness of will and horror of ugliness. Like Kate and Milly, Densher plunges into the abyss, which for him as for the others is both internal and external—the private depths and the social depths. If Milly's descent to the abyss reveals spiritual love and Kate's reveals only will, Densher's reveals, not the will he had sought to find, but a capacity for sanctifying grace. For he remains weak always. His suffering is most acute when he is isolated—after his moral rejection of Kate, but before his acceptance of Milly's love. When Sir Luke leaves the dying Milly to Densher alone, the physician's unspoken plea that he love Milly leads Densher to ask himself "into what abyss it pushed him . . ." (XX, 309). Densher soars from the abyss, too late to save Milly, but not too late to be saved by her; he embraces spirit over flesh.

In a world whose institutional and aesthetic heritage has been drained of moral meaning, there can be no ultimately valid achievement for the James character without "the final authority of selfhood." [21] Thus the romantic epithets that Susan Stringham applies to Milly Theale lack real significance: the heiress of all the ages has an inheritance of corruption only; the princess reigns in a morally bankrupt empire. But Kate and, for the most part, Densher also miss the point by being too prosaic about Milly. To Kate, Milly is identified primarily with her fortune; to Densher she is the "little American girl" (XX, 174). Milly's descent to the abyss precedes the apotheosis of the dove—her transfigured self. Milly can acquire identity only by assaulting life, by risking everything. And not until her great and lonely moral achievement does Milly assume an identity independent of the social, economic, and aesthetic structures which had previously established, for others and for herself, her reality and her being.

## THE GOLDEN BOWL

In *The Golden Bowl* James achieves a resolution of the Europe-America antithesis principally because he is hesitant to place the burden of evil on the Europeans. It is the human situation itself which produces the intense moral evil of the novel, rather than the deeds of particular characters or sets of characters. In *The Golden Bowl* James continues to dramatize the moral, cultural, and temperamental differences between the American and the European, but he reveals that the common denominator of the two is their mutual participation in human sin.

The problem of *The Golden Bowl* is easily formulated, for it is contained in the central symbolism of the bowl itself. The Golden Bowl stands mainly for Maggie Verver's marriage. The bowl contains a flaw, which stands for the defect in the marriage. To define the flaw is to define the evil of the situation.

It is a gross oversimplification to assume that the only evil is the adulterous tie between Prince Amerigo and Charlotte Stant. James stresses the equally grave, though less sensational, moral defects in the wealthy American art collector and his daughter. In *The Golden Bowl* James takes American innocence less at face value than in any previous work; he dispassionately analyzes the serious moral shortcomings of the Ververs. He neither judges them nor implies that they are better or worse than the Europeans, but he dramatizes their role in the creation of the flaw in the golden bowl. The adultery is the objectification of the evil, the prime dramatic act of evil; but behind the actual adultery is a complex of motives and attitudes which leads inexorably to the relatively simple matter of unfaithfulness and comprises the essential evil.

Because of the way the story is told, James's criticism of the Ververs remains implicit rather than explicit. The first half of the novel comes from the point of view of the Prince, whose gentleness and urbanity prevent him from thinking of his wife and father-in-law as anything other than kind and just. Maggie, the center of consciousness in the second half of the novel, rarely realizes her own shortcomings. Fanny Assingham, who provides several illuminating comments about the Prince and Charlotte, seems unaware of the Ververs' flaws—even though some of her general observations are ironically applicable to them—and thus she, the only confidante of the novel, cannot function as a consistently judicious and perceptive chorus.

Nevertheless, through dialogue, action, and imagery, James reveals his attitude toward the Ververs.[22] Their faults stem mainly from their innocence and their power. Both Maggie and Mr. Verver are naïve and simple, incapable of understanding their own lives and those of others. Thus, particularly in the case of Mr. Verver, James describes them as children. Instead of realizing that they are involved in adult marriages, the American father and daughter act as if they are playing games: "They were fairly at times, the dear things, like children playing at paying visits, playing at 'Mr. Thompson and Mrs. Fane,' each hoping that the other would really stay to tea" (XXIII, 252). Often Mr. Verver gives the impression of "handling a relic of infancy—sticking on the head of a broken soldier or trying the lock of a wooden gun" (XXIII, 126–127). The Ververs are "good children, bless their hearts, and the children of good children; so that verily the Principino himself, as less consistently of that descent, might figure to the fancy as the ripest genius of the trio" (XXIII, 334).

The infant king and the princess play the game of living as adults. The fairyland in which they live, however, is the real world: Mr. Verver is the king of a great empire; Maggie, unlike Milly Theale, is a real princess. James does not divest American innocence of its moral sense, but he exposes its ignorance and its inclination to romanticize life. Fanny Assingham, in one of her most clear-sighted observations, remarks that "stupidity pushed to a certain point *is*, you know, immorality. Just so what is morality but high intelligence?" (XXIII, 88). Fanny, in her utilitarian and merely social conception of morality, is ignorant of the implications of her statement and of its application to the Ververs; nevertheless the outcome of their marriages proves her right.

Unlike most American innocents, the Ververs are not taken advantage of because of their ignorance of evil; rather they help create evil because of their ignorance. Curiously the Ververs' ignorance is hardly distinguishable from their selfishness. They are unconcerned with the Prince and Charlotte as persons, for they are unaware of life outside of themselves and they know nothing of the meaning of marriage.

Early in the story, even before his marriage, Prince Amerigo thinks of Americans as "incredibly romantic" (XXIII, 11). Maggie's romanticism is a blend of ignorance, optimism, and sentimentality. The Prince says to her, "You see too much—that's what may sometimes make you difficulties. When you don't at least . . . see too little" (XXIII, 11). If Maggie sees too much, she sees too much of herself in others; she is eventually betrayed by her belief that the Prince can be expected to fit comfortably in the little niche which she has arranged for him. If she sees too little, it is the existence of evil—actual and potential—to which she is blinded. The Prince soon notes Maggie's inclination to shy away from any significant (adult) questions:

> He had perceived on the spot that any *serious* discussion of veracity, of loyalty, or rather of the want of them, practically took her unprepared, as if it were quite new to her. He had noticed it before: it was the English, the American sign that duplicity, like "love," had to be joked about. It couldn't be "gone into" (XXIII, 15).

Fanny Assingham idealizes Maggie consistently. She tells her husband that Maggie "wasn't born to know evil. She must never know it" (XXIII, 78). Undoubtedly James thinks otherwise. He accepts neither Fanny's estimate of Maggie nor Maggie's estimate of herself. He ironically contrasts Maggie's sentiments and words

with her actions, showing that in spite of her optimism and goodness she is a contributor to evil. Maggie's ignorance shields her
from guilt, even though it is because of her ignorance, added to
the power of her wealth, that she is an agent of evil. Maggie
blandly buys herself a prince, then neglects him to be with her
father, and realizes only fitfully her part in undermining her own
happiness.

It is ironic that idealism motivates the "purchases" of the
Ververs. They are not American robber barons in the ordinary
sense; they supplement the acquisitiveness of the American com-
mercialist with a kind of high idealism, unconcerned with simple
profit. Mr. Verver's explicit reason for being in Europe is to stock
an art museum which he has constructed for the edification of the
citizens of "American City." Maggie and her father have much to
say about their unselfishness, but basically they are unselfish only
to each other and exhibit their mutual altruism at the expense of
others, most notably the Prince and Charlotte. Maggie marries
the Prince as a favor to her father: to enrich his personal collection, to free him from the care of her. Mr. Verver, through selfless devotion to his daughter, marries Charlotte. Maggie had suggested his marriage originally; the elder Verver agrees in order to
satisfy her, all the while unconcerned about the nature of marriage
and his duty toward Charlotte.

The trouble with the Ververs' transcendental idealism is that it
is too much removed from ordinary life. The section of the novel
which describes Mr. Verver's proposal to Charlotte conveys the
limitations and shallowness of that idealism. First it is notable
that Mr. Verver suggests that Charlotte accompany him to Brighton, where he plans to purchase a set of rare tiles. The association
of Charlotte with the purchase of the tiles has an obvious symbolic value, which is increased and deepened with the visit to the
owner of the pieces. He is a poor man, burdened by a large family; yet within the house there beats the "pulse of life" (XXIII,
211). Mr. Verver is oblivious of the humanity of the scene.
Furthermore, the Brighton scene is not a golden one: it is un-
embellished by art or money. James dramatizes Mr. Verver's
inability to deal with life realistically, by showing the disparity
between his childish romantic conceptions and unadorned reality.

In his proposal to Charlotte, Mr. Verver demonstrates this deficiency further. He is pathetically unresponsive to Charlotte's humor and vitality:

> It really came home to [him] on the spot that this free range of observation in her, picking out the frequent funny with extraordinary promptness, would verily henceforth make a different thing for him of such experiences, of the customary hunt for the valuable prize, the inquisitive play of his accepted monomania . . . (XXIII, 213).

Mr. Verver at first misrepresents his intentions to Charlotte; he tells her that he wishes simply to be kind to her. But Charlotte, not a deceptive adventuress by any means, spots the weakness of his argument and calls his attention to the disparity between his avowed concern for herself and his obviously deeper love for Maggie: "She's everything to you—she has always been. Are you so certain that there's room in your life—?" Mr. Verver can lie no longer: "To put her at peace is . . . what I'm trying, with you, to do" (XXIII, 222–223).

Mr. Verver's ignorance, his acquisitiveness, his dependence on a lie—all for the sake of "his majestic scheme" (XXIII, 210), his "exciting, inspiring, uplifting" (XXIII, 208) idea—unquestionably place a burden of moral responsibility on him and reveal the insidious and hypocritical side of his magnanimity.

Both he and Maggie, however, are only objectively hypocritical. Neither wishes to deceive. There are many characters in James who bring about evil though they are unaware of its existence, but the Ververs are the only ones whose imperception is unconditioned by either self-interest or self-righteousness. Yet it is precisely James's point that a pure motive and straightforward conduct can lead to evil if the intelligence is deficient. To James a morality based on feeling is dangerous as well as sentimental; the only true morality originates in intelligence.

On the other hand, if the Ververs arrange their marriages with ignorance, the Prince and Charlotte are intelligent and prudent in carrying out their agreements. It is a piece of bad luck that through lack of funds the two lovers have been unable to marry. With maturity and decency they renounce their attachment to each other to marry into the Verver family. James stresses Amerigo's noble intentions prior to his marriage: "If there was one thing in the world the young man at this juncture clearly intended it was to be much more decent as a son-in-law than lots of fellows he could think of had shown themselves in the character" (XXIII, 5). The Prince is obviously disturbed by Charlotte's inopportune visit. Charlotte, however, does not come (at least not consciously) as a marriage-wrecker; she is convinced of her strength of purpose. Fanny Assingham, who is a reliable analyst of her two friends from Italy, believes in the good intentions of Charlotte: "She doesn't deliberately intend, she doesn't consciously wish, the least complication. It's perfectly true that she thinks Maggie a dear—as who doesn't? She's incapable of any *plan* to hurt a hair of her head" (XXIII, 70). Charlotte's hesitance to marry Mr. Verver, because of sincere reservations about his motives, shows her to be seeking neither a fortune nor easy access to the Prince.

Also Charlotte and the Prince combine good intentions with intelligence, while Maggie and her father combine them with ignorance. However, with the Prince and Charlotte good intentions go along with a deficiency of moral strength, so that the insulting treatment accorded them by their *sposi* makes their adultery inevitable. The Prince, as an Italian, and Charlotte, as a Europeanized American, lack the moral sense which the Ververs have in abundance. Early in the novel, Amerigo explains to Fanny Assingham, with acute self-knowledge, the delicate balance in his own nature between his lack of a firm moral foundation and his determination to remain irreproachable: "Of my real honest fear of being 'off' some day, of being wrong, *without* knowing it. That's what I shall always trust you for—to tell me when I am. No—with you people it's a sense. We haven't got it—not as you have" (XXIII, 30–31).

The Prince's latent immorality is hereditary. Amerigo is aware of a side of his nature that is independent of his background—his decency, his good intentions—and a side of his nature which is inherited—his refinement and culture, but also his ancestral guilt, his latent capacity for evil. It is ironic that the Ververs find him attractive as a relic of old Rome, even though the Prince often warns that his history is associated with violence and criminality, remotely with the crimes of the Borgias. It is, therefore, fitting that Maggie discovers ultimately in the Prince the fulfillment of his history which she had originally sought.

The Prince is associated with both his near and his remote past: he is a cultured gentleman, a man of the world. Charlotte, likewise, as an experienced and sophisticated traveller, with a rich past of her own, is associated indirectly but essentially with old Florence. Mrs. Assingham once compares her to a Borgia, alluding to her capacity for evil. Mr. Verver and Maggie habitually think of Charlotte as simply Maggie's playmate, and thus underestimate her as much as they do the Prince—though in a different way.

To complement their tastes and their temperaments, Amerigo and Charlotte require the large public life. The small and retiring Ververs, through a failure in intelligence, ignore these obvious needs; they thus not only provide the opportunity for the Prince and Charlotte to find in each other a means to happiness, but they also help cause such an illicit relationship. The mental unrest that precedes the Prince's actual sin points up again his superiority to the common adulterer. He is sincere and profound in his discontent; he is unable to interpret the Verver's neglect as a wrong against him. The affair begins not as a calculated act, but as an effect of boredom. The Prince is left alone at Portland Place while Maggie pays one of her regular visits to her father. Charlotte, who has left her own home out of a delicate sense of intrusion into the Verver's private life, comes to the Prince, seeking consolation and company. At first they discuss somberly and philosophically their mutual distress. The Prince ponders their curious arrangement; he concludes that "Nothing stranger surely had ever happened to a conscientious, a well-meaning, a perfectly passive pair: no more extraordinary decree had ever been launched against such victims than this of forcing them against their will into a relation of mutual close contact that they had done everything to avoid" (XXIII, 289).

James shows that a difference of personal and national traits causes evil. Moral and cultural differences isolate; they prevent social harmony. One of the cultural differences contributing to the evil in *The Golden Bowl* is between Charlotte's and Amerigo's conception of marriage, on the one hand, and Maggie's and Mr. Verver's, on the other. The spiritual love between father and daughter is not only different from but also inimical to the kind of physical love which Charlotte and the Prince ("The Prince's notion of a recompense to women . . . was more or less to make love to them" [XXIII, 21–22]) associate with marriage. As long as she is so close to her father, Maggie resists the Prince's sexuality. Amerigo desires "the maximum of immersion in the fact of being married" (XXIII, 148). Significantly it is Charlotte's sensuousness which tempts Amerigo: "He was occupied with Charlotte because in the first place she looked so inordinately handsome and held so high, where so much else was mature and sedate, the torch of responsive youth and the standard of passive grace . . ." (XXIII, 321).

In addition, the Prince maintains an ethical standard which he admits to be inferior to that of the Ververs: "it's always a question of doing the best for one's self one can—without injury to others" (XXIII, 58). Consistent with his creed, the Prince marries Maggie to gain for himself a large freedom, a contact with art and wealth, and a desirable social situation. On the other hand, he is satisfied that he is not taking unfair advantage of Maggie or acting from base motives. Charlotte, who also seeks freedom and position, responds similarly to Mr. Verver's proposal of marriage. Furthermore, the joint attitude of Charlotte and Amerigo need undergo no alteration or modification in order to permit an adultery between them. They agree that as long as they keep up appearances and act discreetly, they commit no crime. Thus, with the Prince and Charlotte, an absence of the American moral sense makes adultery possible. Both the Europeans and the Americans, then, have their faults, but it is the combination of European notions of ethics and American ignorance which produces the evil of the situation.

It is to the credit of Charlotte and the Prince that they have ties with Italy rather than with England. Like the Ververs they are on foreign soil in England. The England of *The Golden Bowl* is still the England of *What Maisie Knew*, of *The Awkward Age*, and of *The Wings of the Dove*. It is associated almost exclusively with middle-class materialism, with economic and social competition, with lust and greed, with irreverence and indignity, with a decayed aristocracy. The Assinghams—Fanny with her genius for social planning and the Colonel with his narrow economic viewpoint—symbolize England. They also suggest the element of greed and materialism that is present on all sides of the quadrangular marital arrangement of the Ververs. The Assinghams reveal by contrast the moral superiority of the Ververs and of the Prince and Charlotte, although at the same time they adumbrate the flaws of each. Thus the high idealism of the Ververs overshadows the Assinghams, but so does the integrity of Amerigo and Charlotte, whose consideration for their spouses, even though limited, and whose ability to maintain dignity while committing adultery show their moral superiority to such English adulterers as Maisie's parents. The Prince and Charlotte ennoble what James treats most often as mere lust, so that their sin shares somehow in the rich sensuousness of Renaissance Italy, to which both have ties.

In spite of the many virtues of the adulterers, James reveals their sins as well. R. P. Blackmur observes that "The act of illicit love is the tragic fault . . . the act which can be explained but which cannot be justified." [23] Adultery is always abhorrent to James, and it remains so in *The Golden Bowl*, although here it is equated not with willful betrayal or with animal lust, but with universal human weakness. But since the illicit love occurs within a marital arrangement—unlike the affairs in *The Ambassadors* and *The Wings of the Dove*—it takes on a greater indecency because of its perfidy. Mrs. Assingham and Maggie refer repeatedly to the affair as "lurid," "abominable," and "ugly" (XXIV, 127, 185, 111); unquestionably James's attitude toward it is the same.

When Maggie learns of the affair, she does not consider it a crime against herself. She sees it as a disarrangement of the perfect order she had visualized. Similarly James's attitude is that the adultery is the most obvious deviation from the ideal order, contributing to the general flaw, which all four persons have helped to create.

But the worst sin of the Prince and Charlotte is not adultery, but deceit. As if to stress the seriousness of their deception, James puts weight on their not disclosing to Maggie or her father their previous intimacy. Just as Kate and Densher betray Milly from the beginning by concealing their acquaintance with each other —a deception which leads easily and inevitably to their major deception—so it is the original insincerity of the Prince and Charlotte (whose mission with Amerigo to the gift shop is crucial) which portends the much graver deception that follows. Carl Van Doren writes that "For James, as for Maggie, the evil of the situation consisted less in the sin of adultery than in the ugliness of stealth and deceit." [24] Austin Warren concludes that "the great theme of *The Bowl* is the discovery that evil exists in the forms most disruptive to civilization: in disloyalty and treason." [25] In the second half of the novel, where the sense of evil is especially pervasive, Maggie is most horrified by deception.

Once their affair has begun, the Prince and Charlotte undergo a moral disintegration: they readily abandon the standards of honor and responsibility which had once sustained them. The Prince soon begins to rationalize his guilt, to place all the blame on the Ververs, to assume that because "he was . . . held cheap and made light of" (XXIII, 353), he is justified in his unfaithfulness. When Maggie, once conscious of Amerigo's defection, tries to regain his favor by attentiveness and consideration (in fact, by a deliberate appeal to his sensuality), he evades her; he wishes to maintain the existing arrangement. His intimacy with Charlotte has so affected him that he no longer wishes for Maggie to separate herself from her father. He now supports the evil he had previously condemned.

From the beginning Charlotte is morally unconscious. Her loyalty to Maggie and Mr. Verver restrains her from resuming her affair with the Prince. Once she falters, however, she subsides completely into sensuality. She loses concern for all but propriety; "We're happy—and they're happy" (XXIII, 341), she says. When the question of guilt arises, she blames either Fanny Assingham or, like the Prince, the Ververs.

James uses imagery of gold and golden objects to suggest a complex of motifs which underlies the main action. For example, there are recurrent references to the Golden Age. Mr. Verver

(Adam) and his daughter are often described in terms suggestive of an ideal pastoral state prior to the Fall of Man, especially in the scenes at Mr. Verver's country estate, Fawns. Fawns exists in "a wonderful windless waiting golden hour" (XXIII, 191), and is surrounded by "the general golden peace" (XXIII, 192). Everything at Fawns "with its uncorrected antiquity" is "conscious" of "no violence from the present and no menace from the future" (XXIV, 309). The association of the Ververs with a prelapsarian innocence has an ironic effect. The Ververs are not living in a golden age, but in a fallen world; and their conduct is motivated by a naïve belief in human perfection and, much worse, by the assumption that their "marriage" to each other stands as a normal, even an ideal, relationship. The Prince, who recognizes the absurdity of upholding the standards imposed on him by the Ververs, realizes that the Golden Age cannot be recreated, at least insofar as his relation with Charlotte is concerned.

> What was supremely grotesque in fact was the essential opposition of theories—as if a galantuomo, as *he* at least constitutionally conceived galantuomini, could do anything *but* blush to "go about" at such a rate with such a person as Mrs. Verver in a state of childlike innocence, the state of our primitive parents before the Fall (XXIII, 335).

The extreme innocence of the Ververs amounts to a kind of evil in itself; their ignorance of sin helps to cause a sin. Appropriately James describes the Verver's developing knowledge of evil also in terms of the dissolution of the golden atmosphere. When Maggie first suspects the defection of the Prince, she is forced to pay "tribute . . . to realities looming through the golden mist that had already begun to be scattered. The conditions facing her had yielded for the time to the golden mist—had considerably melted away . . ." (XXIV, 31).

An additional implication of the gold imagery is the suggestion of a contest of power between the old gold of Roman culture and the new gold of American wealth. As Francis Fergusson has stated, "the novel is a struggle for power. The power in question is, literally and in the beginning, that of Adam Verver's vast wealth; and the question is, who shall control it, and to what end?" [26] But the Prince possesses a power of his own, notably that of the ancient Roman Empire, transfigured and enhanced by Renaissance culture and art. Thus the new gold of Mr. Verver attracts and eventually absorbs the old gold of Amerigo. The Americans acquire European elegance and experience; the Europeans acquire American wealth. The Ververs initially refuse to accept the implications of a personal union with Europe, but Amerigo is fully conscious of the significance of his marriage. He sees himself becoming engulfed by a tide of new wealth: his early dealings with Maggie

> had but sweetened the waters in which he now floated, tinted them as by the action of some essence, poured from a gold-topped phial, for making one's bath aromatic. No one before him, never—not even the infamous Pope—had so sat up to his neck in such a bath. It showed for that matter how little one of his race could escape after all from history. What was it but history, and of *their* kind very much, to have the assurance of the enjoyment of more money than the palace-builder himself could have dreamed of? (XXIII, 10).

Maggie's synthesis of her own innocence and Amerigo's experience (each a blend of good and evil) dramatizes the struggle for power and status between the two great worlds. What Fergusson calls "the historic dimension of the novel" [27] is reflected in the personal conflict between the Europeans and the Americans. *The Golden Bowl* is basically a novel of the private life; yet the suggestion that the conflict is emblematic of a larger struggle between empires contributes a related theme. The evil that taints the Verver family likewise taints the historical movement of western civilization from Europe to America. James's point is that an assimilation between American wealth and European tradition cannot come about without a mutual contamination, without European experience in evil, in deceit, in treachery subverting American innocence. The common meeting ground of London stresses the materialism detrimental to an honorable union between Europe and America. Fanny Assingham is much worse than any of the major participants, but her opportunism, her concern for position, her readiness to lie and betray have their counterparts in Adam and Maggie Verver and in the Prince and Charlotte.

British materialism provides a particularly apt background to the novel: it reveals the baseness of the monetary struggle and counteracts the emphasis on the exotic and the golden, on the ancestral and aesthetic connotations of the same wealth that Colonel Assingham values only in terms of pounds and shillings. Naked greed motivates each of the marriage partners: the Ververs "buy" their *sposi;* Amerigo and Charlotte marry mainly because of the Verver fortune. R. W. Short writes that the most pervasive images in *The Golden Bowl* are those of "travel and machinery and 'ownership' (*money* or *property*). If these . . . do not alone set the tone, they create the story, inasmuch as it is the story of ever-moving homeless persons, trapped by the rarefied rigidities of society, all in some sense buying and selling each other." [28] Though not so much as *The Wings of the Dove, The Golden Bowl* is dominated by a drive for wealth and power that is disguised rather than transformed by the heavy golden atmosphere. James is not unaware that gold is also suggestive of money as loot, as unadorned wealth. The novel begins when the Prince, glancing at a London shop window, evaluates the assorted riches as ill-gotten, as sordid, and as representative of nothing more than plunder.

> He had strayed simply enough into Bond Street, where his imagination, working at comparatively short range, caused him now and then to stop before a window in which objects massive and lumpish, in silver and gold, in the forms to which precious stones contribute, or in leather, steel, brass, applied to a hundred uses and abuses, were as tumbled together as if, in the insolence of the Empire, they had been the loot of far-off victories (XXIII, 3).

The Golden Bowl stands for Maggie's marriage, but it is also a focal symbol of luxury and wealth. The gold of the bowl is the combined gold of the Ververs and of the Prince—new and old, American and European. The flashy exterior is, in both cases, misleading, for underneath is the cracked crystal, the evil center.

If the dimensions of evil in *The Golden Bowl* are conveyed through image motifs, the terror of Maggie Verver suggests the force of the evil. In handling Maggie's awakening vision of evil, James indicates that her suffering is not the gratuitous agony of Lambert Strether, but in many ways a just punishment for her sin. Maggie's sin is close in nature though not in gravity to that of Gilbert Osmond. She recognizes that she and her father "liked to think they had given their life this unusual extension and this liberal form, which many families, many couples, and still more pairs of couples, wouldn't have found workable" (XXIV, 5–6). Maggie's *hybris* consists in her view of marriage as an extension of herself. It is fitting that her suffering should consist in a diminishing of herself, in a severing from society, in a limiting of her relationships with life. For Maggie suffers not so much from the shock that follows knowledge as from the isolation that knowledge necessitates. She is isolated first of all from the Prince and Charlotte inasmuch as she cannot allow them to know that she knows without permanently destroying her marriage. What pains Maggie most is her isolation from her father: "I must do everything . . . without letting papa see what I do—at least till it's done" (XXIV, 38).

The second volume of *The Golden Bowl* begins, insofar as Maggie's experience with Europe is concerned, at that point where *The Portrait of a Lady* ends—when the heroine realizes that she has been betrayed. Significantly a greater sense of evil emerges from the second than from the first half of the book. Once Maggie learns of the initial evil, she tries to restore good to the situation, or, in her own terms, to have the bowl "as it *was* to have been. . . . The bowl without the crack" (XXIV, 216–217). It is in the process of recovery that each member of the circle is most oppressed by evil. Though Maggie is successful in patching up the pieces of her smashed happiness, the darkness that attends the restoration prevents *The Golden Bowl* from being anything but a somber novel.

Once the point of view switches to Maggie, once she instead of the Prince dominates the action, the sense of evil increases. One reason is that Maggie more than anyone else suffers from the joint crime of all. Her discovery of the adultery is her first vision of evil, and her native sense of morality and fear of sexuality cause her to be more shocked and dismayed than a European would be.

Yet the full force of evil is not released until Maggie acts. Maggie's intervention augments the suffering of all. When a social situation is grounded in evil, all further behavior, even though motivated by high ideals and executed with intelligence, must intensify and partake of that evil. Maggie becomes deceiver, aggressor, and mistress of intrigue to gain her victory. Employing the techniques of the worldly-wise and practical-minded European, Maggie uses evil means to bring about a good end. No other means are available to her. To be candid would be to wreck the arrangement permanently and to alienate the Europeans. Maggie Verver reconciles American idealism and British practicality, combining, as it were, the spiritual love of Milly Theale and the practical genius of Kate Croy. James does not modify the ugliness of her intrigue, even though, in his ethical relativism, he reveals that moral motives may transcend and convert objectively immoral means.

Maggie's maneuver consists in aligning the Prince with her, thereby alienating him from Charlotte. To this end she bluntly tells the Prince that she knows of his affair. The Prince discovers a vitality in Maggie that previously he had found wanting. Therefore he rejects Charlotte; he refuses to tell her what Maggie knows. Maggie lies to Charlotte when she tells her that she suspects nothing. Maggie deceives her father also by not revealing her knowledge. Fanny Assingham, who also is compelled to lie— she pretends an innocence of the adultery so that Maggie may have a free hand in ending it—tells her husband, "We shall have . . . to lie for her—to lie till we're black in the face" (XXIV, 122).

The lie represents the compromise of good with evil. The Ververs' domestic arrangement is so perverse that only perverse means can improve it. Further evil and suffering must follow; and complete goodness and happiness can never be achieved. Certainly Maggie's solution is not an entirely satisfactory one. If there are gains there are also losses. A necessary loss is the severance of Maggie and her father, which, even though painful for both, is

of course required, for it was the unconscionable closeness of the
two which caused much of the initial evil. But there are gratuitous
losses as well. Charlotte Stant is sacrificed to the well-being of the
others. After her terrified anxiety over the deceit of Maggie and
the Prince, Charlotte's doom is completed when she is led off to a
sterile existence in America with Mr. Verver, who is described
as "holding in one of his pocketed hands the end of a long silken
halter looped round her beautiful neck" (XXIV, 287). Charlotte,
not Maggie, is the sacrificial victim, the scapegoat. Deprived of
her freedom, she is like a wounded beast, instinctive and impulsive
in her suffering as she has been in her happiness. Maggie has the
impression of "gilt wires and bruised wings, the spacious but
suspended cage, the home of eternal unrest, of pacings, beatings,
shakings all so vain, into which the baffled consciousness help-
lessly resolved itself. The cage was the deluded condition . . ."
(XXIV, 229). It may be an instance of poetic justice that Charlotte suffers the anguish of deception, because she has contributed
earlier to the deception of Maggie. But when the punishments
are meted out, there is no absolute justice. The Prince escapes
retribution, deprived only of a mistress whom he no longer loves.
At the conclusion, Charlotte, no more guilty than any of the
other three, is made to endure the most pain. As Maggie says, "It's
as if her unhappiness had been necessary to us—as if we had
needed her, at her own cost, to build us up and start us" (XXIV,
346). Charlotte is not only "doomed to a separation that was like
a knife in her heart" (XXIV, 311) from her beloved Amerigo,
but also to perpetual ignorance—for she will never know how
much Maggie knows. One of Maggie's most insidious stratagems
is to rely upon Charlotte's ignorance to restrain her, to keep her
defenseless. And yet the reader is not to accuse Maggie of malice
or cruelty; she takes the only effective course. As Maggie has
suggested, there must be those to suffer and pay for the evil of
all. For, though in *The Golden Bowl* James dramatizes the sup-
pression of evil by good, he does not alter a truth of his earlier
fiction—that evil is ultimately irremediable and permanent, in its
effects if not in its intensity.

F. W. Dupee states that *"The Golden Bowl* is an unsparing
picture of the inevitable strain of private life . . . ."[29] The private

life becomes a strain to all the members of the Verver circle because each, especially Maggie, seeks desperately to reconcile
private differences with the social unit. James's repeated implication is that society necessarily entails some violation of individual
rights. In reality society is composed of aggressor and prey. In
appearance, however, it consists in the forms of intercourse
which suggest equability and happiness. Though false, appearance
has a certain reality of its own: to James's mind organized society,
based on culture and manners, provides a common ground for
communication and association, and a valuable means of experience. In *The Golden Bowl* Maggie seeks to preserve the appearance of society, and James is sympathetic with her goal.

James's emphasis is on the sinister rather than the beautiful
aspects of society, on its reality rather than its appearance. He
dramatizes a condition in which human relations are made impossible. The morally isolated members are held together by the
weakest of bonds. Each feels the horror of the unspoken reality,
which each perceives—though some more clearly than others—
and each is compelled to preserve the appearance of tranquility,
to remain silent. Superficially, Maggie, the Prince, Charlotte, and
Mr. Verver give the appearance of harmony and bliss:

> The merely specious description of their case would have
> been that, after being for a long time, as a family, delight-
> fully, uninterruptedly happy, they had still a new felicity to
> discover; a felicity for which, blessedly, her father's appetite
> and her own in particular had been kept fresh and grateful
> (XXIV, 72–73).

The actual is most horrible, and its evil most felt, because of its
discrepancy with the apparent. In the late chapters Maggie sees
only "terrors and shames and ruins" instead of what might appear
"serenities and dignities and decencies" (XXIV, 236). Her vision
of evil is far more intense than her first awareness of her husband's
infidelity, for she is confronted with "the horror of finding evil
seated all at its ease where she had only dreamed of good; the
horror of the thing hideously *behind*, behind so much trusted, so
much pretended, nobleness, cleverness, tenderness" (XXIV, 237).

Unlike most of her predecessors, Maggie is not permanently

severed from life by her encounter with evil. Rather she comes to accept it as an unavoidable element of experience and also to revise her childish delusion that one should seek only personal happiness, which she had considered not only eminently good, but also eminently obtainable. The rapidly maturing Maggie finds that "any deep-seated passion has its pangs as well as its joys, and that we are made by its aches and its anxieties most richly conscious of it" (XXIV, 7).

Like Milly Theale, Maggie acquires and exercises spiritual love, which replaces her limited and dangerous love for her father. Maggie can "bear anything," she tells Fanny Assingham, not for the love of her father or of her husband, but "For love" (XXIV, 115–116). Maggie's love shelters her from the selfish emotions of jealously and resentment, but it makes it impossible for her to escape the anguish of a knowledge of evil. As her love is general and universal, so must her sense of evil be deep and inclusive. If Maggie's heroic deeds for love counterbalance the force of evil, they never diminish it. Significantly, the Prince, who is associated with an ultimate in human evil by his Italian ancestry, and not Maggie, has the most appropriate word. He tells his wife, "Everything's terrible, cara—in the heart of man" (XXIV, 349).

### CHAPTER FIVE

# The Last Tales: The Appalled Appalling

THE dominant concern in James's fiction is knowledge. James repeatedly explored means by which the individual might develop his moral and aesthetic consciousness. In the beginning the school of experience is Europe, the spiritual testing ground where New-man and Isabel Archer attain a high degree of moral sensibility. In the nineties the setting is London, hideous in its selfish material-ism, a world which has renounced the aesthetic and traditional past for the modern values of money, efficiency, and lust. In this shallow society the James protagonist—now a child—encounters only pain, with none of the benefits of civilization. His acquired knowledge—Maisie's for example—is mainly of the moral in-adequacy of society. In *The Ambassadors*, *The Wings of the Dove*, and *The Golden Bowl*, European civilization is not vulgar, but sterile. The impotent grace of Mme. de Vionnet and Prince Amerigo and the shrill beauty of Palazzo Leporelli and Matcham are James's symbols of a past without meaning in the present. In these novels the personal drama reflects social disintegration, the ultimate betrayal of the past. The veil of pretense, lending beauty to corruption, is ripped aside with the climax of each novel: Mme. de Vionnet and Chad in the boat, the cataclysmic storm in Venice, the sinister bridge game at Fawns.

James's symbols of social collapse retain their validity in the works that follow, for these stories show James's concern with the possibilities of spiritual expansion outside a social context. The only milieu given in these works is the degenerate money culture of America; in most of the tales there is no society at all, simply the abstracted individual. Especially in "A Round of Visits" and "The Bench of Desolation," but to a degree in the

157

other tales too, James dramatizes the plight of the man of sensibilities in a naked world, institutionally and culturally bankrupt.
The bleak expanse of water and sky before which Herbert Dodd
spends most of his life might well represent the ruined, blasted
world that provides the setting for the last fiction in general. The
characters exist in tight and restricted places: small hotel rooms,
dingy seaside resorts, sealed-off eighteenth-century houses,
empty New York homes. Each is at the beginning homeless and
dislocated; the dominant movement is wandering and search
through vacant rooms and aimless streets.

What these stories show is that nothing—not society or civilization certainly—can define the self except the self. To this purpose James's regular themes are reconsidered. The unspoken plea
continues to be "Live, live all you can," but fulfillment now
comes directly through self-understanding. Thus the lifelong
theme of "what might have been," which reaches its culmination
in Strether, is now the theme of what always has been. The terror
in the ghost visions of Spencer Brydon and Ralph Pendrel derives
from their perception not of what they might have become, but of
what they are.

James's final stories assimilate two of his preoccupying themes
of the nineties: that is, the destructiveness of egotism, which is
treated most pointedly in "The Beast in the Jungle," and the
revelation of unsuspected depravity in the personality, the main
theme of the ghost stories of the middle period. The two themes
are brought together in the character of the detached observer, a
characteristic James type, but one which he treated in mid-career
with much less sympathy than in earlier years. In the course of
their stories, John Marcher, George Stransom, and the narrators of
"The Aspern Papers" and The Sacred Fount are brought face to
face with their egotism; each emerges as a man possessed by an
evil much like Hawthorne's "Unforgivable Sin." Stransom is
saved by his recognition, but the rest become increasingly more
separate from others, as they withdraw into their own worlds.

The theme of the recognition of personal evil is obliquely suggested in the often-quoted nightmare passage in A Small Boy and
Others. According to the dream, set in the Galerie d' Apollon of
the Louvre, James puts to flight a monster who had a moment

before horrified and pursued him. James concludes that "I, in my appalled state, was probably still more appalling than the awful agent, creature or presence . . . ." [1] The resemblance of the action of the nightmare to the action of "The Jolly Corner" has often been pointed out. But the pattern of the appalled man turning out to be more appalling than the monster who confronts him is a fairly common structural principle in James's fiction after 1897. The governess in "The Turn of the Screw," for instance, is a case of the appalled person—she is driven to panic by what the demons are doing to the children—becoming herself the appalling one—she terrifies both children and to some degree causes the death of one. The pattern of the nightmare is duplicated more precisely in *The Ambassadors*; it is as if the governess terrifies the ghosts; here Strether expects to be dismayed by Chad and outraged by his mistress, but he instead frightens them into withdrawal. His New England conscience is a greater force for evil than European impropriety.

It is through his use—possibly unconscious—of the motif of the appalled appalling that James converts a moral principle into aesthetic form. The dramatic revelation of character exposes the inner evil of the one who has had the reader's sympathy. The pattern operates in James's last works with a simplicity that somewhat conceals their resemblance to earlier works. James has eliminated all but the essence of the theme—the sudden revelation of personal pride. Not only is the elaborate social context gone, but the supporting cast, the human antagonists, are reduced in importance. It is as if *The Awkward Age* were written with the emphasis on Vanderbank only and Mrs. Brook not at all. In these bare and intense tales the theme of experience has undergone a strange mutation. To experience life one must come to a full knowledge of the self, without the enriching agency of a social framework. In each case the central character must return to the roots of his being.

In "A Round of Visits" (1910) the standard reversal from appalled to appalling is associated with the theme of suffering, so that we are left in the end with the impression of a bleak and noisy world in which meaning resides in suffering only, that of the victim and the victimizer, who share a moral bond that the others, the barbarous and the vapid, cannot experience. Typical of James's last protagonists, Mark Monteith is a long-time American expatriate who returns to find the New York community of his youth a pile of "broken bits." [2] The stable and responsible society he remembers has degenerated to a gaudy anarchy of selfish women. When he returns to New York he learns that his best friend, Phil Bloodgood, has betrayed his trust and absconded with the money Monteith has asked him to invest. Monteith is so appalled by the treachery that he feels he must have someone share his pain. However, everyone he encounters has a tale of woe of his own, though these complaints are petty and banal. Monteith is finally driven to search out an old companion, Newton Winch, whom he had never liked and always considered dull and boorish. It emerges that Winch, like the characters in *The Sacred Fount*, has undergone a physical, emotional, and intellectual transformation, so that he is now a man of sensibility and intelligence. While Monteith unburdens himself to Winch, who provides him the sympathy he seeks, it becomes apparent that Winch has done to someone else what Bloodgood has done to Monteith. In Winch, Monteith sees Bloodgood. His vision changes from that of Bloodgood causing him pain to that of himself pursuing and paining Bloodgood. The imagery of the hunt, which dominates the nightmare passage, is used with similar effect in "A Round of Visits": "our hero found himself on his feet again, under the influence of a sudden failure of everything but horror. . . . It was as if a far-borne sound of the hue and cry, a vision of his old friend hunted and at bay, had suddenly broken in . . . ." [3] In an act of compassion Monteith escapes his own agony to accept Winch's, and by extension Bloodgood's. In doing so, Monteith, like his predecessors George Stransom, Milly Theale, and Maggie Verver, purges himself of the pride of separateness, which usually assumes the guise of betrayed innocence in James, to unite in sympathy with his betrayer. Winch, on the other hand, and presumably Bloodgood too, unites with the one he has betrayed. His transformed personality suggests the effect of disinterested suffering: it has widened the moral vision and purified the sensibility. Winch's burden of suffering proves unbearable, however, and he kills himself.[4] At the end of the story Monteith is left with the pain alone.

The story suggests that the ultimate experience is suffering itself—that love is a community of suffering, that guilt and innocence are negligible distinctions within the larger territory of pain, for the pain originates in the being and action of all.

"The Bench of Desolation" (1910) has a like theme, although this story is acted out not against the background of a hollow society but in a social vacuum. The characters are completely isolated; there are not even artificial relationships which can be said to constitute a society. The two main figures in "The Bench of Desolation" are homeless, desolate people. In the beginning each sees nothing but his own suffering, and in the end nothing but the other's suffering. Here again is the purposeful ambiguity of guilt and innocence, with the apparently victimized Herbert Dodd made to re-see himself and accept his own guilt.

Dodd breaks his engagement to Kate Cookham, and when Kate demands reparation, Dodd feels all the more confident that he has acted wisely. Kate, to him, has an "appalling nature";[5] when Kate tells him that she will take his breach of promise to the courts Dodd goes into bankruptcy to meet her price and avoid facing the vulgar publicity and possible scandal of a legal battle. He marries Nan Drury, whom he finds a woman of taste, quite the opposite of Kate Cookham. However, he is so broken by the demands of Kate for reparation that his wife and children die. It is here that he is haunted by the fear that Kate had no case against him, that there was no obligation on his part to pay her, that he sacrificed his family to his pride, to what he always considered his "natural taste."[6] When, much later, Kate returns, she appears, like Newton Winch, totally transformed, "another and a totally different person," "a 'real' lady."[7] Kate offers Dodd a large sum of money, the fruits of years of penurious living, hard work at a series of distasteful jobs, and careful investment of Dodd's payment. She too has suffered, in an effort to redeem the past; in abject humility she presents Dodd the testament of her pain and love. Dodd's pride for a time restrains him from acceptance of the gift, but eventually he realizes his role in their mutual woe. As the story ends, "She was beside him on the bench of desolation."[8]

It is apparent that several themes of "A Round of Visits" are present in "The Bench of Desolation." Herbert Dodd, like Mark Monteith, must endure the desolation, first, of a sense of separateness, the isolation brought on by pride and righteousness, and, second, the desolation of common agony. Like Monteith, Dodd is the pursued man who must eventually perceive the evil within himself. The great sin is not what Kate Cookham has done to Dodd, but what Dodd, through pride, has done to Nan Drury. In the same way, it is Monteith's pain that makes living unendurable for Winch and brings him to suicide. In each case, however, with self-knowledge, an acceptance of one's role in the common human sorrow,[9] there comes, not relief, but a deepening of consciousness.[10]

The structural opposition of appearance and reality reveals the ambiguity of guilt and innocence in the tale. Dodd has habitually evaluated himself and the two women in his life as persons of fixed moral natures: in his righteousness he esteems his own superiority to the common herd and Nan Drury's "God-given distinction of type," and scorns Kate's "native indelicacy," "her essential excess of will and destitution of scruple." [11] In accepting Kate's love, Dodd must stoop to vulgarity, renounce his egotistic aloofness from the degrading, and without qualification accept the sins of his past. Kate too must rise above the humiliation of being a rejected fiancée to do all for love. What Dodd takes to be her natural coarseness is refined through years of self-abasing atonement. Likewise, "beautiful, gentle-tender-souled Nan" [12] soon degenerates into a dull, spiteful woman under the pressures of poverty. The meaning of these three reversals from what Dodd believes qualities according to nature is not just that Dodd's pride has distorted his vision, but also that the real self can only emerge through the suffering of desolation. Such pain either refines or destroys.

In "The Jolly Corner" (1908) the dream incident is literally used, and in virtually all its details, especially in Spencer Brydon's routing of the monster who has terrified him. The standard explanation, that Brydon exorcises the ghost he might have become by acknowledging it, does not account for the fright of the beast, who is as thoroughly vanquished by the real Brydon as is the monster in the nightmare by James.[13] The fact that Brydon has for thirty years derived his income from his New York houses, "living in luxury on *those* ill-gotten gains" (XVII, 444), as Alice Staverton puts it, and that Brydon, like John Marcher and Herbert Dodd, has sheltered himself from the love of a woman—in this case, Alice Staverton—suggest that there is a positive as well as a negative beast within him. The actual Brydon is more appalling than the self he has avoided becoming. Brydon's pride in escaping from his past parallels Monteith's feeling of outrage and Dodd's comfort in his taste; like the others Brydon must re-examine his past: he must see the deadening vanity of his "selfish frivolous scandalous life" (XVII, 450).

In *The Sense of the Past* (1917) James follows the pattern of the nightmare almost as closely as in "The Jolly Corner"; however, in the novel he seems little concerned with the moral implications so prominent in the short story. By comparison, *The Sense of the Past* is an elaborate mechanical exercise, a tour de force in which the fantastic psychological complexity of Ralph Pendrel's assuming the identity of a man living a hundred years ago and at the same time retaining his own identity is explored for its own sake. The dramatic emphasis is on Pendrel's alteration from a man frightened by a world he cannot comprehend to a source of fright himself, but James's extensive notes indicate his major concern to have been merely the rarefied problems of Pendrel's incredible situation. One can only speculate what James might have made of the novel had he lived to complete it.

The opening chapter presents a situation like those in other works of the last phase: a man renounces life in the present, specifically marriage, to engage in an exclusively private pursuit. In this way Pendrel's rejection of Aurora Coyne for his sense of the past recalls Dodd's rejection of Kate Cookham for pride in taste and Spencer Brydon's rejection of Alice Staverton for cultivated idleness in Europe. The given situation is contrived and mechanical: Aurora Coyne will not marry Pendrel unless he remains in America. Yet the effect is to pose Pendrel with the conflict of love and selfhood.

This theme is not fully developed in either the novel or the notes, but certain suggestions of what James had in mind are present. Several issues emerge: first, Pendrel creates in the inhabitants of the 1820 world a malaise, a terror which is the effect not of what Pendrel does, but of what he is—a man of the twentieth century; second, Pendrel's great fear is that he may be permanently lost in the past. The point may be that Pendrel is seeing the horror of his real self, which is evil simply in its detachment from any personal relationship, and that through his experience Pendrel finds that real identity can be acquired only through acceptance of the present. "It wasn't for Ralph as if he had lost himself," James writes, ". . . but much rather as if in respect to what he most cared for he had never found himself till now" (XXVI, 66). Ralph can discover the present only after discovering the past. He can live fully through others only —through marriage to Aurora Coyne specifically—and not at all through his retreat into the ego through the past.

Pendrel's pride is reflected not only in his inevitable differences from the older society, but also in his aloofness from the world in which he finds himself. Perception is his sole mode of being; he disregards the responsibilities attendant upon his position—albeit a false one—as relative and prospective husband. According to the notes, Pendrel betrays his alter ego: he "has done the other fellow a violence, has wronged the personality of the other fellow *in him,* in himself, Ralph, by depriving him of the indicated, the consonant union with the fine handsome desirable girl whom the 1820 man would perfectly and successfully have been in love with . . ." (XXVI, 322). James projected that Nan Midmore, who loves Ralph's alter ego without being loved by him, and who attracts Ralph far more than his alter ego's fiancée, shall in some undefined manner "liberate" Ralph from the past: "she gives him up for what is to herself utterly nothing, nothing but the exaltation of sacrifice" (XXVI, 349). Nan's sacrifice, in some ways like Kate Cookham's, would seem to point up by contrast the egotism of Ralph's purely intellectual involvement in other lives.

Thus we may speculate that if *The Sense of the Past* were to have a meaning beyond its fantastic plot, it might have been a reworking of the theme of isolation and self-discovery. In the past

Ralph realizes he is cut off from life; he is made to wish to return to the present, to subdue the self in the experience of love.

The remaining works of James's last phase differ somewhat from the prevailing pattern in that they are fundamentally comic. Especially in "The Velvet Glove" and "Mora Montravers" and less obviously in "Crapy Cornelia" and *The Ivory Tower*, human differences suggest comic incongruity rather than occasions for pain. Significantly, however, these primarily satiric works derive their structures from the same concerns which inform the other late tales.

In theme, the slightest of the stories, "The Velvet Glove" (1909), resembles "The Real Thing"; James, however, has added the pride of the artist, whose vanity permits him to be fooled by an impressive-looking but vacuous woman. "Mora Montravers" (1909) is more typical of James's late work. The story is seen through the eyes of an aesthetic idler, Traffle, an egotist interested in others solely as sources of comic diversion. His wife, Jane, a rigid moralist, is appalled when their niece, Mora, leaves them to live with a bohemian artist, Puddick. What occurs is that each character except Traffle is shown to be considerably more moral and intelligent than he first appeared: Mora and Puddick are quite innocent; the puritanical Jane retreats from her morality of respectability to befriend the artist. The egotist, however, is left unchanged. Having at first esteemed himself the sole person with perception and integrity, he finds himself in the end the only person with neither.

For the purposes of comedy, James has cut short the motif of the appalled appalling. He has been more concerned with the humorous possibilities of hidden character and self-discovery. In "The Velvet Glove" and "Mora Montravers," everyone turns out to be quite different from what he first seemed. But these stories conclude with social reconciliation. Furthermore, the man of pride is observer only; he is engaged in no personal crisis; his vanity has no opportunity to affect others.

"Crapy Cornelia" and *The Ivory Tower* repeat the central situation of "The Jolly Corner" and "A Round of Visits." The American expatriate, after years of unproductive leisure in Europe, returns to America, where he is oppressed by the vulgar materialism of modern American civilization. White-Mason in "Crapy Cornelia" (1909) plans to propose to the dazzling and eminently modern Mrs. Worthingham, but decides against it after he meets a friend from his youth, Cornelia Rasch, whose poverty and age do not disguise her refinement. Through the contrast White-Mason sees the indelicacy of Mrs. Worthingham. There is pride in his condescension toward Cornelia's absurd appearance, but it is overcome through his final preference of her to the younger, richer, and prettier Mrs. Worthingham. White-Mason, like Brydon, is a homeless man who finally abandons the idleness of life in Europe and the barbarism of life in America to accept the comfort of a human relation. In "Crapy Cornelia," however, there is no suggestion of the unconscious sin of dissociation from social responsibility; there is merely the comic manipulation of the appearance and reality theme in the contrast between Cornelia and Mrs. Worthingham.

*The Ivory Tower* (1917) repeats the theme of "A Round of Visits," though with much less intensity. Graham Fielder, who has inherited a large amount of money, asks Horton Vint to watch over it for him. Vint, like Phil Bloodgood, betrays his trust and steals much of the money. Fielder is not appalled though, for he recognizes immediately his own complicity in the crime— through presenting the temptation, through his scornful unconcern with the mechanics of investment and banking, and most of all through his association with money immorally acquired. Like Monteith, but with nothing like his suffering, Fielder is brought to compassion for his betrayer. Fielder finally abandons the money entirely, presumably leaving much of it to Vint; but James's notes do not suggest he is to share the kind of moral bond with his betrayer that unites Monteith and Bloodgood.

It appears that James can conceive of no satisfactory social relationship for his last protagonists. The most tenuous association with the plunder of the American robber barons, with "the awful game of grab" (XXV, 33), involves Spencer Brydon, Mark Monteith, and Graham Fielder in immorality. Furthermore, American society is so vulgar and insipid that social intercourse is necessarily unrewarding. On the other hand, James implies that the American can find little that is permanently valuable in Europe. Europe is a negation: it lacks the oppressiveness of America; life for the American in Europe is "wasted." Ralph Pendrel's inability to live in the past typifies the general impossibility of the American's benefitting from the traditional. Nor do the protagonists find in the persons they love the values of a civilization: Newton Winch and Aurora Coyne cannot be defined as products of a class or a culture; Claire de Cintré and Prince Amerigo cannot be defined otherwise. To the late James there is no salvation beyond the private life. Human love, whether it be the compassion in desolation of Kate Cookham and Herbert Dodd or the more conventional attachment of Graham Fielder and Rosanna Gaw, is the sole means of existence in the empty world of James's last tales.

# Conclusion

According to its traditional meaning, the concept "evil" implies the existence of absolute moral standards. In modern times, however, "evil" is most often but a convenient term loosely applied to any form or agent of injury and pain; rarely is it intended to suggest a deviation from a transcendent and unchanging moral order. Since the early eighteenth century, the notion of uniform standards of "good" on the levels of personal, social, and political behavior has lost much ground to more relativistic views of morality.

In this respect, Henry James's relation to his age is curious. James, I think, assumes absolute standards of good and evil; his approach to morality is reactionary—closer to that of Shakespeare and Milton than that of Zola and Dreiser. Yet, if the moral code is an absolute one in James's fiction, his characters perceive it only in the most subjective way. They apprehend both good and evil through the "moral sense," ultimately a faculty of spiritual intuition. The reason is not just that in the stage of history treated by James there is no uniformity of moral standards or any religious, political, or social body which gives voice and authority to common notions of right and wrong, but that James in part shares the modern skepticism. There can be no externally derived moral knowledge. Evil exists absolutely, but hardly objectively.

Because evil is an absolute to James, it must be distinguished from mere failures in manners or violations of conventions, though it exists in close relation to extremely formal, and relative, social standards. James presumes a traditional conception of evil, yet dramatizes it in rarefied social conflicts. In this respect he can be said to urbanize Hawthorne. It is a tribute to James's range and

168

his sophistication that he retains the absolute moral specifications of religious orthodoxy in his worldly settings, his psychologically complex characters, and his various uses of literary realism.

In attempting to elaborate this view, I have used the term "evil" to refer to a multitude of characters and situations. I am well aware that the term itself may be misleading; it has unavoidable connotations of the grave and the sinister, and can be qualified only with some awkwardness. Though evil in James is an absolute in that it transcends convention, not every individual, situation, or action which partakes of that evil should be considered absolutely malignant. Though I have considered Daisy Miller's ignorance a moral failing, and therefore a condition of evil, I have no wish to group her with the Gilbert Osmonds and Peter Quints. The Gothic, melodramatic, and fundamentalist associations of the word "evil" make it an especially cumbersome approach to the subtleties of James. Evil is real and significant in his fiction, but it is rarely sinister and never grim. Not only is his world one of beauty, honor, and humor, but evil itself is frequently identified with these qualities.

The fact that James takes evil both seriously and absolutely is probably one of the main reasons for the great interest mid-twentieth-century critics and readers have taken in his works. It is not accidental that the increase in James's appeal has coincided with the rising popularity of Melville, Hawthorne, and Emily Dickinson. A greater religious seriousness—to some, a "neo-orthodoxy"—and a disillusionment with political and scientific solutions to human anxiety are at least as influential in the James revival as modern criticism's high regard for fictional technique. In the twenties and thirties no respected critic took the word "sin" at its traditional valuation; but the day of Mencken and Parrington has clearly ended.

Of course, in spite of its orthodox elements, James's view of evil is not rigidly or exclusively Christian. James's conception of the reality and irremediability of sin is common to Christianity, especially the Puritan version. But there is no hint of dogma in James's fiction, no theology, and no divine grace. James's works can never be considered Christian in the way that Greene's or Mauriac's are. In addition, the view of evil which James derived from the Christian tradition is supplemented, though not softened, by elements derived from the American traditions of ethical pragmatism and transcendentalism (its psychology, not its ontology).

If modern criticism has discovered James's link to the New England past, through Hawthorne, it has also discovered his link to the twentieth century, through T. S. Eliot. Stephen Spender in particular has illuminated James's closeness to Eliot, Yeats, Auden, and the other poets and novelists distressed by the religious disorientation of modern man. Particularly appropriate to the present study is Spender's view that in James's late novels, "Once the situation is provided the actors cannot behave otherwise. Their only compensation is that by the use of their intelligence, by their ability to understand, to love, and to suffer, they may to some extent atone for the evil which is simply the evil of the modern world. It is these considerations that make his later books parables of modern Western civilization."[1]

These remarks are suggestive, though not, I think, completely accurate. In James, the breakdown of western civilization—the split between the forms of the past and modern selfhood, primarily greed—leads to a condition in which the moral intelligence finds itself totally isolated. The loss of belief in James's fiction is not a denial of religion, but of traditional secular civilization. Beyond this, however, it is questionable that the evil in James's last novels is "simply the evil of the modern world." It is both more and less than this. These novels are richly symbolic, but hardly parables. Their historical meaning develops from their psychological realism. James's vision of things is almost always dual, perceptive of the private moral aspects of any given situation, and also of the relevance of "the special case" to the larger context of the western world. Though in a tale like "The Beast in the Jungle" there is little or no suggestion of national or international themes, most of James's works to some obvious degree extend beyond the private problem to the larger social condition. Evil is above all personal; if it is an attribute of a civilization or symptomatic of social disintegration, it remains the concern of the private man.

Finally, of course, James is an artist. We do not turn to his fiction for solutions to the problem of evil or of any problem. As Philip Rahv has wisely said, "it is hardly the writer's business to stand in for the scientist and the philosopher." [2] James especially seeks to reflect the fullness and complexity of experience through the ordering agency of art. Though it is a commonplace in James criticism, the most fitting conclusion to this study is surely an insistence on James's conviction that the experience represented in a novel can only be that which is bristling, felt, dramatized. "The high price of the novel as a literary form" is

> its power not only, while preserving that form with close-ness, to range through all the differences of the individual relation to its general subject-matter, all the varieties of outlook on life, of disposition to reflect and project, created by conditions that are never the same from man to man (or, as far as that goes, from woman to woman), but positively to appear more true to its character in proportion as it strains, or tends to burst, with a latent extravagance, its mould. [3]

Ultimately the element of evil remains an indistinct and undefined component of all that comprises "life" in the work of art.

# NOTES

Works referred to in the Preface, listed in order of reference:

Paul, Siwek, *The Philosophy of Evil* (New York: Ronald Press, 1951). Henry, James, *The Complete Plays of Henry James*, ed. by Leon Edel (London: Rupert Hart-Davis, 1949).

### CHAPTER ONE

## The Consciousness of Evil

[1] Charles Baudelaire, *French Poets and Novelists* (London: Macmillan & Co., 1919), p. 61.

[2] "The Aesthetic Idealism of Henry James," *The Question of Henry James*, ed. F. W. Dupee (New York: Henry Holt & Co.), p. 87.

[3] "Maule's Well; or Henry James and the Relation of Morals to Manners," *Maule's Curse* (Norfolk, Conn.: New Directions, 1938), pp. 187–216.

[4] Graham Greene, *The Lost Childhood and Other Essays* (London: Heineman, 1951), p. 26.

[5] *Letters to A. C. Benson and Auguste Monod*, ed. E. F. Benson (London: Elkin Mathews & Marrot, 1930), p. 35. In another letter, however, James seems to minimize the power of evil. When he wrote Vernon Lee about her first novel (dedicated to James), he criticized her "want of perspective and proportion. You are really too savage with your painters and poets and dilettanti; *life* is less criminal, less obnoxious, less objectionable, less crude, more *bon enfant*, more mixed and casual, and even in its most offensive manifestations, more *pardonable*, than the unholy circle with which you have surrounded your heroine" (*The Selected Letters of Henry James*, edited with an introduction by Leon Edel [London: Rupert Hart-Davis, 1956], p. 238). Here James is abhorring Gothic excesses, which overemphasize and exaggerate the noxiousness of evil. James cautions against the artist's falsifying reality and thereby offending "our general sense of 'the way things happen'" (*The Art of the Novel: Critical Prefaces by Henry James*, with an introduction by Richard P. Blackmur [New York: Charles Scribner's Sons, 1934], p. 34). James seems critical of Vernon Lee's use of fiction as a vehicle for moral instruction rather than as a reflection of life: "You have proposed to yourself too little to make a firm, compact work—and you have been too much in a moral passion. . . . Morality is hot—but art is icy" (*Selected Letters*, p. 207).

⁶ "Henry James," *Literary History of the United States,* ed. R. E. Spiller and others (New York: Macmillan Co., 1948), II, 1060.

⁷ All volume and page references cited in the text are to *The Novels and Tales of Henry James,* New York Edition (New York: Charles Scribner's Sons, 1907–17). I have used the text of the New York Edition for the discussions of all the works included therein; however, this study is not confined to the works included in this edition.

⁸ "Emerson," *The Art of Fiction and Other Essays,* introduction by Morris Roberts (New York: Oxford University Press, 1948), p. 224.

⁹ *Hawthorne* (New York: Harper & Bros., 1880), p. 99.

¹⁰ *The Letters of Henry James,* selected and edited by Percy Lubbock (New York: Charles Scribner's Sons, 1920), I, 100.

¹¹ *Notes of a Son and Brother* (New York: Charles Scribner's Sons, 1914), p. 224.

¹² "Ivan Turgenieff," *French Poets and Novelists,* p. 250.

¹³ *Apologia pro Vita Sua* (New York: Sheed and Ward, 1947), p. 220.

¹⁴ *Faith and History* (New York: Charles Scribner's Sons, 1951), p. 120.

¹⁵ Katherine Hoskins, "Henry James and the Future of the Novel," *Sewanee Review,* LIV (January–March, 1946), 98, calls attention to James's habit of neglecting the ordinary emotional reaction to death. Of *The Wings of the Dove,* she writes, "seldom in literature has a death taken place with [such] pagan avoidance of the normal thoughts that attend death."

¹⁶ Janet Adam Smith, ed., *Henry James and Robert Louis Stevenson: A Record of Friendship and Criticism* (London: Rupert Hart-Davis, 1948), p. 33 (introduction).

¹⁷ "The Sacred Fount," *Kenyon Review,* IV (Autumn, 1942), 333.

¹⁸ *A Small Boy and Others* (New York: Charles Scribner's Sons, 1913), pp. 347–348.

¹⁹ *Hawthorne,* p. 4.

²⁰ *The Art of the Novel,* pp. 64–65.

²¹ James's American protagonists live "happily and freely, by spiritual, ethical, and intellectual values"; they have a "firm belief in the goodness of human nature," and they aspire "toward the higher life, the purest humanities, the most spontaneous expression" (Katherine Anne Porter, "The Days Before," *Kenyon Review,* V [Autumn, 1943], 488).

In *The Comic Sense of Henry James* (London: Chatto & Windus, 1960), Richard Poirier calls Isabel Archer "an Emersonian Becky Sharp" (p. 217) and fully examines the significance of Emersonianism in *The Portrait of a Lady.*

²² "The Choice So Freely Made," *The New Republic* (Sept. 26, 1955), p. 27.

²³ James's observations about Zola are relevant: "Zola had had inordinately to simplify—had had to leave out the life of the soul, practically, and confine himself to the life of the instincts, of the more immediate passions, such as can be easily and promptly caught in the fact. He had had, in a word, to confine himself almost entirely to the impulses and agitations that men and women are possessed by in common, and to take them as exhibited in mass and number, so that, being writ larger, they might likewise be more easily read" (*The Question of Our Speech and The Lesson of Balzac* [Boston and New York: Houghton Mifflin Co., 1905], pp. 91–92).

[24] See for example Elizabeth Stevenson, *The Crooked Corridor: A Study of Henry James* (New York: Macmillan Co., 1949), p. 89; and Philip Rahv, "The Heiress of All the Ages," *Image and Idea* (New York: New Directions, 1949), p. 56n.

[25] Nathaniel Hawthorne, *The Scarlet Letter,* in *The Complete Novels and Selected Tales of Nathaniel Hawthorne,* ed. Norman Holmes Pearson (New York: Modern Library, 1937), p. 200.

[26] Osborn Andreas, *Henry James and the Expanding Horizon* (Seattle: University of Washington Press, 1948), p. 22.

[27] *Hawthorne,* p. 132.

[28] In saying that the Jamesian villain is realistic, I do not wish to suggest that his sinfulness can be explained by naturalistic causes; only rarely and partially does evil originate in physical or mental conditions. Lyon N. Richardson, *Henry James: Representative Selections, with Introduction, Bibliography and Notes* (New York: American Book Co., 1941), falls into the error of explaining evil in James as a result of physiological and psychical disorders: "It is a general rule in James's works that when evil appears there is manifest also the sense of a disordered mind which tacitly explains but does not condone the sin" (p. xxiii).

[29] "Marius Bewley, Hawthorne and Henry James," *The Complex Fate* (London: Chatto and Windus, 1952), pp. 11–31, describes in some detail the similarities and differences between *The Blithedale Romance* and *The Bostonians,* pointing out how James converts Hawthorne's Gothic elements into credible characters and situations.

[30] *Notes of a Son and Brother,* p. 7.

[31] *The American Adam* (Chicago: University of Chicago Press, 1955), p. 153.

[32] See Robert Bechtold Heilman, "*The Turn of the Screw* as Poem," *Forms of Modern Fiction,* ed. William Van O'Connor (Minneapolis: University of Minnesota Press, 1948), pp. 211–228.

[33] See Jacques Barzun, "Henry James, Melodramatist," *The Question of Henry James,* pp. 254–266; and Leo B. Levy, *Versions of Melodrama: A Study of the Fiction and Drama of Henry James, 1865–1897* (Berkeley and Los Angeles: University of California Press, 1957).

[34] "Henry James," *Readers and Writers* (New York: A. A. Knopf, 1922), p. 12.

[35] *The Art of the Novel,* pp. 175–176.

[36] "Henry James and the Trapped Spectator," *Explorations* (New York: G. W. Stewart, 1947), p. 179.

CHAPTER TWO

## Evil and the International Theme

[1] *The Art of the Novel,* p. 198.

[2] *A Small Boy and Others,* pp. 122, 161, 234.

[3] *The American Adam,* pp. 152–155.

[4] *Hawthorne,* p. 3.

[5] *Notes of a Son and Brother,* p. 458.

[6] *The Novels and Stories of Henry James,* ed. Percy Lubbock (London: Macmillan & Co., 1921), III, 74.

[7] *Novels and Stories*, III, 35, 38, 39.

[8] *Novels and Stories*, III, 77–78.

[9] As is suggested in Chapter I, James is a moral pragmatist. For discussion, see Eliseo Vivas, "Henry and William (Two Notes)," *Kenyon Review*, V (Autumn, 1943), 580–594; and Joseph Firebaugh, "The Pragmatism of Henry James," *Virginia Quarterly Review*, XXVII (Summer, 1951), 419–435. For a discussion of James's attitude toward the lie, see Marius Bewley, "Appearance and Reality in Henry James," *The Complex Fate*, pp. 79–113.

[10] *Henry James* (New York: Henry Holt & Co., 1916), p. 42.

[11] *The Bostonians* (New York: Dial Press, 1945), pp. 12–13, 25, 149.

[12] "On Henry James," *The Question of Henry James*, p. 113.

[13] "Henry James, the Satirist," *Hound and Horn*, VII (April–May, 1934), 516.

[14] *The History of the English Novel* (London: H. F. and G. Witherby, 1938), IX, 516.

[15] "Lady Windermere's Fan," *Salome, The Importance of Being Earnest, Lady Windermere's Fan* (New York: Boni and Liveright, 1919), p. 141.

[16] "Nature," *Selected Prose and Poetry* (New York: Rinehart & Co., 1950), p. 12.

[17] *The Art of the Novel*, p. 274.

[18] "The Enchanted Kingdom of Henry James," *The Wind Blew from the West* (New York: Harper & Bros.), p. 93.

[19] *A Small Boy and Others*, pp. 50–51.

[20] *Craft and Character in Modern Fiction* (New York: Viking Press), p. 123.

[21] *A Small Boy and Others*, pp. 14, 47.

[22] *The Pilgrimage of Henry James* (New York: E. P. Dutton & Co., 1925), p. 29.

[23] It has been pointed out often that James regards orphanage, like wealth, an essential condition of freedom for his feminine protagonists. Isabel Archer, Fleda Vetch, and Milly Theale are parentless; the parent in James is invariably a severe limitation, as, for example, with Catherine Sloper, Nanda Brookenham, and Maggie Verver. Marius Bewley, "Henry James and 'Life,'" *The Eccentric Design* (New York: Columbia University Press, 1959), in discussing the short story "Europe," observes that "The Image of the Mother, usually a life-symbol, is used in this story as a symbol of life-in-death . . ." (p. 237). Nonetheless, orphanage has a double meaning in James: in my consideration of *The Wings of the Dove*, I try to show that James identifies the catastrophes that have devastated Milly Theale's family with the doom that awaits Milly. The same basic situation exists, though less obviously, in many of James's works.

[24] *Henry James: Man and Author* (Boston and New York: Houghton Mifflin Co., 1927), pp. 249–250.

[25] *Notes of a Son and Brother*, p. 491.

[26] *Washington Square* (New York: Harper & Bros., 1894), p. 244.

[27] See *The Art of the Novel*, p. 187: "if I hadn't had, on behalf of the American character, the negative aspects to deal with, I should practically, and given the limits of my range, have had no aspects at all."

[28] *The Crooked Corridor*, p. 33.

[29] "The Enchanted Kingdom of Henry James," p. 107.

[30] This point has been stressed by Richard Chase in his study of *The Por-*

*trait of a Lady;* see *The American Novel and Its Tradition* (New York: Doubleday Anchor Books, 1957), pp. 117–138.

[31] *The Great Tradition* (New York: George W. Stewart, 1950), p. 150.

[32] *The Crooked Corridor,* p. 125.

[33] *Novels and Stories,* III, 35.

[34] "The Choice So Freely Made," p. 26.

[35] *Henry James* (New York: William Sloane Associates, 1951), p. 122.

[36] "The School of Experience in the Early Novels," *Hound and Horn,* VII (April–May, 1934), 427.

[37] "The Relativism of Henry James," *Journal of Aesthetics and Art Criticism,* XII (December, 1953), p. 239.

CHAPTER THREE

## Evil in London

[1] "*The Turn of the Screw* as Poem," pp. 217, 219, 223.

[2] The governess commits the cardinal Jamesian sin of being direct. With his high regard for human dignity and privacy and corresponding aversion to the concrete "dotting of *i*'s and crossing of *t*'s," James never permits a superior character to force an issue with another person, to accuse him of a crime, or to seek a confession from him. Isabel Archer never confronts Osmond with his past; Lambert Strether never alludes to Mme. de Vionnet's adultery when speaking with her; Milly Theale never questions Densher about his relationship with Kate; and Maggie Verver uses only indirect means to learn of and then to end the adultery of the Prince and Charlotte. But the governess, and later the narrator of *The Sacred Fount,* bluntly compel others to admit their guilt.

[3] "*The Turn of the Screw* as Poem," p. 222.

[4] "The Ambiguity of Henry James," *The Question of Henry James,* p. 165.

[5] My interpretation of "The Turn of the Screw," which maintains both the reality of the ghosts and the emotional immaturity of the governess, is substantially supported by John Lydenberg, "The Governess Turns the Screws," *Nineteenth-Century Fiction,* XII (June, 1957), 37–58. For evidence that the ghosts are real, see Alexander E. Jones's excellent "Point of View in *The Turn of the Screw,*" *PMLA,* LXXIV (March, 1959), 112–122, which may conclude the extensive controversy initiated by Edmund Wilson's "The Ambiguity of Henry James," published in its first form in 1934.

[6] Leon Edel, "An Introductory Essay," *The Sacred Fount* (New York: Grove Press, 1953), pp. xxv–xxix, discusses the theme of depletion in the contexts of both James's earlier fiction and his personal life. Professor Edel also deals with the question of the credibility of the narrator (pp. xvi–xxv), which though highly important in itself, is not directly relevant to the present study.

[7] *The Sacred Fount,* with an introductory essay by Leon Edel, p. 45.

[8] *The Sacred Fount,* pp. 104, 128, 128–129.

[9] *The Sacred Fount,* p. 352.

[10] *American Renaissance* (New York: Oxford University Press, 1941), p. 298.

[11] *The Notebooks of Henry James,* F. O. Matthiessen and Kenneth B. Murdock, eds. (New York: Oxford University Press, 1947), p. 196.

[12] *The Art of the Novel*, p. 59.

[13] *The Art of the Novel*, p. 242.

[14] *The Letters of Henry James*, I, 124.

[15] "London," *Essays in London and Elsewhere* (New York: Harper & Bros., 1893), p. 26.

[16] *The Notebooks of Henry James*, p. 207.

[17] *The Art of the Novel*, p. 244.

[18] See Oliver Evans, "James's Air of Evil: 'The Turn of the Screw,'" *Partisan Review*, XVI (February, 1949), 185; and Joseph J. Firebaugh, "Inadequacy in Eden: Knowledge and 'The Turn of the Screw,'" *Modern Fiction Studies*, III (Spring, 1957), 60.

[19] *The Art of the Novel*, p. 123.

[20] *The Art of the Novel*, p. 105.

[21] *The Art of the Novel*, p. 147.

[22] *Selected Short Stories* by Henry James (New York: Rinehart & Co., 1950), pp. v-xiv (introduction).

[23] See Louise Dauner, "Henry James and the Garden of Death," *University of Kansas City Review*, XIX (Winter, 1952), pp. 137–143. Miss Dauner points out that James consistently uses the garden as the scene of crucial decisions and actions, so that it is alternately a garden of life (Eden) and a garden of death (Gethsemane), and at times both.

[24] *The Novels of Henry James* (New York: G. P. Putnam's Sons, 1905), p. 106.

[25] *The Sacred Fount*, p. 128.

[26] *Henry James*, p. 194.

[27] *The Sacred Fount*, pp. 135–136.

[28] *The Art of the Novel*, p. 129.

[29] See Leon Edel, "Introduction," *The Other House* (London: Rupert Hart-Davis, 1948), p. xv: "She is not a figure of unmitigated Evil—the very juxtaposition of 'bad' and 'heroine' indicates that James thought of her as possessing heroic qualities, despite her 'badness.'"

[30] *The Notebooks of Henry James*, p. 248.

[31] "*The Turn of the Screw* as Poem," p. 227; "Innocence and Evil in James's *The Turn of the Screw*," *University of Kansas City Review*, XX (Winter, 1953), 97; "James's Air of Evil: 'The Turn of the Screw,'" pp. 186–187.

[32] *The Art of the Novel*, p. 146.

[33] *The Notebooks of Henry James*, p. 178.

[34] His moral vision is somewhat offset, however, by his blindness to the intellectual genius of Mrs. Brook's circle.

[35] *The Art of the Novel*, p. 102.

[36] "Henry James, Melodramatist," *The Question of Henry James*, pp. 254–264.

[37] Characteristically, Mrs. Brook makes the perfect comment: "I'm not, as a mother—am I, Van?—bad *enough*. That's what's the matter with me. Aggie, don't you see? is the Duchess's morality, her virtue; which, by having it that way outside of you, as one may say, you can make a much better thing of. The child has been for Jane, I admit, a capital little subject, but Jane has kept her on hand and finished her like some wonderful piece of stitching. Oh as work it's of a *soigné*! There it is—to show. A woman like me has to be *herself*, poor thing, her virtue and her morality" (IX, 310–311).

[38] Even more than Nanda, Mitchy retains a high moral standard though he is outwardly the most corrupt of Mrs. Brook's set. Mrs. Brook tells Mitchy, "You're the most delicate thing I know, and it crops up with effect the oddest in the intervals of your corruption. Your talk's half the time impossible; you respect neither age nor sex nor condition; one doesn't know what you'll say or do next; and one has to return your books—*c'est tout dire*—under cover of darkness. Yet there's in the midst of all this and in the general abyss of you a little deepdown delicious niceness, a sweet sensibility, that one has actually one's self, shocked as one perpetually is at you, quite to hold one's breath and stay one's hand for fear of ruffling or bruising. There's no one in talk with whom . . . I find myself half so suddenly moved to pull up short. You've more little toes to tread on—though you pretend you haven't: I mean morally speaking, don't you know?—than even I have myself, and I've so many that I could wish most of them cut off" (IX, 85–86).

CHAPTER FOUR

## Evil and the Major Phase

[1] See Christof Wegelin. *The Image of Europe in Henry James* (Dallas: Southern Methodist University Press, 1958), pp. 86–88, 189 n. 16.

[2] See *The Notebooks of Henry James*, pp. 169–174.

[3] The three novels comprise a "trilogy" in only the loosest sense of the word; though thematically and stylistically closer to each other than to any other of James's novels, *The Ambassadors*, *The Wings of the Dove*, and *The Golden Bowl* are totally distinct and self-contained. Other critics, however, most notably Quentin Anderson in *The American Henry James* (New Brunswick, N. J.: Rutgers University Press, 1957) have argued that the three novels form a rigid symbolical unity. Anderson's position has been ably refuted, I think, by Leon Edel in his review in *American Literature*, XXIX (January, 1958), pp. 493–495; and by Christof Wegelin, *The Image of Europe in Henry James*, pp. 184–185, n. 11.

[4] *The Letters of Henry James*, II, 104–105.

[5] *The Notebooks of Henry James*, p. 207.

[6] *The Pilgrimage of Henry James*, p. 47.

[7] Gaw is described as a bird of prey. At one point he seems to perch "like a ruffled hawk, motionless but for his single tremor, with his beak, which had pecked so many hearts out, visibly sharper than ever, yet only his talons nervous . . ." (XXV, 6).

[8] Catholic churches and monasteries frequently figure as sanctuaries from evil and anxiety, much in the same way as "the great good place" provides the author George Dane a refuge from the harassments of life. In the fullest discussion of James's treatment of Catholicism, Robert M. Slabey writes, "For James and his young American characters, the beauty and tradition of the Church attracted the person of artistic preferences; its quiet and peace offered solace for the troubled soul . . ." ("Henry James and 'The Most Impressive Convention in All History,'" *American Literature*, XXX [March, 1958], 102).

[9] Robert A. Durr, in "The Night Journey in *The Ambassadors*," *Philological Quarterly*, XXXV (January, 1956), writes that Strether has acquired

the "power to transcend the evil of antitheses by including them in a more encompassing vision . . ." (p. 29).

[10] *Henry James*, p. 245.

[11] Though written later than *The Ambassadors*, *The Wings of the Dove* was published slightly earlier.

[12] I am especially indebted in my discussion of *The Wings of the Dove* to R. P. Blackmur, "The Loose and Baggy Monsters of Henry James," *The Lion and the Honeycomb* (New York: Harcourt, Brace & Co., 1955), pp. 268–288; and R. W. B. Lewis, "The Vision of Grace: James's 'The Wings of the Dove,' " *Modern Fiction Studies*, III (Spring, 1957), 33–40.

[13] *The Art of the Novel*, p. 164.

[14] America is less an operative force in *The Wings* than in *The Ambassadors* and *The Golden Bowl*. However, what James says in his preface about Milly's nationality deserves comment: he speaks of there being "fifty reasons for her national and social status. She should be the last fine flower . . . of an 'old' New York stem . . ." (*The Art of the Novel*, p. 292). In Milly, James is invoking the memory not only of Minny Temple, but also of the New York of his youth, which as his late fiction (for example, "A Round of Visits" and *The Ivory Tower*) makes abundantly clear, has lost its charm and innocence. To James's mind materialism and vulgarity have corrupted America as well as England, so that in the world of *The Wings of the Dove* only an anachronism will serve James as a suitable tragic victim, for the moral attributes which James required of his heroine he could no longer detect in Anglo-American culture.

[15] See Quentin Anderson, *The American Henry James*, pp. 246–247, for additional instances in which the merchandising attitude dominates human affairs.

[16] See Ernest Sandeen, "*The Wings of the Dove* and *The Portrait of a Lady*: A Study of James's Later Phase," *PMLA*, LXIX (December, 1954), pp. 1066–1070.

[17] *The Destructive Element* (London: Jonathan Cape, 1953), p. 67.

[18] *The Art of the Novel*, p. 293.

[19] Jean Kimball, "The Abyss and the Wings of the Dove: The Image as a Revelation," *Nineteenth-Century Fiction*, X (March, 1956), 281–300, discusses the meaning and importance of the "abyss" image in *The Wings of the Dove*. Miss Kimball, however, sees the image only in its relation to Milly Theale's predicament.

Frederick C. Crews, *The Tragedy of Manners: Moral Drama in the Later Novels of Henry James* (New Haven: Yale University Press, 1957), p. 72, calls attention to the recurrent water images, which, in my view, supplement the abyss images.

[20] Especially in *The Wings of the Dove*, James's treatment of the past invites comparison with the "heap of broken images" theme in the poetry of T. S. Eliot.

[21] Morton Dauwen Zabel, *Craft and Character in Modern Fiction*, pp. 280–281.

[22] In recent years a critical controversy has risen over James's attitude towards the Ververs. F. R. Leavis (*The Great Tradition*, pp. 159–161) and F. O. Matthiessen (*Henry James: The Major Phase* [New York: Oxford University Press, 1944], pp. 92–93) find it a weakness in the novel that James seems unaware of certain objectionable traits in them, mainly their

consideration of their marriage partners simply as "pieces" for the elder Verver's collection, and their refusal to view their marriages as anything other than noble deeds enacted for the sake of each other.

Other critics, however, have demonstrated that James's attitude towards the Ververs is definitely critical and ironical. See, for example: Joseph J. Firebaugh, "The Ververs," *Essays in Criticism*, IV (October, 1954), 400–410; Francis Fergusson, "The Drama in *The Golden Bowl*," *Hound and Horn*, VII (April–May, 1934), 407–413; and Christof Wegelin, *The Image of Europe in Henry James*, pp. 122–140.

²³ "Introduction," *The Golden Bowl* (New York: Grove Press, 1952), p. vi.

²⁴ *The American Novel: 1789–1939* (New York: Macmillan Co., 1940), p. 184.

²⁵ "Myth and Dialectic in the Later Novels," *Kenyon Review*, V (Autumn, 1943), 565.

²⁶ "*The Golden Bowl* Revisited," *Sewanee Review*, LXIII (Winter, 1955), 21.

²⁷ "*The Golden Bowl* Revisited," p. 23.

²⁸ "Henry James's World of Images," *PMLA*, LXVIII (December, 1953), 956.

²⁹ *Henry James*, p. 267.

CHAPTER FIVE

## The Last Tales: The Appalled Appalling

¹ *A Small Boy and Others*, p. 348.

² *The Finer Grain* (London: Methuen & Co., 1910), p. 153.

³ *The Finer Grain*, p. 171.

⁴ F. O. Matthiessen, *Henry James: The Major Phase*, p. 117, writes that Winch "had penetrated into a world so corrupted by money that the only escape seemed to be by violence." It seems clear, however, that the public offense of materialism is not so much the reason for Winch's suicide as the private offense of betrayal—the major sin in James's work.

⁵ *The Finer Grain*, p. 233.

⁶ *The Finer Grain*, p. 238.

⁷ *The Finer Grain*, pp. 261, 259.

⁸ *The Finer Grain*, p. 307.

⁹ See Edwin Fussell, "Hawthorne, James and 'The Common Doom,'" *American Quarterly*, X (Winter, 1958), 438–453, for a discussion of this aspect of James's work.

¹⁰ Charles G. Hoffmann, *The Shorter Novels of Henry James* (New York: Bookman Associates, 1957), pp. 114–115, briefly discusses the element of fate in "The Bench of Desolation." Kate's comment, "Of course you've suffered . . . you inevitably had to! We have to . . . to do or to be or to get anything" (*The Finer Grain*, p. 279), suggests a limited but significant concept of fate: suffering is inevitable in the world, but it is a kind of inverted grace (as in the novels of Mauriac and Greene), providing a condition of consciousness hostile to egotism and necessary for spiritual growth. The will is free, however, to accept or reject the grace.

It is interesting to compare the treatment of suffering in "The Bench of

Desolation" with that in works by Melville, Hawthorne, and Faulkner. In James, suffering almost always purifies. In Melville, however, especially in "Benito Cereno" and "Bartleby," suffering overwhelms consciousness and leads to total withdrawal from the world. In Hawthorne, most notably in "Young Goodman Brown," exposure to evil can easily intensify spiritual pride. The same is frequently true in Faulkner, many of whose characters become increasingly withdrawn from the world and ego-centered through suffering.

[11] *The Finer Grain*, pp. 245, 232, 232.

[12] *The Finer Grain*, p. 242.

[13] James is explicit on this point: "My hero's adventure [in "The Jolly Corner"] takes the form so to speak of his turning the tables, as I think I called it, on a 'ghost' or whatever, a visiting or haunting apparition otherwise qualified to appal *him;* and thereby winning a sort of victory by the appearance, and the evidence, that this personage or presence was more overwhelmingly affected by him than he by it" (*The Notebooks of Henry James*, pp. 367–368).

Leon Edel, in quoting this passage, calls it "a curiously inaccurate account of the story [James] had written. The novelist here substitutes the nightmare for the story. In the story the hero does not appal the ghost, but is appalled and overwhelmed by it" (*Henry James: The Untried Years* [Philadelphia and New York: J. B. Lippincott Co., 1953], p. 75). Certainly the issue is ambiguous: the motives and feelings Brydon attributes to the ghost are often questionable. It is clear that until his final night in the house Brydon is the pursuer and the ghost is the pursued: "Who had ever before so turned the tables and become himself, in the apparitional world, an incalculable terror?" (XVII, 451). Brydon becomes frightened only when he believes that the alter ego has entered a particular room in the upper rear of the house; then Brydon descends the stairs in terror. However, at the foot of the stairs he sees the presence, its hands covering its face. At this point Brydon advances; the ghost retreats. The ghost then removes his hands to reveal his hideous face, and Brydon faints. Clearly there is at least a mutual terror. Also it is conceivable that the ghost covers his face not to prevent Brydon from seeing him, but to prevent himself from seeing Brydon. See, in this connection, Floyd Stovall's interesting interpretation, "Henry James's 'The Jolly Corner,'" *Nineteenth-Century Fiction*, XII (June, 1957), 72–84.

## CONCLUSION

[1] *The Destructive Element*, p. 67.

[2] "Attitudes toward Henry James," *The Question of Henry James*, p. 278.

[3] *The Art of the Novel*, pp. 45–46.

# Index

## A NOTE ABOUT THE AUTHOR

JOSEPH ANTHONY WARD, JR. was born in Baltimore, Maryland, in 1931. He received his A.B. degree *cum laude* from the University of Notre Dame in 1952 and his M.A. and Ph.D. from Tulane University (1954, 1957). From 1953 to 1957 he served as a graduate assistant and instructor in English at Tulane, and in 1957 joined the faculty of Southwestern Louisiana University as an assistant professor. He was awarded a Guggenheim fellowship for 1960–1961 for study of Henry James's conception of structure in the novel. Although THE IMAGINATION OF DISASTER is his first book, Professor Ward has contributed articles to a dozen scholarly periodicals, among them *American Literature*, the *Journal of English and Germanic Philology*, *Criticism*, the *Western Humanities Review*, *Nineteenth-Century Fiction*, and *Names*.

Professor Ward is married and has two daughters.

CI'

Everyman, I will go with thee, and be thy guide,
In thy most need to go by thy side.

This is No. 747 of Everyman's Library. A list of authors and their works in this series will be found at the end of this volume. The publishers will be pleased to send freely to all applicants a separate, annotated list of the Library.

J. M. DENT & SONS LIMITED
10–13 BEDFORD STREET LONDON W.C.2

E. P. DUTTON & CO. INC.
286–302 FOURTH AVENUE
NEW YORK

EVERYMAN'S LIBRARY
EDITED BY ERNEST RHYS

POETRY & THE DRAMA

PEER GYNT
BY HENRIK IBSEN · TRANSLATED
BY R. FARQUHARSON SHARP

HENRIK IBSEN, born at Skien, Norway, on 20th March 1828. Obtained work in connection with theatres in Bergen and Christiania. Left Norway in 1864 and lived abroad—mostly in Germany—returning to Norway in 1901. Died at Christiania on 23rd May 1906.

# PEER GYNT

HENRIK IBSEN

# INTRODUCTION

*Peer Gynt* was written in 1867, when Ibsen was nearly forty.[1] It followed his other great dramatic poem, *Brand*, by rather less than two years,—for *Brand*, though not published till 1866, was written in 1865. The contrast offered by the audacious high spirits of *Peer Gynt* to the austere gloom of *Brand* was a reflection of a welcome change in their author's worldly circumstances. Ibsen's growing independence of thought and his increasing frankness in insisting upon it (as he had done in his play *Love's Comedy*) had aroused a tempest of criticism in his own country, and in 1864 he had cast off the embarrassing trammels of national and family ties and had gone into voluntary exile in Italy. This had been rendered possible by a small grant of money that had been awarded him by the Norwegian government and substantially supplemented by the kindness of one or two friends. *Brand* was the first outcome of his detachment from real poverty. It to a great extent rehabilitated his repute at home, and put some money in his pocket; and this success further resulted in the Norwegian government's allotting him a " literary pension " of some ninety pounds a year. This sum, together with what he expected to make by his pen, opened out a prospect of a life of literary activity unhampered by continual anxiety as to his daily bread.

*Peer Gynt* obviously was written when his temperament was on the rebound and he was beginning to feel assurance that he could be as independent in thought and word as he pleased. It was conceived (as he says in a letter to Björnson) in the mood of a " Korstog-Jubel " —a " Crusader's Song of Triumph." " After *Brand* came *Peer Gynt*, as though of itself," he says in another

[1] Further details respecting Ibsen's life and writings will be found in the introductions to the four preceding volumes of Ibsen's plays in " Everyman's Library."

letter; [1] "it was written in Southern Italy, in the Island of Ischia and at Sorrento. So far away from one's future readers, one becomes reckless." Again, in a letter written some five years after *Peer Gynt* appeared, he says: "*Peer Gynt* is the very antithesis of *Brand*. . . . It is reckless and formless, written with no thought of the consequences—as I could only dare to write when far from my own country."

In 1880 Ibsen replied to one of his translators, who had asked for information as to the genesis of *Peer Gynt* in its author's brain: "to make the matter intelligible I should have to write a whole book, and for that the time has not yet come. Everything that I have written has the closest possible connection with what I have lived through, even if it has not been my own personal experience; in every new poem or play I have aimed at my own spiritual emancipation and purification." As a matter of fact one of the outstanding features of *Peer Gynt*—the character of Aase, Peer's mother, and the incidents woven round her—was, as we learn from Ibsen's letters, derived directly from his own experiences. "This poem," he wrote to his friend Hansen in 1870, "contains much that is reminiscent of my own youth; for Aase, my mother—with necessary exaggerations—served as model." Again, in a letter written to Brandes in 1882, he says: "My father was a merchant with a large business and wide connections, and he enjoyed dispensing reckless hospitality. In 1836 he failed, and nothing was left to us except a farm. . . . In writing *Peer Gynt* I had the circumstances and memories of my own childhood before me when I described the life in the house of ' the rich John Gynt.' "

With its obvious satire on the typical Norwegian temperament, as well as on what Ibsen considered a ridiculous aspiration for " national self-realisation," it is not surprising that *Peer Gynt* was not at first as popular in Norway as *Brand* had been. Seven editions of *Brand* had appeared before *Peer Gynt* reached its third. In 1876 Ibsen prepared an abridged version of *Peer Gynt* for representation at the Christiania theatre,

---

[1] I quote from Mary Morison's translation of Ibsen's Correspondence, published in 1905.

where it was performed with Grieg's incidental music; and by degrees it became a stock feature in the repertories of the chief Scandinavian theatres. The earliest German translation of the poem was published in 1881; the first English in 1892; and the first French in 1896. In Germany and in France performances have been given of abridged versions, and in 1906 Richard Mansfield produced an almost complete version at Chicago. In this country there has not yet been any attempt at a complete public performance, though a selection of scenes, translated by Miss I. M. Pagan, has been performed semi-privately.

*Peer Gynt* is (as Ibsen was emphatic in asserting) first and foremost a poetic fantasy, and only incidentally a satire. It is a fantasy woven out of the folklore of its author's country and embroidered by his wealth of thought and keen wit. There is a philosophy to be found in it, no doubt; but Ibsen did not set out to write a philosophical poem, but a fantasy. It contains many a shaft of satire, no doubt; but it was not primarily intended as a satirical poem, but as sheer fantasy. This cannot be too emphatically insisted upon, nor too diligently remembered in reading the poem. In a letter to his publisher, soon after *Peer Gynt* had made its appearance, Ibsen wrote: " I learn that the book has created great excitement in Norway. This does not trouble me in the least; but both there and in Denmark they have discovered much more satire in it than was intended by me. Why can they not read the book as a poem ? For as such I wrote it. The satirical passages are pretty well isolated. But if the Norwegians of to-day recognise themselves, as it would appear they do, in the character of Peer Gynt, that is the good people's own affair."

*Peer Gynt* has been the prey of many commentators; and of the majority of them the question might well be asked: " Why can you not read it as a fantasy ? For as such Ibsen wrote it." Ibsen himself ruefully complained more than once that his critics persisted in reading far more into his work than he had intentionally put there; and *Peer Gynt* has been a sufferer in this respect. The wise reader, approaching the poem for the first time, will simply abandon himself or herself to the current of fancy—now laughing, now tender, now ironical—that sweeps through it ; remembering that it is folklore, and the folklore of a people to whose peasantry Trolls and Witches are even to-day a reality. There are isolated difficulties to be encountered in the reading, no doubt; an attempt has been made to touch on some of them in footnotes to the present translation; but, in the main, if the poem be read with an appreciation of its origin and intention, and with a modicum of common sense, its fantasy need not unduly bewilder nor its philosophy unduly puzzle. Even caprice is permissible in a fantasy; Ibsen, on being asked if he corroborated a suggested explanation of a certain scene in *Peer Gynt*, replied that nothing had been farther from his thoughts than what his commentator suggested, and that he had as a matter of fact "stuck in the scene as a mere caprice."

In sending his publishers the manuscript of the poem, Ibsen wrote: "It may interest you to know that Peer Gynt was a real person, who lived in Gudbrandsdal, probably at the end of last, or the beginning of this, century. His name is still [1867] well known among the peasants there; but of his exploits not much more is known than is to be found in Asbjörnsen's *Norwegian Fairy Tales*. . . . Thus I have not had very much to build upon, but that has left me so much the more liberty." In Asbjörnsen's book Peer Gynt's chief exploits lie in the direction of fighting and conquering Trolls.

It is practically impossible for any translation of *Peer Gynt* to be entirely satisfactory. It must be in verse; a prose version of such a fantasy is unthinkable —even if it were not for the fact that its author declared that he would rather never see it translated than translated into prose. One of the charms of the diction of the original is the ingenious variation of metre for scenes of varying nature; that, translation may attempt to reproduce; but the ingenuity of its rhymes cannot be reproduced, and its verbal brilliance must be dulled, in translation.

The present translator has deliberately avoided two

shackling conditions which, it is permissible to think, have hampered previous translators of the poem; he has not attempted rhymed verse, and he has refused to be fettered by a superstitious regard for purely verbal literalness or for "line for line" rendering. He has made an attempt to follow the metres of the original, in unrhymed verse, keeping as closely to the original's literal meaning as was compatible with intelligibility in another tongue—his aim being to produce a version that might be read with sufficient ease to induce appreciation of this amazing work; and appreciation of *Peer Gynt* is bound to lead to admiration of it.

R. FARQUHARSON SHARP.

# BIBLIOGRAPHY OF ENGLISH TRANSLATIONS

*Separate Works.*—The Emperor and the Galilean, by C. Ray, 1876. Nora (The Doll's House), by T. Weber, 1880; H. F. Lord (with Memoir), 1882; revised edition, 1890; W. Archer, 1889. Rosmersholm, by L. N. Parker, 1889; C. Archer, 1891; revised edition, 1906. The Lady from the Sea, by E. Marx-Aveling, with Introduction by E. Gosse (Camelot Series), 1890; Mrs. F. E. Archer, 1897. Ghosts, by H. F. Lord, revised edition, 1890. Hedda Gabler, by E. Gosse, 1891. Peer Gynt, by W. and C. Archer (with two Tales from Asbjörnsen), 1892; by I. M. Pagan, 1909; by R. E. Roberts, 1912; by R. F. Sharp, 1921. The Master Builder, by E. Gosse and W. Archer, 1893; new edition, with Bibliographical Note and Appendix, 1893. Brand, by W. Wilson, 1891; C. H. Herford, 1894; F. E. Garrett, 1894 (Everyman's Library, 1915). Little Eyolf, by W. Archer, 1895. John Gabriel Borkman, by W. Archer, 1897. Love's Comedy, by C. H. Herford (Johnson and Erichsen, "Modern Plays," etc.), 1900. When We Dead Awaken, by W. Archer, 1900. The Wild Duck, by Mrs. F. E. Archer, revised edition, 1905. The Pretenders, by W. Archer, 1913.

*Collections.*—Prose Dramas, 5 vols., edited W. Archer, 1890–91; revised edition, 1900–1; with Biographical and Critical Introduction, by E. Gosse (Lovell's "Series of Foreign Literature"), 1890. Collected Works, with Introduction by W. Archer, 12 vols., 1906–12. The Pillars of Society and other Plays, edited by Havelock Ellis (Camelot Classics), 1888. A Doll's House, The Wild Duck, and The Lady from the Sea, translated by R. F. Sharp and E. Marx-Aveling (Everyman's Library), 1910. Ghosts, The Warriors at Helgeland, and An Enemy of the People, translated by R. F. Sharp (Everyman's Library), 1911. The Pretenders, Pillars of Society, and Rosmersholm, translated by R. F. Sharp (Everyman's Library), 1913. Lady Inger of Ostraat, Love's Comedy, and The League of Youth, translated by R. F. Sharp (Everyman's Library), 1915. Ibsen's Plays (Boston, U.S.A.), 1915. Lyrical Poems, selected and translated by R. A. Streatfeild (Vigo Cabinet Series), 1902. Lyrics and Poems, and Brand, translated by F. E. Garrett, 1912. Correspondence, translated by M. Morison, 1905.

*Biography.*—H. Jaeger, Life of Henrik Ibsen, translated by Clara Bell (with translation of Verse by E. Gosse), 1890; translated by W. M. Payne, 2nd edition, 1901; G. M. C. Brandes, Critical Studies, translated by J. Muir, 1899; E. W. Gosse, Ibsen (Literary Lives Series), 1907. H. Macfall, Ibsen: the Man, His Art and His Significance, etc., 1907. M. J. Moses, Henrik Ibsen: the Man and his Plays, 1908.

# THE CHARACTERS

AASE, widow of John Gynt, a peasant.

PEER GYNT, her son.

Two Old Women with corn-sacks.

ASLAK, a blacksmith.

Wedding Guests, a Steward at the Wedding, a Fiddler, etc.

A STRANGER and his Wife.

SOLVEIG and little HELGA, their daughters.

The Owner of Hægstad Farm.

INGRID, his daughter.

The BRIDEGROOM and his parents.

Three COWHERD GIRLS. A WOMAN IN GREEN.

The TROLL KING. Several Trolls of his Court.

Troll Boys and Girls. Two Witches. Hobgoblins, Brownies, Elves, etc.

An Ugly Urchin. A Voice in the Gloom. Birds' Cries.

KARI, a cotter's wife.

MR. COTTON, MONSIEUR BALLON, HERR VON EBERKOPF and HERR TRUMPETERSTRAALE, tourists.

A Thief and a Receiver of Stolen Goods.

ANITRA, daughter of a Bedouin Chief.

Arabs, Female Slaves, Dancing Girls, etc.

The Statue of Memnon (with song). The Sphinx at Gizeh (dumb).

PROFESSOR BEGRIFFENFELDT, Ph.D., in charge of the Lunatic Asylum at Cairo.

Lunatics with their Keepers.

HUHU, a language-reformer from the Malabar coast.

HUSSEIN, an Eastern Secretary of State.

A Fellah, carrying a royal mummy.

A Norwegian Skipper and his Crew. A Strange Passenger.

A PRIEST. A Funeral Party. A BUTTON-MOULDER. A THIN MAN.

*(The action, which begins in the early years of the century and ends somewhere about our own day [1867], takes place partly in the Gudbrandsdal and on the surrounding mountain-tops, partly on the coast of Morocco, in the Sahara Desert, in the Cairo Lunatic Asylum, at Sea, etc.)*

# PEER GYNT

## ACT I

### Scene I

(Scene.—*The wooded mountain-side near* Aase's *farm, with a stream rushing past. On the farther bank stands an old mill. It is a hot summer's day.* Peer Gynt, *a sturdy youth of twenty, comes down the path, followed by his mother* Aase, *who is short and slight. She is scolding him angrily.*)

Aase.

Peer, you're lying!

Peer Gynt (*without stopping*).

No, I'm not!

Aase.

Well then, will you swear it's true?

Peer Gynt.

Swear? Why should I?

Aase.

Ah, you daren't!
Your whole tale's a pack of lies!

Peer Gynt.

Every blessed word is true!

1

AASE (*facing him*).

I wonder you can face your mother!
First of all, just when the work
Is at busiest, off you go
To prowl about the hills for weeks
After reindeer in the snow;
Come back with your clothes in rags,
Game-bag empty—and no gun!
Then you have the cheek to think
You can make your mother swallow
Such a pack of lies as this
About your hunting!—Tell me, then,
Where you found this precious buck?

PEER GYNT.
West of Gendin.

AASE (*with a scornful laugh*).
I dare say!

PEER GYNT.
I was leeward of the blast,
And behind a clump of trees
He was scraping in the snow
For some moss——

AASE (*as before*).
Oh yes, no doubt!

PEER GYNT.
I stood and listened, held my breath,
Heard the scraping of his hoof,
Saw the antlers of his horns;
Then upon my belly crawled
Carefully between the rocks;
Peeped from cover of the stones—
Such a buck, so sleek and fat,
I suppose was never seen!

AASE.

I expect not!

PEER GYNT.

Then I fired!
Down the buck came on the ground!
But the moment he had fallen
I was up astride his back,
On his left ear got my grip,
And was just in act of thrusting
With my knife into his gullet
Just behind his head—when, hi!
With a scream the ugly beggar
Scrambled up upon his feet.
From my hand his sudden back-throw
Jerked my hunting-knife and scabbard,
Pinned me to his loins and held me
By the legs between his antlers
Like a pair of mighty pincers;
Then he rushed with bounds gigantic
Right along the ridge of Gendin!

AASE (*involuntarily*).

Christ in Heaven—!

PEER GYNT.

Have you ever
Been upon the ridge of Gendin?
Fully half a mile it stretches,
At the top as sheer and narrow
As a scythe-blade. Looking downward—
Past the slopes and past the glaciers,
Past the grey ravines and gullies—
Either side you see the water
Wrapped in dark and gloomy slumber
Half a mile at least beneath you.
    Right along it he and I
    Clove our passage through the air.
    Never rode I such a steed!

Far ahead the peaks were sparkling
As we rushed along.  Beneath us
In the void the dusky eagles
Fell away like motes in sunshine;
You could see the ice-floes breaking
On the banks, yet hear no murmur.
But the sprites that turn us dizzy
Danced and sang and circled round us—
I could hear and seemed to see them!

AASE (*swaying as if giddy*).

Heaven help us!

PEER GYNT.

On a sudden,
On the precipice's edge,
From the hole where it lay hidden
Almost at the reindeer's feet,
Up a ptarmigan rose, cackling,
Flapping with its wings in terror.
Then the reindeer, madly swerving,
Gave a bound sky-high that sent us
Plunging o'er the edge and downwards.
   [AASE *totters and grasps a tree-trunk.* PEER
     GYNT *continues.*
Gloomy precipice behind us!—
Fathomless abyss below us!
First through clouds of mist we hurtled,
Then a flock of gulls we scattered
Wheeling through the air and screaming.
   Downward still and ever downwards!
But beneath us something glistened
Whitish, like a reindeer's belly.
Mother, 'twas our own reflection
Mirrored in the lake beneath us,
Rushing up, it seemed, to meet us
Just as swiftly and as madly
As we downwards rushed towards it.

AASE (*gasping for breath*).
Peer! God help me—! Tell me quickly!

PEER GYNT.
Buck from air and buck from water
Met with mighty splash together,
Scattering the foam around us.
Then at last we somehow managed
To the northern shore to struggle;
Buck, he swam and dragged me after—
So I got home——

AASE.
But where's the reindeer?

PEER GYNT.
I expect he's where I left him—
[*Snaps his fingers, turns on his heel and adds:*
If you find him, you may keep him!

AASE.
And your neck you haven't broken?
Nor your legs? Nor smashed your backbone?
Praise and thanks to God be given
For His goodness that has saved you!
There's a rent across your breeches,
It is true; but that is scarcely
Worth a mention when one thinks
What the harm might well have been
From a leap like that of yours——
[*She suddenly pauses, stares at him with open
mouth, seems to struggle for speech and at
last breaks out.*
Oh, you lying little devil!—
Christ above us, what a liar!
All that rigmarole you told me
Is the tale of Gudbrand Glesnë [1]

[1] The tale is told in Asbjörnsen's *Norske Huldre-Eventyr*,
from another tale in which collection Ibsen derived the germ
of his " Peer Gynt " idea.

That I heard when I was twenty.
'Twas to him that all this happened,
Not to you, you——

PEER GYNT.

             Yes, it did;
History repeats itself.

AASE.

Lies, I know, can be so furbished
And disguised in gorgeous wrappings
That their skinny carcasses
Not a soul would recognize.
That's what you've been doing now,
With your wonderful adventures—
Eagles' wings, and all that nonsense—
Making up a pack of lies,
Tales of breathless risk and danger,
Till one can no longer tell
What one knows and what one doesn't.

PEER GYNT.

If a man said that to me,
I would beat him to a jelly.

AASE (*in tears*).

Would to God that I were dead
And buried in the cold black earth!
Prayers and tears have no effect.
You're a hopeless ne'er-do-well!

PEER GYNT.

Dearest pretty little mother,
Every word you say is true;
So be gay and happy——

AASE.

             Pshaw!
Don't talk nonsense. How could I

Be happy, if I wanted to,
With such a pig as you for son?
Don't you think it's pretty hard
For a poor weak widow never
To feel anything but shame?    [*Weeps again.*
How much is there left of all
That your grandfather enjoyed
In his days of comfort ?  Where
Are the well-filled money-bags
Left by good old Rasmus Gynt?
'Twas your father emptied them,
Pouring money out like sand—
Buying land in all directions—
Gilded coach to ride about in.
Where's the stuff so freely wasted
At the famous winter banquet,
When each guest sent glass and bottle
Crash against the wall behind him?

### PEER GYNT.

Where are the snows of yester year?

### AASE.

Hold your tongue when I am speaking!
See the farmhouse—scarce a window
But is smashed and stuffed with dish-clout;
Scarce a hedge or fence is standing;
No protection for the cattle
From the wind and wet; the meadows
And the fields all lying fallow;
Every month distraint on something——

### PEER GYNT.

That's enough of dismal wailing!
Often when our luck's been drooping
It has grown as strong as ever.

### AASE.

Where it grew, the soil is poisoned.
Peer, you certainly don't lack

Good opinion of yourself.
You are just as brisk and bumptious,
Just as pert, as when the Parson
Who had come from Copenhagen
Asked you what your Christian name was,
Telling you that where he came from
Lots of men of highest station
Would be glad to be as clever;
And your father was so grateful
For his amiable praises
That a horse and sledge he gave him.
Ah me! All went well in those days.
Parsons, Captains and such people,
Dropping in to see us daily—
Filling up with drink and victuals
Until they were nearly bursting.
But it's when your fortunes alter
That you get to know your neighbours.
Since the day when " rich John Gynt "
Took the road with pedlar's pack,
Not a soul has e'er been near us.
                    [*Wipes her eyes with her apron.*
You're a stout and strapping fellow—
You should be a staff supporting
Your old mother in her troubles.
You should work the farm for profit,
And look after all the little
That your father left behind him. [*Weeps again.*
Heaven knows, it's precious little
Use you've been to me, you rascal.
When you are at home, you're loafing
By the fire, or grubbing idly
In the ashes and the embers;
When you're in the town you frighten
All the girls you meet at dances,
So that I'm ashamed to own you—
Fighting with the lowest tramps——

PEER GYNT (*moving away from her*).
Let me be!

AASE (*following him*).

Can you deny
You were foremost in the brawling
In that dog-fight of a scrimmage
Down at Lundë? Who but you
Cracked the blacksmith Aslak's arm?
Or at any rate disjointed
One of his ten fingers for him?

PEER GYNT.

Who has stuffed you up with that?

AASE (*hotly*).

Why, the cotters heard his howls!

PEER GYNT (*rubbing his elbow*).

Yes—but it was I that howled.

AASE.

What!

PEER GYNT.

Yes, mother, *I* got thrashed.

AASE.

What!

PEER GYNT.

Well, he's a lusty chap.

AASE.

Who is?

PEER GYNT.

Aslak—as I felt!

AASE.

Shame! I'd like to spit upon you!
To let such a scurvy swiller,
Such a worthless drunken rascal,

Beat you!                              [*Weeps again.*
                Often I've endured
Shame and scorn on your account,
But that this disgrace should happen
Is the very worst of all.
If he *is* a lusty fellow,
Need that mean that you're a weakling?


            PEER GYNT (*with a laugh*).

Well, it doesn't seem to matter
If I beat, or if I'm beaten—
Either way you start your wailing.
You may cheer up——


                AASE.

                    Are you lying
Now again?


            PEER GYNT.

                Yes, just this once;
So you may as well stop crying.
                    [*Clenches his left hand.*
See, 'twas with this pair of pincers
That I bent the blacksmith double,
While my right hand was my hammer——


                AASE.

Oh, you brawler! You will bring me
To my grave by your behaviour!


            PEER GYNT.

Nonsense! You're worth something better—
Better twenty thousand times!
Little, homely, dainty mother,
Just believe what I am saying.
All the town shall do you honour;
Only wait till I have done
Something—something really great!

AASE (*contemptuously*).

You!

PEER GYNT.

Who knows what lies before him!

AASE.

If you ever know enough
To mend your breeches when they're torn,
'Tis the most that I could hope for!

PEER GYNT (*hotly*).

I'll be a King, an Emperor!

AASE.

Oh, God help me! Now he's losing
What was left him of his wits!

PEER GYNT.

Yes, I shall! Just give me time!

AASE.

Of course! As the old proverb runs,
Everything comes to him that waits.

PEER GYNT.

Mother, you shall see.

AASE.

          Be quiet!
You are as mad as mad can be.
After all, it's true enough
Something might have come of you
If you'd thought of something else
But your stupid lies and nonsense.
Hægstad's daughter fancied you,
And you might have won the game
If you'd rightly gone to work——

PEER GYNT.

Do you think so?

AASE.

        The old man
Is too weak to stand against her.
He is obstinate enough
In a way; but in the end
It is Ingrid takes the lead,
And where *she* goes, step by step
The old hunks comes stumbling after.
              *[Begins to cry again.*
Ah, Peer—a richly dowered girl,
Heir to his lands, just think of it.
You might, if only you had liked,
In bridegroom's finery be dressed
Instead of in these dirty rags!

PEER GYNT (*quickly*).

Come on, I'll be a suitor now.

AASE.

Where?

PEER GYNT.

Why, at Hægstad!

AASE.

        Ah, poor boy,
The right of way is barred to you.

PEER GYNT.

What do you mean?

AASE.

        Alas, alas!
You've lost the moment—lost your chance—

PEER GYNT.

How's that?

AASE (*sobbing*).

While you were on the hills,
Riding your reindeer through the air,
Mads Moen went and won the girl.

PEER GYNT.

What? He? That guy the girls all laugh at?

AASE.

Yes. Now she's betrothed to him.

PEER GYNT.

Just wait till I have harnessed up
The cart——                    [*Turns to go.*

AASE.

You needn't take the trouble.
The wedding is to-morrow.

PEER GYNT.

Pooh!
I'll get there by this evening.

AASE.

Fie! Do you want to make things worse?
Just think how everyone will mock us!

PEER GYNT.

Cheer up! All will turn out right.
        [*Shouting and laughing at the same time.*
No, mother! We won't take the cart;
We haven't time to put the mare in.
                        [*Lifts her off her feet.*

AASE.

Let me alone!

PEER GYNT.

No, in my arms
You shall be carried to the wedding!
                [*Wades out into the water.*

AASE.

Help! Help! Oh, Heaven protect me!—Peer,
We'll drown——

PEER GYNT.

         Oh no, we shan't—I'm born
To meet a better death.

AASE.

        That's true;
You'll probably be hanged.     [*Pulls his hair.*
        You beast!

PEER GYNT.

You'd best keep quiet, for just here
The bottom's smooth and slippery.

AASE.

                Ass!

PEER GYNT.

Yes, abuse me if you like,
Words don't do any harm. Aha!
The bottom's sloping upwards now——

AASE.

Don't lose your hold of me!

PEER GYNT.

          Gee up!
We'll play at Peer and Reindeer now! [*Prances*
I am the reindeer, you are Peer!

AASE.

I'm sure I don't know what I am!

PEER GYNT.

See here, now—here's an even bottom.
*[Wades to the bank.*
Now give your steed a pretty kiss
To thank him for the ride you've had.

AASE (*boxing his ears*).

That's the thanks I'll give him!

PEER GYNT.

Wow!

That's a scurvy sort of tip.

AASE.

Put me down!

PEER GYNT.

Not till we get
To where the wedding is afoot.
You are so clever, you must be
My spokesman—talk to the old fool—
Tell him Mads Moen is a sot——

AASE.

Put me down!

PEER GYNT.

And tell him, too,
The sort of lad that Peer Gynt is.

AASE.

Yes, you may take your oath I will!
A pretty character I'll give you!
I'll draw a faithful portrait, too,——

And all your devil's pranks and antics
I'll tell them of—in every detail——

PEER GYNT.

Oh, will you!

AASE (*kicking him in her temper*).

        I won't hold my tongue
Till the old man sets his dog
Upon you, as upon a tramp!

PEER GYNT.

Ah, then I think I'll go alone.

AASE.

All right, but I shall follow you!

PEER GYNT.

Dear mother, you're not strong enough.

AASE.

Not strong enough? I'm so worked up
That I could smash a heap of stones!
Oh, I could make a meal of flints!
So put me down!

PEER GYNT.

        Yes, if you promise——

AASE.

Nothing! I'm going there with you,
And they shall know the sort you are!

PEER GYNT.

Oh no, you won't; you'll stay behind.

AASE.

Never! I'm going there with you.

PEER GYNT.

Oh no, you aren't.

AASE.

What will you do?

PEER GYNT.

I'll put you on the mill-house roof!
[*Puts her up there. She screams.*

AASE.

Lift me down!

PEER GYNT.

If you will listen——

AASE.

Bah!

PEER GYNT.

Now, little mother, listen——

AASE (*throwing a bit of turf thatch at him*).
Lift me down this moment, Peer!

PEER GYNT.

If I dared I would, indeed. [*Goes nearer to her.*
Remember to sit still and quiet—
Not to kick your legs about,
Nor the tiles to break or loosen—
Or an accident may happen,
And you might fall off.

AASE.

You beast!

PEER GYNT.

Don't shift!

AASE.

I wish you'd been shifted
Up the chimney, like a changeling! [1]

PEER GYNT.

Mother! Shame!

AASE.

Pooh!

PEER GYNT.

You should rather
Give your blessing on my journey.
Will you?

AASE.

I'll give you a thrashing,
Big as you are!

PEER GYNT.

Oh well, good-bye!
Only have patience, mother dear;
I shan't be long.
[*Is going; but turns, lifts a warning finger,
and says:*
But don't forget
You mustn't try to move from there!    [*Goes.*

AASE.

Peer!—Heaven help me, he is gone!
Reindeer-rider! Liar! Hi!
Will you listen?—No, he's off
Over the meadows.                    [*Screams.*
Help! I'm giddy!
[*Two* OLD WOMEN, *with sacks on their backs,
come down the path towards the mill.*

---

[1] She alludes to a Norwegian superstition that " change
lings " left by the fairies can be blown up the chimney.

FIRST OLD WOMAN.
Who's that screaming?

AASE.
Me!

SECOND OLD WOMAN.
Why, Aase,
You have had a lift in life!

AASE.
One that won't do me much good—
I'll be booked for heaven directly!

FIRST OLD WOMAN.
Pleasant journey!

AASE.
Fetch a ladder!
Get me down! That devil Peer——

SECOND OLD WOMAN.
What, your son?

AASE.
Now you can say
You have seen how he behaves.

FIRST OLD WOMAN.
We'll bear witness.

AASE.
Only help me—·
Help me to get straight to Hægstad——

SECOND OLD WOMAN.
Is he there?

FIRST OLD WOMAN.

You'll be revenged;
The blacksmith's going to the party.

AASE (*wringing her hands*).

Oh, God help me! My poor boy!
They will murder him between them!

FIRST OLD WOMAN.

Ah, we know that lot quite well;
You may bet that's what will happen!

SECOND OLD WOMAN.

You can see she's lost her senses.
                              [*Calls up the hill.*
Eivind! Anders! Hi! come here!

A MAN'S VOICE.

What?

SECOND OLD WOMAN.

          Peer Gynt has put his mother
Up upon the mill-house roof!

## SCENE II

(SCENE.—*A little hill covered with bushes and heather.
The high-road, shut off by a fence, runs at the back.
PEER GYNT comes down a foot-path, goes quickly up
to the fence, and stands looking out over the landscape
beyond.*)

PEER GYNT.

Yonder lies Hægstad. I shall soon be at it.
     [*Climbs half over the fence, then stops and considers.*
I wonder if Ingrid's sitting all alone there?
               [*Shades his eyes and looks along the road.*
No. Folk with gifts are swarming up like midges.
Perhaps I had better turn and go no farther.
               [*Draws his leg back over the fence.*

There'll be their grins behind my back for certain—
Whispers that seem to burn their way right through
    you.
> [*Moves a few steps away from the fence, and begins
>     absently plucking leaves.*

If only I'd a good strong drink inside me—
Or could just slip into the house unnoticed—
Or if no one knew me—. No, some good strong liquor
Would be best; their laughter wouldn't hurt then.
> [*Looks round suddenly as if startled, then hides
>     among the bushes.  Some* COUNTRY FOLK,
>     *carrying presents, pass along the road on their
>     way to the wedding.*

### A MAN (*in conversation*).

With a drunkard for father, and a poor thing of a
    mother——

### A WOMAN.

Yes, it's no wonder the boy is such a wastrel.
> [*They pass on.  After a little,* PEER GYNT *comes
>     forward, blushing with shame, and peeps after
>     them.*

### PEER GYNT (*softly*).

Was it of me they gossiped?          [*With a forced shrug.*
                                   Oh well, let them!
Anyway they can't kill me with their gossip.
> [*Throws himself down on the heather slope, and
>     for some time lies on his back with his hands
>     under his head, staring up into the sky.*

What a curious cloud!  That bit's like a horse,
And there is its rider and saddle and bridle,
And behind them an old crone is riding a broomstick.
                              [*Laughs quietly to himself.*
That's mother!  She's scolding and screaming " You
    beast!
Hi!  Peer, come back!"          [*Gradually closes his eyes.*
                             Yes, now she is frightened.—

There rides Peer Gynt at the head of his henchmen,
His charger gold-shod, silver-crested his harness.
Peer carries gauntlets and sabre and scabbard,
Wears a long coat with a fine silky lining.
Splendid the men in his retinue following;
But there's not one sits his charger as proudly,
Not one that glitters like him in the sunshine.
The people in groups by the wayside are gathered,
Lifting their hats as they stare up in wonder;
The women are curtseying, everyone knows it is
Kaiser Peer Gynt and his thousand retainers.
Half-guinea pieces and glittering shillings
Are strewn on the roadway as if they were pebbles;
Rich as a lord is each man in the parish.
Peer Gynt rides over the seas in his glory;
Engelland's Prince on the shore is awaiting,
And Engelland's maidens all ready to welcome him.
Engelland's nobles and Engelland's Kaiser
Rise from their seats as he deigns to approach them.
Lifting his crown, speaks the Kaiser in welcome——

ASLAK THE SMITH
(*to some others, as they pass by on the other side
of the fence*).

Hullo! Look here! Why, it's Peer Gynt the drunkard!

PEER GYNT (*half rising*).

What, Kaiser—!

ASLAK (*leaning on the fence and grinning*).

Get up on your feet, my young fellow!

PEER GYNT.

What the devil—? The blacksmith! Well, pray,
what do *you* want?

ASLAK (*to the others*).

He hasn't got over our spree down at Lundë.

PEER GYNT (*springing up*).
Just let me alone!

ASLAK.
                    That I will. But, young fellow,
What have you done with yourself since we parted?
It's six weeks ago. Have the troll-folk been at you?

PEER GYNT.
I can tell you I've done something wonderful, Aslak.

ASLAK (*winking to the others*).
Let's hear it then, Peer!

PEER GYNT.
                    No, it won't interest you.

ASLAK.
Shall we see you at Hægstad?

PEER GYNT.
                    You won't.

ASLAK.
                    Why, the gossip
Says there was a time you were fancied by Ingrid.

PEER GYNT.
You dirty-faced crow!

ASLAK.
                    Now don't get in a temper!
If the girl *has* refused you, there surely are others.
Remember the goodly John Gynt was your father!
Come along to the farm! There'll be girls at the
    wedding
As tender as lambkins, and widows well seasoned—

PEER GYNT.

Go to hell!

ASLAK.

You'll be sure to find someone who'll have you.
Good evening. I'll give the bride all your good wishes!
    [*They go off, laughing and whispering.* PEER
        *stands for a moment looking after them, then
        tosses his head and turns half round.*

PEER GYNT.

Well, Ingrid at Hægstad may wed whom she pleases,
For all that I care! I shall be just as happy!
                        [*Looks down at his clothes.*
Breeches all torn—all dirty and tattered.
If only I had something new to put on me—
                    [*Stamps his foot on the slope.*
If I only could carve at their breasts like a butcher,
And tear out the scorn and contempt that they show
    me!                    [*Looks round suddenly.*
What was that? Who is it that's laughing behind
    there?
I certainly thought that I heard—. No, there's no one.
I'll go home to mother.
        [*Moves off, but stops again and listens in the
            direction of Hægstad.*
                    The dance is beginning!
    [*Stares and listens; moves step by step towards the
        fence; his eyes glisten; he rubs his hands
        down his legs.*
How the girls swarm! Seven or eight of them
There for each man! Oh, death and damnation,
I must go to the party!—But what about mother,
Sitting up there on the roof of the mill-house—?
        [*His eyes wander towards the fence again; he
            skips and laughs.*
Haha! I can hear them out dancing a Halling![1]
Guttorm's the boy!—how he handles his fiddle!

---

[1] A boisterous country-dance.

Hear it sparkle and flash like a stream at a waterfall!
And think of the girls—all the pick of the neighbour-
   hood—
Yes, death and damnation, I'm off to the party!
   [*Vaults over the fence and goes off down the road.*

## Scene III

(Scene.—*The courtyard of the farm at Hægstad. The
farm buildings are at the back. A number of guests are
assembled, and a lively dance is in progress on the grass.
The* Fiddler *is seated on a table. The* Steward *stands
in the doorway. Cook-maids pass to and fro between the
buildings. The older folk are sitting about, gossiping.*)

### A Woman
(*joining a group of guests who are sitting on some logs*).

The bride? To be sure she is crying a little,
But that's not a thing that is out of the usual.

### The Steward (*to another group*).
Now then, my friends, you must empty your noggins!

### A Man.
Ah, thank you kindly—you fill up too quickly!

### A Youth
(*as he flies past the* Fiddler, *holding a girl by the hand*).
That's the way, Guttorm! Don't spare your fiddle-
   strings!

### The Girl.
Scrape till it echoes out over the meadows!

### Other Girls
(*standing in a ring round a youth who is dancing*).
That's a good step!

A GIRL.

He's lusty and nimble!

THE YOUTH (*dancing*).

The roof here is high and the walls far apart, you
know![1]
[*The* BRIDEGROOM *comes up whimpering to his*
FATHER, *who is standing talking to some*
*others, and pulls at his jacket.*

THE BRIDEGROOM.

Father, she won't! She is not being nice to me!

HIS FATHER.

What won't she do?

THE BRIDEGROOM.

      She has locked herself in.

HIS FATHER.

Well, you must see if you can't find the key.

THE BRIDEGROOM.

But I don't know how.

HIS FATHER.

      Oh, you are a nuisance!
[*Turns to the others again. The* BRIDEGROOM
*drifts across the courtyard.*

A BOY (*coming from behind the house*).

I say, you girls! Now things will be livelier!
Peer Gynt's arrived!

---

[1] His allusion is to the fact that in dancing the Halling a
great feat is to kick as high as the rafters of the roof; but he
is dancing in the open air.

ASLAK (*who has just come on the scene*).
Who invited him?

THE STEWARD.

No one did.
[*Goes into the house.*

ASLAK (*to the girls*).
If he should speak to you, don't seem to hear him.

A GIRL (*to the others*).
No, we'll pretend that we don't even see him.
[PEER GYNT *comes in, hot and eager, stops in front of the group and rubs his hands.*

PEER GYNT.
Who is the nimblest girl of the lot of you?

A GIRL (*whom he has approached*).
Not I.

ANOTHER.
Nor I.

A THIRD.
No, nor I either.

PEER GYNT (*to a fourth*).
Then *you* dance with me, for want of a better.

THE GIRL (*turning away*).
I haven't time.

PEER GYNT (*to a fifth*).
You, then.

THE GIRL (*moving away*).
I'm off homeward.

PEER GYNT.

Homeward to-night? Are you out of your senses?

ASLAK (*after a little, in a low voice*).

Peer, she has taken an old man to dance with.

PEER GYNT (*turning quickly to another man*).

Where are the disengaged girls?

THE MAN.

Go and look for them.
[*He moves away from* PEER GYNT, *who has suddenly
become subdued. He glances furtively and
shyly at the group. They all look at him, but
no one speaks. He approaches other groups.
Wherever he goes there is a sudden silence;
when he moves away, they smile and look after
him.*

PEER GYNT (*in a low voice*).

Glances—and thoughts and smiles that are cutting—
Jarring on one like a file on a saw-blade!
[*He sidles along by the palings.* SOLVEIG, *holding
little* HELGA *by the hand, comes into the courtyard with her* PARENTS.

A MAN (*to another, close to* PEER GYNT).

These are the newcomers.

THE OTHER.

Living out westward?

FIRST MAN.

Yes, out at Hedal.

THE OTHER.

Ah, yes—of course they are.
[PEER GYNT *advances to meet the newcomers,
points to* SOLVEIG *and addresses her* FATHER.

PEER GYNT.

May I dance with your daughter?

THE FATHER.

You may; but before that
We must go indoors and give our hosts greeting.
[*They go in.*

THE STEWARD
(*to* PEER GYNT, *offering him a drink*).

As you're here, I suppose you must wet your whistle.

PEER GYNT (*looking fixedly after the newcomers*).

Thanks, I'm for dancing. I don't feel thirsty.
[*The* STEWARD *leaves him.* PEER GYNT *looks
towards the house and laughs.*
How fair she is! Was there ever a fairer?
Eyes glancing down at her shoes and white apron—
And the way she held on to her mother's skirt, too—
And carried her prayer-book wrapped in a kerchief—!
I must have a look at her!
[*Is going into the house, but is met by several*
YOUTHS *coming out.*

A YOUTH.

What, off already
Away from the dance?

PEER GYNT.

No.

THE YOUTH.

You're on the wrong road, then!
[*Takes him by the shoulders to turn him round.*

PEER GYNT.

Let me get past!

THE YOUTH.
Are you frightened of Aslak?

PEER GYNT.

I, frightened?

THE YOUTH.
Remember what happened at Lundë!
[*The group laugh and move off to where the danc-
ing is going on.* SOLVEIG *comes to the door.*

SOLVEIG.
Are you the boy who wanted to dance with me?

PEER GYNT.

Of course I am.  Can't you tell by the look of me?
Come on!

SOLVEIG.
But I mustn't go far—mother said so.

PEER GYNT.

Mother said?  Mother said?  Were you only born
    yesterday?

SOLVEIG.

Don't laugh——

PEER GYNT.
It is true you are almost a kiddie still.
Are you grown up?

SOLVEIG.
I shall soon be confirmed, you know.

PEER GYNT.

Tell me your name—then we can talk easier.

SOLVEIG.

My name is Solveig. Tell me what yours is.

PEER GYNT.

Peer Gynt.

SOLVEIG (*drawing back her hand from his*).
Oh, heavens!

PEER GYNT.
Why, what is the matter?

SOLVEIG.

My garter's come loose; I must tie it more carefully.
[*Leaves him.*

THE BRIDEGROOM (*pulling at his* MOTHER'S *sleeve*).
Mother, she won't——

HIS MOTHER.
She won't? What won't she do?

THE BRIDEGROOM.

Mother, she won't——

HIS MOTHER.
What?

THE BRIDEGROOM.
Unbar the door to me!

HIS FATHER (*in a low and angry voice*).
You're only fit to be tied in a stable, sir!

HIS MOTHER.

Poor boy, don't scold him—he'll be all right presently.
[*A* YOUTH *comes in, with a crowd of others who
have been dancing.*

THE YOUTH.

Brandy, Peer?

PEER GYNT.

No.

YOUTH.
Just a drop!

PEER GYNT.

Have you got any?

YOUTH.
Maybe I have.         [*Pulls out a flask and drinks.*
Ah, that's got a bite to it!
Well?

PEER GYNT.

Let me try it.                    [*Drinks.*

SECOND YOUTH.
And now have a pull at mine!

PEER GYNT.

No.

YOUTH.
Oh, what rubbish! Don't be a simpleton!
Have a drink, Peer!

PEER GYNT.
Well, give me a drop of it.
                    [*Drinks again.*

A GIRL (*in an undertone*).
Come, let's be off.

PEER GYNT.
Why, are you afraid of me?

YOUTH.

Do you think there is any that isn't afraid of you?
You showed us what you could do, down at Lundë.

PEER GYNT.

I can do better than that if I'm roused, you know!

YOUTH (*whispering*).

Now he is getting on!

OTHERS (*making a ring round* PEER).

Come on, now—tell us, Peer,
What can you do?

PEER GYNT.

Oh, I'll tell you to-morrow—

OTHERS.

No!

Tell us to-night!

A GIRL.

Can you show us some witchcraft, Peer?

PEER GYNT.

Ah, I can conjure the Devil!

A MAN.

My grandmother,
She could do that long before I was born, they say.

PEER GYNT.

Liar! What *I* can do, no one alive can do.
Why, once I conjured him into a nutshell,
Right through a worm-hole!

OTHERS (*laughing*).

Of course—we can guess that!

PEER GYNT.

He swore and he wept and promised to give me
All sorts of good things——

ONE OF THE GROUP.

But had to go into it?

PEER GYNT.

Yes; and then, when I'd stopped up the worm-hole,
Lord! if you'd heard him buzzing and rumbling!

A GIRL.

Fancy!

PEER GYNT.

'Twas like a great bumble-bee buzzing.

THE GIRL.

And pray have you got him still in the nutshell?

PEER GYNT.

No, the old Devil got right clean away again.
It is his fault the blacksmith dislikes me.

A BOY.

How's that?

PEER GYNT.

Because I took him to the smithy
And asked the smith to crack the nutshell for me.
He said he would. I laid it on the anvil;
But you know Aslak's very heavy-handed,
And with a will he laid on with his hammer——

A VOICE FROM THE GROUP.

Did he kill the Devil?

PEER GYNT.

No; he laid on stoutly,
But the Devil looked after himself and just vanished
Through ceiling and walls in a flame of fire.

SEVERAL VOICES.

And Aslak—?

PEER GYNT.

Stood there with his hands well roasted.
And since that day we have never been friendly.
[*General laughter.*

VOICES.

That's a fine rigmarole!

OTHERS.

Easily his best one!

PEER GYNT.

Do you suggest that I made it up?

A MAN.

Oh no,
I know you didn't; for I've heard the story
Told by my grandfather——

PEER GYNT.

Liar! It happened
To me, I tell you!

THE MAN.

Oh, well—that's all right.

PEER GYNT (*tossing his head*).

Pooh! I can ride through the clouds on horseback!
There are lots of fine things I can do, I tell you!
[*Roars of laughter again.*

ONE OF THE GROUP.

Peer, let us see you ride clouds!

OTHERS.

Yes, dear Peer—!

PEER GYNT.

Oh, you won't need to beg me so humbly—
One day I'll ride like a storm o'er the lot of you!
The whole countryside shall fall at my feet!

AN OLDER MAN.

Why, now he's raving!

ANOTHER.

Yes, the great booby!

A THIRD.

The braggart!

A FOURTH.

The liar!

PEER GYNT (*threatening them*).

Just wait and you'll see, then!

A MAN (*half drunk*).

Yes, wait and you'll get your jacket well dusted!

OTHERS.

A good sound drubbing! A nice black eye, too!
[*The crowd disperses, the older ones angry and the
younger ones laughing and mocking him.*

THE BRIDEGROOM (*edging up to* PEER).

Peer, is it true you can ride through the clouds, then?

PEER GYNT (*shortly*).

Anything, Mads! I'm the boy, I can tell you!

THE BRIDEGROOM.

I suppose you've a coat that will make you invisible?

PEER GYNT.

An invisible hat, do you mean? Yes, I have one.
> [*Turns away from him.* SOLVEIG *comes across the
> courtyard leading* HELGA *by the hand.* PEER
> GYNT *goes to meet them, looking happier.*

Solveig! Ah, I am glad you have come to me!
> [*Grasps her wrists.*

Now I shall swing you round most nimbly!

SOLVEIG.

Oh, let me go!

PEER GYNT.

Why?

SOLVEIG.

You look so wildly.

PEER GYNT.

The reindeer grows wild when summer's approaching.
Come along, girl! Come, don't be sullen!

SOLVEIG (*drawing back her arm*).

No—no, I daren't.

PEER GYNT.

Why?

SOLVEIG.

No, you've been drinking.
> [*Moves away a little, with* HELGA.

PEER GYNT.
I wish I had stuck my knife in the lot of them!

THE BRIDEGROOM (*nudging* PEER's *elbow*).
Can't you help me to get in there where the bride is?

PEER GYNT (*absently*).
The bride? Where is she?

THE BRIDEGROOM.
In the loft.

PEER GYNT.
Oh, is she?

THE BRIDEGROOM.
Oh, come, Peer—dear Peer—you might try to!

PEER GYNT.
No, you must manage to do without me.
[*A thought strikes him. He says, softly and mean-
    ingly:*
Ingrid! The loft!          [*Goes up to* SOLVEIG.
Have you made up your mind, then?
[SOLVEIG *turns to get away, but he bars her path.*
I look like a tramp, and so you're ashamed of me.

SOLVEIG (*hastily*).
Oh no, you don't; that isn't the truth.

PEER GYNT.
It is.
And it's because you think I am fuddled;
But that was for spite, because you had hurt me.
Come along, then!

SOLVEIG.
I daren't, if I wanted to.

PEER GYNT.

Who are you frightened of?

SOLVEIG.

Mostly of father.

PEER GYNT.

Your father? Oh, yes—he's one of the solemn ones!
Sanctimonious, isn't he? Answer me!

SOLVEIG.

What shall I say?

PEER GYNT.

Perhaps he's a preacher?
And you and your mother the same, I dare say?
Are you going to answer me?

SOLVEIG.

Let me alone.

PEER GYNT.

I won't!    [*In a low but hard and threatening voice.*
   I can turn myself into a troll!
I shall come and stand by your bed at midnight;
And if you hear something that's hissing and spitting,
Don't you suppose it's your cat you are hearing.
It is I! And I'll drain your life-blood out of you;
And your little sister—I'll eat her up,
For I turn to a were-wolf whenever the night falls,
Your loins and your back I'll bite all over—
   [*Changes his tone suddenly and entreats her anxiously.*
Dance with me, Solveig!

SOLVEIG (*looking darkly at him*).

Ah—now you are horrid.
   [*Goes into the house.*

THE BRIDEGROOM (*drifting up to* PEER *again*).
I'll give you an ox, if you'll help me!

PEER GYNT.
                              Come!
[*They go behind the house. At the same moment
    a crowd comes back from dancing, most of
    them drunk. Noise and confusion.* SOLVEIG,
HELGA *and their* PARENTS *come out to the door.*

THE STEWARD
(*to* ASLAK, *who is in the front of the crowd*).
Be quiet!

ASLAK (*pulling off his coat*).
        No, here we'll settle the matter.
Peer Gynt or I shall get a thrashing.

SOME OF THE CROWD.
Yes, let them fight!

OTHERS.
        No, no, let them argue!

ASLAK.
No, we must fight; we want no arguing.

SOLVEIG'S FATHER.
Be quiet, man!

HELGA.
Will he hit him, mother?

A BOY.
It's better fun with his lies to tease him!

ANOTHER.
Kick him out, I say!

A THIRD.
No, spit in his face!

A FOURTH (*to* ASLAK).

Are you backing out?

ASLAK (*throwing away his coat*).
I'll murder the beggar!

SOLVEIG'S MOTHER (*to* SOLVEIG).

You see now what they think of the booby.
[AASE *comes in, with a cudgel in her hand.*

AASE.

Is my son here?  He shall have such a drubbing!
Just wait and you'll see what a thrashing I'll give
him!

ASLAK (*turning up his shirt-sleeves*).

No, *your* little body's too weak for that.

VOICES.

Aslak will thrash him!

OTHERS.

Slash him!

ASLAK (*spitting on his hands and nodding to* AASE).
Hang him!

AASE.

What?  Hang my Peer?  Just try, if you dare!
This old Aase's got teeth and claws!—
Where is he?                    [*Calls across the courtyard.*
Peer!

THE BRIDEGROOM (*running in*).
Oh, God in Heaven!

Come, father!  Mother!

HIS FATHER.
Why, what's the matter?

THE BRIDEGROOM.
Oh, Peer Gynt! I—!

AASE (*with a scream*).
What? What? Have you killed him?

THE BRIDEGROOM.
No, Peer Gynt—! Look, up there on the hillside!

VOICES.
With the bride!

AASE (*letting her cudgel fall*).
The beast!

ASLAK (*in amazement*).
Where the hill is steepest
He's climbing, by God!—like a mountain goat!

THE BRIDEGROOM (*in tears*).
And carrying her under his arm like a pig!

AASE (*shaking her fist at* PEER).
I wish he would fall and—!     [*Screams anxiously.*
Take care of your footing!

INGRID'S FATHER
(*coming out bareheaded and white with rage*).
I'll have his life for his rape of the bride!

AASE.
No, may God punish me if I let you!

# ACT II

## Scene I

(Scene.—*A narrow track high up on the mountainside. It is early morning.* Peer Gynt *comes hurriedly and sulkily along the path.* Ingrid, *wearing some of her bridal ornaments, is trying to hold him back.*)

Peer Gynt.

Get away!

Ingrid (*in tears*).
                What, after this?
Where to?

Peer Gynt.
                Anywhere you like.

Ingrid (*wringing her hands*).
What deceit!

Peer Gynt.
                It's no use railing.
We must go our own ways—both.

Ingrid.
Think what binds us two together!

Peer Gynt.
Oh, the devil take all thinking!
And the devil take all women—
Except one—!

43

INGRID.
　　And who is she?

PEER GYNT.
She's not you.

INGRID.
　　Who is it, then?

PEER GYNT.
Get you back to where you came from!
Go back to your father!

INGRID.
　　　　　Dearest——

PEER GYNT.
Pshaw!

INGRID.
　　You surely can't be meaning
What you say.

PEER GYNT.
　　I can and do.

INGRID.
To ruin me, and then forsake me?

PEER GYNT.
Well, what have you got to offer?

INGRID.
Hægstad farm, and something more.

PEER GYNT.
Is your prayer-book in your kerchief?
Where's your mane of hair all golden?

Do you glance down at your apron?
Do you hold on to your mother
By her skirt? Come, answer!

INGRID.

No; but——

PEER GYNT.

Shall you go to Confirmation
Very shortly?

INGRID.
No, but dearest——

PEER GYNT.

Are your glances always bashful?
If I beg, can you deny me?

INGRID.

Christ! I think he's lost his senses—!

PEER GYNT.

Does one feel a holy feeling
When one sees you? Answer!

INGRID.

No, but——

PEER GYNT.

Then what matter what you offer?
[*Turns to go.*

INGRID (*confronting him*).
Remember it's a hanging matter
To forsake me now.

PEER GYNT.
So be it.

INGRID.

Rich you may be, and respected,
If you take me——

PEER GYNT.

I can't do it.

INGRID (*bursting into tears*).

Oh, you tempted——

PEER GYNT.

You were willing.

INGRID.

I was wretched.

PEER GYNT.

I was mad.

INGRID (*threateningly*).

You'll pay a heavy price for this!

PEER GYNT.

I should call the heaviest cheap.

INGRID.

Is your mind made up?

PEER GYNT.

Like stone.

INGRID.

Very well.  You'll see who'll win.

[*Goes down the hill.*

PEER GYNT

(*is silent for a little; then suddenly calls out*).

Oh, the devil take all thinking!
And the devil take all women!

INGRID (*turns her head and calls up mockingly*).

All but one!

### PEER GYNT.

Yes, all but one.
> [*They each go their way.*

## SCENE II

(SCENE.—*By a mountain lake, on boggy moorland. A storm is blowing up. AASE, in despair, is calling and searching in every direction. SOLVEIG can scarcely keep pace with her. Her PARENTS and HELGA are a little way behind. AASE beats the air with her arms and tears her hair.*)

### AASE.

Everything's against me with the might of anger!
The skies and the water and the hateful mountains!
Fogs from the skies are rolling to mislead him—
Treacherous waters will delude and drown him—
Mountains will crush or slip away beneath him—!
And all these people! They are out to kill him!
By God, they shall not! I can't do without him!
The oaf! To think the devil thus should tempt him!
> [*Turns to SOLVEIG.*
Ah, my girl, one simply can't believe it.
He, who was always full of lies and nonsense—
He, who was only clever with his talking—
He, who had never done a thing worth telling—
He—! Oh, I want to laugh and cry together!
We were such friends in our need and troubles.
For, you must know, my husband was a drunkard,
Made us a byword in the neighbours' gossip,
Brought all our good estate to rack and ruin,
While I and Peerkin sat at home together—
Tried to forget—we knew no better counsel;
I was too weak to stand up stoutly to it.

It is so hard to face the fate that's coming;
And so one tries to shake one's sorrows off one,
Or do one's best to rid one's mind of thinking.
Some fly to brandy, others try romancing;
So we found comfort in the fairy stories
All about trolls and princes and such cattle—
Tales, too, of stolen brides—but who would ever
Think that such stories in his mind would linger?
               [*Becomes terrified again.*
Ah, what a screech! A nixie or a kelpie!
Peer! Oh, my Peer!—Up there upon the hillock—!
     [*Runs up on to a little hillock and looks over the
          lake.*   SOLVEIG'S PARENTS *come up to her.*
Not a thing to be seen!


               THE HUSBAND (*quietly*).
               It is worst for him.


               AASE (*in tears*).
Oh, Peer! my Peer! My own lost lamb!


          THE HUSBAND (*nodding his head gently*).
Aye, lost indeed.


                    AASE.
               Say no such thing!
He is so clever; there's no one like him.


               THE HUSBAND.
You foolish woman!


                    AASE.
               Oh yes, oh yes,
I may be foolish, but he is fine!


               THE HUSBAND
     (*always quietly and with a gentle expression*).
His heart is stubborn; his soul is lost.

AASE (*anxiously*).

No, no! God's not so hard as that!

THE HUSBAND.

Do you think he feels the weight of his sinning?

AASE (*hastily*).

No—he can ride through the air on a reindeer!

THE WIFE.

Christ! Are you mad?

THE HUSBAND.

What are you saying?

AASE.

There's nothing that is too great for him.
You'll see, if only he live to do it——

THE HUSBAND.

'Twould be best to see him hang on the gallows.

AASE (*with a scream*).

Good God!

THE HUSBAND.

When he's in the hangman's clutches
Perhaps his heart may turn to repentance.

AASE (*confusedly*).

Your talk will make me dazed and giddy!
We must find him!

THE HUSBAND.

Save his soul.

AASE.

And body!
We must drag him out if he's in the marshes,
And ring church bells if the trolls have got him.

THE HUSBAND.
Ah! Here's a track——

AASE.
          May God repay you
If you help me aright!

THE HUSBAND.
          'Tis our Christian duty.

AASE.
All the others are naught but heathens!
There was only one that would come and wander—

THE HUSBAND.
They knew him too well.

AASE.
          He was much too good for them.
                    [*Wrings her hands.*
And to think—to think his life is in danger!

THE HUSBAND.
Here's a footprint.

AASE.
          That's the way we must go, then!

THE HUSBAND.
We'll scatter and search below the pastures.
                    [*He and his wife go on.*

SOLVEIG (*to* AASE).
Tell me some more.

AASE (*wiping her eyes*).
          About my son?

SOLVEIG.

Yes.

Tell me everything!

AASE (*smiling and holding her head up*).

Everything?
'Twould weary you!

SOLVEIG.

You'd be sooner wearied
With telling me, than I with hearing.


## SCENE III

(SCENE.—*Low treeless hills below the higher mountains, whose peaks show in the distance. It is late in the
day, and long shadows are falling.* PEER *comes running
in at full speed, and stops on a slope.*)


PEER GYNT.

They're after me now—the whole of the parish!
And everyone's taken his stick or his rifle.
The old man from Hægstad is leading them, howling.
It has soon got abroad that Peer Gynt is the quarry!
A different thing from a fight with the blacksmith!
This is life! All my muscles are strong as a bear's.
　　　[*Swings his arms about and leaps into the air.*
To overthrow everything! Breast a waterfall!
Strike! Pull a fir-tree up by the roots!
This is life! It can harden and it can exalt!
To hell with all my trumpery lying!
　　[*Three* COWHERD GIRLS *run across the hill,
　　shouting and singing.*


THE GIRLS.

Trond of Valfjeld! Baard and Kaare!
Listen, trolls! Would you sleep in our arms?

E 747

PEER GYNT.

Who are you shouting for?

THE GIRLS.

Trolls! Trolls! Trolls!

FIRST GIRL.

Trond, come lovingly!

SECOND GIRL.

Come, lusty Baard!

THIRD GIRL.

All the beds in our hut are empty!

FIRST GIRL.

Love is lusty!

SECOND GIRL.

And lustiness love!

THIRD GIRL.

When boys are lacking, one plays with trolls!

PEER GYNT.

Where are your boys, then?

THE GIRLS (*with a burst of laughter*).

They can't come!

FIRST GIRL.

Mine called me dearest and sweetheart too,
Now he is wed to an elderly widow.

SECOND GIRL.

Mine met a gipsy wench up at Lien,
Now they are both on the road together.

THIRD GIRL.

Mine made an end of our bastard brat,
Now on a stake his head is grinning.

ALL THREE.

Trond of Valfjeld! Baard and Kaare!
Listen, trolls! Would you sleep in our arms?

PEER GYNT (*leaping suddenly amongst them*).

I'm a three-headed troll, and the boy for three girls!

THE GIRLS.

Can you tackle the job?

PEER GYNT.

You shall see if I can!

FIRST GIRL.

To the hut! To the hut!

SECOND GIRL.

We have mead!

PEER GYNT.

Let it flow!

THIRD GIRL.

This Saturday night not a bed shall be empty!

SECOND GIRL (*kissing* PEER).

He gleams and glitters like glowing iron!

THIRD GIRL (*kissing* PEER).

Like a baby's eyes from the blackest tarn!

PEER GYNT (*dancing with them*).

Dismal bodings and wanton thoughts,
Laughter in eyes and tears in throat!

THE GIRLS

*(making long noses at the mountain-tops, and
shouting and singing).*

Trond of Valfjeld! Baard and Kaare!
Listen, trolls! Did you sleep in our arms?
      [*They dance away over the hills with* PEER
            GYNT *between them.*


SCENE IV


(SCENE.—*Among the mountains. The snowy peaks
are gleaming in the sunset.* PEER GYNT *comes in,
looking wild and distraught.*)

PEER GYNT.

Palace o'er palace is rising!
See, what a glittering gate!
Stop! Will you stop!—It is moving
Farther and farther away!
The cock on the weather-vane's lifting
Its wings as if for a flight—
Into rifts of rock it has vanished,
And the mountain's barred and locked.
What are these roots and tree-trunks
That grow from the clefts of the ridge?
They are heroes with feet of herons—
And now they are vanished away.
A shimmer like strips of rainbow
My sight and mind assails.
Are they bells that I hear in the distance?
What's weighing my eyebrows down?
Oh, how my forehead's aching—
As if I'd a red-hot band
Pressing—! But who the devil
Put it there I don't know!          [*Sinks down.*
A flight o'er the ridge at Gendin—
Romancing and damned lies!

Over the steepest walls with
The bride—and drunk for a day—
Hawks and kites to fight with—
Threatened by trolls and the like—
Sporting with crazy lasses—
Damned romancing and lies!

            *[Gazes upwards for a long time.*

There hover two brown eagles;
The wild geese fly to the south;
And I have to trudge and stumble
Knee-deep in mud and mire.   *[Springs up.*
I'll go with them! Cleanse my foulness
In a bath of the keenest wind!
Up aloft I'll lave my stains in
That glittering christening-font!
I'll away out over the pastures;
I'll fly till I'm pure and clean—
Fly o'er the ocean waters
O'er the Prince of Engelland's head!
Ah, you may stare, you maidens;
I'm flying, but not to you.
It's of no use your waiting—!
Yet I might swoop below—
  Why, where are the two brown eagles?
  They've gone to the devil, I think!
See, there's the end of a gable,
It's rising bit by bit;
It's growing out of the rubbish—
See, now the door stands wide!
Aha! I recognize it,
Grandfather's farm new built!
Gone are the clouts from the casements
And the fence that was tumbling down;
Lights gleam from every window;
They are feasting there within.
  Listen! The Parson's tapping
His knife upon his glass;
The Captain's hurled his bottle
And broken the mirror to smash.
Let them waste and let them squander!

Hush, mother—there's plenty more!
It's rich John Gynt that is feasting;
Hurrah for the race of Gynt!
What's all the bustle and rumpus?
What are the cries and shouts?
" Where's Peer ? " the Captain is calling—
The Parson would drink my health—
Go in, then, Peer, for the verdict;
You shall have it in songs of praise:
Great, Peer, were thy beginnings,
And in great things thou shalt end.

[*He leaps forward, but runs his nose against a rock,
falls and remains lying on the ground.*

## SCENE V

(SCENE.—*A mountain-side, with trees in full leaf
through which the wind is whispering. Stars are
twinkling through the branches. Birds are singing in
the tree-tops. A* WOMAN IN GREEN *crosses the slope.
After her follows* PEER GYNT, *performing all sorts of
amorous antics.*)

THE WOMAN IN GREEN
(*stopping and turning round*).

Is it true?

PEER GYNT (*drawing his finger across his throat*).

As true as my name is Peer;
As true as that you are a lovely woman!
Will you have me? You'll see how nice I can be;
You shall never have to weave or to spin;
You shall be fed till you're ready to burst;
I promise I never will pull your hair——

THE WOMAN IN GREEN.

Nor strike me, either?

PEER GYNT.

No; is it likely?
We sons of kings don't strike our women.

THE WOMAN IN GREEN.

A king's son?

PEER GYNT.

Yes.

THE WOMAN IN GREEN.

I'm the Dovrë-King's daughter.

PEER GYNT.

Are you really? Well, well! How suitable!

THE WOMAN IN GREEN.

In the mountains my father has his castle.

PEER GYNT.

And my mother a larger one, let me tell you.

THE WOMAN IN GREEN.

Do you know my father? His name's King Brosë.

PEER GYNT.

Do you know my mother? Her name's Queen Aase.

THE WOMAN IN GREEN.

The mountains reel when my father's angry.

PEER GYNT.

If my mother begins to scold, they totter.

THE WOMAN IN GREEN.

My father can kick to the highest rafters.

PEER GYNT.

My mother can ride through the fiercest river.


THE WOMAN IN GREEN.

Besides those rags have you other clothing?


PEER GYNT.

Ah, you should see my Sunday garments!


THE WOMAN IN GREEN.

My week-day garments are gold and silver.


PEER GYNT.

It looks to me more like tow and grasses.


THE WOMAN IN GREEN.

Yes. There's just one thing to remember:
We mountain folk have an ancient custom;
All that we have has a double shape.
So when you come to my father's palace
It would not be in the least surprising
If you were inclined to think it merely
A heap of ugly stones and rubbish.


PEER GYNT.

That's just the same as it is with us!
You may think our gold all rust and mildew,
And mistake each glittering window-pane
For a bundle of worn-out clouts and stockings.


THE WOMAN IN GREEN.

Black looks like white, and ugly like fair.


PEER GYNT.

Big looks like little, and filthy like clean.

THE WOMAN IN GREEN (*falling on his neck*).
Oh, Peer, I see we are splendidly suited!

PEER GYNT.
Like the hair to the comb—or the leg to the breeches.

THE WOMAN IN GREEN (*calling over the hillside*).
My steed! My steed! My wedding steed!
[*A gigantic pig comes running in, with a rope's end
for a halter and an old sack for a saddle.
PEER GYNT swings himself on to its back and
seats the WOMAN IN GREEN in front of him.*

PEER GYNT.
Houp-là! We'll gallop right into the palace!
Come up! Come up, my noble charger!

THE WOMAN IN GREEN (*caressingly*).
And to think I was feeling so sad and lonely—
One never can tell what is going to happen!

PEER GYNT (*whipping up the pig, which trots off*).
Great folk are known by the steeds they ride!


## Scene VI

(SCENE.—*The Royal Hall of the King of the Trolls.
A great assembly of* TROLL COURTIERS, BROWNIES *and*
GNOMES. *The* TROLL KING *is seated on his throne,
with crown and sceptre. His children and nearest
relations sit on either side of him.* PEER GYNT *is
standing before him. There is a great uproar in the
hall.*)

TROLL COURTIERS.
Slay him! The Christian's son has tempted
The fairest daughter of our King!

A YOUNG TROLL.

Let me slash him on the fingers!

ANOTHER.

May I tear his hair out for him?

A TROLL MAIDEN.

Let me bite him on the buttocks!

TROLL WITCH (*with a ladle*).

Let me boil him down for broth!

ANOTHER (*holding a chopper*).

Shall he toast on a spit or be browned in a kettle?

THE TROLL KING.

Quiet! Keep calm!
    [*Beckons to his counsellors to approach him.*
       We must not be too boastful.
Things have been going badly with us lately;
We don't feel sure if we shall last or perish,
And can't afford to throw away assistance.
Besides, the lad is almost without blemish,
And well-built too, as far as I can gather.
It's true enough that he has only *one* head;
But then my daughter hasn't more than one.
Three-headed Trolls are going out of fashion;
Two-headed, even, nowadays aren't common,
And *their* heads usually are not up to much.
                  [*To* PEER GYNT.
And so, my lad, it's my daughter you're after?

PEER GYNT.

Yes, if she comes with a kingdom for dowry.

THE TROLL KING.

You shall have half while I am living
And the other half when I am done for.

PEER GYNT.

I'm content with that.

THE TROLL KING.

                    But stop, young fellow,
*You've* got to give some pledges also.
Break one of them, and our bargain's off
And you don't get out of here alive.
First, you must promise never to give thought to
Aught except what within these hills is bounded;
Shun the day, its deeds, and all the sunlit places.

PEER GYNT.

If I'm called King, 'twill not be hard to do it.

THE TROLL KING.

Secondly—now I'll see how far you're clever——
                    [*Rises from his seat.*

THE OLDEST TROLL COURTIER (*to* PEER GYNT).

Let's see if you've got a wisdom tooth
That can crack the nut of our monarch's riddle!

THE TROLL KING.

What is the difference between Trolls and Men?

PEER GYNT.

There isn't any, as far as I can gather;
Big trolls would roast and little ones would claw you—
Just as with us if only we dared do it.

THE TROLL KING.

True; we're alike in that and other things too.
Still, just as morning's different from evening,
So there's a real difference between us,
And I will tell you what it is.  Out yonder
Under the skies, men have a common saying:

" Man, to thyself be true! " But here, 'mongst Trolls,
" Troll, to thyself be—enough! " it runs.

TROLL COURTIER (*to* PEER GYNT).

Well, do you fathom it?

PEER GYNT.

It seems rather hazy.

THE TROLL KING.

" Enough," my son—that word so fraught with
    meaning—
Must be the motto written on your buckler.

PEER GYNT (*scratching his head*).

Well, but——

THE TROLL KING.

It *must*, if you're to be a king here!

PEER GYNT.

All right; so be it. It is not much worse than——

THE TROLL KING.

Next you must learn to value rightly
Our simple, homely way of living.
    [*He beckons; two* TROLLS *with pigs' heads, wearing
        white nightcaps, bring food and drink.*
Our cows give cakes and our oxen mead;
No matter whether their taste is sour
Or sweet; the great thing to remember
Is that they're home-made and home-brewed.

PEER GYNT (*pushing the things away from him*).

The devil take your home-brewed drink!
I'll never get used to your country's habits.

THE TROLL KING.

The bowl goes with it, and it is golden.
Who takes the bowl gets my daughter too.

PEER GYNT (*thoughtfully*).

Of course we're told that a man should master
His disposition, and in the long run
Perhaps the drink will taste less sour.
So, here goes!                                    [*Drinks.*

THE TROLL KING.
          Now that was sensibly said.
But you spit?

PEER GYNT.
I must trust to the force of habit.

THE TROLL KING.

Next, you must take off all your Christian clothing;
For you must know we boast that in the Dovrë
All's mountain-made; we've nothing from the valleys
Except the bows of silk that deck our tail-tips.

PEER GYNT (*angrily*).

I haven't got a tail!

THE TROLL KING.
          Then you shall have one.
                    [*To one of the courtiers.*
See that my Sunday tail is fastened on him.

PEER GYNT.

No, that he shan't! Do you want to make a fool of
     me?

THE TROLL KING.

Don't try with tail-less rump to court my daughter.

PEER GYNT.

Making a beast of a man!

THE TROLL KING.

              My son, you're wrong there;
I'd only make a courtly wooer of you.
And, as a mark of very highest honour,
The bow you wear shall be of bright flame-colour.

PEER GYNT (*reflectively*).

We're taught, of course, that man is but a shadow;
And one must pay some heed to use and wont, too.
So, tie away!

THE TROLL KING.

You're coming to your senses.

TROLL COURTIER.

Just see how nicely you can wag and wave it!

PEER GYNT (*angrily*).

Now, do you mean to ask anything more of me?
Do you want me to give up my Christian faith?

THE TROLL KING.

No, to keep that you are perfectly welcome.
Faith is quite free, and pays no duty;
It's his dress and its cut that a Troll should be known
    by.
If we're of one mind as to manners and costume
You're free to believe what would give us the horrors.

PEER GYNT.

You are really, in spite of your many conditions,
More reasonable than one might have expected.

THE TROLL KING.

We Trolls are better than our reputation,
My son; and that is another difference
Between you and us. But now we have finished
The serious part of the present assembly.
Our ears and our eyes shall now be delighted.
Let the harp-maid waken the Dovrë-harp's strings,
Let the dance-maiden tread the Dovrë-hall's floor.

*[Music and a dance.*

What do you think of it?

PEER GYNT.

Think of it? H'm——

THE TROLL KING.

Tell me quite openly. What did you see?

PEER GYNT.

See? What I saw was impossibly ugly.
A bell-cow thrumming her hoof on a gut-string,
A sow in short stockings pretending to dance to it.

THE TROLL COURTIERS.

Eat him!

THE TROLL KING.

Remember his understanding
Is only human.

TROLL MAIDENS.

Oh, tear his eyes out
And cut off his ears!

THE WOMAN IN GREEN (*weeping*).

Are we to endure it,
My sister and I, when we've played and danced?

PEER GYNT.

Oho, was it you? Well, you know, at a banquet
A joke is a joke—no offence was intended.

THE WOMAN IN GREEN.

Will you swear to me you were only joking?

PEER GYNT.

The dance and the music were both delightful.

THE TROLL KING.

It's a funny thing, this human nature;
It clings to a man with such persistence.
Suppose we fight it and it is wounded,
There may be a scar, but it heals up quickly.
My son-in-law's now most accommodating;
He has willingly cast off his Christian breeches,
Willingly drunk of the mead-filled goblet,
Willingly tied on a tail behind him—
Is so willing, in fact, to do all we ask him
That I certainly thought the old Adam banished
For good and all; then, all of a sudden,
We find him uppermost. Yes, my son,
You certainly must undergo some treatment
To cure this troublesome human nature.

PEER GYNT.

What will you do?

THE TROLL KING.

        I'll scratch you slightly
In the left eye, and then your vision
Will be oblique, and all you look on
Will seem to you to be perfection.
Then I'll cut out your right-hand window——

PEER GYNT.

You're drunk!

# Peer Gynt

THE TROLL KING

*(laying some sharp instruments on the table).*

   See, here are the glazier's tools.
You must be tamed like a raging bullock;
Then you'll perceive that your bride is lovely,
And never again will your sight deceive you
With dancing sows or bell-cows thrumming—

PEER GYNT.

That's fool's talk.

THE OLDEST COURTIER.

   It's the Troll King's word;
He is the wise man and you the fool.

THE TROLL KING.

Just think what a lot of trouble and worry
You will be rid of for good and all.
Remember, too, that the eye is the source
Of the bitter, searing flood of tears.

PEER GYNT.

That's true; and it says in the family Bible:
" If thine eye offend thee, pluck it out."
But, tell me, when will my sight recover
And be as it is now?

THE TROLL KING.

   Never, my friend.

PEER GYNT.

Oh, really! Then I must decline with thanks.

THE TROLL KING.

But what do you mean to do?

PEER GYNT.

   To leave you.

### The Troll King.

Softly! It's easy to get within here;
But the Troll King's gate doesn't open outwards.

### Peer Gynt.

You surely don't mean to detain me by force?

### The Troll King.

Now listen, Prince Peer, and give way to reason!
You're cut out for a Troll. Why, look, already
You bear yourself quite in a Troll-like fashion!
And you want to become one, don't you?

### Peer Gynt.

Of course.

In return for a bride and a well-found kingdom
I'm not unwilling to sacrifice something;
But all things have their natural limit.
I have taken a tail, it is true; but then
I can undo the knots that our friend has tied,
And take the thing off. I have shed my breeches;
They were old and patched; but that won't prevent
me
From putting them on if I have a mind to.
I shall probably find it just as easy
To deal with your Trollish way of living.
I can easily swear that a cow's a maiden;
An oath's not a difficult thing to swallow.
But to know that one never can get one's freedom—
Not even to die as a human being—
To end one's days as a Troll of the mountains—
Never go back, as you tell me plainly—
That is a thing that I'll not submit to.

### The Troll King.

Now, on my sins, I'm getting angry;
I'm not in the mood to be made a fool of.
You scurvy lout! Do you know who I am?
To begin with, you make too free with my daughter—

PEER GYNT.

That's a lie in your throat!

THE TROLL KING.

And you'll have to marry her.

PEER GYNT.

Do you dare accuse me of—?

THE TROLL KING.

Can you deny
That she was the object of all your desire?

PEER GYNT (*whistles*).

But no more than that. What the deuce does that matter?

THE TROLL KING.

You human beings are always the same.
You are always ready to talk of your souls,
But heed nothing really save what is tangible.
You think desires are things that don't matter?
Wait; your own eyes will prove to you shortly——

PEER GYNT.

It's no use baiting your hook with lies!

THE TROLL KING.

My Peer, ere the year's out you'll be a father.

PEER GYNT.

Unlock the doors. I'm going.

THE TROLL KING.

We'll send you
The brat in a goat-skin.

PEER GYNT (*wiping the sweat from his brow*).
> I wish I could wake up!

THE TROLL KING.

Shall we send to your Palace?

PEER GYNT.
> Oh, send to the Parish!

THE TROLL KING.

As you like, Prince Peer; it's your affair solely.
But one thing is certain—what's done can't be undone,
And you will see how your offspring will grow up!
Mongrels like that grow remarkably quickly——

PEER GYNT.

Oh, come, old chap, don't go at me like a bullock!
Fair maiden, be reasonable! Let's come to terms.
I have to confess that I'm neither a prince
Nor rich; and, however you take my measure,
I'm sure you won't find you've made much of a
    bargain.
> [*The* WOMAN IN GREEN *faints and is carried out
> by the* TROLL MAIDENS.

THE TROLL KING
(*looks at him for a while with a contemptuous
expression, then says*).

Dash him to bits on the rocks, my good children!

YOUNG TROLLS.

Dad, mayn't we first play at Owls and Eagles?
Or the Wolf-Game? Or Grey Mouse and Red-Eyed
    Pussy?

THE TROLL KING.

Yes, but be quick. I'm angry and sleepy.
Good night!                            [*Goes.*

PEER GYNT (*hunted by the* YOUNG TROLLS).
Let me go, you young devils!
[*Tries to climb up the chimney.*

YOUNG TROLLS.

Hobgoblins!
Brownies! Come, bite him!

PEER GYNT.
Ow!
[*Tries to get away through the cellar-flap.*

YOUNG TROLLS.
Stop all the holes up!

TROLL COURTIER.
How the youngsters enjoy it!

PEER GYNT
(*fighting with a little* TROLL *who has bitten deep
into his ear*).

You filth, let go!

TROLL COURTIER
(*rapping* PEER GYNT *over the knuckles*).
A little respect for a king's son, you scoundrel!

PEER GYNT.
Ah! A rat hole!                [*Runs towards it.*

YOUNG TROLLS.
Stop up the holes, Brownie brothers!

PEER GYNT.
The old man was foul, but the young ones are worse!

YOUNG TROLLS.
Flay him!

PEER GYNT.
I wish I were small as a mouse!

YOUNG TROLLS (*swarming about him*).
Don't let him escape!

PEER GYNT.
I wish I were a louse!

YOUNG TROLLS.
Now jump on his face!

PEER GYNT (*smothered in* TROLLS).
Help, mother, I'm dying!
[*Church bells are heard afar off.*

YOUNG TROLLS.
Bells in the Valley! The Blackfrock's Cows!
[*The* TROLLS *disperse in a turmoil and wild
shrieks. The Hall falls to pieces. Everything
disappears.*

SCENE VII

(*Pitch darkness.* PEER GYNT *is heard slashing and
hitting about him with a branch of a tree.*)

PEER GYNT.
Answer! Who are you?

A VOICE IN THE DARKNESS.
Myself!

PEER GYNT.
Let me pass, then!

VOICE.

Go round about, Peer! Room enough on the mountain.
[PEER GYNT *tries to pass another way, but runs
up against something.*

PEER GYNT.

Who are you?

VOICE.

Myself. Can you say as much?

PEER GYNT.

I can say what I like, and my sword can strike!
Look out for yourself! I'm going to smash you!
King Saul slew hundreds; Peer Gynt slays thousands!
[*Hits about him wildly.*

Who are you?

VOICE.

Myself.

PEER GYNT.

That's a silly answer,
And you can keep it. It tells me nothing.
What are you?

VOICE.

The great Boyg.[1]

PEER GYNT.

No, are you really?
Things were black before; now some grey is showing.
Out of my way, Boyg!

VOICE.

Go round about, Peer!

[1] A monstrous invisible Troll whose legend occurs frequently
in Scandinavian folklore.

PEER GYNT.

No, through you!          [*Hits out wildly.*
         He's down!
    [*Tries to get on, but always runs up against some
        thing.*

             Ha, ha! Are there more of you?

VOICE.

The Boyg, Peer Gynt! The one and only.
The Boyg that's unwounded, the Boyg that was hurt.
The Boyg that was dead and the Boyg that's alive.

PEER GYNT (*throwing away his branch*).

My weapon's bewitched; but I have my fists!
            [*Strikes out in front of him.*

VOICE.

Yes, put your trust in your fists and strength!
Ho, ho! Peer Gynt, they'll bring you out top!

PEER GYNT.

Backward or forward, it's just as far—
Out or in, the way's as narrow.
It's there!—and there!—and all about me!
I think I've got out, and I'm back in the midst of it.
What's your name! Let me see you! Say what you
     are!

VOICE.

The Boyg.

PEER GYNT (*feeling round him*).

     Neither dead, nor alive; slime and mistiness;
No shape or form! It's as if one were smothered
Amidst any number of bears that are growling
At being waked up!            [*Shrieks.*
     Why don't you hit out at me!

VOICE.

The Boyg's not so foolish as that.

PEER GYNT.

Oh, strike at me!

VOICE.

The Boyg doesn't strike.

PEER GYNT.

Come, fight! You *shall* fight with me!

VOICE.

The great Boyg can triumph without any fighting.

PEER GYNT.

I'd far rather it were the Brownies tormenting me!
Or even as much as a one-year-old Troll!
Just something to fight with—and not this blank
    nothingness!
It's snoring now! Boyg!

VOICE.

What is it?

PEER GYNT.

Show fight, will you!

VOICE.

The great Boyg can get all he wishes by gentleness.

PEER GYNT (*biting his own hands and arms*).

Oh, for claws and teeth that would tear my flesh!
I must see a drop of my own blood flow!
    [*A sound is heard like the beating of wings of great
    birds.*

BIRDS' CRIES.

Is he coming, Boyg?

VOICE.

Yes, foot by foot.

BIRDS' CRIES.

Sisters afar off, fly to meet us!

PEER GYNT.

If you mean to save me, girl, be quick!
Don't hang your head and look down blushing.
Your prayer-book! Hit him straight in the eye with
    it!

BIRDS' CRIES.

He's failing!

VOICE.

He's ours.

BIRDS' CRIES.

Come, sisters, quickly!

PEER GYNT.

An hour of torture such as this
Is too dear a price to pay for life.      [*Sinks down.*

BIRDS' CRIES.

Boyg, he is down! Boyg, seize him! Seize him!
    [*Church bells and the singing of psalms are heard
       in the distance.*

VOICE

(*with a gasp, as the* BOYG *gradually dwindles away
to nothing*).

He was too strong. There were women behind him.

## SCENE VIII

(SCENE.—*On the hillside outside a hut on* AASE'S *mountain pasture. It is sunrise. The door of the hut is barred. Everything is empty and still.* PEER GYNT *lies asleep by the hut. Presently he wakes and looks around him with listless and heavy eyes.*)

PEER GYNT (*spitting*).

I'd give the world for a pickled herring!
　　[*He spits again; then he sees* HELGA *approaching,
　　　　carrying a basket of food.*
You here, youngster? What do you want?

HELGA.

It was Solveig——

PEER GYNT (*springing up*).
　　　　　　Where is she?

HELGA.
　　　　　　　　　　　　Behind the hut.

SOLVEIG (*from behind the hut*).
If you come any nearer, I'll run away!

PEER GYNT (*standing still*).
Perhaps you're afraid I shall carry you off?

SOLVEIG.

For shame!

PEER GYNT.
　　　Do you know where I was last night?
The Troll King's daughter is hunting me down.

SOLVEIG.
'Twas well done, then, that we rang the bells.

PEER GYNT.

Oh, Peer Gynt's not quite the lad to get caught—
What's that you say?

HELGA (*crying*).

She's running away.
[*Runs after* SOLVEIG.

Wait for me!

PEER GYNT (*gripping her by the arm*).

See what I've got in my pocket!
A fine silver button! And you shall have it
If you speak up for me!

HELGA.

Oh, let me go!

PEER GYNT.

Take it, then.

HELGA.

Oh, let me go!—and my basket!

PEER GYNT.

You had better look out if you don't—!

HELGA.

Oh, you frighten me!

PEER GYNT (*quietly, as he lets her go*).

No; all I meant was: don't let her forget me!
[HELGA *runs off*.

# ACT III

## Scene I

(SCENE.—*The depths of a pine-wood. It is a grey autumn day, and snow is falling.* PEER GYNT *is in his shirt-sleeves, felling timber. He has just tackled a tall tree with crooked branches.*)

### PEER GYNT.

Oh yes, you're tough, my ancient friend,
But that won't help you; you're coming down!
                   [*Sets to work again.*
I know you're wearing a coat of mail;
But I'll slash through, were it never so strong.
Yes, you may shake your crooked arms;
I daresay you're both fierce and angry,
But all the same you shall bow to me—!
             [*Suddenly breaks off sullenly.*
What lies! It's only an ancient tree.
What lies! I'm fighting no mail-clad foe;
It's only a fir with its bark all cracked.
It's toilsome work, this felling timber;
But the devil's own job when all the time
One's dreams get mixed up with one's working.
All that must stop—this daytime dreaming
And always being in the clouds.
My lad, remember that you're an outlaw!
Your only shelter's in this forest.
        [*Works again hurriedly for a while.*
An outlaw, yes. You have no mother
To bring you food and spread your table.
If you want to eat, you must help yourself;
Get what you can from the woods and the stream,
Forage for sticks if you want a fire,

79

Look to yourself for everything.
If you need clothes, you must skin a deer;
If you want a wall to put round your house,
You must break the stones; if you want to build,
You must fell the timber and shoulder it
And carry it to the spot you've chosen.

> [*He lets his axe fall and stares in front of him.*

I'll build a beauty! Up on the roof
I'll have a tower and weather-vane,
And on the gable-end I'll carve
A lovely mermaid. Vane and locks
Shall be of brass, and window panes
Shall shine so bright that from afar
People shall wonder what it is
That they see gleaming in the sun.

> [*Laughs bitterly.*

Damned lies! Why, there I go again!
Remember that you're an outlaw, boy!

> [*Sets to work feverishly.*

A well-thatched hut is quite enough
To keep out both the frost and rain.

> [*Looks up at the tree.*

It's giving way. One more stroke! There!
He's down and fallen all his length,
And all the undergrowth is quivering.

> [*Sets to work to lop off the branches ; all at once
> he stops and listens, with uplifted axe.*

There's someone coming! Ingrid's father—
Trying to catch me treacherously!

> [*Hides behind a tree and peeps out.*

A boy! Just one. And he looks frightened.
He's glancing round him. What is that
He's hiding underneath his jacket?
A sickle. Now he stands and looks—
He lays his hand upon a log——
What now? Why does he brace himself—?
Ugh! He has chopped a finger off!
And now he's bleeding like a pig—
And now he runs off with his hand
Wrapped in a clout.

> [*Comes forward.*

He must be mad!
Chopped it right off!—a precious finger!
And did it, too, as if he meant it.
Oho, I see! If one's not anxious
To serve His Gracious Majesty
That is the only way. So that's it!
They would have called him for the army,
But he, I see, would be exempted.
Still, to cut off—? To lose for ever—?
The thought, perhaps—the wish—the will—
Those I could understand; but really
To *do* the deed! Ah, no—that beats me!
[*Shakes his head a little ; then resumes his work.*

### Scene II

(Scene.—*A room in* Aase's *house. Everything is in disorder. The clothes-chest is standing open ; clothes lie scattered about ; a cat is lying on the bed.* Aase *and* Kari *are trying to put things in order.*)

Aase (*running to one side of the room*).
Kari, tell me——

Kari.
What is it?

Aase.
Tell me——
Where is—? Where shall I find—? Oh, tell me,
Where is—? What am I looking for?
I'm going crazy! Where's the chest key?

Kari.
It's in the keyhole.

Aase.
What's that rumbling?

KARI.

The last load going off to Hægstad.[1]

AASE (*weeping*).

I wish they were taking me in my coffin!
What we poor creatures have to suffer!
God pity me! The whole house emptied!
What Hægstad left, the Judge has taken.
They've scarcely left me with a rag
To put upon my back. It's shameful
To have pronounced so hard a sentence!
        [*Sits down on the edge of the bed.*
The farm's gone now, and all our land.
He's a hard man, but the Law was harder;
No one to help me—none showed mercy—
Peer gone, and no one to advise me.

KARI.

You've got this house until you die.

AASE.

Oh, yes—the bread of charity,
For me and for my cat!

KARI.

         Old mother,
God help you! Peer has cost you dear.

AASE.

My Peer? I think you've lost your senses!
They got their Ingrid, safe and sound.
They should have rightly blamed the Devil;
He is the culprit, and no other;
'Twas he, the ugly beast, that tempted
My poor dear boy!

[1] As sentence for his crime of the rape of Ingrid, Peer Gynt
has been proclaimed an outlaw and the forest his only
sanctuary. All his possessions have become forfeit to Ingrid's
father and to the law.

### KARI.

Had you not better
Send for the priest? For all you know,
Things may be worse than you believe.

### AASE.

Send for the priest? Perhaps I'd better. [*Gets up.*
No, no—I cannot! I'm his mother;
I must help the boy—it's only my duty;
I must do my best, when everyone fails me.
They've left him that coat. I must get it patched.
I wish I had dared to keep the bed-cover!
Where are the stockings?

### KARI.

There, with that rubbish.

### AASE (*fumbling among the things*).

What's this? Look here! An old casting-ladle!
He used to pretend to mould buttons with this,
Melt them and shape them and stamp them too.
Once, when we'd company, in came the boy
And begged of his father a bit of tin.
" Not tin," said John, " King Christian's coin!
A silver coin to melt, and show
That you're the son of rich John Gynt."
May God forgive him, for he was drunk;
And when he was drunk it was all the same,
Tin or gold. Ah, here are the stockings!
They are all in holes; I must darn them, Kari.

### KARI.

They certainly need it.

### AASE.

When that is done,
I must go to bed. I feel so bad,

So wretchedly ill.                    [*Joyfully.*

      Oh, look here, Kari!
Two flannel shirts that they have forgotten!

#### KARI.

Aye, so they have.

#### AASE.

      That's a lucky find.
You might put one of them aside.
Or—no, I think we'll take them both;
The one he has on is so thin and worn.

#### KARI.

But, Aase, you know that it's a sin!

#### AASE.

Oh, yes; but you know the parson tells us
That all our sins may be forgiven.

### SCENE III

(SCENE.—*Outside a newly built hut in the forest.
Reindeer horns over the door. Deep snow everywhere.
It is nightfall. PEER GYNT is standing fixing a heavy
wooden bolt to the door.*)

#### PEER GYNT (*laughing now and then*).

There must be a bolt, to fasten my door
Against the Troll-folk and men and women.
There must be a bolt, to keep me safe
From all the plaguy crowd of goblins.
They'll come when it's dark, and I'll hear them
    knocking:
" Open, Peer, we are quick as thoughts!
Under the bed, on the hearth in the ashes,
You'll hear us creeping and crawling about;

We'll fly down the chimney like fiery dragons.
Hee-hee! Do you think your nails and planks
Can save you from plaguy goblin-thoughts? "
    [SOLVEIG *comes over the snow on ski; she has a*
       *shawl over her head and a bundle in her hand.*

### SOLVEIG.

God bless your work.  You must not reject me.
I had your message, and you must take me.

### PEER GYNT.

Solveig! It can't be—! Yes, it is!
And not afraid to come so near me!

### SOLVEIG.

I had your message from little Helga,
And others I had from the winds and the silence.
There was one in all that your mother told me,
And others that came to me in my dreams.
The dreary nights and the empty days
Brought me the message that I must come.
All light had gone from my life down yonder;
I had neither the heart to laugh nor to weep.
I could not tell what was in your mind;
I could only tell what I needs must do.

### PEER GYNT.
But your father?

### SOLVEIG.

       I've no one on God's wide earth
That I can call father or mother now;
I've left them for ever.

### PEER GYNT.

       Solveig, my dear—
To come to me?

SOLVEIG.

Yes, to you alone;
You must be all to me—friend and comfort.

[*In tears.*

The worst was leaving my little sister;
And worse than that, to leave my father;
And worst of all to leave her who carried me
At her breast; no, God forgive me,
The worst indeed was the bitter sorrow
That I must part from all my dear ones!

PEER GYNT.

And do you know the heavy sentence
The law pronounced? They've taken from me
Everything that I had or might have.

SOLVEIG.

'Twas not for what you had or might have
I gave up what was dearest to me.

PEER GYNT.

And do you know that if I venture
Beyond this forest I am forfeit
If any man can lay hand on me?

SOLVEIG.

When I asked my way as I came hither,
They questioned me—where was I going?
" I'm going home ": that was my answer.

PEER GYNT.

Ah, then I need no bolts to guard me,
No locks against the powers of evil!
My hunter's hut is consecrated
If you deign enter it and live there.
Dear, let me look at you! Not too near you—
I'd only look at you! How lovely,
How pure you are! Let my arms lift you!

How slim and light you are, my Solveig!
I'd carry you for ever, dearest,
And never weary! I'll not soil you;
I'll hold your warm and lovely body
At arms' length from me! Ah, my Solveig,
Can I believe I've made you love me?
Both night and day 'tis what I've longed for.
See, I have built this little dwelling—
It shall come down; it's cramped and ugly——

### SOLVEIG.

Little or big, I'm happy here.
Here one can breathe, in the buffeting wind.
Down yonder 'twas sultry; I felt hemmed in;
It was partly that, that drove me away.
But here, where one hears the fir trees soughing—
Such song and silence!—I feel at home.

### PEER GYNT.

But, dear, are you sure? It means for ever!

### SOLVEIG.

There's no way back on the road I have trodden.

### PEER GYNT.

You're mine, then! Go in! I would see you within!
Go in! I will fetch some wood for a fire,
To warm you snugly and flicker brightly;
You shall sit soft and never shiver.
> [*He unbars the door, and* SOLVEIG *goes in. He
> stands silent for a moment, then laughs aloud
> for joy and leaps into the air.*

My princess! Now she is found and won!
Now my palace shall spring into being!
> [*Seizes his axe and crosses over towards the trees.
> At the same moment an elderly woman in a
> tattered green gown advances out of the wood;
> an ugly child with a flagon in his hand limps
> after her, holding on to her skirt.*

THE WOMAN.

Good evening, Peer Light-Foot!

PEER GYNT.

What is it? Who are you?

THE WOMAN.

Old friends, Peer Gynt! My hut is quite near here.
We're neighbours.

PEER GYNT.

Indeed? I was not aware of it.

THE WOMAN.

As your hut grew up, so mine grew beside it.

PEER GYNT (*trying to get away*).

I'm in a great hurry.

THE WOMAN.

You always were that;
But, trudging along, in the end I come up with you.

PEER GYNT.

Old dame, you're mistaken!

THE WOMAN.

I know I was once;
That day when you made me such wonderful promises.

PEER GYNT.

I made you promises? Why, what the devil—?

THE WOMAN.

Do you mean you've forgotten the night when you
drank
At my father's? Do you mean you've forgotten——

### PEER GYNT.

I mean
I've forgotten what never took place to remember!
What nonsense is this? And when last did we meet?

### THE WOMAN.

The last time we met was the first time we met.
[*To the child.*
Give your father a drink; I think he is thirsty.

### PEER GYNT.

His father? You're drunk! Do you mean that this
urchin—?

### THE WOMAN.

You're not going to say that you can't recognise him?
Have you eyes? Can't you see that he's lame in the
shanks
As you're lame in your mind?

### PEER GYNT.

Do you mean to pretend that—?

### THE WOMAN.

You can't wriggle out of it!

### PEER GYNT.

That long-legged brat—?

### THE WOMAN.

He has grown very fast.

### PEER GYNT.

Why, you ugly old hag,
Do you dare to assert that this—?

THE WOMAN.

Listen, Peer Gynt;
You're as coarse as a bullock.          [*Weeps.*

Oh, how can I help it
If I'm not as fair as I was when you tempted me
Out on the hill-side up there in the mountains?
And when in the autumn my travail came on me,
I'd only the Devil to act as a midwife;
So it isn't surprising I lost all my beauty.
But if you would see me as fair as before,
You've only to turn out that girl that's in there,
Out of your house and your mind and your sight;
Do that, dearest lad, and my ill-looks will vanish!


PEER GYNT.

Get away, you old witch!


THE WOMAN.

You shall see if I will!


PEER GYNT.

I'll break your head for you!


THE WOMAN.

Try, if you dare!
You'll find me, Peer, a hard nut to crack!
Every day I shall be back again,
Peeping at doors and spying on both of you.
When you and your girl are sitting together,
And you are inclined for cuddling and fondling,
You'll find me beside you, claiming my share of it.
She and I will share you—turn about.
Good-bye, dear boy.  If you like the prospect,
Then wed her to-morrow!


PEER GYNT.

You devil's nightmare!

THE WOMAN.

But I had forgotten! You've got to look after
Your little son—this graceful urchin!
Come on, little imp, will you go to your father?

THE BOY (*spitting at* PEER).

If I had an axe, I'd split you in two with it!
Just wait!

THE WOMAN (*kissing the* BOY).

What a head he's got on his shoulders!
When you've grown up you'll be just like your father!

PEER GYNT (*stamping his foot*).

I wish you——

THE WOMAN.

As far off as now we are near you?

PEER GYNT (*clenching his fists*).

And all this comes——

THE WOMAN.

Just of thoughts and desires!
Hard luck for you, Peer!

PEER GYNT.

It's hardest for her—
For Solveig—my loveliest, purest treasure!

THE WOMAN.

Oh, yes; the innocent always suffer—
As the Devil said when his mother thrashed him
Because his father had come home drunk!
[*She moves off into the wood with the* BOY, *who
throws the flagon behind him.*

PEER GYNT (*after a long silence*).

" Round about," said the Boyg; that's how I must
     go.—
My palace has trembled about my ears!
She was so near me; and now there has risen
A wall between us, and all in a moment
My joy is gone and everything's ugly.
" Round about "—ah, yes; there's no straight road
That leads through this from me to her.
No straight road? All the same, there might be.
If I remember aright, the Bible
Says something somewhere about repentance—
But I've no Bible, and I've forgotten
The most of it, and in this forest
There's not a thing that will give me guidance.
Repent? It might take years to do it
Before I found the way. And, meanwhile,
A life that's empty, ugly, dreary;
And in the end from shreds and fragments
To try and patch the thing together?
One can patch up a broken fiddle,
But not a watch-spring. If one tramples
On growing things they're spoiled for ever.—
But, surely, the old witch was lying!
I can put all those ugly doings
Out of my sight! But—can I put them
Out of my mind? I shall be haunted
By lurking memories—of Ingrid—
Of those three girls upon the hillside.
Will they come too, and jeer and threaten,
And beg of me to hold them closely
Or lift them tenderly at arms' length?
It's no use! Were my arms as long
As fir-trees' stems or pine-trees' branches,
I should be holding *her* too near
To set her down again unsullied.
I must find some way round about,
Without a thought of gain or loss;
Some way to free me from such thoughts

And shut them from my mind for ever.

    [*Takes a few steps towards the hut, then stops.*

But—go in now? Disgraced and soiled?
With all these Troll-folk at my heels?
Speak, and yet not tell all? Confess,
And still be hiding something from her?

                [*Throws away his axe.*

No, no—to go and meet her now,
Such as I am, were sacrilege.

    [SOLVEIG *appears at the door of the hut.*


        SOLVEIG.

Are you coming, dear?


       PEER GYNT (*below his breath*).

            " Go round about "!


        SOLVEIG.

What do you say?

        PEER GYNT.

        Dear, you must wait.
It's dark, and I've a heavy load.


        SOLVEIG.

I'll come and help you bear the load.


        PEER GYNT.

No, do not come! Stay where you are!
I'll bear the whole of it.


        SOLVEIG.

          But, dear,
Don't be too long.


        PEER GYNT.

         Be patient, child;
Whether the time is long or short,
You must just wait.

SOLVEIG (*nodding to him*).

Yes, I will wait.
[PEER GYNT *goes off along the forest path.* SOLVEIG *remains standing at the half-open door.*

## SCENE IV

(SCENE.—AASE'S *house. It is evening. A log fire is burning on the hearth and lights up the room. A cat is lying on a chair at the foot of a bed on which* AASE *is lying, fumbling restlessly with the sheets.*)

### AASE.

Ah me, is my son never coming?
The nights are so weary and long.
I've no one to take him a message,
And so much to say to him now,
My time's running short—oh, how quickly!
To think that the end should be this!
If only I'd known, I would never
Have said a hard word to the boy!
[PEER GYNT *comes in.*

### PEER GYNT.
Good evening!

### AASE.

My boy! Oh, God bless you!
My dearest, at last you have come!
But how have you dared to come hither?
Your life is in danger, you know.

### PEER GYNT.

My life?—oh, my life doesn't matter.
I had to come down to you now.

AASE.

And Kari!—she said that you wouldn't!
Ah, now I can leave you in peace.


PEER GYNT.

Leave me? Why, what are you saying?
And where do you think you can go?


AASE.

Ah, Peer, it's the end that's approaching;
I haven't much longer to live.


PEER GYNT
(*turning away abruptly and walking across the room*).

I was running away from my sorrows,
And thought at least here I'd be free—!
Are you cold? Are your hands and your feet cold?


AASE.

Yes, Peer; you'll be done with me soon.
When my eyes lose their light you must close them—
But tenderly, carefully, Peer.
And then you must get me a coffin,
And see that it's handsome and fine.
Ah no, I forgot——


PEER GYNT.

Do be quiet!
Time enough for all that by-and-by.


AASE.

Yes, yes.      [*Looks uneasily round the room.*
    Do you see what a little
They've left me? It's all one to them.

PEER GYNT (*with a grimace*).

There you go!                              [*Harshly.*
          Yes, I know I am guilty.
But what do you think is the good
Of raking it up to remind me?


AASE.

No! It was the drink was to blame.
That damnable drink that destroyed you,
My boy; for you know you were drunk,
And didn't know what you were doing.
Besides—that wild ride on the buck!—
I'm sure it was not to be wondered
If you were not right in your head.


PEER GYNT.

Never mind all that nonsense and rubbish;
Never mind about anything now.
Let's put off serious thinking
Till later—another day.
               [*Sits down on the edge of the bed.*
Now, mother, let's have a gossip,
And talk of all sorts of things,
Except what's ugly and horrid
And hurts—let's forget all that.
Bless me! Why, there's old pussy!
To think that he's still alive!


AASE.

At night he seems so uneasy;
And we all know what that means!


PEER GYNT (*turning away*).

What is the news in the district?


AASE (*smiling*).

They do say that hereabouts
There's a girl that longs for the mountains——

PEER GYNT (*hastily*).

Mads Moen—is he content?

AASE.

They say that she will not listen
To the old folks' prayers and tears.
You ought to go and see her;
Maybe you could find a way——

PEER GYNT.

And what's become of the blacksmith?

AASE.

Oh, bother the dirty smith!
I'd so much rather tell you
Her name—that girl's, you know——

PEER GYNT.

No, we're going to have a gossip,
And talk of all sorts of things,
Except what's ugly and horrid
And hurts—let's forget all that.
Shall I fetch you a drink? Are you thirsty?
Can you stretch in that little bed?
Let me look—why, this is surely
The bed I had as a boy!
Do you remember your sitting
Beside my bed at night
Smoothing the bed-spread over
And singing me rhymes and songs?

AASE.

Yes, and we played at sleighing,
When your father had gone away—
The bed-spread was our apron,
And the floor an ice-bound fjord.

PEER GYNT.

Yes, but do you remember
The finest bit of it all—
Our pair of prancing horses?

AASE.

Why, yes—of course I do.
'Twas Kari's cat we borrowed,
And put up on a stool.

PEER GYNT.

To Soria-Moria [1] Castle,
That's westward of the moon
And eastward of the sunrise,
O'er hill and dale we flew.
A stick that we found in the cupboard
Made you a splendid whip.

AASE.

I sat up like the driver——

PEER GYNT.

Yes, and you shook the reins;
And turned round as we galloped,
To ask if I were cold.
God bless you, you old scolder!
You were a dear to me——
Why do you groan?

AASE.

It's my back, Peer;
It's sore from lying here.

PEER GYNT.

Stretch up and I'll support you.
There—now you're lying snug.

[1] The name is taken from the Arabic name of a group of islands beyond the Red Sea which were fabled to be the Isles of the Blest.

Aase (*uneasily*).

I want to get away, Peer.

Peer Gynt.

To get away?

Aase.

Ah, yes—
It's what I'm always longing.

Peer Gynt.

What senseless talk is that?
See, let me smooth the bed-clothes
And then sit on the bed,—
Now, we will make the time fly
With singing rhymes and songs.

Aase.

No, let me have my prayer-book;
My mind is ill at ease.

Peer Gynt.

In Soria-Moria Castle
They're having a splendid feast.
Rest back upon the cushions;
I'll drive you quickly there——

Aase.

But, dear, am I invited?

Peer Gynt.

Of course—and I am, too.
[*He throws a cord round the back of the chair on
which the cat is lying, takes a stick in his
hand and sits down on the foot of the bed.*
Gee up! Get on with you, Blackie!
Mother, you're sure you're not cold?

Aha! Now we shall be moving,
When Granë kicks up his heels!

AASE.

But, Peer—I hear something ringing——

PEER GYNT.

It's the glittering sleigh-bells, dear.

AASE.

They sound so strange and hollow!

PEER GYNT.

We're driving over a fjord.

AASE.

I'm frightened! What is it that's sighing
And moaning so wild and drear?

PEER GYNT.

It's only the firs on the hillside
Whispering. Just sit still.

AASE.

I seem to see lights in the distance.
What is it that's glistening there?

PEER GYNT.

It's the windows and gates of the Castle
Can you hear the dancers?

AASE.

              Yes.

PEER GYNT.

And outside stands Saint Peter
Asking you to come in.

AASE.

Does he greet me?

PEER GYNT.

                        Yes, with honour,
And offers you sweetest wine.

AASE.

Wine! Does he offer cakes, too?

PEER GYNT.

A plateful of them, yes!
And our parson's wife preparing
Your coffee and your dessert.

AASE.

What! Shall I really meet her?

PEER GYNT.

As soon and as oft as you please.

AASE.

You're driving your poor old mother
To a splendid party, Peer!

PEER GYNT (*smacking his whip*).
Gee up! Get on with you, Blackie!

AASE.

Are you sure that you know the way?

PEER GYNT (*smacking his whip again*).
I can see the road.

AASE.

                        But the journey
Makes me feel ill and tired.

PEER GYNT.

I can see the Castle before me;
The drive will soon be done.


AASE.

I'll lie back with my eyes shut,
And trust to you, my boy!


PEER GYNT.

Now show your paces, Granë!
The Castle is all agog;
The folk all swarm to the gateway;
Peer Gynt and his mother arrive!
Why, what's that, Mister Saint Peter?
You won't let my mother in?
You must look far, I can tell you,
To find a worthier soul.
Of myself I will say nothing;
I can turn back to the gate.
I'll take pot-luck, if you'll have me;
If not, it's all one to me.
Like the Devil in the pulpit,
I've told a heap of lies,
And have called my dear old mother
A silly old hen, I know,
Because she cackled and scolded;
But things must be different here.
You must respect and revere her,
Sincerely and honestly;
You'll not get anyone better
From our parts nowadays.—
Oho! Here's God the Father!
Saint Peter, you'll catch it now!
                [*Speaks in a deep voice.*
" Just stop that bullying, will you!
Mother Aase is welcome here! "
            [*Laughs aloud and turns to his mother.*

I knew how 'twould be! Saint Peter
Is singing small enough now!

        [*His voice takes on an anxious tone.*

Why do you stare so, mother?
Have you lost your senses, dear?

        [*Goes to the head of the bed.*

You mustn't lie and stare so—!
Speak, mother; it's I, your boy!

[*Feels her forehead and hands cautiously ; then
   throws the cord away on to the chair and says
   in a low voice :*

So it's that!—You may rest now, Granë;
Our journey's over and done.

        [*Shuts her eyes and bends over her.*

Thanks, dear, for all you gave me,
Thrashings and kisses alike!
And now it's for you to thank me—

        [*Presses his cheek against her lips.*

There—that was the driver's fee.

        [KARI *comes in.*

### KARI.

What? Peer! Then her deepest sorrow
And grieving will be forgot!
Good Lord, how sound she is sleeping!
Or is she—?

### PEER GYNT.

        Hush, she is dead.

[KARI *weeps by* AASE's *body.* PEER GYNT *walks
   to and fro in the room ; at last he stops by
   the bedside.*

### PEER GYNT.

See that she's decently buried.
I must try to escape from here.

### KARI.

Where shall you go?

PEER GYNT.

To the sea-coast.

KARI.

So far!

PEER GYNT.

Aye, and farther still.    [*Goes out.*

# ACT IV

## Scene I

(Scene.—*A grove of palm trees, on the south-west coast of Morocco. A dining-table is spread under an awning; rush matting underfoot. Farther back in the grove hammocks are hanging. A steam yacht, flying the Norwegian and American flags, is lying off the shore. A jolly-boat is drawn up on the beach. It is nearly sundown.* Peer Gynt, *now a good-looking middle-aged man, dressed in a neat travelling-suit, with a pair of gold-mounted eyeglasses dangling on his breast, is presiding at table as host to* Mr. Cotton, Monsieur Ballon, Herr von Eberkopf *and* Herr Trumpeterstraale. *The party have just finished a meal.* Peer Gynt *is passing the wine.*)

PEER GYNT.

Drink, gentlemen! If man is meant
For pleasure, let him take his pleasure.
The past's the past—what's done is done—
So we are taught. What may I give you?

HERR TRUMPETERSTRAALE.

As host, dear brother Gynt, you're splendid!

PEER GYNT.

The credit's just as much my purse's,
My cook's and steward's——

MR. COTTON.

Very well,
Then here's a health to all the four!

MONSIEUR BALLON.

Monsieur, your taste—your *ton*—is such
As nowadays one seldom meets with
Amongst men living *en garçon*—
A certain *je ne sais quoi*——

HERR VON EBERKOPF.

                 Quite so;
A breath, a gleam, of introspection—
World-citizenship's inspiration;
A glance that pierces clouds, that's free
From any narrow prejudices;
A glimpse of higher criticism;
A simple nature coupled with
A life's experience and thereby
Uplifted to the highest power.
I think that's what you meant—eh, Monsieur?

MONSIEUR BALLON.

Yes, very possibly.  In French
It doesn't sound quite so impressive.

HERR VON EBERKOPF.

Of course not.  French is somewhat cramped.
But if we want to trace the source
Of this phenomenon——

PEER GYNT.

              That's easy;
It's just because I've never married.
Why, gentlemen, the thing's as clear
As daylight.  What's a man's first duty?
The answer's brief: To be himself—
To take good care of all that touches
Himself and what is his.  But how
Can he do this if his existence
Is that of a pack-camel laden
With someone else's weal and woe?

HERR VON EBERKOPF.

But I dare say you've had to fight
For this self-centred concentration?

PEER GYNT.

Oh yes, I've had to fight for it,
But I have always won the honours;
Though once I very nearly fell
Into a trap, for all my cunning.
I was a wild, good-looking spark,
And let my roving fancy capture
A girl who was of royal blood——

MONSIEUR BALLON.

Of royal blood?

PEER GYNT (*carelessly*).

Or very nearly.
You know——

HERR TRUMPETERSTRAALE (*thumping on the table*).

These damned aristocrats!

PEER GYNT (*shrugging his shoulders*).

These bogus Highnesses, whose pride
Is to keep off from their escutcheon
The slightest speck of what's plebeian.

MR. COTTON.

And so it came to nothing, then?

MONSIEUR BALLON.

The family opposed the match?

PEER GYNT.

Quite the reverse!

MONSIEUR BALLON.
Ah!

PEER GYNT (*discreetly*).
               Well, you see,
Things took a turn which made them think
That it was high time we were married.
But, to be candid, the affair
From first to last was most distasteful.
In certain things I'm very dainty,
And also like my independence;
And when her father came and hinted
That he would make it a condition
That I should change my name and status
And lose my own nobility—
With lots of similar conditions
I could not stomach or accept—
I gracefully retired from it,
Refused the father's ultimatum,
And gave my youthful bride her *congé*.
    [*Drums on the table with his fingers, and says
       with a pious air:*
Ah yes, there is a Hand that guides us,
And we poor men can trust to that.
It's very comforting to know it.


MONSIEUR BALLON.
So the affair went by the board?


PEER GYNT.
No, it took on another aspect.
Outsiders meddled in the game
And raised an unexpected pother.
The youngsters of the family
Were much the worst. I had to battle
With seven of them all at once.
I never shall forget that time,
Though I emerged from it the victor.

Some blood was spilt; but still that blood
Sealed my certificate of valour,
And proved what I remarked just now—
That there's a Hand that guides us wisely.

### HERR VON EBERKOPF.

You have an outlook upon life
That proves you a philosopher.
For, while an ordinary thinker
Sees every detail separately
And never grasps the whole completely,
Your vision covers all together.
You have a universal standard
To measure life with. Your perceptions,
Like rays of sunlight, emanating
From a great central contemplation,
Pierce every fallacy.—And yet
You say you had no education?

### PEER GYNT.

I am, as I've already told you,
A self-taught man in every way.
I've never learnt methodically,
But I have thought and speculated
And read a bit on every subject.
I was not young when I began;
And so, of course, it wasn't easy
To plough the field of knowledge up
And do the thing at all completely.
I've learnt my history in scraps;
For more than that I've had no leisure.
And since, when evil days assail,
A man needs certain things to trust in,
I fitfully absorbed religion;
I found that it assimilated
Much easier if taken that way.
No use to glut one's self with reading,
But to select what may be useful——

MR. COTTON.

Ah, now, that's practical!

PEER GYNT.

Dear friends,
Just think what my career has been.
What was I when I first went westwards?
Quite penniless and empty-handed.
I had to work hard for my food—
No easy job, believe me, often;
But life, my friends, is always sweet,
And death, as we all know, is bitter.
Well! Luck, you see, did not desert me,
And good old Fate was always kindly.
Things moved, and I was always careful,
And so things went from good to better;
And, ten years after that, they called me
The Crœsus of the Charlestown traders;
My name was known in every port
And luck pursued me with my shipping——

MR. COTTON.

What was your trade?

PEER GYNT.

I trafficked most
In negro slaves for Carolina
And idols that were sent to China.

MONSIEUR BALLON.

Oh, fie, for shame!

HERR TRUMPETERSTRAALE.

Friend Gynt, how could you?

PEER GYNT.

You think my enterprise was passing
Beyond the bounds of what was lawful?

I felt the same thing very keenly;
I found it hateful in the end.
But, once begun, you may believe me
'Twas difficult enough to end it.
In any case, so big a business
Affected others by the thousand;
To break it off too suddenly
Would have, of course, been most disastrous.
I never like to break things off;
But all the same, I must admit
I've always fully been alive
To what you'd call the consequences;
And, when I've overstepped the bounds,
It's always made me feel uneasy.
Besides, I wasn't growing younger.
By that time I was nearly fifty,
And by degrees my hair was greying;
And, though my health was always perfect,
Thoughts such as this cropped up to plague me:
" Who knows how short the time may be
Before the Great Assize is summoned
And sheep from goats are separated? "
What could I do? To cease my trade
With China was impossible.
I found a way. I opened up
A second traffic to those waters;
And, though each spring I sent to China
Shiploads of idols, every autumn
I sent out Missionaries furnished
With everything that could be needful
To work conversion—stockings, rum,
Bibles and rice——

MR. COTTON.
         All at a profit?

PEER GYNT.
Oh, well, of course.—The plan worked well.
For every idol sold out yonder

There was a duly baptized coolie,
So one thing neutralized the other.
We kept the Missionaries busy,
Because they had to counteract
The idols that we were exporting.


MR. COTTON.

But what about the negro traffic?


PEER GYNT.

Why, there my morals triumphed also.
I felt the trade was scarcely suited
To one whose years were fast increasing;
You never know when death may claim you.
And then there were the thousand pitfalls
Dug by our philanthropic friends,
Besides the chance of being caught
And daily risks from wind and weather.
By taking thought I found a way.
" You'll have to reef your sails, friend Peter,
And see "—so I said to myself—
" How you can best retrieve your error! "
I bought land in a southern state,
And held back my last load of niggers
(Which was of first-class quality)
And settled them on the plantation.
They throve apace, grew fat and sleek,
And they, as well as I, were happy.
Yes, without bragging I may say
I treated them like any father—
And the result was handsome profit.
I built them schools, so as to set
A standard of morality
To be maintained, and saw to it
That it was kept well up to mark.
And then, to make the change complete,
Out of the business I retired,
And sold, with livestock, as it stood,
The whole plantation.  When I left,

To all alike, both young and old,
A gratis gift of grog was issued,
And every nigger got a skinful.
The widows, as an extra gift,
Were given snuff. And so I hope—
Unless the Word is merely froth
Which says one's deeds are surely good
If they are not as surely evil—
That all my errors are forgot,
And that perhaps in greater measure
Than in most people's case, my deeds
Will more than balance out my sins.

HERR VON EBERKOPF (*clinking glasses with him*).

How edifying 'tis to hear
A scheme of life worked out so deftly,
Freed from the fog of theories
And undisturbed by outer clamour!

PEER GYNT
(*who during the foregoing conversation has been
applying steadily to the bottle*).

We northern men are famous hands
At planning a campaign! The secret
Of life's success is very simple—
Merely to keep one's ears shut tight
To the insidious advances
Of a pernicious reptile.

MR. COTTON.

Aye,
But what's the reptile, my dear friend?

PEER GYNT.

A small one, always tempting men
To take irrevocable steps.      [*Drinks again.*
A man can venture without fear,
And keep his courage, if he's careful
Not to get definitely caught
In any of life's cunning pitfalls—

If he looks forward, and beyond
The present moment and its chances,
And always carefully preserves
A bridge behind him to retire on.
That theory has held me up
And always coloured all my conduct—
A theory I inherited
And learnt at home from early childhood.

MONSIEUR BALLON.

You're a Norwegian, I believe?

PEER GYNT.

By birth, yes; but by disposition
I am a citizen of the world.
For the good fortune I've enjoyed,
I have to thank America;
My well-stocked library I owe
To Germany's advanced young thinkers;
From France I get my taste in dress,
My manners, and whatever turn
I have for subtleness of mind;
England has taught me industry
And care for my own interests;
The Jews have taught me how to wait;
From Italy I've caught a dash
Of taste for *dolce far niente*;
And once, when in a sorry fix,
I reached the goal of my desire
By trusting to good Swedish steel.

HERR TRUMPETERSTRAALE (*lifting his glass*).
Ah, Swedish steel—!

HERR VON EBERKOPF.
                    Yes, first and foremost
We offer homage to the man
Who is a swordsman.
[*They clink glasses and drink with* PEER GYNT
    *who is beginning to get heated with wine.*

MR. COTTON.

> All you've said
Is excellent; but now, sir, pray
Tell us what you propose to do
With all your wealth.

PEER GYNT (*smiling*).

> Do with it, eh?

ALL (*drawing nearer to him*).
Yes, let us hear!

PEER GYNT.

> Well, first of all,
To travel; and that's why, you see,
I took you all on board my yacht
As company. I had a mind
To have a choir to worship at
My Altar of the Golden Calf——

HERR VON EBERKOPF.
How witty!

MR. COTTON.

> Yes, but no one sails
For the mere pleasure of a journey.
You have an object, without doubt;
What is it?

PEER GYNT.
To be Emperor.

ALL.
What!

PEER GYNT (*nodding his head*).
To be Emperor.

ALL.
> But where?

PEER GYNT.

Of the whole world.

MONSIEUR BALLON.
> But how, my friend—?

PEER GYNT.

Just simply by the power of gold!
It's not a new idea at all;
It has inspired my every effort.
In boyish dreams I used to travel
Over the sea upon a cloud;
I tried to soar to fancied grandeurs,
And then dropped down on to all-fours;
But to its goal my mind was constant.
Somewhere—I can't remember where—
It says that if a man shall win
The whole wide world, but lose *himself*,
All that he gains is only like
A wreath upon an empty skull.
That's what it says—or something like it—
And, trust me, it is pretty true.

HERR VON EBERKOPF.

But what, then, is the Gyntian Self?

PEER GYNT.

The world which lies within my brain;
Which makes me *me*, and no one else—
No more than God can be the Devil.

HERR TRUMPETERSTRAALE.

Now I can see at what you're driving!

MONSIEUR BALLON.

Sublime philosopher!

HERR VON EBERKOPF.
          Great poet!

PEER GYNT (*with growing exaltation*).

The Gyntian Self!—An army, that,
Of wishes, appetites, desires!
The Gyntian Self! It is a sea
Of fancies, claims and aspirations;
In fact, it's all that swells within
My breast, and makes it come about
That I am I and live as such.
But, just as our Good Lord had need
Of earthly mould to be earth's God,
So I have need of lots of gold
If I'm to be an Emperor.

MONSIEUR BALLON.

But you are rich!

PEER GYNT.

          Not rich enough.
Enough, perhaps, for me to pose
For two or three days as a princeling
In some such place as Lippe-Detmold;
But I must be *myself*—complete—
A Gynt fit for the universe—
Sir Peter Gynt from head to heels!

MONSIEUR BALLON (*in transports*).

To purchase all the loveliest things
The world can offer!

HERR VON EBERKOPF.

          All the bins
Of century-old Johannisberger!

HERR TRUMPETERSTRAALE.

The armoury of Charles the Twelfth!

MR. COTTON.

But, before all, to seize the chance
Of profitable business.

PEER GYNT.

               Well,
I've found a way to get them all,
And that is why we're anchored here;
To-night our course will be to northward.
The newspapers I've just received
Have brought me some important news.
           [*Rises and lifts his glass.*
It shows that fortune always favours
Those who have confidence to grasp it——

ALL.

Well? Tell us—!

PEER GYNT.

           Greece is in an uproar.

ALL (*springing to their feet*).

What, have the Greeks—?

PEER GYNT.

               They have revolted.

ALL.

Hurrah!

PEER GYNT.

And Turkey's in a hole.

MONSIEUR BALLON.

To Greece! The way to glory's open!
I'll help them with my sword of France!

HERR VON EBERKOPF.

I with my voice—but at a distance!

Mr. Cotton.

I'll get a contract to supply them!

Herr Trumpeterstraale.

Let us away! I'll find at Bender [1]
Charles the Twelfth's famous spur-buckles!

Monsieur Ballon
(*falling on* Peer Gynt's *neck*).

Forgive me, friend, if for a moment
I had misjudged you!

Herr von Eberkopf
(*grasping* Peer Gynt *by the hand*).

         I'm a fool!
I almost took you for a scoundrel!

Mr. Cotton.

That's much too strong—say, rather, for
A simpleton——

Herr Trumpeterstraale
(*embracing* Peer Gynt).

         And I, dear friend,
Had put you down as an example
Of the worst type of Yankee rascal!
Forgive me!

Herr von Eberkopf.

         We were all mistaken——

---

[1] A town in Bessarabia, on the Dniester, where Charles
XII. spent his years of exile after his defeat at Pultawa in
1709. The allusion to the spur-buckles is explained as
referring to the spurs with which Charles XII. is said in a
fit of anger to have torn the garments of the Turkish emissary
who brought him the news that the Sultan had concluded
a truce with Russia.

PEER GYNT.

What do you mean?

HERR VON EBERKOPF.

We now can glimpse
The banners of the Gyntian army
Of wishes, appetites, desires—!

MONSIEUR BALLON (*admiringly*).

That's what you meant by " being a Gynt "!

HERR VON EBERKOPF (*in the same tone*).

A Gynt that's worthy of all honour!

PEER GYNT.

But tell me—?

MONSIEUR BALLON.

Don't you understand?

PEER GYNT.

I'm hanged if I can take your meaning.

MONSIEUR BALLON.

Why, aren't you going to help the Greeks
With money and with ships?

PEER GYNT (*whistling*).

No, thank you!
I'm going to help the stronger side,
And lend my money to the Turks.

MONSIEUR BALLON.

Impossible!

### HERR VON EBERKOPF.

That's very funny!—
But you of course must have your joke!
[PEER GYNT *is silent for a moment, then leans on*
*a chair and assumes an air of importance.*

### PEER GYNT.

Gentlemen, we had better part
Before the last remains of friendship
Dissolve like wreaths of smoke. The man
Who hasn't anything may lightly
Take any chances; those whose all
Is no more than the scrap of earth
They stand on, are the fittest far
For sacrifice and cannon-fodder.
But when a man's well off, as I am,
He risks a greater stake than they.
Pray go to Greece. I'll land you there,
And furnish you with weapons gratis;
The more you fan the flames of strife,
The better it will be for me.
Strike hard for Freedom and the Right!
Attack the Turks and give them hell;
And meet a glorious end upon
A janissary's spear-point.—But,
Excuse me if I don't come with you.
[*Slaps his pockets.*
I've money in my pockets, and
I am Myself—Sir Peter Gynt.
[*Puts up his umbrella and goes into the grove*
*where the hammocks are hanging.*

### HERR TRUMPETERSTRAALE.

The swine!

### MONSIEUR BALLON.

He has no sense of honour!

MR. COTTON.

Oh, honour—let that pass. But think
What splendid profits we could make
If only Greece could free herself——

MONSIEUR BALLON.

I saw myself acclaimed a victor
By crowds of lovely Grecian women!

HERR TRUMPETERSTRAALE.

I felt those famous buckles safe
Within my Swedish grasp!

HERR VON EBERKOPF.

                 I saw
My glorious fatherland's *Kultur*
Spread widely over land and sea——

MR. COTTON.

The actual loss is worst of all.
Goddam![1]—I feel inclined to cry!
I saw myself proprietor
Of Mount Olympus, which contains
(Unless what men have said is false)
Rich veins of copper to be worked;
And the renowned Castalian stream—
Its many waterfalls would yield
A thousand horse-power, easily!

HERR TRUMPETERSTRAALE.

I shall go, all the same! My sword
Is worth more, still, than Yankee gold.

MR. COTTON.

Perhaps; but, fighting in the ranks,
We should be merely swamped by numbers.
What profit should we get from that?

[1] So in the original.

MONSIEUR BALLON.

Curse it! So near the heights of fortune—
And then to be dashed down again.

MR. COTTON (*shaking his fist at the yacht*).

To think that all this nabob's gold
That he has sweated from his niggers
Is in that ship!

HERR VON EBERKOPF.

An inspiration!
Come on, and let us act! His empire
Shall come to nothing now! Hurrah!

MONSIEUR BALLON.

What will you do?

HERR VON EBERKOPF.

I'll seize his power!
The crew will easily be bought.
On board! I'll commandeer his yacht!

MR. COTTON.

You'll—what?

HERR VON EBERKOPF.

I mean to bag the lot.
[*Goes towards the jolly-boat.*

MR. COTTON.

It's clearly to my interest
To share with you.                [*Follows him.*

HERR TRUMPETERSTRAALE.

There goes a scamp!

MONSIEUR BALLON.

A proper scoundrel! But—*enfin!*
[*Follows the others.*

HERR TRUMPETERSTRAALE.

Well, I suppose I may as well
Go with them—under protest, though!
                              [*Follows.*


## SCENE II

(SCENE.—*Another part of the coast. Moonlight and
passing clouds. Out at sea the yacht is seen steaming
at full speed.* PEER GYNT *is running along the shore,
now pinching himself in the arm, now staring out to
sea.*)

PEER GYNT.

It's nightmare!—Illusion!—I soon shall wake up!
It's heading to sea! And at top of its speed!
It's a dream, and I'm sleeping! I'm drunk or I'm mad!
                              [*Wrings his hands.*
It's impossible that I should perish like this!
                              [*Tears his hair.*
It's a dream! It *must* be—it *shall* be—a dream!
It's terrible! Ah, but alas it is true!
My scoundrelly friends—! Oh, hear me, Good Lord!
You are Wisdom and Justice—oh, punish them, Lord!
                              [*Stretches up his arms.*
It is *I*—Peter Gynt! Do look after me, Lord!
Take care of me, Father, or else I shall die!
Make them slacken the engines—or cast off the gig!
Stop the robbers! Make something go wrong with
    the works!
Do listen! Leave other folk's matters alone!
The world will look after itself while You do.—
He's not listening. He is as deaf as a post!
It's too much! A God that can't think what to do!
                              [*Beckons up to the sky.*
I say! I've disposed of my negro plantation,
And sent heaps of missionaries out to Asia.

Don't You think that one good turn's deserving
    another?

Oh, help me to get on the ship—!

> [*A sudden glare rises into the sky from the yacht,
> followed by a thick cloud of smoke. A dull
> explosion is heard.* PEER GYNT *utters a
> shriek and sinks down on the sand. The
> smoke gradually disperses and the yacht is
> seen to have disappeared.* PEER GYNT *looks
> up, with a pale face, and says in a low voice:*

                                'Twas a judgment!

Sunk with all hands in a moment of time!

All thanks to the chances of fortune.    [*Emotionally.*

                                    No, no!

There was more than the chances of fortune in this,

That I should be saved while the rest of them perish.

Thanks be to Thee who hast been my protector

And kept an eye on me in spite of my failings!

                        [*Takes a deep breath.*

What a wonderful feeling of safety and comfort

It gives you to know that you're specially guarded!

But where shall I find meat and drink in the desert?

I don't know, I'm sure. But He will understand.

It *can't* be so dangerous.—

            [*In a loud and insinuating voice.*

                          He will not suffer

Such a poor little sparrow as I am to perish!

I must humble myself—and allow Him some time.

The Lord will provide; I must not be downhearted.—

         [*Springs to his feet with a cry of terror.*

Did I hear a lion? That growl in the rushes—?

                        [*His teeth chatter.*

No, it was no lion.          [*Pulls himself together.*

             I'm certain it was!

Those creatures, of course, know to keep at a distance;

They dare not take bites at a lord of creation.

They have instinct, of course; it's by instinct they
    feel

That an elephant's not a safe thing to attack.—

All the same, I will see if I can't find a tree.

Ah, there I see palms and acacias waving,
If I climb one of them, I'll get safety and shelter—
Especially if I can only remember
Some psalms to repeat.—      [*Climbs up a tree.*
         " Lo, morning and evening
Are different things "—that's a verse that is often
Discussed and examined.    [*Settles himself in the tree.*
          How pleasant it is
To feel that one's soul is so nobly uplifted !
Thoughts that ennoble are worth more than riches.
I'll trust myself to Him. He knows just how far
I am able to drink of the cup of affliction.
He takes a most fatherly interest in me—
    [*Looks out over the sea, and whispers with a sigh:*
But He's not what you'd call economical over it !


### SCENE III

(SCENE.—*A Moroccan camp on the edge of the desert, at night.* WARRIORS *are resting by a watch-fire.*)

A SLAVE (*running in and tearing his hair*).
Gone is the Emperor's white charger !

ANOTHER SLAVE
(*running in and rending his garments*).
The Emperor's sacred garb is stolen !

A CHIEF OF THE WARRIORS (*coming in*).
A hundred strokes of the bastinado
To all of you, if the thieves escape !
   [*The* WARRIORS *spring on to their steeds and gallop off in all directions.*

## Scene IV

(Scene.—*A clump of palm-trees and acacias. It is
dawn.* Peer Gynt, *in a tree, is trying to defend himself with a broken-off branch against a swarm of Apes.*)

### Peer Gynt.

I've spent an extremely uncomfortable night.
                              [*Hits about him.*
Is that them again? The infernal creatures!
They're throwing down fruit. No, it's something else.
Apes are the most disgusting beasts!
It is written that one must watch and fight;
But I can't do it—I'm wearied out.
          [*Is disturbed again. Speaks impatiently.*
I must make an end of all this discomfort—
Try and get hold of one of these creatures,
Hang him and flay him and dress myself up
From head to foot in his shaggy hide;
Then the others will think I am one of them.—
We men are but nothing, after all,
And must bow to the force of circumstances.—
Another lot! Why, they swarm like flies!
Away with you! Shoo! They act like madmen.
If only I could get a false tail—
Or something to make me look like a beast——
What's that up there above my head?      [*Looks up.*
An old one—his paws chock-full of filth!
     [*Crouches down nervously and keeps still for a
        little. The Ape makes a movement;* Peer
        Gynt *tries to coax him, as one would a dog.*
Hullo, old man! Is that you up there?
He's a good chap, if you speak to him kindly.
*He* won't throw things down—will he? No!
It's I! Good dog! We're the best of friends.
Wuff, wuff! Do you hear, I can speak your language?
Old man and I are as good as cousins!
Would he like a nice big bit of sugar—?

The dirty beast! He's thrown the lot
All over me! Disgusting brute!—
Or was it food, perhaps? Its taste
Was unfamiliar, certainly.
But taste is mostly a thing of habit.
What is it that some philosopher
Has said: You must just spit, and trust
To force of habit.—Here's the crowd
Of youngsters now!               [*Hits about him.*
          This is too much!
That man, who's his Creator's image,
Should have to suffer.—Murder! Help!
The old one's foul, but the youngsters fouler!

### SCENE V

(SCENE.—*A rocky spot overlooking the desert. It is early morning. On one side, a ravine with the entrance to a cave. A* THIEF *and a* RECEIVER OF STOLEN GOODS *are standing in the ravine, with the Emperor's charger and robe. The charger, richly caparisoned, is tied to a rock.* HORSEMEN *are seen in the distance.*)

THIEF.

Spear-points, gleaming
In the sunshine!
See! see!

RECEIVER.

I hear them galloping
Over the sand!
Woe! Woe!

THIEF (*folding his arms on his breast*).

My father thieved;
His son must steal.

RECEIVER.

My father received;
And so must I.

THIEF.

We must bear our lot,
And be ourselves.

RECEIVER (*listening*).

Footsteps in the thicket!
Away! But where?

THIEF.

The cave is deep
And the Prophet great!

> [*They fly, leaving the stolen goods behind them.*
> *The* HORSEMEN *disappear in the distance.*
> PEER GYNT *comes in, whittling a reed.*

PEER GYNT.

Really a most enchanting morning!
The beetles are busy at work in the sand;
Out of their shells the snails are peeping.
Morning! Ah, morning's worth more than gold!
It's strange what a very remarkable power
There is in daylight. In its beams
You feel so safe—your courage waxes—
You're ready to fight wild bulls, if need be.
What silence around me! These rural joys—
It's strange that I never appreciated
These things so much till now. To think
That men live cooped up in great cities,
Just to be pestered and plagued by people.
Look at those lizards, bustling about
Enjoying the air and thinking of nothing.
What innocence in the life of beasts!
They perform the behest of their great Creator,
Their character stamped indelibly on them;
They are *themselves*, whether playing or fighting—
Themselves, as they were when He first said " Be."

> [*Puts on his eye-glasses.*

A toad—looking out of a piece of sandstone,
Only his head peeping out of his chamber.

He sits, as if looking out of a window
At the world; to himself he is—enough,

                             *[Thoughtfully.*

Enough? Where have I read that before?
Most probably in the Great Book I read
As a boy. Or perhaps it was in the Prayer-book?
Or else set down in Solomon's Proverbs?
Dear me—I notice, as years go on,
I cannot remember times and places
As once I used.          *[Sits down in the shade.*
         Here's a spot that's cool;
I'll sit and rest my bones awhile.
Ah, here are ferns—one can eat the roots.

                               *[Tastes one.*

It's really food for beasts; but then
The Book says we must subdue our natures,
And, further, that pride must be abased.
"Who humbleth himself, shall be exalted." *[Uneasily.*
Exalted? Of course that will happen to me—
The contrary's quite unthinkable.
Fate surely will help me away from here
And set my feet on the road to fortune.
This is but a test; if the Lord will grant me
Strength to endure, I'll be rescued later.
    *[Shakes off such thoughts, lights a cigar, stretches
        himself out and gazes over the desert.*
What an enormous, boundless waste!—
Far off, there, I can see an ostrich.—
It is hard to perceive the Almighty's purpose
In all this dead and empty desert,
Where there is nothing that is life-giving;
A burnt-up waste that profits no one,
This bit of the world that's for ever sterile;
A corpse that never, since it was shaped,
Has brought its Creator anything—
Not even thanks. Why was it made?
Nature is ever extravagant.—
Is that the sea that glitters yonder,
Away in the east? No—only mirage.
The sea's to the west, where, like a dam,

Sandhills protect the desert from it.

                        *[An idea strikes him.*

A dam! Then I might—! The hills are low.
A dam! Then a cutting—a canal—
And through the gap the rushing waters
Would fill the desert with a life-flood,
And all this empty burnt-up grave
Become a fresh and rippling ocean!
Islands would show in it where now
There are oases; to the north,
Atlas would fringe the shore with verdure;
And to the south, like heedless birds,
White sails would skim along, where now
The caravans plod painfully;
A lively breeze would dissipate
This stuffy air, and from the clouds
A gentle dew would fall. In time
Town after town would be established,
And grass grow round the swaying palm-trees.
The country beyond the Sahara's edge,
Away in the south, would become a land
Of busy trade and seamen's ventures.
Steam should drive works in Tombuktu,
New colonies arise in Bornu,
And the explorer should be carried
Safe in his waggon through the land
Of Habes [1] to the Upper Nile.
Then in the middle of my sea,
On the most fertile, rich oasis,
I'll settle Norsemen—for the blood
Of dalesmen is the nearest thing
To that of royalty; a cross
With Arab blood will do the rest.
And on a cape with sloping shore
I'll build Peeropolis, the capital!
The old world's out of date; and now
It is the turn of Gyntiana,[2]

[1] The Arabic name for Abyssinia.
[2] The Norwegian violinist Ole Bull had founded, with disastrous financial results, a Norwegian colony of " Oleana " in America on the model approved by the French Socialists.

My new-born land! [*Springs up.*
                        I only need
Some capital, and the thing is done—
A golden key, and the ocean's gate
Is open! A crusade 'gainst death!
That grisly miser shall disgorge
The hidden treasure that he's hoarding.
There is a world-wide wish for freedom.
Like Noah's donkey in the Ark,
I'll bray my message to the world;
Liberty's baptism I will pour
Over these prisoned shores, till they
Grow lovely in their freedom!—Forward!
In east or west I'll have to seek
The money for the work! My kingdom—
Or half my kingdom—for a horse!
                    [*The horse in the ravine neighs.*
A horse! And robes! And ornaments!
And weapons! [*Goes nearer.*
            It's impossible—
And yet it's true!—I know I've read
Somewhere that faith can move a mountain,
But never thought that it could bring
A horse! I must be dreaming—No,
It is a fact—there stands the horse!
*Ab esse ad posse*, etcetera.—
            [*Puts on the robe and looks himself over.*
Sir Peter—and Turk from head to foot!
Well, truly one can never tell
What's going to happen to one! Come up,
Granë, my steed! [*Climbs into the saddle.*
            Gold stirrups, too!
Great folk are known by the steeds they ride!
            [*Gallops away across the desert.*

## SCENE VI

(SCENE.—*The tent of an Arab Chieftain, on an oasis.*
PEER GYNT, *in his oriental robes, is taking his ease
on a divan, drinking coffee and smoking a long pipe.*
ANITRA *and a troup of* GIRLS *are dancing and singing
to him.*)

### CHORUS OF GIRLS.

The Prophet is come!
The Prophet, the Lord, the All-Wise One,
To us, to us he has come,
Riding over the sea of sand!
The Prophet, the Lord, the Infallible,
To us, to us he has come,
Sailing over the sea of sand!
   Blow flute! Sound drum!
   The Prophet, the Prophet is come!

### ANITRA.

His charger is white as milk
In the streams of Paradise!
Bend the knee! Bow low!
His eyes are stars that flash
And yet are full of love.
No earth-born eyes can meet
The flashing of those stars!
Across the desert he came,
Decked with gold and pearls.
Where he rode it was light;
Behind him all was dark,
Drought and the dread simoom.
The Mighty One has come!
Over the desert he came,
Clothed in mortal shape.
Kaaba is empty now!
Himself has told us so.

CHORUS OF GIRLS.

Blow flute! Sound drum!
The Prophet, the Prophet is come!

[*The girls dance to soft music.*

PEER GYNT.

I have read in a book, and the saying's true,
That no man's a prophet in his own country.—
This life's a deal more to my liking
Than that which I led as a Charlestown trader.
There was something false about it all,
Something foreign to me, and shady;
I never could feel myself at home,
Or feel I had chosen the right profession.
*Qu'allais-je faire dans cette galère,*
Grubbing about with business matters?
I can't understand it, the more I try—
It simply happened, and that is all.
To climb up the world on money-bags
Is just like building a house on sand.
If you wear rings and a watch and so forth,
People will curtsey and bow to you,
Take off their hats if you wear a breast-pin;
But the rings and the pin are not yourself.
Now a Prophet—he has a definite status;
You know exactly where you're standing,
If a man salutes you, it's for *yourself,*
And not because of your pounds and shillings.
You are what you are, without pretence.
Owing nothing to chance or accident,
Independent of patents or concessions.
A Prophet—yes, that's the life for me.
And it happened so unexpectedly—
Simply from riding across the desert
And coming upon these children of nature.
The Prophet had come; it was clear to them.
But indeed it was not my design to deceive them—
An official reply from a Prophet is one thing,
And a lie quite another; in any case, too,

I can always retire from my present position.
I'm in no way bound; so it's not so bad.
It's all, so to speak, like a private arrangement.
I can go as I came; my steed's standing ready;
In short, I am master of the situation.

ANITRA (*at the door of the tent*).
Prophet and Master!

PEER GYNT.
What is it, my slave?

ANITRA.
At the door of the tent stand sons of the desert,
Craving to look on the face of the Prophet——

PEER GYNT.
Stop! You can tell them they must keep their
    distance;
I will receive their petitions at a distance.
Tell them no man may set his foot within here!
Menfolk, my child, are but a set of scoundrels—
They are, in fact, a filthy lot of rascals.
You, my Anitra, cannot well imagine
With what barefaced impertinence they cheat one—
H'm!—I should say, how grievously they sin. Now,
No more of that! Come, dance for me, my children!
I would forget these thoughts that make me angry.

THE GIRLS (*as they dance*).
The Prophet is good! His heart is distressed
For the sins that the sons of earth have committed.
The Prophet is kind! All praise to his kindness
Which leads such poor sinners to Paradise!

PEER GYNT
(*whose eyes have followed* ANITRA *through the dance*).
Her legs flit about like nimble drumsticks!
She's really a tasty morsel, the baggage!

It's true her figure's pronounced in some ways—
Not quite in accord with the standards of beauty
But what is beauty?  A mere convention,
A currency coined for a special purpose.
And it's just these extravagances that tickle
A palate that's sated with what is normal.
In marriage there's always something wanting;
She's either too fat or else too scraggy,
Annoyingly young or alarmingly ancient;
And if she's between the two, she's insipid.—
Her feet, it is true, might well be cleaner,
Also her arms—especially that one.
But, after all, that's nothing to matter;
One might rather call it a qualification.—
Anitra, come here!

ANITRA.

Thy slave, my Master!

PEER GYNT.

You attract me, child!  The Prophet is moved.
If you don't believe me, I'll prove it to you—
I'll make you a Houri in Paradise!

ANITRA.

Impossible, Master!

PEER GYNT.

         You don't believe me?
As I am alive, I'm in real earnest!

ANITRA.

But I've no soul!

PEER GYNT.

Then you shall have one!

ANITRA.

How shall I, Master?

PEER GYNT.

That's my affair.
I shall look after your education.
No soul? It's true you are pretty stupid;
I've noticed that fact with some regret;
But there's room enough in you for a soul.
Come here! Let me measure your head. Oh, yes,
There's plenty of room, as I knew there was.
True enough, you'll never be anything much;
A great soul will be quite beyond you.
But, pshaw! it really doesn't matter;
You'll have enough to prevent your feeling
Ashamed of it——

ANITRA.

My Lord is kind——

PEER GYNT.

You're hesitating? What is the matter?

ANITRA.

I'd rather have——

PEER GYNT.

Speak out, at once!

ANITRA.

I don't care so much about having a soul;
I'd rather have——

PEER GYNT.

What?

ANITRA (*pointing to his turban*).

That lovely opal!

PEER GYNT (*in raptures, as he hands her the jewel*).

Anitra, you're one of Eve's true daughters!
Your charm attracts me—for I'm a man;
And, as a noted writer puts it:
" *Das ewig weibliche ziehet uns an.*"


## SCENE VII

(SCENE.—*A grove of palm-trees outside* ANITRA'S *tent. The moon is shining.* PEER GYNT, *with an Arabian lute in his hands, is sitting under a tree. His beard and hair have been trimmed, which makes him look considerably younger.*)

PEER GYNT (*plays and sings*).

I locked the gate of Paradise
And took away the key.
    My bark afar the north wind bore,
    While lovely women on the shore
Were weeping there for me.

Southward I sailed the salty depths
Before the die was cast;
    Where palms were waving proud and free
    Around an inlet of the sea,
I burned my ship at last.

A desert-ship I mounted then—
A four-legged ship, I trow—
    To bear me o'er the desert dark.
    I am a bird of passage! Hark!
I'm twittering on a bough!

Anitra, thou art like the wine
Of palm-trees, sparkling clear!
    Angora-goats'-milk cheese is good,
    But it's not half so sweet a food
As thou, Anitra dear!

[*Slings the lute over his shoulder and approaches the tent.*

All is silent! Now I wonder
If she heard my little song?
Is she there behind the curtain,
Peeping out with nothing on?
What's that sound? It's like a bottle
Someone is uncorking!—There!
There again I heard it!—Is it
Sighs of love?—a lover's song?—
No, it's clearly someone snoring.
Lovely sound! Anitra sleeps!
Nightingales, desist from singing!
You shall suffer if you dare
With your silly cluck and gurgle—.
Oh, well, after all—sing on!
Every nightingale's a songster,
Just as I am one myself;
With their notes, like me, they capture
Tender, delicate young hearts.
Night's cool hours are meant for singing;
Singing is our common sphere;
Singing is the art of being
*Us*—Peer Gynt and nightingale.
And to hear Anitra sleeping
Is the topmost bliss of love;
It's like lifting up a goblet
To the lips, but drinking naught.—
Oh, but here she comes! Well, really,
After all that is the best.

ANITRA (*at her tent door*).
Did I hear my Master calling?

PEER GYNT.
Yes, my dear, the Prophet called.
I was wakened by a hubbub;
Cats were fighting all around——

ANITRA.
Ah, they were not fighting, Master.
It was something worse than that.

PEER GYNT.

What was it?

ANITRA.
Oh, spare me!

PEER GYNT.
Tell me!

ANITRA.
I am blushing!

PEER GYNT (*going close to her*).
Do you mean
The emotion I was feeling
When you had my opal, dear?

ANITRA (*horrified*).
Don't compare yourself, great Master,
To an old disgusting cat!

PEER GYNT.
Child—considered just as lovers,
There's perhaps not much to choose
'Twixt a tom-cat and a Prophet.

ANITRA.
Honeyed jests, great Master, fall
From your lips.

PEER GYNT.
My little friend,
You, like other girls, pass judgment
Solely by a great man's looks.
I am really very playful—
Especially when *tête-à-tête*.
My position makes it needful
For me to put on a mask

Of most serious behaviour;
I'm constrained by daily duties,
And the nature of the business
Relative to my great office,
To assume a weighty manner,
And at times may seem to others
Too prophetically abrupt;
But 'tis all upon the surface.—
Away with all that bosh! In private
I am Peer—that's who I am.
Come, now, I will drop the Prophet;
You shall know my very self!

[*Sits down under a tree and draws* ANITRA *closer
to him.*

Come, Anitra, let us dally
Underneath this waving palm!
You shall smile and I shall whisper
Nothings in your ear; and then
We'll reverse the parts we're playing,
Your sweet lips shall whisper love
In my ear while I sit smiling!

ANITRA (*lying at his feet*).

All you say is sweet as music,
Though I don't quite understand.
Tell me, Master, can your daughter
Get a soul by listening?

PEER GYNT.

Presently you shall be dowered
With that light of life—a soul;
When upon the rosy portals
Of the dawn we see in gold
" I am daybreak " clearly written,—
Then it will be time enough
To begin your education.
But for me to play schoolmaster,
And to waste this lovely night
Trying to collect together

Weatherbeaten bits of lore,
Would be stupid altogether,
Even if I wanted to.
And, besides, considered rightly,
Souls are not the chiefest things
In our lives; it's hearts that matter.

ANITRA.

Speak on, Master! When you speak,
It's like opals flashing fire.

PEER GYNT.

Too much cleverness is folly;
And the fruit of cowardice
Pushed too far, is cruelty.
Truth, if it's exaggerated,
Is no more than wisdom's self
Turned hind-foremost.—Yes, my child,
You may take my word for it,
There are people in the world
Gorged with soul but dull of vision.
I once knew a chap like that;
He seemed brighter than his fellows;
Yet he let resounding phrases
Which he did not understand
Quite mislead him from his business.—
Look around this fair oasis,
At the desert; if my turban
I took off and fluttered gently
Once or twice, the mighty ocean
At my bidding would invade it,
Filling up its every corner.
But I'd be a silly cuckoo
If I set about creating
Seas and continents. Do you know,
My child, what life is?

ANITRA.

           No, instruct me.

## PEER GYNT.

Life means passing safe and dry-shod
Down the rushing stream of time.
Manly strength is what is needed
To be what I am, my dear.
Age makes eagles lose their feathers,
Makes old fogies' footsteps fail,
Sets an old crone's teeth decaying,
Gives an old man withered hands,—
And they all get withered souls.
Give me youth! I mean as Sultan,
Ardent and vigorous, to rule—
Not the realms of Gyntiana
With their palm-trees and their vines—
But the realm of fresh young beauty
That lies in a maiden's thoughts.
   So you see, my child, the reason
Why I graciously was pleased
To bestow my love upon you;
Why I chose your little heart,
So to speak, to be the empire
That shall be my caliphate.
None but I shall know your longings;
In the empire of my love
I must reign supreme, unquestioned!
For you must be mine alone.
I shall be your gentle gaoler,
Binding you with gold and gems.
If we part, life will be empty—
Or, at any rate, for you!
Not a fibre of your being,
Not an instinct of your will,
But shall know me as their master—
You shall be so filled with me.
And your raven locks—your beauty—
All in you that can allure—
These shall be a pleasant garden
For your Sultan's foot to tread.
   And that's why it's really lucky

You've an empty little head.
Souls are apt to make their owners
Too absorbed about themselves.
And—while we're upon the topic—
If you like, I'll seal the pact
By bestowing on your ankle
This fine bangle. That, I think,
Fairly meets the situation.
Me—instead of soul—you'll have;
Otherwise, the *status quo*.      [ANITRA *snores*.
What? Is she sleeping? Have my words
Fallen on unheeding ears?
No; it shows the power lying
In my words—that, like a stream,
They transport her gently with them
To the land of dreams.
        [*Gets up and puts some jewels in her lap.*
        Anitra!
Here are jewels! Here are more!
Sleep, Anitra! Dream of Peer!
Sleep, for in your sleep you've set
A crown upon your Emperor's head!
Peer Gynt has won a victory
Of personality to-night.

### SCENE VIII

(SCENE.—*A caravan route. The oasis is visible in the
remote background.* PEER GYNT, *on his white horse, is
galloping over the desert, holding* ANITRA *before him on
the pommel of his saddle.*)

        ANITRA.
Let go! I'll bite you!

        PEER GYNT.
            You little rogue!

ANITRA.

What do you want to do?

PEER GYNT.

           To play
At dove and falcon! To carry you off,
And do all sorts of reckless things!

ANITRA.

For shame! An old Prophet, too!

PEER GYNT.

                Oh, bosh!
The Prophet is not old, you goose!
Do you think this looks as if he were old?

ANITRA.

Let me go! I want to go home!

PEER GYNT.

              You flirt!
Home! To father-in-law! That's good!
We birds that have flown out of our cage
Dare not be seen by him again.
Besides, my child, no one should stay
Too long in the same place; he's apt
To lose as much in estimation
As he can gain by making friends;
And this is specially the case
When he's a Prophet, or the like.
His should be flying visits—seen
As snatches of a song are heard.
It was time that my visit should come to an end;
These sons of the desert are shifty creatures,—
Incense and gifts have both been lacking
For some days.

ANITRA.

Yes, but *are* you a Prophet?

PEER GYNT.

I am your Emperor!
> *[Tries to kiss her, but she draws back.*

           Oh, come!
Don't be a proud little birdie, now!

ANITRA.

Give me the ring that's on your finger.

PEER GYNT.

Take the lot if you wish, dear!

ANITRA.

Your words are like life-giving music!

PEER GYNT.

What happiness 'tis to be loved like this!
Let me dismount! I will lead the horse
And be your slave!
> *[Hands her the whip and dismounts.*

           See now, my pretty,
My beautiful rose—here am I now,
And here I'll tread the sands until
I get a sunstroke and have to stop.
I am young, Anitra! Remember that!
You mustn't look at my deeds too closely;
Jokes and fun are what youth is known by!
And, if you were not quite so stupid,
My graceful flower, you'd understand
That, since your lover is full of fun,
*Ergo* he's young!

ANITRA.

           Yes, you are young.
Have you any more rings?

PEER GYNT.

           Of course I'm young!
Look, I am bounding like a deer!

If there was any green-stuff handy,
I'd make myself a wreath! Aha!
Of course I'm young! Just see me dance!

*[Dances and sings.*

 I am a happy little cock!
 Peck me, my little pullet!
 Houp-là! Just see me foot it!
 I am a happy little cock!

### ANITRA.

You're sweating, my Prophet; I'm afraid you will
 melt.
Let me carry that bag that weighs down on your belt.

### PEER GYNT.

What tender concern! You shall carry the purse;
Hearts that are loving have no need of gold!

*[Dances and sings again.*

 He is a madcap, your little Peer!
 He doesn't know what he is doing!
 And doesn't care—if he keeps going!
 He is a madcap, your little Peer!

### ANITRA.

How joyful 'tis to see the Prophet dancing!

### PEER GYNT.

Oh, drop that " Prophet " nonsense! Let's put on
Each other's clothes! Come on! You take yours off!

### ANITRA.

Your caftan is too long, your belt too roomy,
Your stockings much too small.

### PEER GYNT.

     *Eh bien !* [1] Instead,
Inflict some pain upon me; for 'tis sweet

[1] So in the original.

For loving hearts to suffer for their love!
And, when we come to where my castle stands——

ANITRA.

Your Paradise? Have we got far to ride?

PEER GYNT.

A thousand miles or so!

ANITRA.

Oh, what a way!

PEER GYNT.

Then you shall have the soul I promised you——

ANITRA.

No, thanks; I think I'll do without the soul.
But you were asking for some pain——

PEER GYNT.

Ah, yes!
Something severe but brief—a passing pang—!

ANITRA.

Anitra must obey the Prophet! So—
Farewell!
[*Hits him smartly over the fingers with the whip,
and gallops back over the desert at full speed.*

PEER GYNT
(*after standing for a long time as if thunderstruck*).

Well, I am—!

## SCENE IX

(SCENE.—*The same as the preceding, an hour later.*
PEER GYNT *is taking off his Turkish dress bit by bit,
deliberately and thoughtfully. When he has finished,
he takes a travelling-cap out of his coat pocket, puts it
on, and stands once more in European dress. He flings
the turban far away from him.*)

### PEER GYNT.

There lies the Turk, and here stand I!
A pagan existence is no good at all.
It's lucky that I can throw it away
With the clothes, and that it's not bred in the bone.
*Qu'allais-je faire dans cette galère?*
It's certainly best to live as a Christian,
Avoid the temptation of sumptuous garments,
Fashion your life by what's lawful and moral;
In fact, be yourself—and deserve at the last
A funeral oration and wreaths on your coffin.
                              [*Takes a few steps.*
The baggage!—Only a little more,
And I believe she'd have turned my head.
But I'll be hanged if I understand
What it was in her that so upset me.
I am well out of it! If the joke
Had been pursued a little farther,
It would have made me ridiculous.—
I have erred, no doubt; but it's comforting
To feel that my erring was the result
Of the position I had assumed;
It was not I, myself, that erred.
It was, as a fact, the prophetic life—
Devoid of any savouring salt
Of active work—that caused in me
These lapses into want of taste.
It's a sorry business being a Prophet!
In the course of your duties you're apt to get heedless.

You're sober and dignified; all of a sudden
You find you're nothing of the sort.
I certainly gave proof of it
By paying homage to that goose,
Still, all the same—          [*Bursts out laughing.*
                    Just think of it!
Spending the time in wanton dancing!
Trying to stem the stream of life
By fooling like that!—sweet music,
Caresses, sighs—and in the end
Be plucked like any silly hen!
Prophetically wild behaviour!—
Plucked!—To my shame, I've been plucked badly!
Still, I've a little left in hand,—
Some in America, and some
Safe in my pocket; so I'm not
Quite on the rocks. And, after all,
A moderate amount of wealth
Is best. I am no longer tied
By horses, coachmen and the like;
I've neither carriages nor luggage
To give me trouble. In a word,
I'm master of the situation.—
Which way shall I choose? Many are open.
It's in such choice that wisdom counts.
My business life is a finished chapter;
My love affairs, discarded garments;
And I have no mind to retrace my steps.
" Forward or back it's just as far;
Out or in, it's just as narrow "—
As I think it says in some clever book.
I must find some new, some ennobling task;
An object that's worth my pains and money.
Suppose I wrote, without concealment,
The story of my life—a book
To serve as a guide and an example
To others after me? Or, wait—!
I've lots of time at my command—
Suppose I become a travelling scholar,
Making a study of bygone ages?

That, I believe, is the thing for me!
I'd always a fancy for history,
And lately I've improved my knowledge.
I'll trace the story of mankind!
Float like a feather upon the stream
Of history; and live again,
As in a dream, the days of old;
See the fierce fights the heroes waged—
But from a vantage-point that's safe,
That of an onlooker; see how
Thinkers were slaughtered, martyrs bled;
How kingdoms rose and kingdoms fell;
Watch epochs of world-history
Grow from their birth; and, in a word,
Skim all the cream of history.—
I must try and get hold of a book of Becker's,[1]
And go chronologically about it.
It's true that my previous knowledge is sketchy,
And history's rather an intricate matter,—
But what is the odds! It frequently happens
That very unusual methods of starting
Lead to the most original outcome.—
To see one's goal and drive towards it,
Steeling one's heart, is most uplifting!

[*With restrained emotion.*

Breaking through every bond that hinders,
Sundering ties of home and friendship,
Bidding adieu to love's soft promptings,
To solve the mystery of truth!

[*Wipes a tear from his eye.*

*That* is the test of a real enquirer!
It makes me happy beyond measure
To feel I have solved the great enigma
Of my destiny. I've only, now,
To hold my course through thick and thin!
I think I may be well forgiven
If I feel proud, and call Peer Gynt
A Man, and Manhood's Emperor!

[1] Becker's *Weltgeschichte*, which had been translated into Danish.

The Past shall be a lock to which
I have the key; I will desert
The sordid paths of modern life.
The Present is not worth a shoe-lace.
The ways of men are empty, faithless;
Their minds are dull, their deeds are futile—
                    [*Shrugs his shoulders.*
And women—well, their name is frailty!
                    [*Moves on.*


## SCENE X

(SCENE.—*Outside a hut in a forest in the far north of Norway. It is a summer's day. The door, which stands open, is furnished with a massive wooden bolt; above the door a pair of reindeer horns is fixed. A herd of goats are feeding by the wall.* SOLVEIG, *now a fair and handsome middle-aged woman, is sitting spinning in the sunshine.*)

SOLVEIG (*looks down the path and sings*).

It may not be till winter's past,
And spring and summer—the whole long year;
But I know that you will come at last,
And I shall wait, for I promised you, dear.
    [*Calls to her goats, then resumes her spinning and
        singing.*
God guard you, dear, where'er you be!
If in Heaven, God have you in His care!
I shall wait till you come back to me;
If you're waiting above, I shall meet you there!


## SCENE XI

(SCENE.—*In Egypt, at the foot of the statue of Memnon, at dawn.* PEER GYNT *comes walking along, stops, and looks around him.*)

PEER GYNT.

I think that this place will do for a start.—
Now, for a change, I'm an Egyptian;

But Egyptian always upon the basis
Of the Gyntian Self. I'll wander later
Into Assyria. I'll stop short
Of going back to the Creation,
For that would only lead to danger.
I'll skirt the edges of Bible history.
No doubt I'll discover certain traces
That will confirm it; but to go
Minutely into it is not
According to my plan of action.
               [*Sits down on a stone.*
I'll rest awhile and wait with patience
Until I've heard the Statue singing
Its customary morning song;
And, after I have had my breakfast,
I'll climb the Pyramid, and then,
If I have time I'll look inside it.
Then to the Red Sea, where perhaps
I shall discover King Potiphar's grave.
Then I will be an Asiatic;
In Babylon I'll seek the famous
Hanging Gardens and Concubines—
The fairest products, that's to say,
Of civilization. Then a leap,
And I'll be at the walls of Troy;
And thence the sea-route is direct
To beautiful old Athens. There,
I shall examine, stone by stone,
The pass Leonidas defended;
I'll make myself familiar
With all the best philosophies;
Find out the gaol where Socrates
Laid down his life as sacrifice—
But, stop a minute, I forgot—!
Greece is at war, so for the present
I must put Hellenism aside.     [*Looks at his watch.*
What a ridiculous time the sun
Takes in rising! My time's precious.
Well, then,—from Troy—that's where I'd got to—
               [*Gets up and listens.*

I wonder what that curious murmur—?

[*The sun rises.*

THE MEMNON STATUE (*singing*).

From the demi-god's ashes [1] arise new-born
      Singing birds.
    Zeus, the all-knowing,
    Shaped them for conflict.
     Owl of Wisdom,
    Where sleep my birds?
You must die if you read not
    The Riddle of the Song!

PEER GYNT.

I really do believe I heard
Sounds from the Statue! That would be
The music of the past. I heard
The rise and fall of the Statue's voice.
I'll note that down for consideration
At experts' hands.

[*Makes a note in his pocket-book.*
    " The Statue sang.
I heard the sounds quite plainly, but
Could not completely understand
The words. I have, of course, no doubt
The whole thing was hallucination.
Otherwise, I have not observed
Anything of importance so far."    [*He moves on.*

[1] At Memnon's death, Jove changed the hero's companions into birds that sang wildly and fought fiercely with each other. Ibsen's satire here is said to be directed against the University Professors of Norway, the Owl of Wisdom being the crest of the University. He regarded the professorial wisdom as a dead thing, insomuch as it merely concerned itself with the past and took no proper part in the conflict for the future of Norway. The Statue here asks Peer, as the representative of the Norwegian people, where the fighting spirit that should have arisen from the ashes of the past is sleeping.

## SCENE XII

(SCENE.—*Near the village of Gizeh, by the great Sphinx carved out of the rock. In the distance are seen the spires and minarets of Cairo. PEER GYNT arrives; he examines the Sphinx carefully, sometimes through his eye-glass, sometimes through the hollow of his hand.*)

### PEER GYNT.

Now where in the world have I met before
Something I only half remember
That this ugly thing reminds me of?
For met it I have—either north or south.
Was it a man? And, in that case, who?
The Memnon Statue reminded me
Of the Troll King of our fairy tales,
Sitting like that, all stiff and rigid,
Resting his rump on a piece of rock;
But this remarkable mongrel here,
This monster, half lion and half woman—
Have I known it, too, in a fairy tale?
Or have I some real recollection of it?
A fairy tale?—No, I know the chap!
It's the Boyg, if you please, whose skull I cracked—
I mean to say that I dreamt I did,
For I was lying ill of a fever.

[*Goes nearer to the Sphinx.*

The selfsame eyes, the selfsame lips!
Not quite so sluggish—a bit more cunning—
But in the main points just the same.
Well, Boyg, old fellow, you're like a lion,
Seen from behind and in the daylight!
Are you still full of riddles? We'll try, and see;
We'll see if you answer as you did before.

[*Calls to the Sphinx.*

Hi, Boyg! Who are you?

VOICE (*from behind the Sphinx*).
> *Ach, Sfinx, wer bist du?*

PEER GYNT.

What's that? An echo in German? Astounding!

VOICE.

*Wer bist du?*

PEER GYNT.

It's got a perfect accent!
The observation's new, and my own.
> [*Makes a note in his book.*
" Echo in German—with Berlin accent."
> [BEGRIFFENFELDT *comes from behind the Sphinx.*

BEGRIFFENFELDT.

A man!

PEER GYNT.

Oh—it was *he* that was talking.
> [*Makes a further note.*
" Came later to another conclusion."

BEGRIFFENFELDT
(*with signs of great excitement*).

Excuse me, Sir—! A vital question—!
What was it brought you here to-day?

PEER GYNT.

A visit. I'm greeting a friend of my youth.

BEGRIFFENFELDT.

The Sphinx?

PEER GYNT.

Yes, I knew him in days gone by.

BEGRIFFENFELDT.

Splendid!—And after the night I've spent!
My forehead is throbbing as if it would burst!—
You know him, Sir? Then speak! What is he?
Can you tell me that?

PEER GYNT.

What is he? Yes,
I can tell you that. He is *himself.*

BEGRIFFENFELDT (*with a start*).

Ha! Like a flash I see the answer
To life's enigma!—Is it certain
That he's himself?

PEER GYNT.

Yes; at least, he said so.

BEGRIFFENFELDT.

Himself! The great awakening's come!
[*Takes off his hat.*
Your name, sir?

PEER GYNT.

I am called Peer Gynt.

BEGRIFFENFELDT
(*with an air of quiet amazement*).

Peer Gynt! Allegorical! What one expected.
Peer Gynt? That means: the Great Unknown—
The Messiah that was announced to me——

PEER GYNT.

No—really? And you came here to find him--?

BEGRIFFENFELDT.

Peer Gynt! Profound! Enigmatic! Incisive!
Each word is full of deepest teaching!
What are you?

PEER GYNT (*modestly*).

        I have always tried
To be myself. And, for the rest,
My passport——

BEGRIFFENFELDT.

        Enigmatic too!
All an enigma!      [*Grasps him by the hand.*
       Come to Cairo!
Come! I have found the Emperor
Of Exegesis!

PEER GYNT.

Emperor?

BEGRIFFENFELDT.

        Come!

PEER GYNT.

Am I really known—?

BEGRIFFENFELDT
(*dragging him away with him*).

        The Emperor
Of Exegesis—based on Self!

SCENE XIII

(SCENE.—*In a lunatic asylum at Cairo. A big court-yard surrounded by high walls and buildings with barred windows. Iron cages on the ground level. Three of the* KEEPERS *are in the courtyard. A fourth comes in.*)

FOURTH KEEPER.

I say, Schafmann—where's the Director?

ANOTHER KEEPER.

He went out this morning, long before dawn.

FOURTH KEEPER.

I'm afraid something's happened that has upset him,
Because in the night——

ANOTHER.

Hush! Here he comes!

[BEGRIFFENFELDT *shows* PEER GYNT *in, locks the
gate and puts the key in his pocket.*

PEER GYNT (*aside*).

He is a remarkably learned man;
Almost all that he says is beyond understanding.

[*Looks round him.*

So this, then, is your Savants' Club?

BEGRIFFENFELDT.

Yes, here you'll find them, bag and baggage——
The coterie of seventy
Professors of Exegesis. Lately
A hundred and three new ones joined them.——

[*Calls to the* KEEPERS.

Mikkel, Schlingelberg, Schafmann, Fuchs——
Into the cages with you! Quick!

THE KEEPERS.

We!

BEGRIFFENFELDT.

Yes—who else? Get on! get on!
As the world's topsy-turvy, we
Must follow suit!          [*Shuts them up in the cage.*

The mighty Peer
Has come to us to-day; so you
Can join the others.—I will say
No more.

[*Locks the cage and throws the key into a well.*

PEER GYNT.
But why—my dear Director—?

BEGRIFFENFELDT.
Don't call me that! I *was* Director
Until—— Sir, can you keep a secret?
I must unburden myself——

PEER GYNT.
What is it?

BEGRIFFENFELDT.
Promise me that you will not tremble.

PEER GYNT.
I will try not to.

BEGRIFFENFELDT
(*takes him into a corner and whispers*).
Absolute Reason
Expired at eleven o'clock last night!

PEER GYNT.
God help us—!

BEGRIFFENFELDT.
Yes, it's a great disaster.
In *my* position, too, you see,
It's doubly disagreeable;
Because this place, until it happened,
Was known as a lunatic asylum.

PEER GYNT.
A lunatic asylum!

BEGRIFFENFELDT.
Ah,
Not *now*, you understand!

PEER GYNT (*aside, growing pale*).

I see
Exactly how it is; this fellow
Is mad—and not a soul suspects it. [*Moves away.*

BEGRIFFENFELDT (*following him*).

I hope you have really understood me?
To say it's dead is not accurate.
It has left itself—got out of its skin
Like my friend Baron Munchausen's fox.[1]

PEER GYNT (*trying to get away*).

Excuse me——

BEGRIFFENFELDT (*holding on to him*).

No, it was like an eel,
Not a fox. A nail right through its eye—
And there it was, squirming on the wall——

PEER GYNT.

How on earth am I to save myself?

BEGRIFFENFELDT.

Just one slit round the neck—and pop!
Out of its pelt it came!

PEER GYNT.

Quite mad!

BEGRIFFENFELDT.

And now the fact is evident
That this same exit-from-itself
Entails a revolution
In all the world. All persons who

[1] In one of Baron Munchausen's tales, he relates an encounter with a fox in which he thrust his hand down the fox's throat and onwards till he felt its tail; having grasped that, he pulled till he turned the fox inside out.

Up to that time were known as mad
At eleven o'clock last night became
Normal; this, in conformity
With Reason in its newest phase.
And, if you consider the matter farther,
It's clear that from the selfsame hour
Our so-called wise men all went mad.

PEER GYNT.

Speaking of time, my time is precious——

BEGRIFFENFELDT.

Your time? You've jogged my memory!
                    [*Opens a door and calls out.*
Come out! The appointed time has come!
Reason is dead. Long live Peer Gynt!

PEER GYNT.

No, my dear friend—!
    [*The mad folk come one after another into the
        courtyard.*

BEGRIFFENFELDT.

                    Good morning to you!
Come out and greet the dawn of freedom!
Your Emperor's here!

PEER GYNT.
                    Their Emperor?

BEGRIFFENFELDT.

Certainly!

PEER GYNT.
            It's too great an honour—
Far more than——

BEGRIFFENFELDT.

          No false modesty
At such a time as this!

PEER GYNT.

          At least
Give me some respite!—I'm not fit
For such a task; I'm quite dumbfounded!

BEGRIFFENFELDT.

The man who guessed the Sphinx's riddle!
Who is himself!

PEER GYNT.

        That's just my trouble.
I am myself in every way;
But here, so far as I can see,
Everyone gets outside themselves.

BEGRIFFENFELDT.

Outside themselves? Oh no, you're wrong.
It's here that men are most themselves—
Themselves and nothing but themselves—
Sailing with outspread sails of self.
Each shuts himself in a cask of self,
The cask stopped with a bung of self
And seasoned in a well of self.
None has a tear for others' woes
Or cares what any other thinks.
We are ourselves in thought and voice—
Ourselves up to the very limit;
And, consequently, if we want
An Emperor, it's very clear
That you're the man.

PEER GYNT.

        I wish to goodness—!

M 747

BEGRIFFENFELDT.

Don't be downhearted; everything
That's new, at first seems strange to one.
" One's self "—well, as a specimen,
I'll choose the first that comes to hand.
          [*To a gloomy figure that is passing.*
Good morning, Huhu! Still, my lad,
Looking the picture of misery?

HUHU (*a Language-Reformer* [1] *from Malabar*).

What can I do, when generation
After generation dies
Lacking an interpreter?     [*To* PEER GYNT.
You're a stranger; will you listen?

PEER GYNT (*bowing*).

By all means.

HUHU.

          Then pay attention.—
Away in the East, like a bridal crown,
Lie the shores of Malabar.
Portuguese and Hollanders
Try to civilize the place,
Where there still survive a lot
Of original Malabari.
These good folk have muddled up
Their language, and now rule supreme
In that land. But, long ago,
That same countryside was ruled
By Orang-outangs. The woods
Were all theirs; and they could fight,
Growl and snarl to hearts' content—
Live, in fact, as Nature made them;
They could screech without permission,

---

[1] The satire in this episode is directed against the " Maal-
strävere," as a group of national language-reformers were
called, whose aim was to rid the Norwegian language of its
Danish taint and get back to the old Norse tongue.

And were lords of all the country.
Then there came this horde of strangers
And disturbed the primal language
That was spoken in the forests.
Now four hundred years have passed—
That means many generations—
And so long a time as that,
As one knows, can easily
Stamp out aborigines.
The forest cries have long been dumb,
Not a growl is ever heard;
If we want to speak our minds,
We must have recourse to words.
It applies to all alike—
Portuguese and Hollanders,
Hybrid races, Malabari—
All are equally affected.
I have tried my best to fight
For our real forest-tongue;
Tried to bring its corpse to life;
Upheld people's right to screech,
Screeched myself, and pointed out
The necessity of screeching
In our folk-songs. But my efforts
Met with no result whatever.—
Now I think you understand
What my grievance is. I thank you
For your courtesy in listening.
If you think you can advise me
What to do, I beg you'll tell me!

PEER GYNT (*aside*).
They say that when you are in Rome
You should do as the Romans do.          [*Aloud.*
My friend, if I remember rightly,
There are forests in Morocco
Where there are Orang-outangs
That have neither songs nor teacher;
And their language much resembles
That of Malabar; if you

Were, like many other statesmen,
To expatriate yourself
For the good of these same people,
It would be a noble action
And a fine example also.

HUHU.

Let me thank you, sir, for listening;
I will follow your advice.
                    [*With an impressive gesture.*
In the east they flout their singer!
The west has its Orang-outangs!     [*Goes out.*

BEGRIFFENFELDT.

Now, surely you'll say that *he's* himself!
He's full of himself and nothing else;
Himself in every word he says—
Himself when he's beside himself.
Come here! I want to show you another,
Who's been no less conformable
To Reason since last night's occurrence.
    [*To a* FELLAH *who is carrying about a Mummy
        on his back.*
King Apis, how goes it, my noble sir?

FELLAH (*fiercely, to* PEER GYNT).
Am I King Apis?

PEER GYNT
(*getting behind* BEGRIFFENFELDT).
                    I'm afraid
I'm not quite qualified to say;
But I should think, if I may judge
From what your voice suggests to me——

FELLAH.
Now you are lying, too!

BEGRIFFENFELDT.

Your Highness
Must kindly deign to let us have
An explanation.

FELLAH.

Well, I will.
[*Turns to* PEER GYNT.
You see this man I'm carrying?
King Apis was his name.
They call him now a Mummy;
And, what is more, he's dead.

He built up all the Pyramids,
And carved the mighty Sphinx,
And fought—so the Director says—
With Turks on every side.

And therefore the Egyptians
Worshipped him as a God,
And set up in their temples
His statue as a bull.

But *I* am that King Apis—
It's just as clear as day;
If you don't understand it,
I'll make you very soon.

King Apis was out a-hunting,
And got down from his horse,
And stepped aside for a moment
In my grandfather's field.

The soil King Apis fertilized
Has nourished *me* with corn;
And, if more proof is needed,
I have invisible horns.

Then don't you think it's damnable
That I can't get my due?
By my birth I am King Apis,
But only a Fellah here.

If you think you can advise me,
Tell me, without delay,

What I'm to do to make myself
Like Apis, the great king.

PEER GYNT.

Your Highness must build Pyramids
And carve a mighty Sphinx,
And fight—as the Director says—
With Turks on every side.

FELLAH.

Yes, that's a likely story!
A Fellah! A hungry louse!
It's all I can do to keep my hut
Clear of the rats and mice.
Come, think of something better,
To make me great and safe,
And also make me look like
King Apis that's on my back.

PEER GYNT.

Suppose your Highness hanged yourself,
And then, deep in the ground,
Within a coffin's sheltering walls
Behaved like one that's dead——

FELLAH.

I'll do it! Let me have a rope!
To the gallows with my head!
I'll not be quite like him at first,
But time will alter that.
    [*Goes away and makes preparations to hang
        himself.*

BEGRIFFENFELDT.

A great personality that, my friend—
A man with method——

PEER GYNT.

Yes, so I see.—
But he really *is* hanging himself! God help us!
I feel quite sick—and my brain is turning!

BEGRIFFENFELDT.

A transitional stage; it won't last long.

PEER GYNT.

Transition? To what? I really must go——

BEGRIFFENFELDT (*holding him back*).

Are you mad?

PEER GYNT.

Not yet! Mad? God forbid!
[*Amidst an uproar,* HUSSEIN, *a Minister of State,
pushes his way through the other lunatics.*

HUSSEIN.

They tell me an Emperor's come to-day.
[*To* PEER GYNT.

Is it you?

PEER GYNT (*desperately*).

They've settled that it is!

HUSSEIN.

Good.—Here are papers that need an answer.

PEER GYNT (*tearing his hair*).

Aha! Go on! The more the merrier!

HUSSEIN.

Perhaps you will honour me with a dip?
[*Bows low.*

I am a pen.

PEER GYNT (*bowing still lower*).
        And I am merely
A trumpery imperial parchment.

HUSSEIN.

My history, Sir, is briefly this:
They think me a sand-box, and not a pen.

PEER GYNT.

And mine, Sir Pen, succinctly told:
I'm a paper that's never been written on.

HUSSEIN.

They never will understand what I'm meant for;
They all want to use me to sprinkle sand!

PEER GYNT.

I was a book with silver clasps,
When I belonged to a woman once.
Madness or wisdom is merely a misprint.

HUSSEIN.

But, think—how wretched to be a pen
That never has tasted the edge of a knife!

PEER GYNT (*leaping into the air*).

Think what it is to be a reindeer
That's always jumping down from a height
And never reaching solid ground!

HUSSEIN.

A knife! I am blunt; I need repairing!
The world will perish if I'm not mended!

PEER GYNT.

That would be sad when, like all that He made,
Our Heavenly Father admired it so much.

BEGRIFFENFELDT.

Here's a knife!

HUSSEIN (*grasping it*).
Ah, how I shall lick up the ink!
How lovely to cut one's self!  [*Cuts his throat.*

BEGRIFFENFELDT (*moving to one side*).
Don't splash me!

PEER GYNT (*with growing terror*).
Hold him!

HUSSEIN.
Yes, hold me! That's the word!
Hold! Hold the Pen! Is the paper there—?  [*Falls.*
I'm worn out. A postscript—don't forget it:
He was a pen in the hands of others.

PEER GYNT.

What shall I—? What am I? Oh, Thou—keep hold!
I am what Thou wilt—a Turk, a Sinner,
A Troll; only help me! Something has burst
Within me!  [*Shrieks.*
I cannot remember Thy name—
Help me, Thou—Guardian of all madmen!
  [*Sinks down in a swoon.* BEGRIFFENFELDT,
    *holding a straw crown in his hand, leaps on
    to* PEER GYNT *and sits astride of him.*

BEGRIFFENFELDT.

See how he sits enthroned in the mud!—
He's out of himself! Let us crown him now!
  [*Puts the crown on* PEER GYNT'S *head, and shouts :*
Long live the Emperor of Self!

SCHAFMANN (*in the cage*).
*Es lebe hoch der grosse Peer !*

# ACT V

## SCENE I

(SCENE.—*On board a ship in the North Sea, off the coast of Norway. Sunset and a threatening sky.* PEER GYNT, *now a vigorous old man with grey hair and beard, is on the poop. His clothes, which are somewhat the worse for wear, are half sailor-like; he wears a pilot-jacket and sea-boots. He looks weather-beaten, and his expression has hardened. The* CAPTAIN *is at the wheel with the* HELMSMAN. *The crew is forward.* PEER GYNT *is leaning his arms on the gunwale and gazing at the land.*)

PEER GYNT.
There's Hallingskarven in winter dress;
He shows up well in the evening light.
And there's his brother Jöklen behind,
Still wearing his ice-green glacier cap;
And, like a lady dressed in white,
Lies Folgefond behind them both.—
Don't try any follies, my ancient friends!
Stay where you are—you are made of stone.

CAPTAIN (*calling forward*).
Two men to the wheel—and hoist the light!

PEER GYNT.
It's blowing.

CAPTAIN.
Aye, we'll have a storm.

PEER GYNT.
Can one see Rondë from the sea?

CAPTAIN.

No—it lies hidden behind Faanen.

PEER GYNT.

Or Blaahö?

CAPTAIN.

No; but, from aloft,
Galdhöpiggen when the weather's clear.

PEER GYNT.

Which way's Harteigen?

CAPTAIN (*pointing*).

Over there.

PEER GYNT.

Of course.

CAPTAIN.

You seem to know the country.

PEER GYNT.

I passed this way when I sailed from home;
And early impressions, as they say,
Last longest.
   [*Spits over the side, and continues gazing at
      the coast.*
It is over there—
Where the hillside glens are blue,
In the dark and narrow valleys,
And along the open fjords—
That is where the people live.
                [*Looks at the* CAPTAIN.
Not many houses on this coast.

CAPTAIN.

No, they are few and far between.

PEER GYNT.

Shall we be in by morning?

CAPTAIN.

                     Aye,
I hope so, if the night is not
Too bad.

PEER GYNT.

     It's gathering in the west.

CAPTAIN.

It is.

PEER GYNT.

     Oh, by the way, look here—
Remind me, when we're settling up,
That I intend to make a present
To the crew——

CAPTAIN.

          You're very good.

PEER GYNT.

It will only be a small one.
I made money, but I've lost it;
Fate and I have fallen out.
You know what I have got on board;
Well, that's the lot. The rest of it
Has taken wings and flown away.

CAPTAIN.

Oh, what you've got is quite enough
To win respect from folk at home.

PEER GYNT.

I have no folk. There's no one waiting
For this rich ugly uncle.—Well,
I shall be spared some fuss at landing.

CAPTAIN.

The storm is brewing.

PEER GYNT.

Now remember,
If any of you need it badly
I'm not close-fisted with my money.

CAPTAIN.

That's kind.  They're mostly badly off;
They all have wives and families—
Can scarcely live upon their pay—
And, if your kindness sends them home
With something extra in their pockets,
To-morrow's home-coming will never
Be forgotten.

PEER GYNT.

What's all that?
Do you say they've wives and children?
Married?

CAPTAIN.

Yes, married—all the lot.
The poorest of them all's the Cook;
His house is never free from hunger.

PEER GYNT.

Married?  And someone waiting there
To greet them when they come?  Is that it?

CAPTAIN.

Of course, like all poor folk.

PEER GYNT.

Supposing
It's evening when they come—what then?

CAPTAIN.

Then I expect that something tasty
Will have been got for the occasion——

PEER GYNT.

A lamp upon the table?

CAPTAIN.

           Aye,
And maybe two; a dram to drink——

PEER GYNT.

They'll sit at ease, in warmth and comfort,
With children round them? And such hubbub
In the room that no one hears
Half the other says to them,
Just because they are so happy?

CAPTAIN.

Very likely; and that's why
It's so kind of you to promise
They shall have a little present.

PEER GYNT (*banging his fist on the gunwale*).
No, I'm damned if they shall have it!
Do you think me such a fool
As to fork out for the pleasure
Of helping other people's children?
I've worked too hard to get my money!
No one's waiting for old Peer Gynt.

CAPTAIN.

Just as you please; it's your own money.

PEER GYNT.

Quite so. It's mine and no one else's.
Directly you have cast your anchor
I'll settle up for what I owe you
For my cabin passage hither
From Panama; and then I'll give you
Something for a dram of brandy
For the crew; but not a penny
More than that. You may have leave
To knock me down if I give more!

CAPTAIN.

You'll get my receipt, and nothing else.
Now please excuse me; the storm is rising.
    [*He crosses the deck. It has become dark, and the
        cabin lamps are being lit. The sea grows
        rougher. Fog and thick clouds gather.*

PEER GYNT.

Provide for a crowd of others' children—?
Fill others' hearts with happiness,
And so be always in their thoughts—?
There's no one wasting thoughts on me.
Lamps on their tables? I'll put them out!
I'll find some way—! I will make them drunk;
Not one of these fellows shall go home sober.
They shall go drunk to their wives and children;
They shall swear—bang loudly on the table—
Frighten their families out of their wits!
Their wives shall scream and run out of the house,
And their children too! I'll spoil their pleasure!
    [*The ship rolls heavily; he stumbles, and has
        difficulty in holding on.*
That was a bad one! The sea's as busy
As if it were paid for what it's doing.
It's the same always, up here in the north;
The sea to fight with, fierce and angry——
                        [*Listens.*
What was that cry?

THE WATCH (*forward*).
        A wreck to leeward!

CAPTAIN (*amidships*).

Starboard the helm! Keep her close to the wind!

HELMSMAN.

Are there men on the wreck?

THE WATCH.

> I can make out three.

PEER GYNT.

Lower a boat—!

CAPTAIN.

> It would only capsize.
> > [*Goes forward.*

PEER GYNT.

Who thinks of that?            [*To the crew.*
> If you're men, you'll save them!
You're surely not afraid of a wetting?

BOATSWAIN.

It's impossible in such a sea as this.

PEER GYNT.

They're calling again! The wind is raging.—
Cook, won't you try? Come on! I'll pay you——

COOK.

Not if you gave me twenty guineas.

PEER GYNT.

You dogs! You cowards! Don't you know
That these are men that have wives and children
Who are waiting—?

BOATSWAIN.

> Patience will do them good.

CAPTAIN.

Keep her stern to the breakers!

HELMSMAN.

> The wreck's gone under.

PEER GYNT.

Was that sudden silence—?

BOATSWAIN.

If they are married,
As you suggest, then the world's the richer
By three newly-created widows.

*[The storm increases in violence.* PEER GYNT *goes aft.*


PEER GYNT.

There's no more Faith among men any longer—
No more Christianity worth the name;
There's little that's good in their words or their deeds,
And they pay no heed to the Powers Above.
In a storm like to-night's, one may very well
Be afraid of God; these brutes should cower
And remember that, as the saying goes,
It's risky to play with elephants,—
And then they defy Him openly!
*I'm* guiltless enough; if it comes to judgment,
I can prove that I made an offer to pay them.
But what do I get in return for that?
I know they say that your head lies easy
If your conscience is clear. That may be true
On *terra firma*; but on the sea,
Where an honest man's quite the exception,
I don't consider it worth a rush.
At sea you never can be yourself;
You simply sink or swim with the others;
Should the hour of vengeance chance to strike
For the Cook and the Boatswain, I most likely
Should be swept along to perdition with them:
There's no respect for individuals,—
You're nothing more than one of the crowd.
    My mistake has been that I've been too meek,
And get the blame for all that has happened.
If I were younger, I do believe
I'd change my tune and play the boss.
There's time for it yet! It shall get abroad
That Peer has come overseas a winner!
By hook or crook I'll get back the farm;
I'll build on it—it shall look like a castle.

But not a soul shall come into my house!
They shall stand at the door and twiddle their caps,
They shall beg—I'll let them do *that* with pleasure—
But I'll not give them a single farthing;
If I've had to smart from the lash of fortune,
They'll find out that I can hit back again——

[*A* STRANGER *is seen standing beside* PEER GYNT
*in the gloom, bowing politely to him.*

STRANGER.

Good evening!

PEER GYNT.

Good evening!  What—?  Who are you?

STRANGER.

Your fellow-passenger, at your service.

PEER GYNT.

Indeed?  I thought I was the only one.

STRANGER.

A wrong impression, corrected now.

PEER GYNT.

But it's very strange I have never seen you
Until this evening——

STRANGER.

I don't go out

In daytime.

PEER GYNT.

Perhaps you are not well?
You're as white as a sheet——

STRANGER.

I'm quite well, thank you.

PEER GYNT.

What a storm!

STRANGER.

Yes, what a blessing, man!

PEER GYNT.

A blessing?

STRANGER.

The waves are mountains high.
It makes one's mouth water to think
Of the wrecks that there will be to-night!—
Of the corpses that will be washed ashore.

PEER GYNT.

God forbid!

STRANGER.

Have you ever seen a man
That has been strangled—or hanged—or drowned?

PEER GYNT.

What on earth do you mean?

STRANGER.

There's a grin on their faces;
But the grin is ghastly, and for the most part
They've bitten their tongues.

PEER GYNT.

Do go away!

STRANGER.

Only one question! Suppose, for instance,
That the ship should run aground to-night
And sink——

PEER GYNT.

Then do you think there's danger?

STRANGER.

I really don't know what to answer.
Suppose I'm saved and you get drowned——

PEER GYNT.

Oh, bosh—!

STRANGER.

       Well, it's just possible.
With one foot in the grave, a man
Inclines to charitable thoughts——

PEER GYNT (*putting his hand in his pocket*).

I see, it's money that you want!

STRANGER.

No; but if you would be so kind
As to present me with your corpse—?

PEER GYNT.

This is too much!

STRANGER.

       Merely your corpse!
It's for a scientific purpose——

PEER GYNT.

Get out!

STRANGER.

      But, my dear friend, consider—
The thing would be to your advantage!
I'd have you opened and laid bare.
It really is the seat of dreaming
That I am seeking; but, besides,
I'd have you thoroughly examined——

PEER GYNT.

Get out!

STRANGER.

But, sir—a mere drowned corpse!

PEER GYNT.

Blasphemous man! You encourage the storm!
What folly! In all this wind and rain
And heavy seas and every sign
That some fatality may happen—
Here are you asking for something worse!

STRANGER.

I see that you're not disposed, for the moment,
To carry the matter farther. But time
So very often will alter things. [*Bows politely.*
We shall meet when you're sinking, if not before;
Then, perhaps, you'll be in a better humour.
[*Goes into the cabin.*

PEER GYNT.

Unpleasant fellows, these men of science!
Freethinkers, too——
[*To the* BOATSWAIN *who is passing.*
A word, my friend!
Who is that lunatic passenger?

BOATSWAIN.

I did not know we had any but you.

PEER GYNT.

No other? Why, this gets worse and worse.
[*To a* SAILOR *who comes out of the cabin.*
Who went into the cabin just now?

SAILOR.

The ship's dog, sir! [*Passes on.*

THE WATCH (*calling out*).
Land close ahead!

PEER GYNT.

My trunk! My box! Bring them up on deck!

BOATSWAIN.

We have something else to think about now.

PEER GYNT.

Captain, I wasn't serious
In what I said! I was only joking!
Of course I'm going to help the Cook—!

CAPTAIN.

The jib has gone!

MATE.

There went the foresail!

BOATSWAIN (*calling from forward*).

Breakers ahead!

CAPTAIN.

She'll go to pieces!

[*The ship strikes. Noise and confusion.*

SCENE II

(SCENE.—*Off the coast, amongst rocks and breakers. The ship is sinking. Through the mist, glimpses are caught of a boat with two men in it. A breaking wave fills it; it capsizes; a scream is heard, then all is still for a while. Soon afterwards the boat comes into sight, floating keel uppermost.* PEER GYNT *comes to the surface near the boat.*)

PEER GYNT.

Help! Help! A boat!—Help! I shall sink!
God save me—as the Bible says!

[*Clings tight to the keel of the boat. The* COOK *comes to the surface on the other side of the boat.*

COOK.

Oh, God—for my dear children's sake
Be pitiful! Let me be saved!

[*Holds on to the keel.*

PEER GYNT.

Let go!

COOK.

Let go!

PEER GYNT.

I'll push you off!

COOK.

I'll push *you* off!

PEER GYNT.

I'll kick you off!
Let go your hold! It won't bear two!

COOK.

I know. Get off!

PEER GYNT.

Get off yourself!

COOK.

Not likely!
[*They fight. The* COOK *gets one hand hurt, but
clings fast to the boat with the other hand.*

PEER GYNT.

Take your hand away!

COOK.

Be kind! Be merciful!—Just think
Of my young children there at home!

PEER GYNT.

I have more need to live than you,
For I have got no children yet.

COOK.

Let go! You've had your life; I'm young!

PEER GYNT.

Be quick and sink; you're much too heavy.

COOK.

Have mercy! For God's sake let go!
There's no one that will mourn for you——
                    [*Shrieks and slips down.*
I'm drowning!

PEER GYNT (*catching hold of the* COOK'S *hair*).
No, I've got you tight
By your back hair; repeat " Our Father "!

COOK.

I can't remember—all seems dark——

PEER GYNT.

Say what is most essential! Quick!

COOK.

" Give us this day "——

PEER GYNT.

Oh, skip all that;
You have got all that you will need.

COOK.

" Give us this day "——

PEER GYNT.

The same old song!
It's easy seen you were a cook——
[*His grip gives way.*

COOK (*sinking*).

" Give us this day our "——        [*Goes under.*

PEER GYNT.

Amen, lad!
You were yourself up to the end.
[*Swings himself up on to the keel of the boat.*
Where there is life there's always hope——
[*The* STRANGER *is seen in the water, catching hold of the boat.*

STRANGER.

Good morning!

PEER GYNT.
Eh!

STRANGER.

I heard a cry;
It's funny I should find you here.
Well? Do you see I spoke the truth?

PEER GYNT.

Let go! There's barely room for one!

STRANGER.

I'll swim quite well with my left leg.
I'll float if only I insert
My finger-tip into this crack.
But what about your corpse?

PEER GYNT.

Be quiet!

STRANGER.

The rest is absolutely done for——

PEER GYNT.

Do hold your tongue!

STRANGER.

Just as you wish.

[*Silence.*

PEER GYNT.

Well?

STRANGER.

I am silent.

PEER GYNT.

Devil's tricks!—
What are you doing?

STRANGER.

I am waiting.

PEER GYNT (*tearing his hair*).

I shall go mad! What are you?

STRANGER (*nodding to him*).

Friendly!

PEER GYNT.

Go on! What more?

STRANGER.

What do you think?
Don't you know anyone that's like me?

PEER GYNT.

I know the Devil——

STRANGER (*lowering his voice*).

Is he wont
To light us on the darkest paths
Of life when we're beset by fear?

PEER GYNT.

Oh! So it seems, on explanation,
That you're a messenger of the light?

STRANGER.

Friend, have you known—say, twice a year—
What terror really means?

PEER GYNT.

Of course.
One is afraid when danger threatens;
But your words are ambiguous——

STRANGER.

Well, have you ever, even once,
Triumphed as the result of terror?

PEER GYNT (*looking at him*).

If you have come to guide my steps,
'Twas stupid not to come before.
It's not much good to choose the time
When I'm most likely to be drowned.

STRANGER.

And would your triumph be more likely
If you sat snugly by your fire?

PEER GYNT.

Perhaps not; but your talk was foolish.
How could you think it would affect me?

STRANGER.

Where I come from, they think a smile
Worth quite as much as any pathos.

PEER GYNT.

There is a time for everything.
Things which a publican may do
Are most disgraceful in a bishop.

STRANGER.

The souls of those of bygone days
Whose ashes rest in funeral urns
Aren't always in a solemn humour.

PEER GYNT.

Leave me, you bugbear! Get away!
I won't die! I must get to land!

STRANGER.

As far as that goes, make your mind
Quite easy; no one ever dies
Until he's seen the fifth act through.

[*Disappears.*

PEER GYNT.

Ah, it slipped out of him at last;—
He was a wretched Moralist.


## SCENE III

(SCENE.—*A churchyard high up in the mountains. A
funeral is going on. The* PRIEST *and the* MOURNERS
*are just finishing the last verse of a hymn.* PEER GYNT
*is passing on the road, and stops at the churchyard gate.*)

PEER GYNT.

Here's another man going the way of all flesh.
Well, God be praised that it isn't me!

[*Goes into the churchyard.*

### PRIEST.

Now that his soul has gone to meet its God,
And this poor dust waits like an empty husk,—
Let us, dear friends, in a few words recall
The dead man's journey on this earth of ours.

He wasn't rich, nor was he very clever;
His voice was weak, his bearing scarcely manly;
He had no strength of mind, nor much decision;
Nor in his own home did he seem the master.
His manner when he came to church was such
As if he felt he must request permission
To take his seat among the congregation.

Of Gudbrandsdal he was, you know, a native,
And he was scarce a boy when he came hither;
And, to the last, as you no doubt have noticed,
He always kept his right hand in his pocket.

That same peculiarity I mention
Was probably the only thing that stamped
His picture on our minds; that, and the shyness—
The almost shamefaced diffidence—with which
He bore himself when he came in amongst us.

But, though he was so diffident and quiet,
And to the last was almost like a stranger,
You know quite well, in spite of his concealment,
The hand he hid had no more than four fingers.—

I well remember, many years ago,
During the war, one morning a Conscription
Was held at Lundë. Everyone was full
Of Norway's troubles and her doubtful future.
Behind a table, I remember, sat
A Captain and the Mayor, and several Sergeants;
And one by one our lads came in, were measured,
Enrolled, and duly sworn in to the army.
The room was full; and outside in the courtyard
Was heard the noise of the young people's laughter.

A name was called out, and a lad came in
With face as white as snow upon the hilltops.
They told him to come forward to the table.
His right hand was all swathed up in a napkin;

He gasped and swallowed—tried to find his voice—
But seemed as if he had no words to answer
The Captain's questions. Still, at last, he did;
And then, with crimson face and faltering tongue
That sometimes let the words out with a rush,
He mumbled some tale of an accident—
A reaping-hook that slipped and cut his finger
Clean off his hand. There was a sudden silence.
Men exchanged glances; lips were curled in scorn;
Looks of disdain were flashed upon the lad,
Who stood there staring with unseeing eyes;
He felt their scorn although he did not see it.
And then the Captain, an old grey-haired man,
Stood up, and spat, and pointed to the door
And said: " Begone! "—and so the lad went out.
Those in the room divided to make way,
So that he ran the gauntlet of them all.
He reached the door, and then took to his heels;
Ran up the hillside—through the woods and pastures,
Up over rocks and stones, stumbling and slipping—
To where his home was, far up in the mountains.
    'Twas six months after that when he came hither,
Bringing his mother, children and betrothed.
He leased some land upon the mountain-side
Near to where Lomb is bounded by the moor.
As soon as it was possible, he married
The mother of his children; built a house;
Broke up the stony ground with such success
That yellow grain in patches soon appeared
Amidst the rocks. It's true that when he went
To church he kept his right hand in his pocket;
But on his farm I know he worked as well
With nine fingers as others with their ten.—
Then, one wet spring, a flood swept all away.
    They saved their lives, but nothing else; and, poor
And naked as he was, he set to work
To clear the soil afresh; and by the autumn
He'd built himself a house on safer ground.
Safer? Yes, from the flood but not the mountains.
For, two years later, in an avalanche

All that he had was overwhelmed again.
But even avalanches had no power
To daunt his soul.  He set to work to dig
And clear the snow and save what might be left;
And, ere the winter's snow had come again,
He'd built his little house a third time up.

　　Three sons he had—three fine young lads—and they
Must go to school, and school was far away;
And so, from where the public roadway ended,
He had to cut a steep and narrow path
Through the hard snow.  And then—what did he do?
The eldest boy had to climb up and scramble
As best he could; and where it was too steep
His father roped him to him for support.
The other two he carried in his arms
And on his back.

　　　　　　　And thus, year after year,
He drudged; and his three sons grew to be men.
Then came a time when he might surely ask
For something in return from them; but they,
Three prosperous men in far America,
Had quite forgotten their Norwegian father
And how he used to help them to the school.

　　He was a man whose vision never saw
Farther than what lay nearest to his hand.
Words which resound in other people's hearts
Were meaningless to him as tinkling bells;
Family, Country—all that's best and brightest—
Was blurred and hidden by a veil of tears.

　　But never did I know a man so humble.
From that Conscription Day he carried with him
The sense of guilt, which showed as plainly on him
As did the blush of shame upon his cheek
And his four fingers hidden in his pocket.
A breaker of his country's laws?  Perhaps!
But there is something that outshines the law
As certainly as Glittertinde's peaks
Stand gleaming in the sun above the clouds.
He was a bad citizen, no doubt;
For Church and State alike, a sterile tree;

But up there on the rocky mountain side,
In the small circle of his hearth and home,
Where his work lay, *there* I say he was great,
Because he was himself. 'Twas only there
The metal he was made of could ring true.
His life was like a melody that's played
On muted strings. — And therefore, peace be with
    you,
Poor silent warrior, who fought and fell
Waging the little war of peasant's life!
   We will not seek to search the heart and reins,
That's not a task for us, but for his Maker.
Still, this I hope—and hope with confidence:
That this man, as he stands before the Throne,
Is not a cripple in the eyes of God!

    [*The congregation disperses.* PEER GYNT *remains
      alone.*

#### PEER GYNT.

Well, *that's* what I call Christianity!
Nothing in it to make one feel uneasy.
Indeed the theme of the Priest's address—
That we should all strive to be ourselves—
Is really extremely edifying.    [*Looks into the grave.*
Was it he, I wonder, who slashed his knuckles
When I was felling trees in the forest?
Who knows? If I were not standing here
By the grave of this congenial spirit,
I might believe that it was myself
That was sleeping there and was listening
In dreams to praises that I deserved.
It's really a beautiful Christian practice
To take a kindly retrospect
Of the whole life of the departed.
I'd readily accept a verdict
From this most worthy priest.—However,
I've still some time left, I expect,
Before the sexton comes and claims me;
And, as the Scripture says: " The best
Is still the best "; and, in like manner:

" Sufficient for the day is the evil thereof ";
And, further: " Do not borrow trouble."—
The Church is the only comforter.
Up till now I have never given
The credit to it that is its due;
But now I know what good it does you
To hear authority proclaim:
" As you have sowed, so must you reap."
We must be ourselves; in everything,
Both great and small, we must look after
Ourselves and what concerns ourselves.
Though Fortune fail us we shall win
Respect, if our careers have been
Shaped in accordance with this doctrine.—
And now for home! What though the way
Be steep and narrow—what though Fortune
Be still malicious—old Peer Gynt
Will go his own way, and remain,
As always: poor but virtuous.                    [*Goes.*

## SCENE IV

(SCENE.—*A hillside showing the dried-up bed of a
stream, by which stands a ruined mill. The ground is
torn up, and everything is in a ruinous state. Outside
the mill an auction is taking place ; there is a large and
noisy gathering of people, and drinking is going on.*
PEER GYNT *is sitting on a heap of rubbish near the
mill.*)

### PEER GYNT.

Backward or forward, it's just as far;
Out or in, the way's as narrow.
Time destroys and the stream cuts through.
" Round about," said the Boyg; and we needs must,
        here.

A MAN IN MOURNING.[1]

Now there's nothing left but the rubbish.

[*Looks at* PEER GYNT.

Strangers, too? God save you, sir!

PEER GYNT.

Well met! This is a merry scene;
Is it a christening, or a wedding?

MAN IN MOURNING.

I should rather say a house-warming;
The bride, poor thing, is food for worms.

PEER GYNT.

And worms are fighting for rags and scraps.

MAN IN MOURNING.

It's a finished story, and this is the end.

PEER GYNT.

Every story ends the same;
I've known them all since I was a boy.

A YOUNG BOY (*holding a casting-ladle*).

Look what a fine thing I have bought!
Peer Gynt used to mould buttons with this.

ANOTHER.

I got a fine purse for a farthing!

A THIRD.

A pedlar's pack for twopence halfpenny!

PEER GYNT.

Peer Gynt? Who was he?

MAN IN MOURNING.

I only know
He was brother-in-law to the bridegroom, Death,
And also to the blacksmith Aslak.

[1] The Man in Mourning is Aslak, who apparently has
married Ingrid and is now in mourning for her death.

A MAN IN GREY.[1]
You're forgetting me; you must be drunk!

MAN IN MOURNING.
You're forgetting the loft-door at Hægstad.

MAN IN GREY.
So I was; but you were never dainty.

MAN IN MOURNING.
If only she doesn't play Death a trick——

MAN IN GREY.
Come on! Have a drink with your relation!

MAN IN MOURNING.
Relation be damned! Your drunken fancies——

MAN IN GREY.
Oh, nonsense! Blood is thicker than that;
At least we're both Peer Gynt's relations.
                              [*They go off together.*

PEER GYNT (*aside*).
I'm meeting old friends.

A BOY (*calling after the* MAN IN MOURNING).
                    My poor dead mother
Will come after you, Aslak, if you get drinking.

PEER GYNT (*getting up*).
The Agriculturalists are wrong;
It doesn't smell better the deeper you dig.

A BOY (*with a bearskin*).
Here's the Dovrë-Cat!—or at least his skin!
It was he chased the Troll on Christmas Eve.

ANOTHER (*with a pair of reindeer-horns*).
Here's the fine buck on which Peer Gynt
Rode right along the ridge of Gendin.

[1] The Man in Grey is Mads Moen.

A THIRD
(*with a hammer, calls to the* MAN IN MOURNING).
Hi! Aslak! Do you know this hammer?
Was it this you used when the Devil escaped?

A FOURTH (*showing his empty hands*).
Mads Moen, here's the invisible cloak
In which Peer Gynt and Ingrid vanished.

PEER GYNT.
Some brandy, boys! I'm feeling old;
I'll hold an auction of all my rubbish.

A BOY.
What have you got to sell?

PEER GYNT.
A castle;
It's up at Rondë, and solidly built.

BOY.
I bid one button!

PEER GYNT.
A drink with it, then;
It's a sin and a shame to offer less.

ANOTHER BOY.
He's a merry old chap!
[*The crowd gathers round* PEER GYNT.

PEER GYNT.
Granë, my horse!—
Who bids?

ONE OF THE CROWD.
Where is he?

PEER GYNT.
Away in the West!
Near the sunset, boys! He can trot as fast
As Peer Gynt could make up his lies.

VOICES.

What more have you?

PEER GYNT.

                    Both gold and rubbish!
I bought them at a loss, and now
I'll sell them at a sacrifice.

A BOY.

Put them up!

PEER GYNT.

                    A vision of a prayer-book!
You may have it for a hook and eye.

BOY.

Deuce take your visions!

PEER GYNT.

                    Then—my Empire!
I throw it to you; you may scramble for it!

BOY.

Does a crown go with it?

PEER GYNT.

                    A lovely crown
Of straw, and it will fit the first
That puts it on.—Here's something more!
An empty egg!  Grey hair of a madman!
The Prophet's beard!—You may have them all,
If you'll only show me on the hillside
A signpost marked: " This is the way "!

THE MAYOR (*who has come up*).

The way you're going on, my man,
I think will lead you to the lock-up.

PEER GYNT (*with his hat in his hand*).

Very likely.  But, tell me, who was Peer Gynt?

THE MAYOR.

Oh, bother—!

PEER GYNT.

Excuse me—I want to know—!

THE MAYOR.

Well,—they say, an incurable romancer.

PEER GYNT.

Romancer?

THE MAYOR.

Yes; romanced about
All sorts of glorious deeds as if
He had done all of them himself.
Excuse me now, my friend, I'm busy——
*[Goes away.*

PEER GYNT.

And where's this wonderful fellow now?

AN ELDERLY MAN.

He went oversea to a foreign land,
And came to grief as one might have expected.
It's many years now since he was hanged.

PEER GYNT.

Hanged? Dear me! I was sure of it;
The late Peer Gynt was himself to the last.
*[Bows.*
Good-bye. I'm much obliged to you all!
*[Takes a few steps, then stops.*
You merry boys and lovely women,
May I tell you a story in return?

VOICES.

Yes, if you know one!

PEER GYNT.

Certainly.

[*Comes back to them. His face takes on an
altered expression.*

I was in San Francisco, gold-digging,
And the whole town was full of freaks;
One played the fiddle with his toes,
One danced fandangos on his knees,
A third, I heard, kept making verses
While holes were bored right through his skull.
To this freak-show the Devil came,
To try his luck like so many others.
His line was this: he could imitate
The grunting of a pig exactly.
His personality attracted
Although he was not recognized.
The house was full, and on tenterhooks
Of expectation. In he strode,
Dressed in a cape with flowing wings;
*Man muss sich drappieren,* as the Germans say.
But no one knew that in his cape
He had a little pig concealed.
And now he started his performance.
The devil pinched; the pig gave tongue.
The whole was a fantasia
On a pig's life, from birth to slaughter,
Ending up with a shriek like that
Which follows on the slaughterer's stroke;
With which, the artist bowed and went.—
Then there arose a keen discussion
Among the experts in the audience.
The noises were both praised and censured;
Some found the tone of them too thin,
Others declared the dying shriek
Was far too studied; but they all
Were of the same mind on one point:
That the performance was, *qua* grunt,
Exceedingly exaggerated.
You see, that's what the Devil got,

Because he'd made the sad mistake
Of reckoning without his public.
    [*Bows and goes away.   An uneasy silence falls
      on the crowd.*

## Scene V

(Scene.—*A clearing in a great forest, on the Eve of
Pentecost.  In the background is seen a hut, with a pair
of reindeer-horns over the door.  Peer Gynt is on all-
fours on the ground, grubbing up wild onions.*)

### Peer Gynt.

This is one standpoint.  Where is the next?
One should try all things and choose the best.
I have done that; I've been a Cæsar,
And now I'm behaving like Nebuchadnezzar.
So I might go through Bible history.
This old boy's back to mother earth.
I remember the Book says: " Dust thou art."
The great thing in life is to fill your belly.
Fill it with onions?  It matters little;
I'll fit some cunning traps and snares.
There is a brook; I'll not go thirsty;
And all wild things shall do my bidding.
And, suppose I die—which perhaps may happen—
I'll creep beneath a fallen tree;
Like the bear, I'll cover myself with leaves,
And scratch in the bark, in great big letters:
" Here lies Peer Gynt, a decent chap,
Who was Emperor of all the Beasts."—
Emperor?                                   [*Laughs to himself.*
      You absurd old humbug!
You're not an emperor, you're an onion!
Now, my dear Peer, I'm going to peel you,
However little you may enjoy it.
      [*Takes an onion and peels it, layer by layer.*
There's the untidy outer husk;
That's the shipwrecked man on the wreck of the boat;
Next layer's the Passenger, thin and skinny—

Still smacking of Peer Gynt a little.
Next we come to the gold-digger self;
The pith of it's gone—someone's seen to that.
This layer with a hardened edge
Is the fur-hunter of Hudson's Bay.
The next one's like a crown. No, thank you!
We'll throw it away without further question.
Here's the Antiquarian, short and sturdy;
And here is the Prophet, fresh and juicy;
He stinks, as the saying goes, of lies
Enough to bring water to your eyes.
This layer, effeminately curled,
Is the man who lived a life of pleasure.
The next looks sickly. It's streaked with black.
Black may mean missionaries or negroes.
                    [*Pulls off several layers together.*
There's a most surprising lot of layers!
Are we never coming to the kernel?
                    [*Pulls all that is left to pieces.*
There isn't one! To the innermost bit
It's nothing but layers, smaller and smaller.
Nature's a joker!   [*Throws the bits away from him.*
                    Deuce take all thinking!
If you begin that, you may miss your footing.
Well, anyway *I* don't run that risk
As long as I'm down on all-fours here.
                    [*Scratches the back of his head.*
Life's an uncommonly odd contraption;
It plays an underhand game with us;
If you try to catch hold of it, it eludes you,
And you get what you didn't expect—or nothing.
          [*Goes closer to the hut, looks at it, and starts.*
That hut? In the forest—! Eh?    [*Rubs his eyes.*
                    I'm certain
I must have seen that hut before.
The reindeer-horns there, over the door—!
A mermaid carved on the end of the gable—!
That's a lie! No mermaid—just logs and nails—
And the bolt that should keep out plaguy thoughts—!
          [SOLVEIG'S *voice is heard from the hut.*

SOLVEIG (*singing*).

Now all is ready for Pentecost.
Dear lad far away, are you coming near?
If your burden's heavy, then rest awhile;
I shall wait, because I promised you, dear.
[PEER GYNT *rises to his feet, deathly pale and quiet.*

PEER GYNT.

One who remembered—and one who forgot;
One who has kept what the other has lost.
Life's serious, not a foolish jest!
Ah, misery! *Here* my Empire lay!
[*Runs into the wood.*

## SCENE VI

(SCENE.—*A moor with firs, at night. A forest fire has laid it waste. Charred tree-trunks for miles around. Patches of white mist are lying here and there over the ground.* PEER GYNT *comes running over the moor.*)

PEER GYNT.

Ashes, mists and dust-clouds flying—
Fine material to build with!
Stench and rottenness within them;
All a whited sepulchre.
Fancies, dreams and still-born wisdom
For a base, while lies shall serve
For a staircase for the building
Of a lofty pyramid.
Flight from everything that's worthy;
No repentance—only terror;
These shall cap a building labelled:
" Petrus Gyntus Cæsar fecit "!          [*Listens.*
What is that sound like children's weeping?—
Weeping that is half a song?
What are these that I see rolling
At my feet, like balls of thread?
[*Kicks his feet about.*
Get away! You block the path up!

THE THREADBALLS [1] (*on the ground*).
>We are thoughts;
>You should have thought us;
>Little feet, to life
>You should have brought us!

PEER GYNT (*going round them*).
I've only brought *one* thought to life,—
And it was wry and bandy-legged!

THE THREADBALLS.
>We should have risen
>With glorious sound;
>But here like threadballs
>We are earth-bound.

PEER GYNT (*stumbling*).
Threadballs! You infernal rascals!
Are you tripping up your father? [*Runs away.*

WITHERED LEAVES (*flying before the wind*).
>We are a watchword;
>You should have used us!
>Life, by your sloth,
>Has been refused us.
>By worms we're eaten
>All up and down;
>No fruit will have us
>For spreading crown.

PEER GYNT.
Still, you have not been born for nothing;
Lie still, and you will serve for manure.

A SIGHING IN THE AIR.
>We are songs;
>You should have sung us!
>In the depths of your heart

---

[1] The idea of Trolls incorporated in threadballs is frequently met with in Scandinavian folklore.

Despair has wrung us!
We lay and waited;
You called us not.
May your throat and voice
With poison rot!

PEER GYNT.

Poison yourselves, you silly doggerel!
Had I any time for verse and twaddle?

[*Goes to one side.*

DEWDROPS (*dropping from the branches*).

We are tears
Which were never shed.
The cutting ice
Which all hearts dread
We could have melted;
But now its dart
Is frozen into
A stubborn heart.
The wound is closed;
Our power is lost.

PEER GYNT.

Thanks!—I wept at Rondesvalen,
And got a thrashing on the backside!

BROKEN STRAWS.

We are deeds
You have left undone;
Strangled by doubt,
Spoiled ere begun.
At the Judgment Day
We shall be there
To tell our tale;
How will you fare?

PEER GYNT.

Rubbish! You can't condemn a man
For actions that he *hasn't* done!

AASE'S VOICE (*from afar off*).
  Fie, what a driver!
  Ugh! You've upset me
  Into a snowdrift,
  Muddied and wet me.
  Peer, where's the Castle?
  You've driven madly;
  The whip in your hand
  The Devil's used badly!

PEER GYNT.
I'd best be off while I am able.
If I have to bear the burden
Of the Devil's sins, I'll sink
Into the ground. I find my own
Quite a heavy enough load.          [*Runs off.*

SCENE VII

(SCENE.—*Another part of the moor.*)

PEER GYNT (*singing*).
A sexton! a sexton! Where are you all?
Open your bleating mouths and sing!
We've bands of crape tied round our hats,
And plenty of corpses for burying!
  [*The* BUTTON MOULDER, *carrying his box of
    tools and a big casting-ladle, comes in by
    a side path.*

BUTTON MOULDER.
Well met, gaffer!

PEER GYNT.
    Good evening, my friend!

BUTTON MOULDER.
You seem in a hurry. Where are you going?

PEER GYNT.

To a funeral.

BUTTON MOULDER.

Really? My sight's not good—
Excuse me—is your name by any chance Peer?

PEER GYNT.

Peer Gynt's my name.

BUTTON MOULDER.

What a piece of luck!
It was just Peer Gynt I was looking for.

PEER GYNT.

Were you? What for?

BUTTON MOULDER.

Well, as you see,
I am a button moulder; and you
Must be popped into my Casting-ladle.

PEER GYNT.

What for?

BUTTON MOULDER.

So as to be melted down.

PEER GYNT.

Melted?

BUTTON MOULDER.

Yes; it's clean and it's empty.
Your grave is dug and your coffin ordered;
Your body will make fine food for worms;
But the Master's orders bid me fetch
Your soul at once.

PEER GYNT.

Impossible!
Like this?—without the slightest warning?

BUTTON MOULDER.

Alike for funerals and confinements
The custom is to choose the day
Without giving the slightest warning
To the chief guest of the occasion.

PEER GYNT.

Quite so. My head is going round!
You are—?

BUTTON MOULDER.

You heard; a button moulder.

PEER GYNT.

I understand! A favourite child
Is called by lots of names.—Well, Peer,
So *that's* to be the end of your journey!—
Still, it's a scurvy trick to play me.
I deserved something a little kinder.
I'm not so bad as perhaps you think;
I've done some little good in the world.
At worst I might be called a bungler,
But certainly not an out-and-out sinner.

BUTTON MOULDER.

But that is just the point, my man.
In the highest sense you're not a sinner;
So you escape the pangs of torment
And come into the Casting-ladle.

PEER GYNT.

Oh, call it what you like—a ladle
Or the bottomless pit—it's just the same!
Ginger is always hot in the mouth,
Whatever you may be pleased to call it.
Satan, away!

BUTTON MOULDER.

You are not so rude
As to think that I've a cloven hoof?

### PEER GYNT.

Cloven hoof or fox's claws—
Whichever you like. So now pack off!
Mind your own business, and be off!

### BUTTON MOULDER.

My friend, you're under a great delusion.
We're both in a hurry; so, to save time,
I'll try to explain the matter to you.
You are, as you yourself have said,
Nothing great in the way of a sinner—
Scarcely a middling one, perhaps——

### PEER GYNT.

Now you are talking reasonably.

### BUTTON MOULDER.

Wait a bit!—I think it would be going
Too far to call you virtuous——

### PEER GYNT.

I certainly don't lay claim to that.

### BUTTON MOULDER.

Well, then, say, something betwixt and between
Sinners in the true grand style
Are seldom met with nowadays;
That style of sin needs power of mind—
It's something more than dabbling in mud.

### PEER GYNT.

That's perfectly true; one should go at it
With something of a Berserk's fury.

### BUTTON MOULDER.

You, on the contrary, my friend,
Took sinning lightly.

### PEER GYNT.

                    Just, my friend,
A little mud-splashed, so to speak.

BUTTON MOULDER.

Now we're agreed. The bottomless pit
Is not for you who played with mud.

PEER GYNT.

Consequently, my friend, I take it
That I may have your leave to go
Just as I came?

BUTTON MOULDER.

        Oh no, my friend—
Consequently you'll be melted down.

PEER GYNT.

What's this new game that you've invented
While I have been abroad?

BUTTON MOULDER.

           The practice
Is just as old as the Creation,
And was invented for the purpose
Of keeping things up to the standard.
You know in metal work, for instance,
It sometimes happens that a casting
Turns out a failure, absolutely—
Buttons are turned out without loops.
What would you do in such a case?

PEER GYNT.

I'd throw the trash away.

BUTTON MOULDER.

         Exactly.
Your father had the reputation
Of reckless wastefulness as long
As he had anything to waste.
The Master, on the other hand,
Is economical, you see,
And therefore is a man of substance.
He never throws away as useless

A single thing that may be dealt with
As raw material.—Now, *you*
Were meant to be a gleaming button
On the World's waistcoat, but your loop
Was missing; so you've got to go
Into the scrap-heap, to be merged
Into the mass.

### PEER GYNT.

But do you mean
That I've got to be melted down
With any Tom and Dick and Harry
And moulded fresh?

### BUTTON MOULDER.

That's what I mean.
That's what we've done to not a few,
It's what they do at the mint with money
When the coin is too much worn with use.

### PEER GYNT.

But it's simply disgusting niggardliness!
My dear friend, won't you let me go?
A loopless button—a smooth-worn coin—
What are they to a man of your master's substance?

### BUTTON MOULDER.

The fact of your having a soul's enough
To give you a certain intrinsic value.

### PEER GYNT.

No, I say! No! With tooth and nail
I'll fight against it! I'd rather, far,
Put up with anything than that!

### BUTTON MOULDER.

But what do you mean by " anything "?
You must be reasonable, you know;
You're not the sort that goes to Heaven——

PEER GYNT.

I'm humble; I don't aim so high
As that; but I'm not going to lose
A single jot of what's myself.
Let me be sentenced in ancient fashion;
Send me to Him with the Cloven Hoof
For a certain time—say, a hundred years,
If the sentence must be a very severe one.
That's a thing I daresay one might put up with;
The torture would then be only moral,
And perhaps, after all, not so very tremendous.
It would be a transition, so to speak,
As the fox said.[1] If you wait, there comes
Deliverance and you may get back;
Meanwhile you hope for better days.
But the other idea—to be swallowed up
Like a speck in a mass of strange material—
This ladle business—losing all
The attributes that make a Gynt—
*That* fills my inmost soul with horror!

BUTTON MOULDER.

But, my dear Peer, there is no need
For you to make so great a fuss
About so small a thing; because
You never yet have been yourself.
What difference can it make to you
If, when you die, you disappear?

PEER GYNT.

*I*'ve never been myself! Haha!
You almost make me laugh. Peer Gynt
Anything but himself!—No, no,
Friend Button Moulder, you are wrong;
You're judging blindly. If you searched
My inmost being, you would find
I'm Peer right through, and nothing else.

[1] " As the fox said when they skinned him." A Norwegian
proverb.

BUTTON MOULDER.

Impossible. Here are my orders.
See, they say: " You will fetch Peer Gynt.
He has defied his destiny.
He is a failure, and must go
Straight into the Casting-ladle."

PEER GYNT.

What nonsense! It must surely mean
Some other Gynt. Are you quite sure
That it says Peer?—not John, or Rasmus?

BUTTON MOULDER.

I melted them down long ago.
Now, come along and don't waste time.

PEER GYNT.

No, that I won't! Suppose to-morrow
You found that it meant someone else?
That would be pleasant! My good man,
You must be careful, and remember
What a responsibility——

BUTTON MOULDER.

I've got my orders to protect me.

PEER GYNT.

Give me a little respite, then!

BUTTON MOULDER.

What for?

PEER GYNT.

I will find means to prove
That, all my life, I've been myself;
That is, of course, the point at issue.

BUTTON MOULDER.

Prove it? But how?

PEER GYNT.
        With witnesses
And testimonials.

BUTTON MOULDER.
        I fear
That you won't satisfy the Master.

PEER GYNT.
I'm quite sure that I shall! Besides,
We'll talk about that when the time comes.
Dear man, just let me have myself
On loan for quite a little while.
I will come back to you. We men
Are not born more than once, you know,
And naturally we make a fight
To keep the self with which we came
Into the world.—Are we agreed?

BUTTON MOULDER.
So be it. But, remember this:
At the next crossroads we shall meet.
                    [PEER GYNT *runs off.*


SCENE VIII

(SCENE.—*Another part of the moor.*)

PEER GYNT (*running in*).
Time is money, as people say.
If I only knew where the crossroads are—
It may be near, or it may be far.
The ground seems to burn my feet like fire.
A witness! A witness! Where shall I find one?
It's next to impossible, here in the forest.
The world's a bungle! It's managed wrong,

If it's necessary for a man to prove
His rights that are clear as the noonday sun!

*[A bent* OLD MAN, *with a staff in his hand and a
bag on his back, hobbles up to* PEER GYNT.

OLD MAN.

Kind sir, give a homeless old man a penny!

PEER GYNT.

I'm sorry—I have no change about me——

OLD MAN.

Prince Peer! Can it be that we meet at last?

PEER GYNT.

Why, who—?

OLD MAN.

He's forgotten the old man at Rondë!

PEER GYNT.

You surely are never—?

OLD MAN.

The King of the Dovrë.

PEER GYNT.

The Troll King? Really? The Troll King?—Answer!

OLD MAN.

I'm he, but in different circumstances.

PEER GYNT.

Ruined?

OLD MAN.

Aye, robbed of everything;
A tramp, and as hungry as a wolf.

PEER GYNT.

Hurrah! Such witnesses as this
Don't grow on every tree!

OLD MAN.

          Your Highness
Has grown grey too since last we met.

PEER GYNT.

Worry and age, dear father-in-law.
Well, let's forget our private affairs;
And, above all, our family squabbles.
I was a foolish youth——

OLD MAN.

          Yes, yes;
You were young, and youth must have its fling.
And it's lucky for you that you jilted your bride;
You've escaped a lot of shame and bother,
For afterwards she went clean to the bad——

PEER GYNT.

Dear me!

OLD MAN.

       Now she may look after herself.
Just think—she and Trond have gone off together.

PEER GYNT.

What Trond?

OLD MAN.

      Of the Valfjeld.

PEER GYNT.

          He? Aha,
I robbed him of the cowherd girls.

OLD MAN.

But my grandson's grown a fine big fellow
And has bouncing babies all over the country.

PEER GYNT.

Now, my dear man, I must cut you short;
I am full of quite a different matter.—

I'm in rather a difficult position,
And have to get a certificate
Or a testimonial from someone;
And I think you'll be the very person.
I can always raise the wind enough
To stand you a drink——

### OLD MAN.

Oh! Can I really
Be of assistance to Your Highness?
Perhaps, if that is so, you'll give me
A character in return?

### PEER GYNT.

With pleasure.
I'm a little short of ready money
And have to be careful in every way.—
Now, listen to me. Of course you remember
How I came that night to woo your daughter——

### OLD MAN.

Of course, Your Highness!

### PEER GYNT.

Oh, drop the title!
Well, you wanted to do me violence—
To spoil my sight by cutting my eyeball,
And turn Peer Gynt into a Troll.
What did I do? I strongly objected;
Swore I would stand on my own feet;
Gave up my love, and power and honours,
Simply and solely to be myself.
I want you to swear to that in court——

### OLD MAN.

I can't do that!

### PEER GYNT.

What's that you're saying?

OLD MAN.

You'll surely not force me to swear a lie?
Remember that you put on Troll breeches,
And tasted our mead——

PEER GYNT.

Yes, you tempted me;
But I resolutely made up my mind
That I would not give in. And *that*'s the way
A man shows what he's worth. A song
Depends on its concluding verse.

OLD MAN.

But the conclusion, Peer, was just
The opposite of what you think.

PEER GYNT.

What do you mean?

OLD MAN.

You took away
My motto graven on your heart.

PEER GYNT.

What motto?

OLD MAN.

That compelling word—

PEER GYNT.

Word—?

OLD MAN.

—that distinguishes a Troll
From Mankind: " Troll, to thyself be——
*Enough* "!

PEER GYNT (*with a shriek*).
*Enough !*

OLD MAN.

And, ever since,
With all the energy you have,
You've lived according to that motto.

PEER GYNT.

I? I? Peer Gynt?

OLD MAN (*weeping*).

You're most ungrateful.
You've lived like a Troll, but have kept it secret.
The word I taught has enabled you
To move in the world like a well-to-do man;
And now you begin abusing me
And the word to which you owe gratitude.

PEER GYNT.

*Enough!*—A mere Troll! An egoist!
It must be nonsense—it can't be true!

OLD MAN (*producing a bundle of newspapers*).

Don't you suppose that we have our papers?
Wait; I will show you in black and white
How the *Bloksberg Post* has sung your praises;
The *Heklefjeld News* has done the same
Ever since the winter you went abroad.
Will you read them, Peer? I'll be pleased to let you.
Here's an article signed: " Stallion's Hoof."
Here's one: " On the National Spirit of Trolldom ";
The writer shows how true it is
That it doesn't depend upon horns or tails,
But on having the spirit of Trollhood in one.
" Our 'Enough,'" he concludes, " is what gives the
        stamp
Of Troll to Man "; and he mentions you
As a striking instance.

PEER GYNT.

I—a Troll?

OLD MAN.

It seems quite clear.

PEER GYNT.

                    Then I might have stayed
Where I was, and lived in peace and comfort
At Rondë! I might have saved shoe leather,
And spared myself much toil and trouble!
Peer Gynt—a Troll! It's a pack of lies!
Good-bye! Here's a penny to buy tobacco.

OLD MAN.

But, dear Prince Peer—!

PEER GYNT.

                    Oh, drop this nonsense!
You're mad, or else you're in your dotage.
Go to a hospital.

OLD MAN.

                    Aye, it's that
I'm looking for. But, as I told you,
My grandson's very influential
In all this part, and tells the people
I don't exist except in legends.
The saying goes that one's relations
Are always the worst; and now, alas,
I feel the truth of it. It's sad
To be looked on as being merely
A legendary personage——

PEER GYNT.

Dear man, you're not the only one
To suffer that mishap.

OLD MAN.

                    And then,
We Trolls have nothing in the way

Of Charities or Savings Banks
Or Alms-boxes; such institutions
Would never be acceptable
At Rondë.

### PEER GYNT.

No; and there you see
The work of your confounded motto—
Your fine " To thyself be *enough* "!

### OLD MAN.

Your Highness has no need to grumble.
And if, in some way or another—?

### PEER GYNT.

You're on the wrong scent altogether;
I'm at the end of my resources.

### OLD MAN.

Impossible! Your Highness ruined?

### PEER GYNT.

Cleared out. Even my princely self
Is now in pawn. And that's your fault,
You cursed Trolls! It only shows
What comes of evil company.

### OLD MAN.

So there's another of my hopes
Destroyed!—Good-bye! I'd better try
And beg my way down to the town——

### PEER GYNT.

And when you're there, what will you do?

### OLD MAN.

I'll try and go upon the stage.
They're advertising for National Types
In the papers.

PEER GYNT.

          Well, good luck to you!—
And give my kind regards to them!
If I can only free myself,
I'll go the same way too.  I'll write
A farce that shall be both profound
And entertaining, and its title
Shall be: " Sic Transit Gloria Mundi."
     [*Runs off along the path, leaving  the* OLD
     MAN *calling after him.*

SCENE IX

(SCENE.—*At crossroads.*)

PEER GYNT.

This is the tightest corner, Peer,
You've ever been in.  The Trolls' " Enough "
Has done for you.  Your ship's a wreck;
You must cling to the wreckage—anything—
To avoid the general rubbish heap.

BUTTON MOULDER (*at the parting of the ways*).
Well, Peer Gynt?  And your witnesses?

PEER GYNT.

What, crossroads here?  This is quick work.

BUTTON  MOULDER.

I can read your face as easily
As I can a book, and know your thoughts.

PEER GYNT.

I'm tired from running—one goes astray——

BUTTON  MOULDER.

Yes; and, besides, what does it lead to?

PEER GYNT.

True enough; in the woods, in this failing light——

BUTTON MOULDER.

There's an old man trudging along; shall we call him?

PEER GYNT.

No, let him alone; he's a drunken scamp.

BUTTON MOULDER.

But perhaps he could——

PEER GYNT.

        Hush! No—don't call him!

BUTTON MOULDER.

Is that the way of it?

PEER GYNT.

        Just one question:
What is it really to " be one's self "?

BUTTON MOULDER.

That's a strange question from a man
Who just now——

PEER GYNT.

        Tell me what I asked you.

BUTTON MOULDER.

To be one's self is to slay one's self.[1]
But as perhaps that explanation
Is thrown away on you, let's say:
To follow out, in everything,
What the Master's intention was.

[1] *i.e.*, to kill the base part of one's nature that one's better self may live.

PEER GYNT.

But suppose a man was never told
What the Master's intention was?

BUTTON MOULDER.

Insight should tell him.

PEER GYNT.

             But our insight
So often is at fault, and then
We're thrown out of our stride completely.

BUTTON MOULDER.

Quite so, Peer Gynt. And lack of insight
Gives to our friend with the Cloven Hoof
His strongest weapon, let me tell you.

PEER GYNT.

It's all an extremely subtle problem.—
But, listen; I give up my claim
To have been myself; it very likely
Would be too difficult to prove it.
I'll not attempt to fight the point.
But, as I was wandering all alone
Over the moor just now, I felt
A sudden prick from the spur of conscience.
I said to myself: " You are a sinner——"

BUTTON MOULDER.

Oh, now you're back to where you started——

PEER GYNT.

No, not at all; I mean a *great* one,—
Not only in deed, but in thought and word.
I lived a dreadful life abroad——

BUTTON MOULDER.

May be; but have you anything
To show to prove it?

PEER GYNT.

Give me time;
I'll find a priest, and get it all
In writing, properly attested.

BUTTON MOULDER.

If you can do that, it will clear things up,
And you will be spared the Casting-ladle.
But my orders, Peer——

PEER GYNT.

They're on very old paper;
It certainly dates from a long time back,
When the life I lived was loose and foolish.
I posed as a Prophet and Fatalist.—
Well, may I try?

BUTTON MOULDER.

But——

PEER GYNT.

Be obliging!
I'm sure you have no great press of business.
It's excellent air in this part of the country;
They say it adds years to the people's lives.
The parson at Justedal used to say:
" It is seldom that anyone dies in this valley."

BUTTON MOULDER.

As far as the next crossroads—no farther.

PEER GYNT.

I must find a parson, if I have
To go through fire and water to get him!

## Scene X

(Scene.—*A heathery slope. A winding path leads up to the hills.*)

### Peer Gynt.

You never can tell what will come in useful,
As Esben [1] said of the magpie's wing.
Who would have thought that one's sinfulness
Would, in the end, prove one's salvation?
The whole affair is a ticklish business,
For it's out of the frying-pan into the fire;
But still there's a saying that's very true—
Namely, that while there's life there's hope.

> [*A* Thin Person, *dressed in a priest's cassock which is well tucked up, and carrying a bird-catcher's net over his shoulder, comes running down the hill.*

Who's that with the bird-net? It's a parson!
Hurrah! I am really in luck to-day!—
Good afternoon, sir! The path is rough——

### Thin Person.

It is; but what would not one put up with
To win a soul?

### Peer Gynt.

               Oh, then there's someone
Who's bound for heaven?

### Thin Person.

                    Not at all;
I hope he's bound for another place.

---

[1] Esben Askeladd, in a folk-tale, where his finding of a dead magpie led to his winning the hand of the fair Princess.

PEER GYNT.

May I walk with you a little way?

THIN PERSON.

By all means; I'm glad of company.

PEER GYNT.

Something is on my mind——

THIN PERSON.

Speak on!

PEER GYNT.

You have the look of an honest man.
I have always kept my country's laws
And have never been put under lock and key;
Still, a man misses his footing sometimes
And stumbles——

THIN PERSON.

That's so, with the best of us.

PEER GYNT.

These trifles, you know——

THIN PERSON.

Only trifles?

PEER GYNT.

Yes;
I have never gone in for wholesale sinning.

THIN PERSON.

Then, my dear man, don't bother me.
I'm not the man you seem to think.
I see you're looking at my fingers;
What do you think of them?

PEER GYNT.
                                    Your nails
Seem most remarkably developed.


THIN PERSON.
And now you're glancing at my feet?


PEER GYNT (*pointing*).
Is that hoof [1] natural?


THIN PERSON.
                        Of course.


PEER GYNT (*lifting his hat*).
I would have sworn you were a parson.
And so I have the honour to meet—?
What luck! If the front door is open,
One doesn't use the servants' entrance;
If one should meet the King himself,
One need not seek approach through lackeys.


THIN PERSON.
Shake hands! You seem unprejudiced.
My dear sir, what can I do to serve you?
You must not ask me for wealth or power;
I haven't such a thing to give you,
However willing I might be.
You wouldn't believe how bad things are
With us just now; nothing goes right;
Souls are so scarce—just now and then
A single one——


PEER GYNT.
                        Have people, then,
Improved so wonderfully?

[1] In Scandinavian folklore the Devil is traditionally represented with a horse's hoof for a right foot.

THIN PERSON.

No,
Just the reverse,—deteriorated
Shamefully; the most of them
End in the Casting-ladle.

PEER GYNT.

Ah!
I've heard a little about that;
It really was on that account
That I approached you.

THIN PERSON.

Speak quite freely!

PEER GYNT.

Well, if it's not too much to ask,
I'm very anxious to secure——

THIN PERSON.

A snug retreat, eh?

PEER GYNT.

You have guessed
What I would say before I said it.
You say you're not doing much business,
And so perhaps my small suggestion
May not be irksome——

THIN PERSON.

But, my friend——

PEER GYNT.

I do not ask for much. Of course
I shouldn't look for any wages,
But only as far as possible
To be treated as one of the family.

THIN PERSON.

A nice warm room?

PEER GYNT.

But not too warm.
And, preferably, I should like
An easy access, in and out,
So that I could retrace my steps
If opportunity should offer
For something better.

THIN PERSON.

My dear friend,
I really am extremely sorry,
But you can't think how very often
Exactly similar requests
Are made to me by people leaving
The scene of all their earthly labours

PEER GYNT.

But when I call to mind my conduct
In days gone by, it seems to me
I am just suited for admittance——

THIN PERSON.

But they were trifles——

PEER GYNT.

In a sense;
Still, now that I remember it,
I did some trade in negro slaves——

THIN PERSON.

I have had folk who carried on
A trade in minds and wills, but still
Did it half-heartedly,—and they
Didn't get in.

### PEER GYNT.

      Well—I've exported
Idols of Buddha out to China.

### THIN PERSON.

Rubbish! We only laugh at those.
I have known folk disseminating
Uglier idols, far—in sermons,
In art and literature—and yet
Not getting in.

### PEER GYNT.

      Yes, but—look here!
I've passed myself off as a Prophet!

### THIN PERSON.

Abroad? That's nothing! Such escapades
End mostly in the Casting-ladle.
If you've no stronger claim than that,
I can't admit you, however much
I'd like to do it.

### PEER GYNT.

      Well, but—listen!
I had been shipwrecked, and was clinging
Fast to a boat that had been capsized.
" A drowning man clings to a straw,"
The saying goes; but there's another:
" Everyone for himself ";—and so
The fact that the ship's cook was drowned
Was certainly half due to me.

### THIN PERSON.

It would have been more to the point
If you had been responsible
For stealing half a cook-maid's virtue.

Begging your pardon, what's the good
Of all this talk of half a sin?
Who do you think, in these hard times,
Is going to waste expensive fuel
On worthless rubbish such as that?
Now, don't be angry; it's your sins
And not yourself I'm sneering at.
Excuse my speaking out so plainly.
Be wise, my friend, and give it up;
Resign yourself to the Casting-ladle.
Suppose I gave you board and lodging,
What would you gain by that? Consider—
You are a reasonable man;
Your memory's good, it's very true;
But everything you can recall,
Whether you judge it with your head
Or with your heart, is nothing more
Than what our Swedish friends would call
" Very poor sport." There's nothing in it
That's worth a tear or worth a smile,
Worth boasting or despairing of,
Nothing to make one hot or cold—
Only, perhaps, to make one angry.


PEER GYNT.

You can't tell where the shoe is pinching
Unless you've got it on, you know.


THIN PERSON.

That's true; and—thanks to so-and-so—
I only need one odd one. Still,
I'm glad you mentioned shoes, because
It has reminded me that I
Must push along. I've got to fetch
A joint I hope will prove a fat one.
I haven't any time to spare
To stand here gossiping like this——

PEER GYNT.

And may I ask what sort of brew
Of sin this fellow has concocted?

THIN PERSON.

As far as I can gather, he
Has been persistently himself
By day and night; and that is what
Is at the root of the whole matter.

PEER GYNT.

Himself? Does your domain include
People like *that*?

THIN PERSON.

       Just as it happens;
The door is always left ajar.
Remember that there are two ways
A man can be himself; a cloth
Has both a right side and a wrong.
You know they've lately invented in Paris
A method by which they can take a portrait
By means of the sun. They can either make
A picture like the original,
Or else what is called a negative.
The latter reverses the light and shade;
To the casual eye it's far from pretty;
But the likeness is in it, all the same,
And to bring it out is all that is needed.
If in the conduct of its life
A soul has photographed itself
So as to make a negative,
They don't on that account destroy
The plate; they send it on to me.
I take in hand the rest of the process,
And proceed to effect a transformation.
I steam it, dip it, burn it, clean it,
With sulphur and other ingredients,

Till I get the likeness the plate should give,—
That's to say, what is called a positive.
But when, as in your case, it's half rubbed out,
No sulphur or lye is of any use.


PEER GYNT.

So, then, one may come to you like soot
And depart like snow?—May I ask what name
Is on the particular negative
That you're on the point of converting now
Into a positive?


THIN PERSON.
Yes—Peer Gynt.


PEER GYNT.
Peer Gynt? Indeed! Is Peer Gynt himself?


THIN PERSON.
He swears he is.


PEER GYNT.
He's a truthful man.


THIN PERSON.
You know him, perhaps?


PEER GYNT.
Just as one knows
So many people.


THIN PERSON.
I've not much time;
Where did you see him last?

PEER GYNT.

At the Cape.

THIN PERSON.
The Cape of Good Hope?

PEER GYNT.
Yes—but I think
He's just on the point of leaving there.

THIN PERSON.
Then I must start for there at once.
I only hope I'm in time to catch him!
I've always had bad luck at the Cape—
It's full of Missionaries from Stavanger.
[*Goes off southwards.*

PEER GYNT.
The silly creature! He's off at a run;
On a wrong scent, too. He'll be disappointed.
It was quite a pleasure to fool such a donkey.
A nice chap, he, to give himself airs
And come the superior over me!
He has nothing to give himself airs about!
He won't grow fat on his trade, I'll warrant;
He'll lose his job if he isn't careful.
H'm! *I*'m not so very secure in the saddle;
I am out of the " self "-aristocracy
For good and all, as it seems to me.
[*A shooting-star flashes across the sky. He nods
to it.*
Peer Gynt salutes you, Brother Star!
To shine,—to be quenched, and lost in the void—.
[*Pulls himself together apprehensively and plunges
deeper into the mist. After a short silence he
calls out :*
Is there no one in the universe—

Nor in the abyss, nor yet in heaven—?
> [*Retraces his steps, throws his hat on the ground
> and tears his hair. By degrees he grows
> calmer.*

So poor, so miserably poor
May a soul return to the darkling mists
And become as nothing. Beautiful earth,
Forgive me for having trodden thee
All to no purpose. Beautiful sun,
Thy glorious rays have shone upon
An empty shell—no one within
To receive warmth and comfort from thee,
The owner never in his house.
Beautiful sun, beautiful earth,
'Twas but for naught you warmed and nourished
My mother. Nature is a spendthrift,
And the Spirit but a greedy miser.
One's life's a heavy price to pay
For being born.—I will go up,
Up to the highest mountain-tops;
I'll see the sun rise once again,
And gaze upon the promised land
Until my eyes are weary. Then
The snow may fall and cover me,
And on my resting-place be written
As epitaph: " The tomb of *No One* "!
And—after that—well, come what may.

CHURCHFOLK (*singing on the road*).

Oh, blessed day when the Gift of Tongues
Descended on earth in rays of fire!
O'er all the world creation sings
The language of the heavenly quire!

PEER GYNT (*crouching down in terror*).

I will not look! There's nothing there
But desert waste.—I am in terror
Of being dead long ere my death.
> [*Tries to steal into the thickets, but finds himself
> standing at crossroads.*

## SCENE XI

(SCENE.—*Crossroads.* PEER GYNT *is confronted by
the* BUTTON MOULDER.)

### BUTTON MOULDER.
Good morning, Peer Gynt! Where's your list of sins?

### PEER GYNT.
I assure you that I have shouted and whistled
For all I knew!

### BUTTON MOULDER.
But yet found no one?

### PEER GYNT.
Only a travelling photographer.

### BUTTON MOULDER.
Well, your time is up.

### PEER GYNT.
Everything's up.
The owl smells a rat. Do you hear him hooting?

### BUTTON MOULDER.
That's the matins bell——

### PEER GYNT (*pointing*).
What's that, that's shining?

### BUTTON MOULDER.
Only a light in a house.

PEER GYNT.
                    That sound
Like wailing?

BUTTON MOULDER.
Only a woman's song.

PEER GYNT.
'Tis there—there I shall find my list
Of sins!

BUTTON MOULDER (*grasping him by the arm*).
          Come, set your house in order!
[*They have come out of the wood, and are standing
    near* SOLVEIG'S *hut. Day is dawning.*

PEER GYNT.

Set my house in order? That's it!—Go!
Be off! Were your ladle as big as a coffin,
I tell you 'twould not hold me and my list!

BUTTON MOULDER.
To the third crossroads, Peer; but *then*—!
                    [*Moves aside and disappears.*

PEER GYNT (*approaching the hut*).

Backward or forward, it's just as far;
Out or in, the way's as narrow.          [*Stops.*
No! Like a wild unceasing cry
I seem to hear a voice that bids me
Go in—go back—back to my home.
          [*Takes a few steps, then stops again.*
" Round about," said the Boyg!
          [*Hears the sound of singing from the hut.*
                    No; this time

It's straight ahead in spite of all,
However narrow be the way!

[*Runs towards the hut. At the same time* SOLVEIG
*comes to the door, guiding her steps with a
stick (for she is nearly blind). She is dressed
for church and carries a prayer-book wrapped
up in a handkerchief. She stands still, erect
and gentle.*

PEER GYNT (*throwing himself down on the threshold*).

Pronounce the sentence on a sinner!

SOLVEIG.

'Tis he! 'Tis he! Thanks be to God!
[*Gropes for him.*

PEER GYNT.

Tell me how sinfully I have offended!

SOLVEIG.

You have sinned in nothing, my own dear lad!
[*Gropes for him again, and finds him.*

BUTTON MOULDER (*from behind the hut*).

Where is that list of sins, Peer Gynt?

PEER GYNT.

Cry out, cry out my sins aloud!

SOLVEIG (*sitting down beside him*).

You have made my life a beautiful song.
Bless you for having come back to me!
And blest be this morn of Pentecost!

PEER GYNT.

Then I am lost!

SOLVEIG.
There is One who will help.


PEER GYNT (*with a laugh*).
Lost! Unless you can solve a riddle!


SOLVEIG.
What is it?


PEER GYNT.
What is it? You shall hear.
Can you tell me where Peer Gynt has been
Since last we met?


SOLVEIG.
Where he has been?


PEER GYNT.
With the mark of destiny on his brow—
The man that he was when a thought of God's
Created him! Can you tell me that?
If not, I must go to my last home
In the land of shadows.


SOLVEIG (*smiling*).
That riddle's easy.


PEER GYNT.
Tell me, then—where was my real self,
Complete and true—the Peer who bore
The stamp of God upon his brow?


SOLVEIG.
In my faith, in my hope and in my love.

### PEER GYNT.

What are you saying? It is a riddle
That you are speaking now. So speaks
A mother of her child.

### SOLVEIG.

Ah, yes;
And that is what I am; but He
Who grants a pardon for the sake
Of a mother's prayers, He is his father.
[*A ray of light seems to flash on* PEER GYNT.
*He cries out.*

### PEER GYNT.

Mother and wife! You stainless woman!
Oh, hide me, hide me in your love!
[*Clings to her and buries his face in her lap.
There is a long silence. The sun rises.*

### SOLVEIG (*singing softly*).

Sleep, my boy, my dearest boy!
I will rock you to sleep and guard you.

The boy has sat on his mother's lap.
The two have played the livelong day.

The boy has lain on his mother's breast
The livelong day. God bless you, my sweet!

The boy has lain so close to my heart
The livelong day. He is weary now.

Sleep, my boy, my dearest boy!
I will rock you to sleep and guard you.
[*The* BUTTON MOULDER'S *voice is heard from
behind the hut.*

BUTTON MOULDER.

At the last crossroads I shall meet you, Peer;
*Then* we'll see—whether—! I say no more.

SOLVEIG (*singing louder in the sunshine*).

I will rock you to sleep and guard you!
Sleep and dream, my dearest boy!

MADE AT THE
TEMPLE PRESS ❀ LETCHWORTH
IN GREAT BRITAIN